The Great
Indian Elephant Book

'Bisgaum Charges The Dying Tiger.'

The Great Indian Elephant Book

An Anthology of Writings on Elephants in the Raj

edited by

Dhriti K. Lahiri-Choudhury

OXFORD
UNIVERSITY PRESS

YMCA Library Building, Jai Singh Road, New Delhi 110001

Oxford University Press is a department of the University of Oxford. It furthers the University's objective of excellence in research, scholarship, and education by publishing worldwide in

Oxford New York

Athens Auckland Bangkok Bogota Buenos Aires Calcutta
Cape Town Chennai Dar es Salaam Delhi Florence Hong Kong Istanbul
Karachi Kuala Lumpur Madrid Melbourne Mexico City Mumbai
Nairobi Paris Sao Paolo Singapore Taipei Tokyo Toronto Warsaw

with associated companies in Berlin Ibadan

Oxford is a registered trade mark of Oxford University Press
in the UK and in certain other countries

Published in India
By Oxford University Press, New Delhi

Front endpaper: Mural on the wall of Dariya Daulåt,
Tipu Sultan's summer palace near Seringapatnam, Mysore
shows the combined forces of the British and the
Nizam marching against him.

Back endpaper: A view of the state entry at Coronation Durbar 1903

First published 1999

ISBN 019 564 8927

Typeset by Wordsmiths, New Delhi 110 034
Printed by Pauls Press, New Delhi 110 020
Published by Manzar Khan, Oxford University Press
YMCA Library Building, Jai Singh Road, New Delhi 110 001

Acknowledgements

The tropics are not kind to old books. Predictably, while putting this volume together, accessing rare printed material in reasonable shape, fit for handling and photocopying, turned out to be a major hurdle which I could overcome largely with the help of my good friend Arijit Choudhury, unfailingly generous with his time and resources. Kalyan Bannerjee kindly lent me his copy of 'Snaffle'. Pradip Shukla of the Indian Forest Service serving with West Bengal Forest Department, went out of his way to dig up for me the meaning of some dialectal words used in sub-Himalayan western Uttar Pradesh. OUP's 'reader' made many valuable suggestions which helped me to winnow out the chaff from the grain. Amiya Bagchi and Gautam Bhadra helped to guide my reading round the subject in the nineteenth century. I am grateful to C. Panda, Secretary and Curator, Victoria Memorial Hall, Calcutta, for a colour slide of the enormous oil by Vassili Verestchagin (1876) in the Hall's collection, depicting the procession taking Edward, Prince of Wales, later King Edward VII, through the streets of Jaipur, which appears here on the book's cover. My special thanks are due to Anuradha Roy of OUP, Delhi. The book was her idea. With enormous patience and care she saw it translated into reality. The editorial staff of OUP, Delhi, carried out the onerous and tedious job of seeing the book through the press, for which I can never thank them enough.

All very generously left me to find my own pitfalls.

Contents

Maps ix
Introduction xi

Prologue
Thackeray's Grandfather in Bengal
W.W. Hunter 3

I. Romance to Realism: Changing Perceptions of the Elephant

Elephants and Sport
Thomas Williamson 11
The King of Beasts
Samuel White Baker 17
The Wild Elephant
John Emerson Tennent 23
The Asiatic Wild Elephant
G.P. Sanderson 49
The Elephant in Captivity
G.P. Sanderson 70
A Temperamental Elephant
Samuel Baker 86
Elephants
Douglas Hamilton 94
The Elephant
A.J.O. Pollock 100
Big Game of Lower Burma
F.T. Pollok 102

Asiatic Elephant
V.M. Stockley 115

Elephants
F.W. Champion 129

Photographing Wild Elephants
F.W. Champion 132

Dev Raj and Chota Hathi
John Symington 145

Tame Elephants
Frank Nicholls 152

II. The Most Dangerous Game: Indian Elephants

Shikar as a Part of Life
J.G. Elliott 167

The Mad Elephant of Mandla
A. Bloomfield 181

The Narrowest Escape
G.P. Sanderson 213

The Asiatic Elephant
A.A.A. Kinloch 220

Records of Sport in South India
Douglas Hamilton 232

Elephants
A.J.O. Pollock 246

The Indian Elephant
C.E.M. Russell 256

Charged by a Rogue Elephant: A Nilgiris Man-killer
E.E. Bull 270

'Peer Bux', the Terror of Hunsur
A. Mervyn Smith 276

Elephant
A.E. Wardrop 292

An Elephant Shoot on the Baragur Hills
Randolph C. Morris 298

Elephants from Above and Below
H.S. Wood 306

Sona Dant, Rogue Elephant
John Symington 315

Experiences with Elephants
Frank Nicholls 322

III. Brushes in Burma

An Elephant Hunt
F.T. Pollok 331

Elephants
W.S. Thom 340

The Indian Elephant
G.P. Evans 360

Asiatic Elephant
V.M. Stockley 387

How John Nestall Escaped the Elephant
S. Eardley-Wilmot 401

Some Experiences Amongst Elephant and the Other Big Game of Burma 1887 to 1931
W.S.Thom 407

IV. The Most Dangerous Game: Encounters in Ceylon

The Rifle and Hound in Ceylon
Samuel White Baker 417

Brothers in Arms Against the Game of Ceylon
Samuel White Baker 424

Elephant Shooting
J. Emerson Tennent 435

After Elephants on the Kambukenaar River
'Snaffle' 441

Select Bibliography 451

Glossary 455

Maps

(i)	Sanderson's India	48
(ii)	The principal big game shooting areas	176
(iii)	Map showing the localities over which the Mad Elephant of Mandla roamed	182
(iv)	Map of Lower Burma	339
(v)	Map of Upper Burma	359

Waiting for the Raja by J.Lockwood Kipling Courtesy: National Library, Calcutta.

Introduction

> It should always be remembered that the professional ecologist has to rely, and always will have to rely, for great many of his data, upon the observation of men like fishermen, gamekeepers, local naturalists, and, in fact, all manners of people who are not professional naturalists at all... . It is therefore worth emphasizing the vital importance of keeping in touch with all practical men who spend much of their lives among wild animals.
>
> (C. Elton, *Animal Ecology*, 1927)

Indian Elephant lore has a long history, dating back to the *Rigveda* (1500 BC). The chosen area for this anthology, however, is the modern period. It may be said to have begun with the exposure of the West to the Asian elephant when the British established their rule in South Asia and adjoining Burma (now Myanmar), sometimes loosely called the Raj. This anthology of writings on the Asian elephant offers excerpts from books and in a few cases from periodical articles published in this period, most of the material not easily accessible to the general or even the specialist reader.

The beginning of the British rule in India was spread out in time and space. By the Regulating Act of 1773 the British Parliament established its control over the affairs of the Company and the administration of its territories in India. This would be a convenient starting date for us here.

Burma (Myanmar) was taken over by the British piecemeal as had been done in India and Sri Lanka. The First Anglo-Burmese War of 1824–6 established British control over the northern part of the Burmese empire including Assam, Cachar, and Manipur. F.T. Pollok's hunting experiences predate the Third Burmese War (1886). His first book, published in 1879, took Assam and Upper Burma as one unit. Thus for our purpose the story in Burma begins after the War of 1824–6.

Ceylon (Sri Lanka) ran altogether a different political course. It was only following the defeat of the Kandyan king in 1815 that the sovereignty of the entire island passed to Britain. But for the initial two years, 1796 to 1798, of administration of coastal Ceylon by the East India Company from Madras, Ceylon actually was never under the Raj, if one accepts the Indian association of the word, as the country was never administered from India. This anthology takes in Ceylon nevertheless because of the geo-cultural unity of the region, and its historical links with the main land. India kept her tryst with destiny in 1947; Sri Lanka and Myanmar, less eloquently, in early 1948. India, Burma and Ceylon come here together in what was a widely accepted package of the times, as in the title of Blanford's Book: *British India including Ceylon and Burma*.

The anthology seeks to examine a powerful cultural phenomenon, a way of life, centred round the elephant, 'the king of beasts', as Baker put it in 1847 in an era of the 'lion rampant', a valuation enthusiastically endorsed later by Sanderson. The elephant here is an indicator species, as the biologists like to put it, or an emblem of the Raj, the imperial power.

This book has been structured on two themes: the changing perception of the elephant and the sportsman's ways with them. Because of the thematic division of the collection into sections, observations by the same author, often from the same book, had to be split between separate sections. For some sportsmen the elephant was a hunter's quarry; for others an indispensable vehicle when hunting big game in tall grass. The latter is a fascinating story with a long history which, for lack of space here, must be relegated to a future volume. The second part of the introduction tries to explore the compulsions which drove the new rulers to big game hunting, especially elephants. One account in this collection, Samuel Baker's 'A Temperamental Elephant', offers a perception of the value of a 'good' elephant in shikar, apart from its usefulness as a beast of burden in difficult terrain.

The ancillary subjects of capture, training, care, and post-capture sale of elephants are the foundation on which the use of elephants was based. The subjects of wild and tame elephants constantly intermingle. Wild elephants are tamed, and tame elephants are then put to capturing wild ones. Sometimes captive animals go back to the wild; a few of them are recaptured, some return on their own after years of playing truant. All this will be worth recounting separately in future.

When selecting pieces for this collection the need to keep a balance between the regions of India was kept in mind. Kinloch's inglorious account is included here with Uttar Pradesh specially in sight. This is finely counterpoised by Champion, notable, among other things, for its sharp criticism of Kinloch, without mentioning names, of course. The fact is, there were not too many wild elephants around in Uttar Pradesh at the end of the nineteenth century. The observations of Sir John Hewett, a keen sportsman, a civil servant, and a former governor of the province are worth noting:

> Towards the close of the last century occasional Kheddah operations were undertaken by the Maharaja of Balarampur for the capture of elephants in Garhwal district. These operations left only a few big males still wild in those jungles. The only other wild elephants left in the United Provinces were in a herd which lived partly in Eastern Tarai and partly in Nepal. ... The latest reports estimate that there are not more than a hundred elephants in the forests between Baramdeo on the Sarda and Hardwar on the Ganges in the United Provinces. ... A proposal was recently made that kheddah operations should be once more undertaken in the Garhwal district. It is good news that the Government of the United Provinces, influenced to a great extent by a note I wrote when I was Lieutenant-Governor in 1912, has negatived the proposal.

Public memory is notoriously short, but official memory is sometimes no better. When after a good many years these part-Eastern Tarai and part-Nepal elephants reappeared in the Dudhwa region, the official reaction, generally, was one of bewilderment. Champion noted in 1927:

> They were at one time fairly common in these forests [sub-montane forests of the United Provinces], but their numbers were sadly depleted during the earlier part of the last century, and it was only the protection afforded by the Government 'Elephant Preservation Act' which saved

> them from complete annihilation. They now number only from 100–150 individuals, divided into several small herds with a large number of solitary bulls and maknas. ...

It is, therefore, not surprising that in this period there are few accounts of wild elephants from northern India, the present Uttar Pradesh. While Kinloch gives a fair and unedifying picture of the prevailing state of affairs prior to the passing of the Elephant Preservation Act of 1879, Champion represents the emerging consciousness of the need for conservation for the animal's sake, and not only as a valuable resource. It is in south and north-east India, therefore, that we find most of the accounts of wild elephants.

The select bibliography at the end is restricted to the book's chosen themes, and therefore excludes such classics as Forsyth Evans, Deraniyagala, Milroy, Shebbeare and others.

Our story begins with W.W. Hunter's account of Thackeray the novelist's grandfather in Bengal. He arrived in Calcutta in 1766, the year after the Company had obtained the Dewani of Bengal. Thackeray, also William Makepeace as in the case of the novelist, was appointed the first Collector of Sylhet (now in Bangladesh) in 1772. As was customary for the Company's servants under the 'Dual System' of Clive, he augmented his official income by private enterprise. Two of his sources of such income were destruction of tigers for bounty, and hunting and capture of wild elephants. He was also a supplier of elephants to the Company's troops, collaborating with an official contractor.

We have earlier accounts of the Company being in possession of elephants. On 7 December 1752 a minute in the Proceedings of the Fort William records a 'letter from the Nawab forwarding a *serpaw* [sar-o-pa] and an elephant'. But this is soon smothered in items of purely commercial interest such as 'explaining the method of sorting and prizing cloths at the Export Warehouse'; 'weavers settling down under the Protection of the Company'; 'examination of shop keeper's accounts', 'controversy over 650 bags of rice' and so forth. To the early Company-wallahs, elephants were just another form of merchandise out of which one made money. Old Thackeray was a factor at Dacca before taking up his position in Sylhet.

Captain Thomas Williamson in 1807 kick-starts the nineteenth-century search for the *real* Asian elephant, the elephant of facts rather than of western fiction. Emerson Tennent publishing in 1867 and Sanderson in 1878 are the acknowledged authorities on the Asian elephant throughout the nineteenth century, Sanderson continuing to enjoy the distinction even today. Tennent's authority lost out to Sanderson's in course of time. By 1913 Sanderson had become 'a great—if not the greatest authority' (Stockley). Sanderson's *Thirteen Years* ran seven editions between 1878 and 1912. Sir Samuel Baker (1854), however, predates both, and despite his rather drastic ways with the hapless Sri Lankan elephants, deserves recognition for his pioneering observations on the wild elephant. It is a fact of life that till very recently, our knowledge of wild elephants came mainly from hunters, as this anthology will testify. They alone observed the animal in the wild, albeit over the barrels of a rifle. Williamson limited himself to captive animals; Tennent was an exception. Many years later, in the next century, Champion opened a new way of looking at wild animals: through the viewfinder of a camera.

Williamson describes elephants in shikar. He puts the subject of capture of elephants under different 'plates', which do not concern us here. Writing from first-hand experience, the general accounts of the elephant, says Williams, 'may be attributed to fiction'. His declared objective is to 'keep within the limits of reality' and present his findings 'to the more enlightened circles of the community' and not to 'a number of Calcutta as well as London cockneys'. It is fascinating to follow from now on the slow groping forward towards a thorough and complete understanding of the species with occasional fumbling even as late as 1900. He notes the 'docility and wondrous discrimination of the noble animal', and goes on to make the famous observation that 'the elephant may be said to possess, the energy of the horse, the sagacity of the dog, and a large portion of the monkey's cunning'. Notable here is Williamson's deliberate attempt to move to the area of direct experience. The elephant is no longer a remote creature of one's imagination but a part of everyday life of the colonial English man. There were many careful observations of the natural world in medieval England. The Bird Psalter in the Fitzwilliam Museum in Cambridge and the sketchbook in the Pepysian Library are excellent examples. Yet these were exceptions, and the usual intentions of the artists were mainly emblematic (Thomas). Book perceptions overrode direct observation of nature. Mathew Paris (*c*. 1200–59) drew from life an African elephant, lodged in a special enclosure in the Tower of London, presented in February 1255 by Louis IX of France to Henry III of England. In his rendering the animal stands stiff as a wooden doll; for according to contemporary belief elephants had no joints in their legs. Since they had no joint in their legs, it was obvious, therefore, that once down on the ground, they could not get up again. They were thus forced to sleep standing, reclining against trees. This belief had sanction in classical antiquity. In spite of some direct observations on the habit and morphology of the elephant, Mathew's main authorities for the elephant were the Bible, Virgil, Horace, Bernard Sylvester and medieval Bestiary (Vaughan). A change is marked in the Tudor times. Although by 1800 direct observation had become the key, for elephants it continued to be anthropocentric, the main interest in animals being in their utility for man (Thomas).

Apart from his informative chapter on various methods of capturing elephants, Williamson introduces two themes that engage most of the elephant literature of the nineteenth century: the nature of the elephant and its intelligence. These points get thoroughly threshed out in the course of the years that follow. To Samuel Baker (1854) they are 'naturally savage, wary and revengeful. ... The fact of their great natural sagacity renders them more dangerous as foes'. 'Natural sagacity' is, of course, a variation on the theme introduced by Williamson earlier. Tennent's view is the polar opposite of Baker's: 'So peaceable and harmless is the life of the elephant that nature appears to have left it unprovided with any special weapon of offence'. Working out the theme of Williamson, Tennent feels that 'rather simplicity than sagacity' is the key to the elephant's mind. To Sanderson 'one of the strongest features in the domesticated elephant's character is its obedience'. The nineteenth-century mammalogists, Blanford or Lydekker for example, were inclined to agree with Sanderson on this point. As for its sagacity, Sanderson observes: 'its reasoning faculties are far below those of the dog [an obvious reference to Williamson]. ... It is in many things a stupid animal.' Despite Tennent and especially Sanderson, Douglas Hamilton continues to be impressed by the 'wonderful sagacity and intelligence of the animal' as also by its obedience. Following Tennent, the elephant to him is 'the knowing old engineer who makes paths over the ranges of hills' which are 'quite wonderful feats of engineering'.

Sanderson, carried away by his theory of 'obedience, gentleness, and patience' asserts: 'their vices are few and only occur in exceptional animals' and goes on to add that except when in *musth*, 'at all other times the elephant is perfectly safe, rarely suddenly cable in temper'. Despite Sanderson, F.T. Pollok is probably nearer the mark when he notes: 'I have never known an elephant that could be invariably depended upon for dangerous shooting [i.e. under stress]; they are like women—uncertain, coy, and difficult to please.' He hits the nail on the head when he observes that while the elephant is 'naturally very gentle and would not hurt a worm', yet 'some elephants are vicious by nature—those born in captivity more than those caught wild'. Again, contra Sanderson, he observes: 'Full-grown males cannot be trusted to live in amity.' The experience of present-day elephant men confirms this. To Pollok's co-author Thom, the elephant is 'the most docile, timid, and *intelligent* of animals' (emphasis added). Pollok and Thom assert, in stated defiance of Sanderson, that the *maknas* are a separate species, and not intraspecific variations. The cobwebs obviously had not cleared yet.

In this trophy-conscious age, size of tusks and of the animal were constant preoccupations of the hunter-naturalists, which continued well into the present century (Daniel). It was only in the 1980s that enquiries in India about the Asian elephant took a new turn, following the trend of research in Africa and by the Smithsonian scientists in Sri Lanka. For tusks the benchmark was set by Sir Victor Brooke's elephant shot in Hassanoor in south India in 1863, against which later hunters measured their prowess. Regarding height, all agreed that the 'natives' tended to exaggerate the height of the animal. The new insistence was on measuring the elephant as one would a horse: perpendicularly at the withers. The old method of throwing a tape over the shoulder of an elephant, making both ends touch the ground, and halving the length, came to be rejected as this was not the method employed to measure horses 'at home'. That the traditional local method attempted to measure the dimension rather than just the height of the animal did not bother anyone too much, although it was later realized that the bulk of an elephant was a crucial factor for judging an animal's serviceability. Sanderson recognized this when he took into account the indigenous classification of the elephant's body structures: *Koomeriah*, *Mirga*, *Dosala*, but his obsession with height remained. Hence his famous assertion that 'there is little doubt that there is not an elephant 10 feet at the shoulder in India.' Sanderson, however, had to change his opinion later when he travelled some days by bullock cart to measure personally a male elephant belonging to the Raja of Simoor which stood 10' 7½" at the shoulder.

Another problem which intrigued the nineteenth-century naturalists was the life span of wild elephants. It all starts with Tennent who mentions that according to people familiar with domesticated animals the expected duration of life is about 70 years. So far, fine. But then he proceeds to refer to the papers of one Colonel Robertson, who was in Ceylon in 1799. Robertson found a domesticated animal in the elephant establishment at Matura which, according to records, had served during the entire period of more than 140 years of Dutch occupation, and it was said to have been already in the stables when the Dutch arrived. This Sri Lankan report continued to be the crux for later observers of the elephant. When Sanderson put the average life-expectancy of an elephant in the wild at around 150 years, he probably had this Sri Lankan report in mind and was just playing it safe. In all fairness it should be pointed out that the idea of relating life expectancy of the elephant to the condition of its molars had not yet been recognized in Sanderson's time. I feel that the solution to the Sri Lankan crux came finally from Nuttall, Sanderson's predecessor in office at the Government Kheddah establishment for thirty years, quoted by Pollok and Thom: mahouts tend to give elephants some stock names, and Robertson's 150-year old elephant was probably more than one elephant of the same name. Having known umpteen numbers of Paban Pearies, Chanchal Pearies, Rupkalis, Gulab Kalis, and Champa Kalis in my time, I am inclined to agree with Nuttall on this point.

Lastly, the question of a universal graveyard, a chosen valley of death for elephants. A topic introduced by Tennent as a 'Singhalese superstition', it is, however, taken up in all seriousness by subsequent writers on the subject including Sanderson, and the topic continues to be seriously debated as late as Champion in his *With a Camera in Tigerland* and Thom in 1933 before it is finally and comprehensively rejected.

Although roundly rubbished by Sanderson later as 'full of errors', 'mostly romancing', 'confessedly no sportsman, probably, never saw a wild tusker', Tennent assumes an approach which is closer in spirit to the modern conservationists' than that of any other nineteenth-century specialist writing on the subject. Undoubtedly he slipped badly when commenting on an elephant 'jumping' a 9' high fence, and describing the tusks of elephants as placed almost vertically down, and therefore being 'useless appendages to elephants and of little service for offence'. Tennent's acquaintance with male Ceylonese elephants was probably limited to *maknas*, the tusks of which sometimes protrude several inches beyond the lip, going vertically downward, and hence probably the confusion which Sanderson was so prompt to pounce upon. Tennent warns against the declining number of elephants in Ceylon as well as in south India, and their disappearing habitat—quite a lone voice in that age.

By the time Sanderson in 1878 comes to make his observations, a definite change is noticed in the perceived value of the elephant. There is also an attempt to see the elephant through 'native eyes'. The realization dawns at last that an elephant was not a horse, and trying to understand one in terms of the other might not be a fruitful exercise. Sanderson's following remarks in this context are significant:

> The elephant is essentially a native animal. Natives alone have fully studied his peculiarities and classified him into castes; his capture, training, and keeping are in native hands, as well as his trade. ...

The change in the perception of the value of the elephant can be related to changing British attitude to India, culminating in the Queen's proclamation of 1858 making the British rule over India direct. In the seventeenth and the eighteenth centuries the English viewed man's authority over the natural world as absolute. He might use it as he pleased, said John Day in 1620 'for his profit and his pleasure' (Thomas). Old Thackeray used the elephant for his immediate, short-term profit; Williamson valued it for pleasure (sport): both legitimate English pursuits and both completely exploitative in attitude. It was all a part of the theology of man's, and by unconscious implication the White Man's, subjugation and exploitation of nature. In the colonial period, the theory of the primacy of the human race soon became the primacy and superiority of the colonizing race. Up to 1858 the attitude to natural resources was primarily that of the predatory merchant-adventurer's, best illustrated in this volume by Baker in Sri Lanka and Kinloch in India: maximize hay-making while the climate is favourable. This almost became a philosophy. The attitude of the colonizers to Sri Lanka was, however, somewhat different from that adopted in India. Sri Lanka was small and manageable enough to be thought of in terms of complete colonization. When Baker himself in his *Wild Beasts and their Ways* came to regret his indiscriminate shooting of elephants in the past after realizing the importance of elephant in tiger hunting, he was still reacting on the principle of pleasure bringing legitimate happiness and appreciating the elephant for its utility in sport.

The new rulers, unlike the 'natives', were not encumbered by any superstitious veneration for the animal; for any animal for that matter, except perhaps the horse, the emblem of the Northern People's culture. It was only after the emergence of the idea of a permanent empire that the approach changed from one of short-term profit to long-term investment (Hutchins). Steel in 1885 adequately sums up the role of the elephant in post-1858 India:

> Recent warlike operations by the British in the East [Burma] have been associated with the elephant. In Abyssinia and Afghanistan he has done his work well. We see him in India engaged in drawing heavy field guns, carrying fodder and baggage, penetrating jungles in tiger hunting, and carrying magnates in religious and state processions.

Apart from its long-recognized role in the commissariat, elephants now had a new emblematic role to play in the grand imperial design. One does not have to move far to find where Viceroys found their role models for the use of elephants on state occasions like durbars. As Theodore Morison put it,

> If any tourist ... wishes to enter into the political ideas of people of India let him accompany the Rajah on his evening ride. From the gateway of Fort, the Rajah's elephant, in long housings of velvet and cloth of gold, comes shuffling down the steep declivity; on his back, in a silver howdah, sits the Rajah, laden with barbaric pearl and gold; behind him clatter his kinsmen and relations on brightly caparisoned horses; ... and make a brave show. Cavalcade winds down the narrow streets; the men pick up their sword and hurry forward; the women

> and children rush to the doors of their houses, and all the people gaze upon their prince with an expression of almost ecstatic delight; as the elephant passes, each man puts one hand to the ground and shouts 'Maharaj Ram Ram'. The most indolent tourist cannot fail to notice the joy upon all the people's faces. ...

Elephants played a spectacular role in religious processions, particularly in feudatory India, as in Mysore, Travancore, Gwalior, and Indore. Elephants' ceremonial role extended to the great zamindary estates as well. The procession at Darbhanga (Bihar) on the occasion of Indra Puja was a notable event. Such processions of elephants, richly caparisoned and with silver and gilt accoutrements, was common on Dashami Day, the day of the ceremonial immersion of the image of the Goddess Durga in Bengal. One such famous annual religious procession was at Dacca (now Dhaka, the capital of Bangladesh) on Janmashtami day (the day of the birth of Lord Krishna) to which local zamindars lent their elephants. The use of elephants by the British in state processions was perhaps the most important visual symbol of the process of orientalization of the Raj.

When India formally came under direct British rule in 1858, it was but a crystallization of ideas which had been floating around for some time. Early in the nineteenth century state visits to courts in feudatory India were made on elephants, the sahibs dismounting from their horses to get on to elephants for the actual ceremonial entry (Mundy). The Persian loan word 'durbar', used in English as early as 1609, was in common use throughout the nineteenth century. Thackeray the novelist published his 'The Story of Koompanee Jehan' in the *Punch* of 17 March 1849, a burlesque of the Mughal rule which still obtained, and a satirical jibe at the airs of the Company.

Men like Thomas Macaulay and C.E. Trevelyan had wanted to reform Indian society on an English model. What eventually transpired was a transformed English society in the colonial mould: a life of curry and rice, brandy and *blighty pawnee* (soda), *quoi hais, khidmatgars,* and tiger-shooting parties (Trevelyan).

When Canning became the first Viceroy of India, the last of the Great Mughals safely out of the way in Rangoon (present Yangon), the temptation to play the Great White Mughal was irresistible. He was obviously badly bitten by the durbar bug (Cohn). He hopped across northern India, from durbar to durbar, from Calcutta to Peshawar, and back to Calcutta (Cunningham). The object of Lytton's 'Imperial Assemblage' in 1877 was to 'place the Queen's authority upon the ancient throne of the Moguls, with which the imagination and tradition of [our] Indian subjects associate the splendour of supreme power' (Lytton, quoted in Cohn). Hence the choice of the location was imperial Delhi, rather than commercial Calcutta. The bug was active, expectedly, in Curzon as well. He held a number of durbars. The crowning event was the great coronation durbar in Delhi in 1903, the 'Curzon Durbar', where the procession of elephants occupied centre stage. Even here Kitchener sought to make his separate point. An eyewitness gleefully noted: 'In the elephant state entry Kitchener was a fine and conspicuous figure, mounted on his thoroughbred "Democrat", a runner in the Derby of 1902. As the horse insisted on doing the whole processional route sideways, it must have been very uncomfortable for K. Nor can one blame the horse much, for Derby runners do not often see elephants' (Woodyatt). The hallowed tradition of the Orderly Room in the army (Regimental Court) was redesignated 'durbar' in some regiments. In the 9th Punjabis durbar was held twice a week (Woodyatt). In some regiments the 'wise Colonels' made it a rule never to make a sit-down of a durbar 'for the simple, though perhaps unworthy, reason that once a circle of Indians is firmly seated they take hours to dig up' (Younghusband). The fascinating story of elephants in state processions and durbars is best told in the visual rather than in the narrative mode; and hence would be out of place in this volume.

Sanderson represents this new post-1858 attitude: realization of the value of the elephant as an important natural resource of strategic importance. His attitude in the chapter on captive elephants is essentially that of a manager. He discusses the state of the market, and the supply position. He explains why an all-out effort to capture elephants in south India was a compulsion for the government because large-scale mortality made import from Burma cost-prohibitive. In fact attempts had been made to march them overland from Burma, with disastrous results, to avoid the journey by sea. To quote Steel,

> In 1857–60 between 800–900 elephants were brought to Dacca from Moulmein or Rangoon in sailing vessels, but a vast number of casualties

> resulted...; so it was decided in future to march them up by land. Some escaped and others died *en route*, and over 30 per cent died in 1866–67 as a result of their being subjected to native mismanagement at Chittagong. The introduction of European management materially lessened the fatality.

Things, of course, did not work out quite like that on the ground. Tennent provides us with figures of elephant mortality in government stables in Ceylon. It was reported to A.J.O. Pollock in 1881 that the last of Sanderson's first catch of elephants in Mysore had died that year. He adds, 'there would appear to be something wrong in this method of capture'. Something out of joint there certainly was in the prevailing state of affairs, as mortality figures of 25 to 30 per cent were common in government Kheddahs during and immediately after capture. Sanderson kept quiet over these figures, except in official annual reports. It remained for Milroy early in the next century to set things right, but that is another story.

In his chapter on wild elephants, Sanderson's is essentially a hunter's perception of the animal. 'Hunting' here includes 'capture', as in the current legal definition in India. He obviously learnt from expert 'native' elephant catchers the basic behaviour of elephants, when and how they moved, their number, the status of the adult male about which the catching party always had to be wary. We owe to him the first clear assertion in plain English that the leader of a herd was a female, never a male, and that the prevalent ideas about 'solitary' males were wrong. Sanderson had learnt his lessons well from the professional elephant catchers around him who actually carried out the job.

Elephants were protected in Sri Lanka under the Kandyan kings. When the English took Sri Lanka, they soon started to encourage mass destruction of elephants by offering bounty, and in the name of sport. Tennent narrates part of this sad story. Recently this has been updated by Jayewardene; but the complete account is yet to be pieced together.

A similar approach prevailed in south India as well, particularly in Madras Presidency (now Tamil Nadu), directly administered by the British, and the puppet regime in the adjacent feudatory State of Mysore (now Karnataka), set up by the British after the overthrow of Tipoo Sultan in 1799. The only feudatory State in south India to protect elephants, as tradition and custom demanded, and to resist issuing licences to English sportsmen to shoot elephants was Travancore (now Kerala). Contemporary accounts suggest that the killing of elephants in south India was extensive, significantly reducing the elephant population. Full details are yet to be dug up from the old government files. Historians of ecology one day would like to find out the number of elephants.thus culled, and assess the impact of the policy of exterminating elephants from south India on human land-use pattern, with particular reference to the establishment of plantations of coffee etc. by British entrepreneurs, and extension of settled agriculture to increase revenue earning by the government. The perilous situation in north India has already been reviewed. Only in eastern India was the situation different. Williamson noted that early in the nineteenth century private contractors supplying elephants to the Company had estasblished their own stud. By 1825–6, the official Dhaka stud already had about 300 elephants (Mundy). The south Indian elephants were useless and, therefore, expendable; for local expertise was lacking to make them useful. Only when it was thought that the necessary expertise could be transferred to the south from eastern India was a convincing case for their protection made. Elephants, to justify their existence, had to prove their usefulness. The main point is that realization had dawned that elephants were useful for services other than that of sport, and needed a long-term policy of sustainable exploitation.

Madras Presidency by a ukase executive order of 1871 put elephants under protection, and Mysore government, following suit, passed a similar order the same year. Madras passed an Act in 1872 'to prevent indiscriminate destruction of elephants', which came in force in October 1873. We gather from A.J.O. Pollock (see Sec. I) that actually these 'indiscriminate destructions' had been deliberately engineered by the government by offering a bounty of Rs 70-00 for each animal killed. The 1871 decision shows how total the reversal was of the previous attitude and policy.

The all-India Elephant Preservation Act of 1879 settled the issue, and the scope of the Act was gradually extended to the rest of India, and eventually to Burma. More than 'preservation', the 1879 Act was meant to establish government monopoly of this important and strategically vital natural resource. This changed approach had led earlier to the setting up of Reserve Forests in India in the

1860s. In Sri Lanka the first attempt at curbing wanton destruction of elephants and buffalo came in 1891 (Jayewardene). Exactly how important elephants had become to the British government in India can be deduced from the figures of government elephants gathered by Sanderson in 1882:

Commissariat: Bengal and North India	1,016
Bombay	78
Madras and Burma	213
Forest, Frontier, Police, Railway, Telegraph and Public Works Department in India and Burma	300
Grand Total	1,607

(Quoted by Steel)

Champion, breaking away from the traditional utilitarian view, opens a new chapter in the history of the Raj's perception of the elephant, when he lashes out at Kinloch's reckless shooting at elephants: 25 hits on 10 elephants of which 3 were cows, and only 1 secured, a makna without any trophy value. His is a new voice defiantly telling the British sporting gentry at large: 'Nothing whatever would induce me to attempt to destroy one of these magnificent creatures ... perhaps the finest of God's wild creatures.' Woodyatt is admiringly quoted for refusing to shoot elephants. The great Sanderson himself, introduced as 'a desperately [*sic*] keen shikari', is quoted only for his expression of revulsion after killing an elephant. With Champion people and elephants start acquiring faces—for example, the mahout Karim Baksh and Champion's favourite mount Balamati. The elephants Dev Raj and Chhota Hathi are distinct personalities whom Symington 'knew well and came to admire'. Nicholls lived for long periods in remote camps with his own personal elephants. His bald statement 'I have the greatest admiration and love for elephants' says it all. This was how Thom in 1933 responded to the contrary wind:

> Big game shooting nowadays is, I am afraid, very much decried. People look askance upon any one who may happen to have shot a few more animals than other people and refer to them as butchers. The filming and photography of wild animals in their natural habitat is now all to the fore.

He then takes a nostalgic stroll down memory lane, reminiscing about the good old days. Yet, when he proudly displays the photograph of the tusker he took in Thayetmyo Yoma (Myanmar), he feels obliged to explain: 'It may be asked why I did not shoot this fine specimen. My reply is that I had quite a few already and would much rather have the photograph I obtained. I had a heavy rifle at the time [with me] ...' This laying aside of the heavy rifle for the camera is symbolic of the beginning of a new era.

II

Elephant hunting was not in the mainstream culture of northern or peninsular India. 'Elephants were something one shot from, not shoot at'. Elephant hunting as a sport was not favoured by the Indian upper classes. In fact to orthodox Hindus killing elephants was taboo. However, tribals in the remote areas of south and north-east India had no such qualms. Williamson in 1807 declares that 'no native of Bengal nor any European resident there, would undertake such a piece of rashness as to go out shooting elephants', and is frankly sceptical of one Monsieur Vaillant's account of shooting elephants in Africa. The idea of elephant hunting as a sport of the upper classes was introduced by the English sometime after 1807. We learn from Major Forbes that elephant hunting by 1826 had become an accepted form of sport by the English in Sri Lanka, a distinct change from complete protection the species had enjoyed under the Kandyan kings. Not hunting, but capturing elephants had been the recognized royal sport, from the Mughal court to distant Siam. Abu'l Fazl gives an account of this form of court entertainment in Akbar's time. However, under the British, officers, military and civil, could seek entertainment in elephant hunting when 'lucky enough' to be posted in south or north-east India.

Hunting has always been a cherished ideal of the English upper classes. It featured prominently in the code of conduct for the ruling class, the governors, drawn up by Sir Thomas Elyot in 1531. Sundry manly exercises are highly recommended, 'but the most honourable exercise, in my opinion', declares Elyot, 'and that beseemeth the estate of every noble person, is to ride surely and clean on a great horse and a rough, which undoubtedly ... importeth a majesty and dread to inferior persons, beholding above the common course of other men ...' Hunting in ancient times is reverentially recalled: how the 'chief hunting of the valiant Greeks was at the lion, the leopard, the tiger, the wild swine, and the bear, and sometimes the wolf and the hart'; how 'Theseus, which was companion to Hercules, attained the greatest part of his renown for fighting with the great boar, which Greeks called *phera*'; how Alexander fought alone with a lion; how Pompeii, Sertorius, and 'diverse other noble Romans ... in the vacation seasons from wars' while in North Africa, 'hunted lions, leopards, and such other beasts, fierce and savage'. Adds Elyot, 'But Almighty God be thanked, in this realm there be no such crul beasts to be pursued.' But Almighty God be thanked again, at the beginning of the nineteenth century in the realms acquired overseas, the new governors could now play at being Theseus, Alexander, Meleager, Pompeii, and 'diverse other noble Romans', pursuing 'beasts fierce and savage', to their glory and fame. The northern horse culture missed the great horses when establishing their heroic image in the colonies; but a great tusker had its majesty surpassing that of any horse, as Curzon realized, and Kitchener did not.

Shikar in the colonies opened up an avenue to heightened social status and self-esteem, despite a growing concern for animal welfare in eighteenth- and nineteenth-century England (Thomas). Blood sports in England were still the closely guarded privilege of the upper classes. This class was much more broadly defined in the colonies; but there were stratifications within its broad base itself. All sahibs to the 'native' were *pucca,* but to the sahibs themselves some were more *pucca* than others. This difference was keenly felt in the post-Hailebury era of 'competition-wallahs'. The Hon'ble J.W. Best states the position candidly:

> I think that in the old days in my father's time, Europeans could discriminate between one Indian and another as we discriminate in our own native country. In those days of class distinction at home, a gentleman knew when he met another in the East. It was a matter of breeding and education. I do not agree, however, with the view that one hears expressed regarding the present personnel of the I.C.S. and other services, namely that they are now recruited through examinations from all classes and they include many of those known as 'board-school boys'. Many of the most able, and the most courteous, and the most successful in dealing with the Indians are men of humble birth who have often educated themselves by their ability to pass examinations for scholarships.

Despite the liberal views aired at the end, Best's patronizing tone is unmistakable. These competition-wallahs, though not gentlemen, could have good points. Recruitment of army officers stopped short of this kind of egalitarianism. So, the phrase 'officer and gentleman' still held good. Then there was the great divide between those in the government machinery, and the 'interlopers', those outside in business and trade. Even among the interlopers, those connected with land, such as coffee or tea planters in south India and Assam, or indigo planters in Bihar, were allowed a privilege not enjoyed by mere traders. A man growing tea or coffee held a certain position not granted to sellers of the same product, the box-wallahs. The class hierarchy among the new governors was thus multi-layered.

At the beginning of this century K.N. Chaudhuri was a leading light of the Calcutta Bar and one of Bengal's most renowned sportsmen. He was also considered one of the leading Brown Sahibs of his day. He is better than best in his reactions to changes in the social structure of the ruling community:

> Tent clubs are things of the past, the planter has vanished with the discovery of synthetic indigo and other causes, and the Haileyburian has been supplanted by Jews, Germans, aliens and all sorts and conditions of men, and few Englishmen of the good old type, who are still to be found, are so shuffled up with these undesirables and with some of our non-sporting *bhaibund* in the same service, that in no district in Bengal will you find any ardour or endeavour to resuscitate this noble form of sport [pig sticking]. Big-game shooting is not also one of their failings ... And the service is fast losing touch with the people ... the District Officer is to be found confined to plying his pen at leisure, inditing unnecessary reports, while he should be out with a hog spear or an up-to-date rifle. ...

It has been argued that 'shikar or game hunting was one of the sites on which the colonial project tried to construct and affirm the difference between its "superior self" and the inferiorised "native" other'. The whole object was to establish hunting as 'an ideological marker which confirmed the colonising white male as super-masculine' (Pandian). I may point out that it would take a very brave soul to try to 'inferiorise' a K.N. Chaudhuri. More to the point perhaps is the approach of Elyot who divides people into 'noble' and 'inferior' classes in his own country. The situation is not too difficult to understand in the context of colonial India. Best explains it in the passage just quoted. The new rulers of India did not always come from the ruling class in their own country. So, those who did not, had to prove their credentials to their peers. They were not out to impress the 'inferiorised' natives—they were out to impress their own tribe in India and 'at home'. Big-game hunting was a short-cut to the status of being a gentleman.

Kitchener was the C-in-C when new leave rules were being framed for the Indian Army. A combined leave of eight months was proposed including six months on furlough allowance. There were murmurs of dissatisfaction. One of the objections was that the period being restricted to from March to November, no officer of the Indian Army would be able to hunt; whereupon the great K. of K. asked with his characteristic bluntness, how many officers of the Indian Army could afford to hunt at home. This composition of the Army started to change at the beginning of the twentieth century when British Territorials, Terriers as they were commonly called, started to come over to India with scions of aristocracy in their ranks.

Williamson's declared target readership was the elite in London and Calcutta. He dedicated his volume to George III. Sir Samuel Baker dedicated his *Wild Beasts and their Ways* to the Prince of Wales, later King Edward VII. Tennent extended the courtesy to Major Skinner in *The Wild Elephant.* Sanderson coming from a modest background in Bangalore sought the patronage of Col. G.B. Malleson, 'late guardian to His Highness the Maharaja of Mysore', for his *Thirteen Years,* but not of the Maharaja himself. All published in England, certainly not with a 'native' readership in view.

Hunting and outdoor activities of the English Royalty visiting India were officially chronicled in lavishly produced volumes, obviously not intended for the 'natives'. Exploits of British hunters regularly appeared in *Country Life* and *Field* in England. *Oriental Sporting Magazine* and other such periodicals published in India were emphatically by the British, and for the British. Sporting columns in English language dailies published in India, such as *South of India Observer*, the *Pioneer* or the *Statesman* had about the same kind of target readership in view.

Stratifications within the ruling class led to hierarchical arrangement among the sporting communities of the colonizers. The army formed a separate brotherhood of their own, pig sticking featuring prominently in their calendar of annual sporting events. There were the Vice Regal and gubernatorial shoots, frequently organized by local Princes and big zamindars. The planters had their own niche, in easy coexistence with the district-level government officials, sometimes even with patronage from those higher up. The Nilgiri Game Association was the preserve of the planters in south India, as the Tista-Torsa Game Association was of tea planters in the Dooars in North Bengal. Inglis was an indigo planter in Bihar moving in his own circle.

Sir Samuel Baker in his *Rifle and Hound in Ceylon* wrote the manifesto of English big-game hunters in the colonial period. One did not have to cross the Red Sea to meet the 'other'; they were right there across the Channel, incapable of understanding the great English sense of sportsmanship. Baker painted the ideal, which the ground reality did not always match. Baker himself along with his friends in Sri Lanka did not hesitate to wipe out entire herds of elephants, collecting only their tails as trophy from these tuskless elephants, male and female. His sporting diary records 22 elephants, cows and calves included, accounted for in three weeks. On another occasion, out of four herds, 31 elephants were killed in a 'few days' shooting'. The story runs on. Five elephants, an entire family group, were exterminated within 30 seconds in November 1851. At the end of a three weeks' trip the party had bagged 50 elephants, 5 deer and two buffaloes. Thus the trip ended, writes Baker, showing 'the habits and character of elephants in a most perfect manner'.

Kinloch after righteously declaring it 'a great shame to slaughter a number of female elephants which might be caught and made useful; and which have no tusks to make them worth the shooting', nevertheless found the 'temptation too strong' to refrain from firing at three separate cow elephants in a herd. It was a cold-blooded affair; for he had previously determined that the herd was without a tusker.

As for English sportsmanship, it was common gossip in shikar camps that the Viceroy's tigers were measured with specially marked tapes which had eleven inches to a foot. Sir Henry Ramsay, commonly called in his days the 'king of Kumaon', the Commissioner of Kumaon and Garhwal for 35 years, was the Controller of the Prince of Wales's shoot in 1875. Woodyatt tells us that though there were plenty of wild tigers around, Sir Henry thought it necessary to introduce a few tame ones 'to make the bagging of at least two or three by the Prince an absolute certainty'. A Nepal-style ring of three hundred shikar elephants was used. When the ring was closing in, one of the party fired a shot, and the Prince called out sharply, 'who fired that shot?' The name was known to all, but never given away, demonstrating an exemplary *esprit de corps.* So much for the much-disapproved field manners of 'hogging the game'. Woodyatt goes on to describe how a few minutes later one of the tame tigers would not go away from in front of Sir Henry's elephant, and he had to pelt it with oranges to get it to move on. The irrepressible Woodyatt, himself no stranger to tiger shooting, does not forget to mention at the end how delighted the Prince was with his first tiger.

Baker fixed the place of the elephant at the top of the hierarchy of game animals, as elephant hunting was 'the most dangerous of all sort of sports', a view shared by all hunters who came after him, including Sanderson and Stracey. This made it logical for those seeking fame and recognition for their hunting prowess to go after elephants, and helped to fix the pecking order among the would-be gentlemen. Here again privilege and, if we believe K.N. Chaudhuri, inclination ruled. Mostly army officers, not many competition-wallahs, appear to have made the most of the opportunity. This, not counting the planters and people actually living near forests who were frequently asked to help in putting down a rogue elephant.

How did the Asian 'other' fare in this game? Mostly as the 'insignificant other', like the Sherpas in recent times, who carried the Himalayan 'summiteers' to the heights of their glory while remaining faceless themselves. This attitude prevailed even after Hillary had decided to share with Tenzing the honour of conquering the Everest. They were not Prince Hamlet, nor were meant to be. They helped 'to swell the progress, advise the Prince, were easy tools, deferential, glad to be of use, at times almost ridiculous,— almost at times the fool'. Baker's type-cast 'Cingalese' servant in *Rifle and Hound,* in a state of abject terror implores Baker to run: 'Buffalo's coming sar! Master, run plenty, quick! Buffalo's coming sar! Master, get big tree!' Equally true to preconceived type is Baker's 'rascally horse-keeper' who is soundly thrashed for handing him the wrong weapon, though handing out suitable weapons was hardly the business of the horse-keeper.

Actually, Baker did not hold the nation of the 'Cingalese' in too high an esteem, as one gathers from his following remarks in *Rifle and Hound*:

> You see a native woman clad in snow-white petticoat a beautiful tortoise shell fastened to her raven hair; you pass her—you look back—wonderful!—she has a beard! Deluded stranger, this is another disappointment; it [*sic*] is a Cingalese Appo—a man—no, not a man,—something male in petticoats; a petty thief, a treacherous, cowardly villain, who would perpetuate the greatest rascality had he only the pluck to dare it. In fact in this petticoated wretch you see a type of the nation of the Cingalese.

Indians, although *sans* 'petticoats', were not much better off in the eyes of the average British administrator, the Pathans excepted.

Sanderson, when after the wounded Kakankote makna, did not hesitate to send two of his unarmed, leading trackers fifty yards in advance of himself. A separate party of Kuruba trackers had been sent two days earlier after another elephant, a tusker. This tusker was then tracked down, fired at, and injured. Again an advance-party of trackers was sent to locate the injured beast. It was found and fired at once more. Once again leading trackers sallied forth to bring back report on its location and condition to the hunter who then approached the animal. This was a common pattern of behaviour among the elephant hunters, and Sanderson was reputed to be one of the best. It seems obvious that Sanderson's target readership were not the Kurubas.

J.G. Elliott attempted to divide the history of shikar in colonial India into periods: up to 1880, post-1880 (period of game laws), and so forth. Another valid period division would be between the black-powder regime and the age of cordite; the former again with subdivisions into successive periods of muzzle loaders and breech loaders. The history of the development of the modern sporting rifle has been well outlined by Samuel Baker in the long first chapter of his *Wild Beasts and their Ways,* which the interested reader might care to look up. These improvements made all the difference to elephant shooting. Baker in Sri Lanka carried a battery of seven heavy muzzle-loading, black-powder rifles to ensure rapid shooting. 'Dastardly gun-bearers', therefore, were a necessity. Even then, the hardened spherical lead balls fired through these rifles, actually, more mini-cannons than rifles, lacked the power to penetrate the massive skull of an elephant to the brain, unless one got the correct angle. Body shots had to be *behind* the shoulder, not *through,* as ordinary sporting ammunition or charge lacked the power to smash through the heavy shoulder-blades of an elephant. Hence body shots often resulted in messy lung-shots. Much of the drama of nineteenth-century elephant hunting arose out of bungled brain shots. Sanderson was the *arbiter elegantiae* in these matters:

> To steal up to ten paces, and drop an elephant before he is aware of the danger, is the poetry of the sport; to kill him by body shots is the prose.

Unfortunately, one is not always conscious that good prose may be preferable to bad poetry. Sanderson himself was lucky on more than one occasion to escape from the consequences of muffed brain-shots.

The second hazard of black powder was the smoke obscuring the view of the hunter after firing the shot. F.T. Pollock and W.S. Thom made sure of a handy tree or clump of bamboo before firing at an elephant, and stepped behind it immediately after the shot; for the assumption was that the animal was not going to drop to the shot and the smoke would prevent the hunter from seeing what had happened to it. This was often the most suspenseful moment.

Most of the writers on elephant shooting add elaborate notes on suitable weapons and the vital spots to aim at in an elephant. These have been excised from the stories in this collection, as unlikely to be of immediate interest to the present-day readers.

Finally the question, why are hunting stories here at all? This anthology has sought to argue that elephant hunting for the British in India, had a socially significant role. It helped to establish some as 'super-gentlemen' among their peers. These stories help us to understand the motivation which drove these people to big game, and especially elephant hunting, and help us to understand the spirit of an age that has gone by. Apart from these rather heavy socio-cultural considerations related to elephant-hunting stories, the fact is, people rather like reading hunting stories for the vicarious thrill and excitement they offer. Corbett has firmly held his place for decades in the bestseller list. In fact, such literature can be said to make up a distinct sub-genre of adventure literature with a very long history. We can start with Hercules bagging the Nemean Lion, and carrying its pelt as trophy on his person all his life. St George, in the absence of anything more interesting by way of big game, went after the dragon. Beowulf established his rank in society after killing Grendel's mother. Stories collected here are, in a way, in the same tradition.

The curtain came down on the Raj in India in 1947; in Sri Lanka and Myanmar a few months later. J.G. Elliott describes the last scene of the drama with a touching vividness. Crowds of those pulling out stand around; stacks of luggage on the platform, all looking remarkably similar—gun cases 'canvas-clad and stained with oil. ... They were all marked "not wanted on voyage": some of them would never be wanted again in the hands of those who owned them. These were part of a way of life, symbols of a passing era.' The days of playing Alexander and Pompeii were over.

REFERENCES*

Best, James W. (1935). *Forest Life in India*. London: James Murray.

Blanford, W. T. (1888–91) *The Fauna of British India including Ceylon and Burma Mammalia*. London: Taylor & Francis.

Chaudhuri, K.N. (1918). *Shikar in Jheel and Jungle*. Calcutta: Thacker, Spink.

Cohn, Bernard S. (1987). *An Anthropologist among the Historians*. Oxford: Oxford University Press.

Cunningham, H.S. (1891). *Rulers of India: Earl Canning*. Oxford: Clarendon Press.

Elyot, Sir Thomas (1513). *The Book named the Governor,* Ed. with intro. by S.E. Lamberg. London: Dent. Bk I, xvii.

Forbes. *Eleven Years in Ceylon*. 2 vols. (1840). London: Richard Bentley.

Hewett, Sir John (1938). *Jungle Trials in Northern India.* London: Methuen.

Hutchins, Francis G. (1967). *The Illusion of Permanence: British Imperialism in India*. Princeton: Princeton University Press.

Jayewardene, J. (1994). *The Elephant in Sri Lanka.* Colombo.

Lydekker, R. (1903). *Mostly Mammals.* London: Hutchinson.

Morison, Sir Theodore (1899). *Imperial Rule in India*. Westminster: Archibald Constable.

Mundy, Gen. Godfrey Charles (1858). *Pen and Pencil Sketches in India*. London: John Murray.

Pandian, M.S.S. (1998). 'Hunting and Colonialism in the Nineteenth-Century Nilgiri Hills of South India'. In *Nature and the Orient.* Ed. R.H. Groves et al. Delhi: Oxford University Press.

Steel, J.H. (1885). *A Manual of the Diseases of the Elephant*. Madras: Lawrence Asylum Press.

Sterndale, R.A. (1884). *Natural History of the Mammalia of India*. Calcutta: Thacker, Spink.

Thackeray, W.M. 'The Story of Koompanee Jehan', *Punch* 17 March 1849

*Excluding references to texts in this anthology.

(reproduced in *Oxford Thackeray*, ed. G. Saintsbury, London: Oxford University Press, 1908, vol. VII).

Thomas, Keith (1983). *Man and the Natural World.* Repr. Harmondsworth: Penguin 1994.

Trevelyan, G.O. (1864). *The Competition Wallah*. Repr. Delhi: HarperCollins, 1992.

Vaughan, Richard, ed. (1958). *Mathew Paris*. Cambridge: Cambridge University Press.

Woodyatt, Major-General Nigel (1922). *Under Ten Viceroys.* London: Herbert Jenkins.

Younghusband, Maj-General Sir George (1933). 'The Regimental Durbar' in *Blackwood Tales from the Outposts*, Vol. VII: 'Soldier's Tales'. London: Blackwood.

Prologue

W.W. HUNTER

Thackeray's Grandfather in Bengal

The Thackerays formed a typical family of the Bengal Civil Service in the days of John Company. They threw out branches into the sister services, military and medical, and by a network of intermarriages created for themselves a ruling connexion both in India and in the Court of Directors at home. The first Thackeray in India went as a covenanted civilian in 1766, and four of his sons, with at least fourteen of his descendants and collaterals, have been traced in the same profession. ...

Harrow School, although far on in its second century, had declined, under 'a drunken, disorderly, idle' headmaster, to thirty-three boys, a number which increased to 130 during the vigorous rule of Dr Thomas Thackeray. He died in 1760.

The heavily weighted widow thankfully accepted a Writership in the East India Company's service for her sixteenth and youngest child, William Makepeace, born in 1749. ... William Makepeace Thackeray, grandfather of the novelist, was placed at the age of fourteen with a 'Writing-Master' at Bromley-by-Bow, to learn book-keeping—at that time essential for entering the Company's service. In August 1765, his preceptor certified his capacity to the Court of Directors in somewhat guarded terms.

Excerpted from *The Thackerays in India and Some Calcutta Graves*, London: Henry Frowde, 1897.

He 'has been under my care and instruction since midsummer, 1764', wrote this worthy, 'has gone through a regular set of merchants' accounts and the practical rules of arithmetic, and I believe he understands what he has learned as well as most young gentlemen of his age and experience.' Accordingly in February 1766, the lad sailed by the *Lord Camden* for Calcutta, with a family Bible which his mother had used for fifty-three years, and which she gave him as her parting gift. ...

The shipload of young civilians arrived in stirring times. The previous year, 1765, had brought the grant of Bengal from the Mughal Emperor to the East India Company, followed by Clive's despairing effort, as he said, 'to cleanse the Augean stable' of Anglo-Indian abuses. The elder civilians were banded against the Governor's attack on their private trade, while the English officers of the army formed a mutinous league against his military retrenchments. ...

[Thackeray's] 'arrival as Writer' is dated in the Company's books, June 20, 1766, his seventeenth birthday, although the *Lord Camden* did not actually reach Calcutta till some weeks later. Placed with three others of his shipmates in the Secretary's office, he attracted the notice of his superiors, and was next year promoted to be assistant treasurer or 'cash keeper' under the new Governor, Verelst. ...

Except during a brief appointment in the Calcutta Court, his first five years were passed in the financial and correspondence departments of the Government. Mr Cartier, who succeeded to the Governorship of Bengal in 1769, also employed him under his own eye. ...

That position gave him a thorough insight into the mechanism of the Government. Clive had left behind a dual system, under which the actual administration remained apart from the superior control. The actual administration continued in the hands of the old native officials who collected the revenue. The superior control was exercised by a handful of Englishmen who could do little more than see the revenue duly forwarded to headquarters, and invest it in calicoes or other country products for the yearly shipment home. Their business was not to dispense justice to the people, but to provide dividends for Leadenhall Street. ...

In conducting the Company's commerce, its servants also did business on their own account. Their nominal salaries scarcely yielded a subsistence. These meagre stipends, which they looked on as retainers rather than as pay, they augmented sometimes a hundredfold by private trade and by presents from natives. ...

During Thackeray's whole residence in Bengal the officials continued, without social disapproval or self-reproach, to do business on their own account. ... Whatever success Thackeray had in his early ventures, he conducted them under the eye of the Governor, apparently from the Governor's own house, and certainly in such a spirit as to retain the confidence and esteem of his master.

After five years of training at the centre of government, he was appointed to a more independent position in the interior. The Governor, Mr Cartier, had spent his whole inland service at Dacca, except when he volunteered as an ensign with Clive's army in 1757 after the Black Hole. He knew the advantages of the place for private trade, and he determined to give to his young favourite the same opportunity of making a fortune as he himself had enjoyed. In 1771 he accordingly appointed Thackeray to be Factor and Fourth in Council at Dacca. The brother and two sisters put themselves and their belongings into large country boats, and wended their way eastwards across the delta of the Ganges. The journey was a slow one amid tropical swamps and vast jungles, in which the roar of the tiger could be heard through the night, and his foot-prints seen at his drinking places in the morning. After days of rowing, and poling, and towing from the banks, they emerged on the confluence of waters over which Dacca reigned as a queen. ...

His nominal salary, as Fourth in the Dacca Council, appears on the Company's pay-sheet for 1771 as only Rs 495, or say £62 per annum—about half his allowances during previous years under Governor Cartier in Calcutta. But whatever restrictions were placed on the personal dealings of the Chief of Council, who drew a compensating grant, the junior members had the privilege of private trade. They could not have bought their daily food and kept a roof over their heads without it. In making the Annual Investment for the Company they made investments for themselves. ...

Under the old system, against which the Court of Directors inveighed, the Company's servants claimed exemption from the transit duties levied on all other merchandise. This unfair privilege was abolished by Lord Clive's reforms, and the Company's servants had to conduct their private dealings subject to well-understood restrictions. ...

Thackeray soon had an opportunity of still further increasing his fortune. The Dual Government left behind by Clive had visibly broken down, and in 1772 the Company resolved to stand forth as the sole responsible Government in Bengal. Under its orders Warren Hastings, the new Governor-General, appointed a British 'Collector' or Chief for the administration of each circle or the District. Thackeray was selected as the first 'Collector' of the dangerous frontier province of Sylhet. In this great outlying angle of north-eastern Bengal new branches of commerce opened to him. Sylhet, with its virgin forests and mineral wealth, supplied the materials for the new fortress and city of Calcutta, several hundred miles off at the other end of the great river highway. The Hon. Robert Lindsay, a son of the Earl of Balcarres, who succeeded as Resident or 'Collector' of Sylhet in 1778, four years after Thackeray left, grew quickly rich as a wholesale lime merchant and shipbuilder. 'My pay as Resident,' wrote the candid Robert, 'did not exceed £500 per annum, so that fortune could only be acquired by my own industry.' During the period of Thackeray's residence, from 1772 to 1774, there were not only similar contracts open to him, but also the profitable business of supplying elephants for the Company's troops.

These two men, William Makepeace Thackeray and the Hon. Robert Lindsay, are the first British administrators who left their mark in that remote District. They converted what had been a wild borderland into a British Province, and 'Thackeray's House' was still pointed out when I visited Sylhet a century later. Their rule was a simple one. 'Black tax-farmers' brought the £17,000 of land-tax to the treasury in the local currency of cowries—41,000 of which equalled one pound sterling. The British head of the district shipped off to Dacca the heaped-up masses of little shells; or kept part of them in payment for the lime, timber, and elephants which he supplied to the Company. Such local products formed in fact a means of remitting the revenue, alike profitable to the British Resident and convenient to the central government. The Dacca Council asked few questions as long as the fixed amount of cowries, or their equivalent in the articles ordered for the Company, came down the river.

The serious business of the Resident of Sylhet, or 'Collector' as he began to be called in 1772, was to hold the District against the frontier tribes and rebellious chiefs. Each autumn the hillmen burst out upon the valley: if in any year they did not come, it was because the floods had already swept away the crops. Murderous affrays still took place between the Hindu and Musalman cultivators. At the greater festivals of the rival religions, temples were sacked, cows were slain within the holy precincts, mosques were defiled, and bloody reprisals followed on both sides. It must be remembered that when Thackeray went to Sylhet in 1772, it had only been under nominal British control for six years. He found it as it was left by centuries of native rule. ...

Thackeray, the first British 'Collector' of the District, found it in a [wild] state. Two of his sources of income were the destruction of tigers and the capture of wild elephants. Half a dozen years later, Lindsay [Thackeray's successor] continued to bag sixty or seventy tigers yearly, for which the Government allowed liberal rewards. Thackeray's name survives as a mighty hunter of elephants. Herds of these animals roamed through the mountains and forests, at times forcing the hillmen to lodge in trees for shelter, and sallying forth to devastate the villages and crop-lands of the plains. ...

If the supply of elephants for the Company's troops yielded a good profit, it was apt to bring the purveyor into unpleasant disputes. For the newly caught elephant is a delicate monster, apt to die on his travels, and with as infinite a capacity for unsoundness as a young horse. The difficulty of judging an elephant forms, indeed, the subject of many shrewd stories among the Bengal peasantry. One relates how a merchant who believed he had a really sound elephant, and was just about to complete its sale, espied a villager looking fixedly at the animal's hind legs. Fearing that the man detected some unknown flaw, he whispered, 'Say nothing till the bargain is struck, and I shall give you fifty rupees.' The villager stood silent and stolid as before, and presently the merchant handed him the money. 'But now tell me, what was it you discovered?' asked the merchant. 'Discovered? What could I discover?' replied the peasant, tying up the silver in his waistband. 'I had never seen an elephant before, and I was watching how far his tail could reach in flapping off the flies.'

In 1774 a batch of elephants, for which Thackeray was the real although not the ostensible contractor, turned out badly. Only sixteen out of sixty-six survived their trying march across India to Belgram—a distance of about a thousand miles. The price of the animals averaged Rs 1000 each, and the Government, having given an advance of Rs 33,000, disputed the balance and called on Thackeray to divulge his connexion with the nominal contractors. He refused, on the ground that if he were to do so, 'he might, by breaking his promise, forfeit the character of a man of principle and honour, and suffer in the opinion of his friends.' He preferred to bring the matter before a judicial tribunal, boldly sued the Company in the Supreme Court of Bengal, and obtained a decree for Rs 29,600 (say £3700) and costs.

The Court of Directors in England resented the loss. A couple of years after Thackeray had left India, they made it the subject of one of the carping despatches with which they rewarded the hard and faithful service of their Governor-General, Warren Hastings. The Bengal Government, it appears, had gone carefully into the matter, but did not find it possible to resist Thackeray's claim in court. Francis and his partisans, as usual, turned the action of the Governor into material for a malignant charge. But there can be little doubt that the pure-handed Hastings did his best in this as in other cases to see justice done. He himself, at an earlier period, held a contract for the supply of commissariat bullocks. Hastings had thus a personal knowledge of the very class of transactions in which Thackeray was engaged, and he knew perfectly what was permissible and what was not under the system of anonymous trade then practised in Bengal. His whole career, and especially his strict control as Governor-General, make it certain that if, in the interests of the Company, he could have defended the suit he would have done so. ...

I
Romance to Realism: Changing Perceptions of the Elephant

Fig. 1

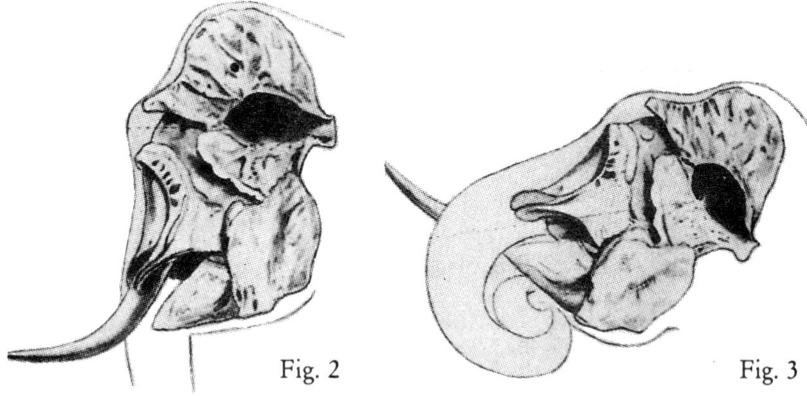

Fig. 2 Fig. 3

Fig 1: A manuscript of the 15th century in the British Museum, containing the romance of *Alexander*, which is probably of the fifteenth century, is interspersed with drawings illustrative of the strange animals of the East. Amongst them are two elephants whose trunks are literally in the form of trumpets with expanded mouths. See Wright's *Archaeological Album*, p. 176, and M.S. Reg. 15, e. VI. Brit. Mus.

Fig 2 and 3: Diagrams showing the position of the elephant's brain.

THOMAS WILLIAMSON

Elephants and Sport

The Public have at times been amused with various tales relating to Elephants, of which the generality may be attributed to fiction; because they are either repugnant to the disposition and nature of that noble animal, or, from local circumstances, highly improbable. Such as evince nothing contrary to docility and wondrous discrimination, may be viewed in general, without too severe a scrutiny: for the Elephant may be said to possess the energy of the horse, the sagacity of the dog and a large portion of the monkey's cunning. Were it not that these qualities may be fully proved by a visit to the several museums, I should hardly venture to give such a character, lest I might be suspected of an intention to impose.

Many of the instances quoted in this Work are from personal information; others are from the descriptions of those whose veracity could be relied on. I may possibly be wanting in a few particulars; but I can safely aver, that, the spirit of the facts is given, and that the whole will be found most completely to support the several circumstances to be illustrated, or confirmed. Generally speaking, I have been anxious to keep within the limits of reality; not venturing, on many occasions, to amplify to the extent I should be warranted by truth. I am aware that many things by no means

From *Oriental Field Sports*, 1807 edn, vol. I. The title is not the author's.

wonderful or uncommon in one country, are upheld to ridicule in another, as being monstrous and absurd! Thus, when the sailor boy related to his father and mother, that the flying fishes used to drop on board the ship; they silenced him with a severe rebuke, for attempting to impose on them with so palpable a falsehood: but when Jack, altering his tone to make friends with the old folks, said that in weighing their anchor while up the Red Sea, a large carriage wheel of solid gold and studded with diamonds, was found hanging to one of its flukes, they acknowledged his fiction as a truth; observing, that 'Pharoah and his host were devoured there; and that no doubt it was one of the wheels of his Majesty's chariot.'

I am sensible that not a few will treat large portions of this Work as a downright apocrypha; however, as it is not intended for the ignorant, but for the more enlightened circles of the community, I have less diffidence in venturing upon some of the more curious details; which, happily, may be corroborated by numbers in the first ranks of society. India has been frequented by many of that class; its customs and curiosities are becoming daily more known. As yet no complete description of them has been given to the World, and an intimate knowledge of the many interesting natural curiosities of that country remains among our desiderata.

In a Publication so respectably patronized as is the present, and where detection might, through a variety of channels, easy of access, be immediately effected, neither credit nor profit could result were the smallest attempt indulged in, to substitute falsehood for truth. That many matters may be considered marvellous, I freely admit. Where the candid reader may find difficulty in accrediting, he will not pass an illiberal sentence, but by seeking for information among the many who may have been in India, especially in Bengal, his doubts will be removed, and his misconceptions be rectified. The issue of such references must prove satisfactory, and at least preserve me from anathema. It may be proper to remark, that there are a number of Calcutta as well as London cocknies: to such I do not appeal!

Before I close this introduction, I must answer to some queries which, I am persuaded, the generality of my readers will have in their minds. They will ask, 'Why all the characters introduced as sportsmen, are European?' This certainly may appear strange, but is nevertheless perfectly correspondent with facts. The natives of India consider what we call sporting, to be quite a drudgery, and derogatory from the consequence and dignity of such as are classed among the superior orders. Nabobs, and men of rank, often have hunting parties; but an ignorant spectator would rather be led to enquire, against what enemy they were proceeding? The reader will form to himself an idea of what sport is to be expected, where perhaps two or three hundred elephants, and thirty or forty thousand horse and foot, are in the field. The very dust must often preserve the game from view! As to energy and personal exertion, except in the case of a few individuals, who, either from vanity, or a partiality to British customs and diversions, partake of our conviviality and recreations, more will never be seen: and even such demi-anglified personages cannot be expected to do much. In truth, they generally become objects of ridicule to both parties: their countrymen detest their apostasy, while we smile at their awkward attempts, like the bear in the boat, to conduct themselves with propriety in their new element!

It will, no doubt, be farther enquired, 'Whether such a number of menials as are described in the Plates, can be absolutely necessary?' A reference to that copious and admirable display of Indian costume, published by Mr Orme, the proprietor of this Work, will be found to contain a very complete answer to this question. For the present it may be sufficient to state, that owing to the customs peculiar to India, and principally dependent on superstitious ordinations, the services of menials are much confined; each having but one particular office to attend to, never interfering in the department of any other of the household. ...

Having premised thus much, I shall proceed to state the manner in which a party usually repairs to the hunting-ground.

To those who have but one horse, which is a common case, especially among gentlemen of the army, it is an object of moment to keep him fresh for the sport. This motive, added to the refreshment produced by change of seat and position, induces many to proceed to and from the field on elephants, which are variously accoutred for the occasion: some having only the pads used when carrying burthens; others, if of small stature, furnished with saddles, or cushions and stirrups; and others again with *howdahs*, or carriages, with or without hangings. These are respectively exhibited

Elephants in Sport.

in the present Plate, and their construction will be found particularly detailed in the subsequent Numbers, in such parts as may require more complete elucidation. Suffice it for the present to state, that the carriage pad is formed of canvas, stuffed hard with straw, and lashed securely to the elephant's back by strong hempen cords. It is in general spacious enough to hold about four persons, though I have seen some so large, being in proportion to the elephant's bulk, as to carry eight or nine with ease. It requires a good spring to jump up; and those not possessed of such active powers are aided by servants, or avail themselves of the benefit of a chair, &c. to facilitate their mounting. Saddles are appropriate to such elephants as may be of rather low stature, that is about six feet or less; they are placed on pads lined with cotton or wool, and are girted on as with horses. In this manner only one person can ride each elephant; it is, however, in my mind, the most pleasant mode. Some, instead of a saddle, have a long cushion fastened on with one or two pairs of stirrups. These are certainly convenient and easy; besides which they possess the advantage of carrying double. The howdah being made on a strong frame, and of a heavy construction, requires not only to be very effectually secured to the pad, but should be borne by elephants of good stature; that is from seven feet upwards. They are of various forms. That exhibited in this Plate is an *Hindostanee*, such as has been ever in use among natives, and was at first the only form adopted by Europeans, who have since considerably varied this conveyance. All howdahs, however, require a ladder to ascend into them; after which the ladder is slung at the side of the elephant, in a horizontal position, by means of rope-loops made for that purpose. The iron rails in the front were introduced by gentlemen for the purpose of supporting their firearms; and some have added a similar guard all around the back, filled up with cord or wire netting, as a security against falling out. The *coosah*, or back division of the howdah, behind the front seat, is usually allotted to a servant, who conveys either an umbrella or ammunition, or furnishes the sportsmen with refreshment. Into this the menials generally ascend by climbing up the elephant's rump, in which they are aided by the ropes that pass, like a crupper, under the insertion of its tail.

The elephant is invariably driven by a *mohout*, let the form of conveyance be what it may. He sits on the neck, with his legs behind the ears, and his feet within a kind of collar of loose cords passed ten or twelve times round the neck. With his toes he guides the elephant; pressing under the ear opposite the way he would proceed: thus, if he would turn to the right, he presses with his left toe; and *vice versa*. He governs the elephant by means of an iron instrument about two feet long, having a large hook affixed near the top. This is called a *haunkus*, literally a driver: with the pointed end of it he either accelerates, or causes the elephant to lie down: in the former case he urges the point forward; in the latter, he presses it perpendicularly on the centre of the skull; accompanying each mode with words of command in general use, and for the most part so well understood by elephants as to suffice without recourse to the *haunkus*. As many elephants are impatient while mounting, or loading, it is not only proper to keep a certain pressure on the head, but to cause a grass cutter, who ordinarily attends, provided with a spear, spiked at both ends, and used chiefly to goad the elephant forward, to stand on one of the forelegs; pressing, if necessary, the end of the spear, so as to deter the animal from rising prematurely.

SAMUEL WHITE BAKER

The King of Beasts

The king of beasts is generally acknowledged to be the lion; but no one who has seen a wild elephant can doubt for a moment that the title belongs to him in his own right. Lord of all created animals in might and sagacity, the elephant roams through his native forests. He browses upon the lofty branches, upturns young trees from sheer malice, and from plain to forest he stalks majestically at break of day, 'monarch of all he surveys'.

A person who has never seen a wild elephant can form no idea of his real character, either mentally or physically. The unwieldy and sleepy-looking beast who, penned up in his cage at a menagerie, receives a sixpence in his trunk, and turns round with difficulty to deposit it in a box; whose mental powers seem to be concentrated in the idea of receiving buns tossed into a gaping mouth by children's hands,—this very beast may have come from a warlike stock. His sire may have been the terror of a district, a pitiless highwayman, whose soul thirsted for blood; who, lying in wait in some thick bush, would rush upon the unwary passer-by, and know no pleasure greater than the act of crushing his victim to a shapeless mass beneath his feet. How little does his tame sleepy son resemble him! Instead of browsing on the rank vegetation of wild pasturage,

From *The Rifle and Hound in Ceylon*. London: Longmans Green, 1854 (new impression 1890, 1904). The title is not the author's.

he devours plum-buns; instead of bathing his giant form in the deep rivers and lakes of his native land, he steps into a stone-lined basin to bathe before the eyes of a pleased multitude, the whole of whom form their opinion of elephants in general from the broken-spirited monster which they see before them.

I have even heard people exclaim upon hearing anecdotes of elephant-hunting, 'Poor things!'

Poor things, indeed! I should like to see the very person who thus expresses his pity, going at his best pace, with a savage elephant after him, give him a lawn to run upon if he likes, and see the elephant gaining a foot in every yard of the chase, fire in his eye, fury in his headlong charge; and would not the flying gentleman who lately exclaimed 'Poor thing!' be thankful to the lucky bullet that would save him from destruction?

There are no animals more misunderstood than elephants; they are naturally savage, wary, and revengeful; displaying as great courage when in their wild state as any animals known. The fact of their great natural sagacity renders them the more dangerous as foes. Even when tamed, there are many that are not safe for a stranger to approach, and they are then only kept in awe by the sharp driving hook of the mohout.

In their domesticated state I have seen them perform wonders of sagacity and strength; but I have nothing to do with tame elephants; there are whole books written upon the subject, although the habits of an elephant can be described in a few words.

All wild animals in a tropical country avoid the sun. They wander forth to feed upon the plains in the evening and during the night, and they return to the jungle shortly after sunrise.

Elephants have the same habits. In those parts of the country where such pasturage abounds as bamboo, lemon grass, sedges on the banks of rivers, lakes, and swamps, elephants are sure to be found at such seasons as are most propitious for the growth of these plants. When the dry weather destroys this supply of food in one district, they migrate to another part of the country.

They come forth to feed about 4 p.m., and they invariably retire to the thickest and most thorny jungle in the neighbourhood of their feeding-place by 7 a.m. In these impenetrable haunts they consider themselves secure from aggression.

The period of gestation with an elephant is supposed to be two years, and the time occupied in attaining full growth is about sixteen years. The whole period of life is supposed to be a hundred years, but my own opinion would increase that period by fifty.

The height of elephants varies to a great degree, and in all cases is very deceiving. In Ceylon, an elephant is measured at the shoulder, and nine feet at this point is a very large animal. There is no doubt that many elephants far exceed this, as I have shot them so large that two tall men could lie at full length from the point of the forefoot to the shoulder; but this is not a common size: the average height at the shoulder would be about seven feet.[1]

Not more than one in three hundred has tusks; they are merely provided with short grubbers, projecting generally about three inches from the upper jaw, and about two inches in diameter; these are called 'tushes' in Ceylon, and are of so little value that they are not worth extracting from the head. They are useful to the elephants in hooking on to a branch and tearing it down.

Elephants are gregarious, and the average number in a herd is about eight, although they frequently form bodies of fifty and even eighty in one troop. Each herd consists of a very large proportion of females, and they are constantly met without a single bull in their number. I have seen some small herds formed exclusively of bulls, but this is very rare. The bull is much larger than the female, and is generally more savage. His habits frequently induce him to prefer solitude to a gregarious life. He then becomes doubly vicious. He seldom strays many miles from one locality, which he haunts for many years. He becomes what is termed a 'rogue'. He then waylays the natives, and in fact becomes a scourge to the neighbourhood, attacking the inoffensive without the slightest provocation, carrying destruction into the natives' paddy-fields, and perfectly regardless of night fires or the usual precautions for scaring wild beasts.

The daring pluck of these 'rogues' is only equalled by their extreme cunning. Endowed with that wonderful power of scent peculiar to elephants, he travels in the daytime *down* the wind; thus nothing can follow upon his track without his knowledge. He winds his enemy as the cautious hunter advances noiselessly upon his track, and he stands with ears thrown forward, tail erect,

[1]The males 7 ft 6 in., the females 7 ft., at the shoulder.

trunk thrown high in the air, with distended tip pointed to the spot from which he winds the silent but approaching danger. Perfectly motionless does he stand, like a statue in ebony, the very essence of attention, every nerve of scent and hearing stretched to its cracking point; not a muscle moves, not a sound of a rustling branch against his rough side; he is a mute figure of wild and fierce eagerness. Meanwhile, the wary tracker stoops to the ground, and with a practised eye pierces the tangled brushwood in search of his colossal feet. Still farther and farther he silently creeps forward, when suddenly a crash bursts through the jungle; the moment has arrived for the ambushed charge, and the elephant is upon him.

What increases the danger is the uncertainty prevailing in all the movements of a 'rogue'. You may perhaps see him upon a plain or in a forest. As you advance he retreats, or he may at once charge. Should he retreat, you follow him; but you may shortly discover that he is leading you to some favourite haunt of thick jungle or high grass, from which, when you least expect it, he will suddenly burst out in full charge upon you.

Next to a 'rogue' in ferocity, and even more persevering in the pursuit of her victim, is a female elephant when her young one has been killed. In such a case she will generally follow up her man until either he or she is killed. If any young elephants are in the herd the mothers frequently prove awkward customers.

Elephant-shooting is doubtless the most dangerous of all sports if the game is invariably followed up; but there is a great difference between elephant-killing and elephant-*hunting;* the latter is sport, the former is slaughter.

Many persons who have killed elephants know literally nothing about the sport and they may even leave Ceylon with the idea that an elephant is not a dangerous animal. Their elephants are killed in this way, viz:

The party of sportsmen, say two or three, arrive at a certain district. The headman is sent for from the village; he arrives. The enquiry respecting the vicinity of elephants is made; a herd is reported to be in the neighbourhood, and trackers and watchers are sent out to find them.

In the meantime the tent is pitched, our friends are employed in unpacking the guns, and, after some hours have elapsed, the trackers return: they have found the herd, and the watchers are left to observe them.

The guns are loaded and the party starts. The trackers run quickly on the track until they meet one of the watchers who has been sent back upon the track by the other watchers to give the requisite information of the movements of the herd since the trackers left. One tracker now leads the way, and they cautiously proceed. The boughs are heard slightly rustling as the unconscious elephants are fanning the flies from their bodies within a hundred yards of the guns.

The jungle is open and good, interspersed with plots of rank grass; and quietly following the head tracker, into whose hands our friends have committed themselves, they follow like hounds under the control of a huntsman. The tracker is a famous fellow, and he brings up his employers in a masterly manner within ten paces of the still unconscious elephants. He now retreats quietly behind the guns, and the sport begins. A cloud of smoke from a regular volley, a crash through the splintering branches as the panic-stricken herd rush from the scene of conflict, and it is all over. X has killed two, Y has killed one, and Z knocked down one, but he got up again and got away; total, three bagged. Our friends now return to the tent, and, after perhaps a month of this kind of shooting, they arrive at their original headquarters, having bagged perhaps twenty elephants. They give their opinion upon elephant-shooting, and declare it to be capital sport, but there is no danger in it, as the elephants *invariably run away*.

Let us imagine ourselves in the position of the half-asleep and unsuspecting herd. We are lying down in a doze during the heat of the day, and our senses are half benumbed by a sense of sleep. We are beneath the shade of a large tree and we do not dream that danger is near us.

A frightful scream suddenly scatters our wandering senses. It is a rogue elephant upon us! It was the scream of his trumpet that we heard! And he is right among us. How we should bolt! How we should run at the first start until we could get a gun! But let him continue this pursuit and how long would he be without a ball in his head?

It is precisely the same in attacking a herd of elephants or any other animals unawares; they are taken by surprise, and are for the moment panic-stricken. But let our friends X, Y, Z, who have just bagged three elephants so easily, continue the pursuit, hunt the remaining portion of the herd down till one by one they have nearly all fallen to the bullet—X, Y, Z, will have had enough of it; they will be blinded by perspiration, torn by countless thorns, as they have rushed through the jungles determined not to lose sight of their game, soaked to the skin as they have waded through intervening streams, and will entirely have altered their opinion as to elephants invariably running away, as they will very probably have seen one turn sharp round from the retreating herd, and charge straight into them when they least expected it. At any rate, after a hunt of this kind they can form some opinion of the excitement of the true sport.

The first attack upon a herd by a couple of first-rate elephant shots frequently ends the contest in a few seconds by the death of every elephant. I have frequently seen a small herd of five or six elephants annihilated almost in as many seconds after a well-planned approach in thick jungle, when they have been discovered standing in a crowd and presenting favourable shots. In such an instance the sport is so soon concluded that the only excitement consists in the cautious advance to the attack through bad jungle.

As a rule, the pursuit of elephants through bad, thorny jungles should if possible be avoided: the danger is in many cases extreme, although the greater portion of the herd may at other times be perhaps easily killed. There is no certainty in a shot. An elephant may be discerned by the eye looming in an apparent mist formed by the countless intervening twigs and branches which veil him like a screen of network. To reach the fatal spot the ball must pass through perhaps fifty little twigs, one of which, if struck obliquely, turns the bullet, and there is no answering for the consequence. There are no rules, however, without exceptions, and in some instances the following of the game through the thickest jungle can hardly be avoided. ...

JOHN EMERSON TENNENT

The Wild Elephant

With the exception of the narrow but densely inhabited belt of cultivated land, that extends along the seaborde from Chilaw on the western coast towards Tangalle on the south-east, there is no part of Ceylon in which elephants may not be said to abound; even close to the environs of the most populous localities of the interior. They frequent both the open plains and the deep forests; and their footsteps are to be seen wherever food and shade, vegetation and water, allure them, alike on the summits of the loftiest mountains, and on the borders of the tanks and lowland streams.

From time immemorial the Singhalese have been taught to capture and tame them, and the export of elephants from Ceylon to India has been going on without interruption from the period of the first Punic War.[1] In later times in all forests elephants were the property of the Kandyan crown; and their capture or slaughter without the royal permission was classed amongst grave offences in the criminal code.

In recent years there is reason to believe that their numbers

From *The Wild Elephant*, 1867.

Note: The serial numbers of the footnotes have been changed here because of a different page set-up. All the footnotes have not been included in this reprint.—DKLC.

[1] Ælian, *de Nat. Anim.* lib. xvi.c. 18; Cosmas Indicopl., p. 128.

have become considerably reduced. They have entirely disappeared from localities in which they were formerly numerous;[2] smaller herds have been taken in the periodical captures for the public service, and hunters returning from the chase report them to be growing year by year more and more scarce. In consequence of this diminution the natives in some parts of the island have even suspended the ancient practice of keeping watchers and fires by night to scare away elephants from their growing crops.[3] The opening of roads too in the hill districts, and the clearing of the mountain forests of Kandy for the cultivation of coffee have forced the animals to retire to the low country, where again they have been followed by large parties of European sportsmen; and the Singhalese themselves, being more freely provided with arms than in former times, have assisted in swelling the annual slaughter.[4]

Had the motive that incites to the destruction of the elephant in Africa and India prevailed in Ceylon, that is, had the elephants there been provided with tusks, they would long since have been annihilated for the sake of the ivory.[5] But it is a curious fact that,

[2]Le Brun, who visited Ceylon AD 1705, says that in the district round Colombo, where elephants are now never seen, they were then so abundant, that 160 had been taken in a single corral (*Voyage, etc.* tom. ii, ch. lxiii. p. 331.)

[3]In some parts of Bengal, where elephants were formerly troublesome specially near the wilds of Ramgur, the natives got rid of them by mixing a preparation of the poisonous Nepal root called *dakra* in balls of grain, and other materials of which the animal is fond. In Cuttack, above fifty years ago, mineral poison was laid for them in the same way, and the carcasses of eighty were found which had been killed thus. (*Asiat. Res.* xv. 183.)

[4]The number of elephants has been similarly reduced throughout the south of India, and as in the advancing course of enclosure and cultivation, the area within which they will be driven must become more and more contracted, the conjecture is by no means problematical, that before many generations shall have passed away, the species may become extinct in Asia.

[5]The annual import of ivory into Great Britain alone, for the last few years, has been about *one million* pounds which, taking the average weight of a tusk at sixty pounds, would require the slaughter of 8333 male elephants.

But of this quantity the importation from Ceylon has generally averaged only five or six hundred weight; which, making allowance for the lightness of the tusks, would not involve the destruction of more than seven or eight in each year. At the same time, this does not fairly represent the annual number of tuskers shot in Ceylon, only because a portion of the ivory finds its way to China and to other places, but because the chiefs and Buddhist priests have a passion for collecting tusks, and the finest and largest are to be found

whilst in Africa and India both sexes have tusks,[6] with some slight disproportion in the size of those of the females; in Ceylon, not one elephant in a hundred is found with tusks, and the few that possess them are exclusively males. Nearly all, however, have those stunted processes called *tushes*, about ten or twelve inches in length and one or two in diameter. These I have observed them to use in loosening earth, stripping off bark, and snapping asunder small branches and climbing plants; and hence tushes are seldom seen without a groove worn into them near their extremities.

Amongst other surmises more ingenious than sound, the general absence of tusks in the elephant of Ceylon has been associated with the profusion of rivers and streams in the island; whilst it has been thrown out as a possibility that in Africa, where water is comparatively scare, the animal is equipped with these implements in order to assist it in digging wells in the sand and in raising the juicy roots of the mimosas and succulent plants for the sake of their moisture. In support of this hypothesis, it has been observed, that whilst the tusks of the Ceylon species, which are never required for such uses, are slender, graceful and curved, seldom exceeding fifty or sixty pounds' weight, those of the African elephant are straight and thick, weighing occasionally 150 pounds, and even 300 pounds. But it is manifestly inconsistent with the idea that tusks were given to the elephant to assist in digging for food, to find that the females are less bountifully supplied with them than the males, whilst the necessity for their use extends alike to both sexes. The same consideration serves to demonstrate the fallacy of the conjecture, that the tusks of the elephant were given as weapons of offence, for if such were the case the vast majority of them in Ceylon, males as well as females, would be left helpless in the presence of an assailant. But although in their conflicts with one another, those which are provided with tusks may occasionally push clumsily with them at an opponent, it is a misapprehension

---

ornamenting their temples and private dwellings. The Chinese profess that for their exquisite carvings the ivory of Ceylon excels all other, both in density of texture and in delicacy of tint; but in the European market, the ivory of Africa, from its more distinct graining and other causes, obtains a higher price.

[6]A writer in the *Indian Sporting Review* for October 1857 says, 'In Malabar a tuskless male elephant is rare. I have seen but two.' (p. 157).

to imagine that tusks are designed, as has been stated, to serve 'in warding off the attacks of the wily tiger and furious rhinoceros, often securing the victory by one blow which transfixes the assailant to the earth'.

So peaceable and harmless is the life of the elephant, that nature appears to have left it unprovided with any special weapon of offence: the trunk is too delicate an organ to be rudely employed in a conflict with other animals and although on an emergency it may push or gore with its tusks (to which the French have hastily given the designation of '*defenses*'), their almost vertical position, added to the difficulty of raising its head above the level of the shoulder, is inconsistent with the idea of their being designed for attack, since it is impossible for the animal to deliver an effectual blow, or to 'wield' its tusks as the deer and the buffalo can wield their horns. ...

Towards man the elephant evinces shyness, arising from love of solitude and dislike of instruction; any alarm exhibited at his appearance may be reasonably traced to the slaughter which has reduced their numbers; and as some evidence of this, it has always been observed in Ceylon that an elephant manifests greater impatience of the presence of a white man than of a native. Were its instincts to carry it further, or were it influenced by any feeling of animosity or malignity, it must be apparent that, as against the prodigious numbers that inhabit the forests of the island, man would wage an unequal contest, and that of the two, one or other must long since have been reduced to a helpless minority.

Official testimony is not wanting in confirmation of this view: in the returns of 108 coroner's inquests in Ceylon, during five years from 1849 to 1855 inclusive, held in cases of death occasioned by wild animals, 15 are recorded as having been caused by buffaloes, 6 by crocodiles, 2 by boars, 1 by a bear, and 68 by serpents (the great majority of the last class of sufferers being women and children, who had been bitten during the night), and 16 by elephants. Little more than three fatal accidents occurring annually on the average of five years, is certainly a very small proportion in a population estimated at a million and a half, in an island abounding with wild elephants, with which, independently of casual encounters, voluntary conflicts are daily stimulated by the love of sport or the hope of gain. Were the elephants instinctively vicious or even highly irritable in their temperament, the destruction of human life under the circumstances must have been infinitely greater. It must also be taken into account, that some of the accidents recorded may have occurred in the rutting season, when even tame elephants are subject to fits of temporary fury, known in India by the term *must,* in Ceylon *mudda,*—a paroxysm which speedily passes away, but during the fury of which it is dangerous even for the mahout who has charge of them to approach those ordinarily the gentlest and most familiar.

Again, the elephant is said to 'entertain an extraordinary dislike to all quadrupeds; that dogs running near it produce annoyance; that it is alarmed if a hare start from her form;' and from Pliny to Buffon every naturalist has asserted its supposed aversion to swine. These alleged antipathies are in as great degree, if not altogether, imaginary. The habits of the elephant are essentially harmless, its wants lead to no rivalry with other animals, and the food to which it is most attached flourishes in such luxuriance that abundance of it is obtained without an effort. In the quiet solitudes of Ceylon, elephants may be seen browsing peacefully in the immediate vicinity of other animals, and often in close contact with them. I have seen groups of deer and wild buffaloes reclining in the sandy bed of a river in the dry season, and elephants plucking the branches above and beside them. They show no impatience in the company of the elk, the bear, and the wild hog; and on the other hand, I have never discovered an instance in which these animals have evinced any apprehension of the elephant. Its natural timidity, however, is such that it becomes alarmed on the appearance in the jungle of any animal with whose form it is not familiar. It is said to be afraid of the horse; but from my own experience, I should say it is the horse that is disquieted at the aspect of the elephant. In the same way, from some unaccountable impulse, the horse has an antipathy to the camel, and evinces extreme impatience, both of the sight and the smell of that animal. When enraged, an elephant will not hesitate to charge a rider on horseback; but it is against the man, not against the horse, that his fury is directed; and no instance has been ever known of his wantonly assailing a horse. ...

Pigs are constantly to be seen feeding about the stables of tame elephants, which manifest no repugnance to them. As to smaller animals, the elephant undoubtedly evinces uneasiness at the presence of a dog, but this is referable to the same cause as its impatience of a horse, namely, that neither is habitually seen by it in the forest; and it would be idle to suppose that this feeling could amount to hostility against a creature incapable of inflicting on it the slightest injury. The truth I apprehend to be that, when they meet, the impudence and impertinences of the dog are offensive to the gravity of the elephant, and incompatible with his love of solitude and noiseless repose. Or, as regards the horse and the dog, may it be assumed as an evidence of the sagacity of the elephant, that the only two animals to which it manifests an antipathy, are the two which it has seen only in the company of its greatest enemy, man? ... On the whole, therefore, I am of opinion that in a state of nature the elephant lives on terms of amity with every animal in the forest, that it neither regards them as its foes, nor provokes their hostility by its acts; and that, with the exception of man, its greatest enemy is a fly! ...

Amongst elephants themselves, jealousy and other causes of irritation frequently occasion contentions between individuals of the same herd; but on such occasions their general habit is to strike with their trunks, and to bear down their opponents with their heads. It is doubtless correct that an elephant, when prostrated by the force and fury of an antagonist of its own species, is often wounded by the downward pressure of the tusks, which in any other position it would be almost impossible to use offensively.

Mr Mercer, who in 1846 was the principal civil officer of Government at Badulla, sent me a jagged fragment of an elephant's tusk, about five inches in diameter, and weighing between twenty and thirty pounds, which had been brought to him by some natives, who, being attracted by a noise in the jungle, witnessed a combat between a tusker and one without tusks, and saw the latter with his trunk seize one of the tusks of his antagonist and wrench from it the portion in question, which measured two feet in length.

Here the trunk was shown to be the more powerful offensive weapon of the two; but I apprehend that the chief reliance of the elephant for defence is on its ponderous weight, the pressure of its foot being sufficient to crush any minor assailant after being prostrated by means of its trunk. Besides, in using its feet for this purpose, it derives a wonderful facility from the peculiar formation of the knee-joint in the hind leg, which, enabling it to swing the hind feet forward close to the ground, assists it to toss the body alternately from foot to foot, till deprived of life. ...

But here there arises a further and a very curious enquiry, as to the specific objects in the economy of the elephant, to which its tusks are conducive. Placed as it is in Ceylon, in the midst of the most luxuriant profusion of its favourite food, in close proximity at all times to abundant supplies of water, and with no natural enemies against whom to protect itself, it is difficult to conjecture any probable utility which it can derive from such appendages. Their absence is unaccompanied by any inconvenience to the individuals in whom they are wanting; and as regards the few who possess them, the only operation in which I am aware of their tusks being employed in relation to the habits of the animal, is to assist in ripping open the stem of the jaggery palms and young palmyras to extract the farinaceous core; and in splitting up the juicy shaft of the plantain. Whilst the tuskless elephant crushes the latter under foot, thereby soiling it and wasting its moisture; the other, by opening it with the point of its tusk, performs the operation with delicacy and apparent ease.

These, however, are trivial and almost accidental advantages: on the other hand, owing to irregularities in their growth, the tusks are sometimes an impediment to the animal in feeding; and in more than one instance in the Government studs, tusks which had so grown as to approach and cross one another at the extremities, have had to be relieved by the saw; the contraction of space between them so impeding the free action of the trunk as to prevent the animal from conveying branches to its mouth. ...

Between the African elephant and that of Ceylon, with the exception of the striking peculiarity of the infrequency of tusks in the latter, the distinctions are less apparent to a casual observer than to a scientific naturalist. In the Ceylon species the forehead is higher and more hollow, the ears are smaller, and, in a section of the teeth, the grinding ridges, instead of being lozenge-shaped, are transverse bars of uniform breadth.

The Indian elephant is stated by Cuvier to have four nails on the hind foot, the African variety having only three; but amongst the perfections of a high-bred elephant of Ceylon, is always enumerated the possession of *twenty* nails, whilst those of a secondary class have but eighteen in all.

So conversant are the natives with the structure and 'points' of the elephant, that they divide them readily into castes, and describe with particularity their distinctive excellences and defects.[7]

Amongst the Singhalese, however, a singular preference is evinced for elephants that exhibit those flesh-coloured blotches which occasionally mottle the skin of an elephant, chiefly about the head and extremities. The front of the trunk, the tips of the ears, the forehead, and occasionally the legs, are thus diversified with stains of a yellowish tint, inclining to pink. These are not natural; nor are they hereditary, for they are seldom exhibited by the younger individuals in a herd, but appear to be the result of some eruptive affection, the irritation of which has induced the animal in its uneasiness to rub itself against the rough bark of trees, and thus to abrade the outer cuticle.

To a European these spots appear blemishes, and the taste that leads the natives to admire them is probably akin to the feeling that has at all times rendered a *white elephant* an object of wonder to Asiatics. The rarity of the latter is accounted for by regarding this peculiar appearance as the result of albinism; ...

In 1633 a white elephant was exhibited in Holland; but as this was some years before the Dutch had established themselves firmly in Ceylon, it was probably brought from some other of their eastern possessions.

Habits When Wild

Although found generally in warm and sunny climates, it is a mistake to suppose that the elephant is partial either to heat or to light. In Ceylon, the mountain tops, and not the sultry valleys, are its favourite resort. In Ouvah, where the elevated plains are often crisp with the morning frost, and on Pedura-talla-galla, at the height of upwards of eight thousand feet, they may be found in herds at times when the hunter will search for them without success in the hot jungles of the low country. No altitude, in fact, seems too lofty or too chill for the elephant, provided it affords the luxury of water in abundance; and, contrary to the general opinion that the elephant delights in sunshine, it seems at all times impatient of

[7]Here follows a detailed description of these 'points' from *Hastisilpe*, an old Sri Lankan work.—DKLC.

glare, and spends the day in the thickest depth of the forests, devoting the night to excursions, and to the luxury of the bath, in which it also indulges occasionally by day. ...

All the elephant hunters and natives with whom I have spoken on the subject, concur in opinion that its range of vision is circumscribed, and that it relies more on the ear and the sense of smell than on its sight, which is liable to be obstructed by dense foliage; besides which, from the formation of its short neck, the elephant is incapable of directing the range of the eye much above the level of the head. ...

On the other hand, the power of smell is so remarkable as almost to compensate for the deficiency of sight. A herd is not only apprised of the approach of danger by this means, but when scattered in the forest, and dispersed out of range of sight, they are enabled by it to reassemble with rapidity and to adopt precautions for their common safety. The same necessity is met by a delicate sense of hearing, and the use of a variety of noises or calls, by means of which elephants succeed in communicating with each other upon all emergencies. 'The sounds which they utter have been described by the African hunters as of there kinds: the first, which is very shrill, produced by blowing through the trunk, is indicative of pleasure; the second, produced by the mouth, is expressive of want; and the third, proceeding from the throat, is a terrific roar of anger or revenge.' These words convey but an imperfect idea of the variety of noises made by the elephant in Ceylon; and the shrill cry produced by blowing through his trunk, so far from being regarded as an indication of 'pleasure', is the well-known cry of rage with which he rushes to encounter an assailant. Aristotle describes it as resembling the hoarse sound of a 'trumpet'. The French still designate the proboscis of an elephant by the same expression 'trompe' (which we have unmeaningly corrupted into *trunk*), and hence the scream of the elephant is known as 'trumpeting' by the hunters in Ceylon. ...

Should the attention of an individual in the herd be attracted by any unusual appearance in the forest, the intelligence is rapidly communicated by a low suppressed sound made by the lips, somewhat resembling the twittering of a bird, and described by the hunters by the word '*prut*'.

A very remarkable noise has been described to me by more than one individual,. who had come unexpectedly upon a herd during the night, when the alarm of the elephants was apparently too great to be satisfied with the stealthy note of warning just described. On these occasions the sound produced resembled the hollow booming of an empty tin when struck with a wooden mallet or a muffled sledge. Major Macready, Military Secretary in Ceylon in 1836, who heard it by night amongst the wild elephants in the great forest of Bintenne, describes it as 'a sort of banging noise like that of a cooper hammering a cask', and Major Skinner is of opinion that it must be produced by the elephant striking his ribs rapidly and forcibly with his trunk. Mr Cripps informs me that he has more than once seen an elephant, when surprised or alarmed, produce this sound by beating the ground forcibly with the flat side of the trunk; and this movement was instantly succeeded by raising it again, and pointing it in the direction whence the alarm proceeded, as if to ascertain by the sense of smell the nature of the threatened danger. As this strange sound is generally mingled with the bellowing and ordinary trumpeting of the herd, it is in all probability a device resorted to, not alone for warning their companions of some approaching peril, but also for the additional purpose of terrifying unseen intruders.

Elephants are subject to deafness; and the Singhalese regard as the most formidable of all wild animals, a 'rogue' afflicted with this infirmity.

Extravagant estimates are recorded of the height of the elephant. In an age when popular fallacies in relation to him were as yet uncorrected in Europe by the actual inspection of the living animal, he was supposed to grow to the height of twelve or fifteen feet. Even within the last century, in popular works on natural history, the elephant, when full grown, was said to measure from seventeen to twenty feet from the ground to the shoulder.[8] At a still later

[8]*Natural History of Animals.* By Sir John Hill. M.D. London 1748– 52, p. 565. A probable source of these false estimates is mentioned by a writer in the *Indian Sporting Review* for October 1857. 'Elephants were measured formerly, and even now, by natives, as to their height, by throwing a rope over them, the ends brought to the ground on each side, and half the length taken as the true height. Hence the origin of elephants fifteen and sixteen feet high. A rod held at right angles to the measuring rod, and parallel to the ground, will rarely give more than ten feet, the majority being under nine' (p. 159).

period, so imperfectly had the truth been ascertained, that the elephant of Ceylon was believed 'to excel that of Africa in size and strength'. But so far from equalling the size of the African species, that of Ceylon seldom exceeds the height of nine feet; even in the Hambangtotte country, where the hunters agree that the largest specimens are to be found, the tallest in ordinary herds do not average more than eight feet. ...

For a creature of such extraordinary weight it is astonishing how noiselessly and stealthily the elephant can escape from a pursuer. When suddenly disturbed in the jungle, it will burst away with a rush that seems to bear down all before it; but the noise sinks into absolute stillness so suddenly, that a novice might well be led to suppose that the fugitive had only halted within a few yards of him, when further search will disclose that it has stolen away, making scarcely a sound in its escape; and, stranger still, leaving the foliage almost undisturbed by its passage. ...

The real peculiarity in the elephant in lying down is, that he extends his hind legs backwards as a man does when he kneels, instead of bringing them under him like the horse or any other quadruped. The wise purpose of this arrangement must be obvious to anyone who observes the struggle with which the horse *gets up* from the ground, and the violent efforts which he makes to raise himself erect. Such an exertion in the case of the elephant, and the force requisite to apply a similar movement to raise his weight (equal to four or five tons) would be attended with a dangerous strain upon the muscles, and hence the simple arrangement, which by enabling him to draw the hind feet gradually under him, assists him to rise without a perceptible effort.

From the same causes I am disposed to think that the elephant is too weighty and unwieldy to leap, at least to any considerable height or distance; and yet I have seen in the *Colombo Observer* for March 1866, an interesting account of a corral, written by an able and accurate describer, in which it is stated that an infuriated tusker, the property of the Government, made a rush to escape from the enclosure, 'and fairly leaped the barrier, of some fifteen feet high, only carrying away the top cross beam with a great crash'.

The same construction rendered his gait not a 'gallop', as it has been somewhat loosely described, which would be too violent a motion for so vast a body; but a shuffle, that he can increase at pleasure to a pace as rapid as that of a man at full speed, but which he cannot maintain for any considerable distance.

It is to the structure of the knee-joint that the elephant is indebted for his singular facility in ascending and descending steep acclivities, climbing rocks and traversing precipitous ledges, where even a mule dare not venture; and this again leads to the correction of another generally received error, that his legs are 'formed more for strength than flexibility and fitted to bear an enormous weight upon a level surface without the necessity of ascending or descending great acclivities'. The same authority assumes that, although the elephant is found in the neighbourhood of mountainous ranges, and will even ascend rocky passes, such a service is a violation of its natural habits.

Of the elephant of Africa I am not qualified to speak, nor of the nature of the ground which it most frequents; but certainly the facts in connection with the elephant of India are all irreconcilable with the theory mentioned above. In Bengal, in the Nilgherries, in Nepal, in Burmah, in Siam, Sumatra, and Ceylon, the districts in which the elephants most abound, are all hilly and mountainous. In the latter, especially, there is not a range so elevated as to be inaccessible to them. On the very summit of Adam's Peak, at an altitude of 7420 feet and on a pinnacle which the pilgrims climb with difficulty, by means of steps hewn in the rock, Major Skinner, in 1840, found the spoor of an elephant.

Prior to 1840, and before coffee-plantations had been extensively opened in the Kandyan ranges, there was not a mountain or a lofty feature of land of Ceylon which they had not traversed, in their periodical migrations in search of water; and the sagacity which they display in 'laying out roads' is almost incredible. They generally keep along the *backbone* of a chain of hills, avoiding steep gradients: and one curious observation was not lost upon the Government surveyors, that in crossing valleys from ridge to ridge, through forests so dense as to obstruct a distant view, the elephants invariably select the line of march which communicates most judiciously with the opposite point, by means of the safest ford.[9] So sure-footed are they, that there are few places where man

[9]Dr Hooker, in describing the ascent of the Himalayas, says, the natives in making their paths despise all zigzags, and run in straight lines up the steepest hill faces, whilst 'the elephant's path is an excellent specimen of engineering—

can go that an elephant cannot follow, provided there be space to admit his bulk, and solidity to sustain his weight. ...

A *herd* of elephants is a family, not a group whom accident or attachment may have induced to associate together. Similarity of features and caste attest that, among the various individuals which compose it, there is a common lineage and relationship. In a herd of twenty-one elephants, captured in 1844, the trunks of each individual presented the same peculiar formation—long and almost of one uniform breadth throughout, instead of tapering gradually from the root to the nostril. In another instance, the eyes of thirty-five taken in one corral were of the same colour in each. The same slope of the back, the same form of the forehead, is to be detected in the majority of the same group.

In the forest several herds sometimes browse in close contiguity, and in their expeditions in search of water they may form a body of possibly one or two hundred; but on the slightest disturbance each distinct herd hastens to re-form within its own particular circle, and to take measures on its own behalf for retreat or defence.

The proportion of males is generally small, and some herds have been seen composed exclusively of females; possibly in consequence of the males having been shot. A herd usually consists of from ten to twenty individuals, though occasionally they exceed the latter number; and in their frequent migrations and nightly resort to tanks and water-courses, alliances are formed between members of associated herds, which serve to introduce new blood into the family.

In illustration of the attachment of the elephant to its young, the authority of Knox has been quoted, that 'the shees are alike tender of anyone's young ones as of their own'. Their affection in this particular is undoubted, but I question whether it exceeds that of other animals; and the trait thus adduced of their indiscriminate kindness to all the young of the herd,—of which I have myself been an eye-witness,—so far from being an evidence of the intensity of parental attachment individually, is, perhaps, somewhat inconsistent with the existence of such a passion to any extraordinary degree. In fact, some individuals, who have had extensive facilities for

---

the opposite of the native tracks—for it winds judiciously.' (*Himalayan Journal*, vol. i ch. iv.)

observation, doubt whether the fondness of the female elephants for their offspring is so great as that of many other animals; as instances are not wanting in Ceylon, in which, when pursued by the hunters, the herd has abandoned the young ones in their flight, notwithstanding the cries of the latter for protection.

In an interesting paper on the habits of the Indian elephant, published in the *Philosophical Transactions* for 1793, Mr Corse says: 'If a wild elephant happens to be separated from its young for only two days, though giving suck, she never after recognises or acknowledges it', although the young one evidently knows its dam, and by its plaintive cries and submissive approaches solicits her assistance.

It is believed by the Singhalese that these are either individuals, who by accident have lost their former associates and become morose and savage from rage and solitude; or else that being naturally vicious they have become daring from the yielding habits of their milder companions, and eventually separated themselves from the rest of the herd which had refused to associate with them. Another conjecture is, that being almost universally males, the death or capture of particular females may have detached them from their former companions in search of fresh alliances. It is also believed that a tame elephant escaping from captivity, unable to rejoin its former herd, and excluded from any other, becomes a '*rogue*' from necessity. In Ceylon it is generally believed that the *rogues* are all males (but of this I am not certain), and so sullen is their disposition that although two may be in the same vicinity, there is no known instance of two *rogues* associating, or of a *rogue* being seen in company with another elephant.

They spend their nights in marauding, often around dwellings of men, destroying plantations, trampling down gardens, and committing serious ravages in rice grounds and young coconut plantations. ... By day they generally seek concealment, but are frequently to be met with prowling about the by-roads and jungle paths, where travellers are exposed to the utmost risk from their assaults. It is probable that this hostility to man is the result of the enmity engendered by measures which the natives, who have a constant dread of their visits, adopt for the protection of the growing crops. ...

To return to the herd: one member of it, usually the largest and stand most powerful, is by common consent implicitly followed as leader. A tusker, if there be one in the party, is generally observed to be the commander; but a female, if of superior energy, is as readily obeyed as a male. ...

In drinking, the elephant, like the camel, although preferring water pure, shows no decided aversion to it when discoloured with mud; and the eagerness with which he precipitates himself into the tanks and streams attests his exquisite enjoyment of fresh coolness, which to him is the chief attraction. In crossing deep rivers, although his rotundity and buoyancy enable him to swim with less immersion than other quadrupeds, he generally prefers to sink till no part of his huge body is visible except the tip of his trunk, through which he breathes, moving beneath the surface, and only now and then raising his head to look that he is keeping the proper direction. In the dry season the scanty streams which, during the rains, are sufficient to convert the rivers of the low country into torrents, often entirely disappear, leaving only broad expanses of dry sand, which they have swept down with them from the hills. In this the elephants contrive to sink wells for their own use by scooping out the sand to the depth of four or five feet, and leaving a hollow for the percolation of the spring. But as the weight of the elephant would force in the side if left perpendicular, one approach is always formed with such a gradient that he can reach the water with his trunk without disturbing the surrounding sand.

I have reason to believe, although the fact has not been authoritatively stated by naturalists, that the stomach of the elephant will be found to include a chamber analogous to that possessed by some of the ruminants, calculated to contain a supply of water as a provision against emergencies. The fact of his being enabled to retain a quantity of water and discharge it at pleasure has been long known to every observer of the habits of the animal; but the proboscis has always been supposed to be 'his water-reservoir', and the theory of an internal receptacle has not been discussed. The truth is that the anatomy of the elephant is even yet but imperfectly understood, and, although some peculiarities of his stomach were observed at an early period by Aristotle and others; and even their configuration described; the function of the abnormal portion remained undetermined, and has been only recently conjectured. An elephant which belonged to Louis XIV died at Versailles in 1681 at the age of seventeen, and an account of its dissection was published in the *Mémoires pour servir à l'Histoire Naturelle*, under the authority of the Academy of Sciences, in which the unusual appendages of the stomach are pointed out with sufficient particularity, but no suggestion is made as to their probable uses. ...

The *food* of the elephant is so abundant that in eating he never appears to be impatient or voracious, but rather to play with the leaves and branches on which he leisurely feeds. In riding by places where a herd has recently halted, I have sometimes seen the bark peeled curiously off the twigs, as though it had been done in mere dalliance. In the same way in eating grass the elephant selects a tussac he draws from the ground by a dexterous twist of his trunk, and nothing can be more graceful than the ease with which, before conveying it to his mouth, he beats the earth from its roots by striking it gently upon his fore-leg. A coco-nut he first rolls under foot, to detach the strong outer bark, then stripping off with his trunk the thick layer of fibre within, he places the shell in his mouth, and swallows with evident relish the fresh liquid which flows as he crushes it between his grinders.

The natives of the peninsula of Jaffna always look for the periodical appearance of the elephants, at the precise time when the fruit of the palmyra palm begins to fall to the ground from ripeness. In like manner in the eastern provinces where the custom prevails of cultivating what is called *chena* land (by clearing a patch of forest for the purpose of raising a single crop, after which the ground is abandoned, and reverts to jungle again), although a single elephant may not have been seen in the neighbourhood during the early stages of the process, the Moormen, who are the principal cultivators of this class, will predict their appearance with almost unerring confidence so soon as the grains shall have begun to ripen; and although the crop comes to maturity at different periods in different districts, herds are certain to be seen at each in succession, as soon as it is ready to be cut. ...

There is something still unexplained in the dread which an elephant always exhibits on approaching a fence, and the reluctance which he displays to face the slightest artificial obstruction to his passage. ...

Sportsmen observe that an elephant, even when enraged by a wound, will hesitate to charge an assailant across an intervening hedge, but will hurry along it to seek for an opening. ...

At the same time, the caution with which the elephant is supposed to approach insecure ground and places of doubtful solidity, appears to me, so far as my own observation and experience extend, to be exaggerated, and the number of temporary bridges which are annually broken down by elephants in all parts of Ceylon, is sufficient to show that, although in captivity, and when familiar with such structures, the tame ones may, and doubtless do, exhibit all the wariness attributed to them; yet, in a state of liberty, and whilst unaccustomed to such artificial appliances, their instincts are not sufficient to ensure their safety. Besides, the fact is adverted to elsewhere, that the chiefs of the Wanny, during the sovereignty of the Dutch, were accustomed to take in pitfalls the elephants which they rendered as tribute to Government.

A fact illustrative at once of the caution and the spirit of curiosity with which an elephant regards an unaccustomed object has been frequently mentioned to me by officers engaged in opening roads through the forest. On such occasions the wooden 'tracing pegs' which they drive into the ground to mark the levels taken during the day, will often be withdrawn by the elephants during the night, to such an extent as frequently to render it necessary to go over the work a second time, in order to replace them. ...

As regards the general sagacity of the elephant, although it has not been over-rated in the instances of those whose powers have been largely developed in captivity, an undue estimate has been formed in relation to them whilst still untamed. The difference of instincts and habits renders it difficult to institute a just comparison between them and other animals. Cuvier is disposed to ascribe the exalted idea that prevails of their intellect to the feats which an elephant performs with that unique instrument, its trunk, combined with an imposing expression of countenance: but he records his own conviction that in sagacity it in no way excels the dog, and some other species of carnivora. If there be a superiority, I am disposed to award it to the dog, not from any excess of natural capacity, but from the higher degree of development consequent on his more intimate domestication and association with man. Coleridge has remarked that 'the ant and the bee seem to come nearer to man in understanding, and in the faculty of adapting means to proximate ends'. ...

When free in its native woods the elephant evinces rather simplicity than sagacity, and its intelligence seldom exhibits itself in cunning. The rich profusion in which nature has supplied its food, and anticipated its every want, has made it independent of those devices by which carnivorous animals provide for their subsistence; and, from the absence of all rivalry between it and the other denizens of the plains, it is never required to resort to artifice for self-protection. For these reasons, in its tranquil and harmless life, it may appear to casual observers to exhibit even less than ordinary ability; but when danger and apprehension call for the exertion of its powers, those who have witnessed their display are seldom inclined to undervalue its sagacity. ...

The working elephant is always a delicate animal, and requires watchfulness and care. As a beast of burden it is unsatisfactory; for although in point of mere strength there is scarcely any weight which could be conveniently placed on it that it could not carry, it is difficult to pack the load without causing abrasions that afterwards ulcerate. The skin is easily chafed by harness, especially in wet weather. During either long droughts or too much moisture, an elephant's feet become liable to sores, that render it non-effective for months. Many attempts have been made to provide some protection for the sole of the foot, but from the extreme weight and the peculiar mode of planting the foot, they have all been unsuccessful. The eyes are also liable to frequent inflammations, and the skill of the native elephant-doctors, which has been renowned since the time of Ælian, is nowhere more strikingly displayed than in the successful treatment of such attacks. In Ceylon, the murrain among the cattle is of frequent occurrence, and carries off great numbers of animals, wild as well as tame. In such visitations the elephants suffer severely, not only those at liberty in the forest, but those carefully tended in the Government stables. Out of a stud of about 40 attached to the department of the Commission of Roads, the deaths between 1841 and 1849 were on an average *four* in each year, and this was nearly doubled in those years when murrain prevailed.

Of 240 elephants employed in the public departments of the Ceylon Government, which died in twenty-five years, from 1831 to 1856, the length of time each lived in captivity has only been recorded in the instances of 138. Of these there died:

Duration of captivity	No.	Male	Female
Under 1 year	72	29	43
From 1 to 2 years	14	5	9
From 2 to 3 years	8	5	3
From 3 to 4 years	8	3	5
From 4 to 5 years	3	2	1
From 5 to 6 years	2	2	-
From 6 to 7 years	3	1	2
From 7 to 8 years	5	2	3
From 8 to 9 years	5	5	-
From 9 to 10 years	2	2	-
From 10 to 11 years	2	2	-
From 11 to 12 years	3	1	2
From 12 to 13 years	3	-	3
From 13 to 14 years	-	-	-
From 14 to 15 years	3	1	2
From 15 to 16 years	1	1	-
From 16 to 17 years	1	-	1
From 17 to 18 years	-	-	-
From 18 to 19 years	2	1	1
From 19 to 20 years	1	-	1
Total	138	62	76

Of the 72 who died in one year's servitude, 35 expired within the first six months of their captivity. During training, many elephants die in the unaccountable manner already referred to, of what the natives designate a *broken heart*.

On being first subjected to work, the elephant is liable to severe and often fatal swellings of the jaws and abdomen.

From these causes there died, between 1841 and 1849	9
Of cattle murrain	10
Sore feet	1
Colds and inflammation	6
Diarrhoea	1
Worms	1
Of diseased liver	1
Injuries from a fall	1
General debility	1
Unknown causes	3

Of the entire, twenty-three were females and eleven males.

The ages of those that died could not be accurately stated, owing to the circumstance of their having been captured in corral. Two only were tuskers. Towards keeping the stud in health, nothing has been found so conducive as regularly bathing the elephants, and giving them the opportunity to stand with their feet in water, or in moistened earth.

Elephants are said to be afflicted with toothache; their tushes have likewise been found with symptoms of internal perforation by some parasite, and the natives assert that, in their agony, the animals have been known to break them off short.[10] I have never heard of the teeth themselves being so affected, and it is just possible that the operation of shedding and the subsequent decay of the milk-tushes, may have in some instances been accompanied by incidents that gave rise to this story. At the same time the probabilities are in favour of its being true. Cuvier committed himself to the statement that the tusks of the elephant have no attachments to connect them with the pulp lodged in the cavity at their base, from which the peculiar modification of dentine, known as 'ivory' is secreted; and hence, by inference, that they would be devoid of sensation. But independently of the fact that ivory is permeated by tubes so fine that at their origin from the pulpy cavity they do not exceed the 1/15,000 part of an inch in diameter, Owen had the tusk and pulp of the great elephant which died at the Zoological Gardens in London in 1847 longitudinally divided, and found that, 'although the pulp could be easily detached from the inner surface of the cavity, it was not without a certain resistance; and when the edges of the co-adapted pulp and tusk were examined by a strong lens, the filamentary processes from the outer surface of the former could be seen stretching, as they were drawn from the dental tubes, before they broke. The filaments are so minute, he adds, that to the naked eye the detached surface of the pulp seems to be entire; and hence Cuvier was deceived into supposing that there was no organic connection between the pulp and the ivory. But if, as there seems no reason to doubt, these delicate nervous processes traverse the tusk by means of the numerous tubes already described, if attacked by caries the pain occasioned to the elephant would be excruciating.

As to maintaining a stud of elephants for the purposes to which

[10]See a paper entitled 'Recollections of Ceylon', in *Fraser's Magazine,* December 1860.

they are now assigned in Ceylon, there may be a question on the score of prudence and economy. In the wild and unopened parts of the country, where rivers are to be forded, and forests are only traversed by jungle paths, their labour is of value, in certain contingencies in the conveyance of stores, and in the earlier operations for the construction of fords and rough bridges of timber. But in more highly civilized districts, and where macadamised roads admit of the employment of horses and oxen for draught, I apprehend that the services of the elephant might, with advantage, be gradually reduced, if not altogether dispensed with.

The love of the elephant for coolness and shade renders it at all times more or less impatient of work in the sun, and every moment of leisure it can snatch is employed in covering its back with dust, or fanning itself to diminish the annoyance of the insects and heat. From the tenderness of the skin and its liability to sores, the labour in which the elephant can most advantageously be employed is that of draught; but the reluctance of horses to meet or pass them renders it difficult to work them with safety on frequented roads. Besides, were the full load which an elephant is capable of drawing, proportionally to its muscular strength, to be placed upon wagons of corresponding dimension, the injury to roads from the extra weight would be such that the wear and tear of the highways and bridges would prove too costly to be borne. On the other hand, by restricting it to a somewhat more manageable quantity, and by limiting the weight, as at present, to about *one ton and a half*, it is doubtful whether an elephant performs so much more work than could be done by a horse or by bullocks, as to compensate for the greater cost of his feeding and attendance.

Add to this, that from accidents and other causes, from ulcerations of the skin, and illnesses of many kinds, the elephant is so often invalided, that the actual cost of its labour, when at work, is very considerably enhanced. Exclusive of the salaries of higher officers attached to the Government establishments, and other permanent charges, the expenses of an elephant, looking only to the wages of its attendants and the cost of its food and medicines, varies from *three shillings to four shillings and sixpence* per diem, according to its size and class.[11] Taking the average at three shillings and

[11]An ordinary-sized elephant engrosses the undivided attention of *three* men. One, as his mahout or superintendent, and two as leaf-cutters, who

ninepence, and calculating that hardly any individual works more than four days out of seven, the charge for each day so employed would amount to *six shillings and sixpence.* The keep per day of a powerful dray-horse, working five days in the week, would not exceed half-a-crown, and two such would unquestionably do more work than any elephant under the present system. I do not know whether it be from a comparative calculation of this kind that the strength of the elephant establishments in Ceylon has been gradually diminished of late years, but in the department of the Commissioner of Roads, the stud, which formerly numbered upwards of sixty elephants, was reduced, some years ago, to thirty-six, and is at present less than half that number.

The fallacy of the supposed reluctance of the elephant to breed in captivity has been demonstrated by many recent authorities; but with the exception of the birth of young elephants at Rome, as

---

bring him branches and grass for his daily supplies. An animal of larger growth would probably require a third leaf-cutter. The daily consumption is two cwt. of green food with about half a bushel of grain. When in the vicinity of towns and villages, the attendants have no difficulty in procuring an abundant supply of the branches of the trees to which elephants are partial; and in journeys through the forests and unopened country, the leaf-cutters are sufficiently expert in the knowledge of those particular plants with which the elephant is satisfied. Those that would be likely to disagree with him he unerringly rejects. His favourites are the palms, especially the cluster of rich, unopened leaves, known as the 'cabbage', of the coconut and areca; and he delights to tear open the young trunks of the palmyra and jaggery (*Caryota urens*) in search of the farinaceous matter contained in the spongy pith. Next to these come the varieties of fig-trees, particularly the sacred *Bo* (*F. religiosa*) religious which is found near every temple, and the *na gaha* (*Messua ferrea*), with thick dark leaves and a scarlet flower. The leaves of the jak-tree and bread-fruit (*Artocarpus integrifolia*, and *A. incisa*) the wood apple (*Ægle masmelos*), Palu (*Mimusops indica*) and a number of others well known to their attendants, are all consumed in turn. The stems of the plantain, the stalks of the sugar-cane, and the feathery tops of the bamboos, are irresistible luxuries. Pine-apples, water-melons and fruits of every description, are voraciously devoured, and a coconut when found is first rolled under foot to detach it from the husk and fibre, and then raised in his trunk and crushed almost without an effort, by his ponderous jaws.

The grasses are not found in sufficient quantity to be an item of daily fodder; the Mauritius or the Guinea grass is seized with avidity; lemon grass is rejected from its overpowering perfume, but rice in the straw, and every description of grain, whether growing or dry; gram (*Cicer arietinum*), Indian corn, and millet, are his natural food. Of such of these as can be found, it is the duty of the leaf-cutters, when in the jungle and on march, to provide a daily supply.

mentioned by Ælian, the only instances that I am aware of their actually producing young under such circumstances, took place in Ceylon. Both parents had been for several years attached to the stud of the Commissioner of Roads, and in 1844 the female, whilst engaged in dragging a wagon, gave birth to a still-born calf. Some years before, an elephant that had been captured by Mr Cripps, dropped a female calf, which he succeeded in rearing. As usual, the little one became the pet of the keepers; but as it increased in growth, it exhibited the utmost violence when thwarted; striking out with its hind-feet, throwing itself headlong on the ground, and pressing its trunk against any opposing object.

The duration of life in the elephant has been from the remotest times a matter of uncertainty and speculation. Aristotle says it was reputed to live from two to three hundred years, and modern zoologists have assigned to it an age very little less; Cuvier allots two hundred and de Blainville one hundred and twenty. The only attempt which I know of to establish a period historically or physiologically is that of Fleurens, who has advanced an ingenious theory on the subject in his treatise '*De la Longévité Humaine*'. He assumes the sum total of life in all animals to be equivalent to five times the number of years requisite to perfect their growth and development;—and he adopts as evidence of the period at which growth ceases, the final consolidation of the bones with their *epiphyses*; which in the young consist of cartilages; but in the adult become uniformly osseous and solid. So long as the epiphyses are distinct from the bones, the growth of the animal is proceeding, but it ceases as soon as the consolidation is complete. In man, according to Fleurens, this consummation takes place at 20 years of age, in the horse at 5, in the dog at 2; so that conformably to this theory the respective normal age for each would be 100 years for man, 25 for the horse, and 10 for a dog. As a datum for his conclusion, Fleurens cites the instance of one young elephant in which, at 26 years old, the epiphyses were still distinct, whereas in another, which died at 31, they were firm and adherent. Hence he draws the inference that the period of completed solidification is thirty years, and consequently that the normal age of the elephant is *one hundred and fifty*.

Amongst the Singhalese the ancient fable of the elephant attaining to the age of two or three hundred years still prevails; but the Europeans, and those in immediate charge of tame ones, entertain the opinion that the duration of life for about *seventy* years is common both to man and the elephant; and that before the arrival of the latter period, symptoms of debility and decay ordinarily begin to manifest themselves. Still instances are not wanting in Ceylon of trained decoys that have lived for more than double the reputed period in actual servitude. One employed by Mr Cripps in the Seven Korles was represented by the cooroowe people to have served the king of Kandy in the same capacity sixty years before; and amongst the papers left by Colonel Robertson (son to the historian of 'Charles V') who held a command in Ceylon in 1799, shortly after the capture of the island by the British, I have found a memorandum showing that a decoy was then attached to the elephant establishment at Matura, which the records proved to have served under the Dutch during the entire period of their occupation (extending to upwards of one hundred and forty years); and it was said to have been found in the stables by the Dutch on the expulsion of the Portuguese in 1656.

It is perhaps from this popular belief in their almost illimitable age, that the natives generally assert that the body of a dead elephant is seldom or never to be discovered in the woods. And certain it is that frequenters of the forest with whom I have conversed, whether European or Singhalese, are consistent in their assurances that they have never found the remains of an elephant that had died a natural death. One chief, the Wannyah of the Trincomalie district, told a friend of mine, that once after a severe murrain, which had swept the province, he found the carcasses of elephants that had died of the disease. On the other hand, a European gentleman, who for thirty-six years without intermission has been living in the jungle, ascending to the summits of mountains in the prosecution of the trigonometrical survey, and penetrating valleys in tracing roads and opening means of communication,—one, too, who has made the habits of the wild elephant a subject of constant observation and study,—has often expressed to me his astonishment that after seeing many thousands of living elephants in all possible situations, he had never yet found a single skeleton of a dead one, except of those which had fallen by the rifle.[12]

[12]This remark regarding the elephant of Ceylon does not appear to extend to that of Africa, as I observe that Beaver, in his *African Memoranda*, says that 'the skeletons of old ones that have died in the woods are frequently found'.

It has been suggested that the bones of the elephant may be so porous and spongy as to disappear in consequence of an early decomposition; but this remark would not apply to the grinders or to the tusks; besides which, the inference is at variance with the fact, that not only the horns and teeth, but entire skeletons of deer, are frequently found in the districts inhabited by the elephant.

The natives, to account for this popular belief, declare that the survivors of the herd bury such of their companions as die a natural death.[13] It is curious that this belief was current also amongst the Greeks of the Lower Empire; and Phile, writing early in the fourteenth century, not only describes the younger elephants as tending the wounded, but as burying the dead.[14]

The Singhalese have a further superstition in relation to the close of life in the elephant: they believe that, on feeling the approach of dissolution, he repairs to a solitary valley, and there resigns himself to death. A native who accompanied Mr Cripps, when hunting in the forests of Anarajapoora, intimated to him that he was then in the immediate vicinity of the spot '*to which the elephants come to die*', but that it was so mysteriously concealed, that although every one believed in its existence, no one had ever succeeded in penetrating to it. ...

African Memoranda relative to an attempt to establish British Settlements at the Island of Bulama, London, 1815, p. 353).

[13]A corral was organized near Putlam in 1846, by Mr Morris, the chief officer of the district. It was constructed across one of the paths to which the elephants resort in their frequent marches, and during the course of the proceedings two of the captured elephants died. Their carcasses were left of course within the enclosure, which was abandoned as soon as the capture was complete. The wild elephants resumed their path through it, and a few days afterwards the headman reported to Mr Morris that the bodies had been removed and carried outside the corral to a spot to which nothing but the elephants could have borne them.

[14]*Expositio de Eleph.* 1, 243.

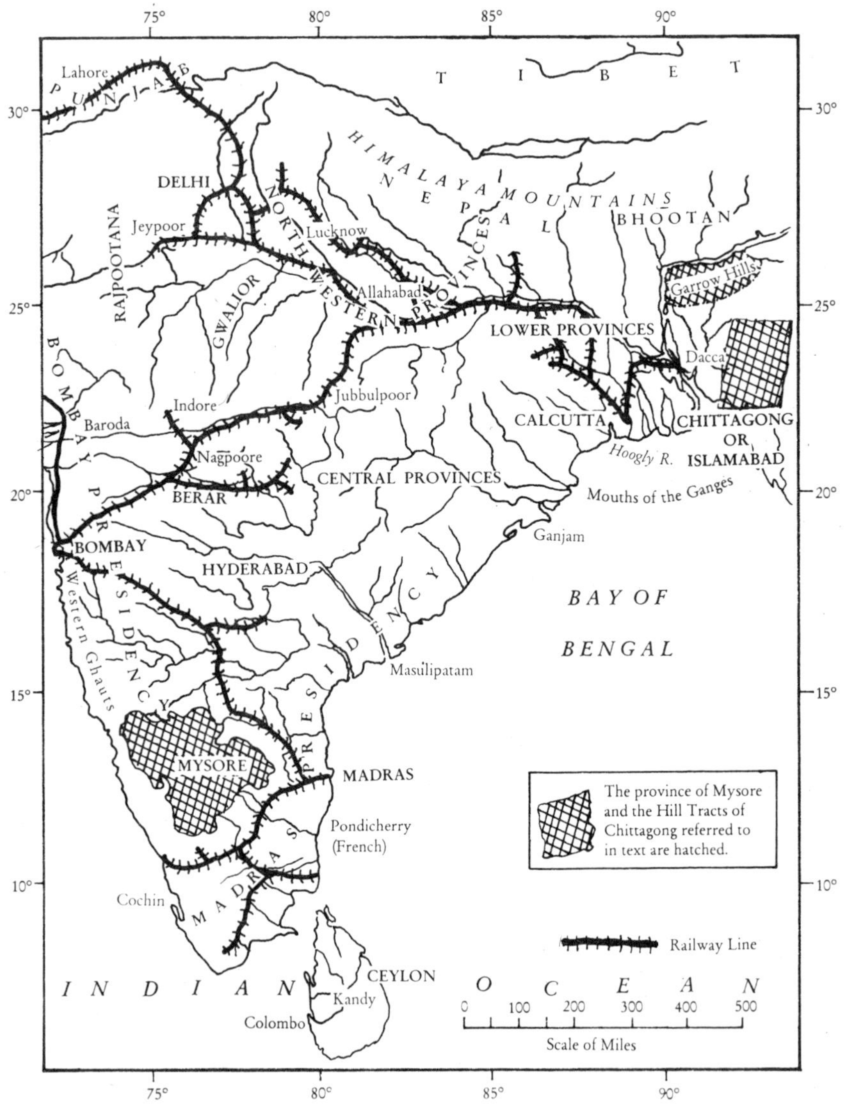

Sanderson's India.

G.P. SANDERSON

The Asiatic Wild Elephant
(*Elephas Indicus*)

My observations of the habits of wild elephants have been made chiefly at Morlay, near the Billiga-rungun hills, where I commenced elephant-catching in Mysore, and also in the Goondulpet and Kakankote forests, where I had shot elephants previously, as well as in the Garrow and Chittagong hills in Bengal.

The wild elephant abounds in most of the large forests of India, from the foot of the Himalayas to the extreme south, and throughout the peninsula from the east of the Bay of Bengal—viz., Chittagong, Burmah, and Siam; it is also numerous in Ceylon. There is only one species of elephant throughout these tracts.

In Mysore large numbers frequent the forests of the Western Ghats which bound Mysore on the west and south, the Billiga-rungun hills in the south-east, and a few are found in portions of the Nugger Division in the extreme north. There being no heavy forests in the interior elephants do not, as a rule, occur far within the borders of the province, but are commonly met with in the belt of lighter jungle which intervenes between the virgin forest and cultivation.

Herds of elephants usually consist of from thirty to fifty

From *Thirteen Years Among the Wild Beasts of India,* 1878.

individuals, but much larger numbers, even one hundred, are by no means uncommon. When large herds are in localities where fodder is not very plentiful, they divide into parties of from ten to twenty; these remain separate, though within two or three miles of each other. But they all take part in any common movement, such as a march into another tract of forest. The different parties keep themselves informed at all times of each other's whereabouts, chiefly by their fine sense of smell. I have observed that tame elephants can wind wild ones at a distance of three miles when the wind is favourable. Each herd of elephants is a family in which the animals are nearly allied to each other. Though the different herds do not intermix, escaped tame female elephants, or young males, appear to find no difficulty in obtaining admittance to herds.

In a herd of elephants the females with their calves form the advance-guard, whilst the tuskers follow leisurely behind; though, if terrified and put to flight, the order is speedily reversed, the mothers with calves falling behind, as the unencumbered tuskers have no one to see to but themselves. I have never known a case of a tusker's undertaking to cover the retreat of a herd. A herd is invariably led by a female, never a male, and the females with young ones are at all times dangerous if intruded upon. The necessity for the convenience of the mothers of the herd regulating its movements is evident, as they must accommodate the length and time of their marches, and the localities in which they rest or feed at different hours, to the requirements of their young ones; consequently the guidance of a tusker would not suit them.

Elephants make use of a great variety of sounds in communicating with each other, and in expressing their wants and feelings. Some are uttered by the trunk, some by the throat. The conjunctures in which either means of expression is employed cannot be strictly classified, as pleasure, want, and other emotions, are sometimes indicated by the trunk, sometimes by the throat. An elephant rushing upon an assailant trumpets shrilly with fury, but if enraged by wounds or other causes, and brooding by itself, it expresses its anger by a continued hoarse grumbling from the throat. Fear is similarly expressed in a shrill brassy trumpet, or by a roar from the lungs. Pleasure by a continued low squeaking through the trunk, or an almost inaudible purring sound from the throat. Want—as a calf calling its mother—is chiefly expressed by the throat. A peculiar sound is made use of by elephants to express dislike or apprehension, and at the same time to intimidate, as when the cause of some alarm has not been clearly ascertained, and the animals wish to deter an intruder. It is produced by rapping the end of the trunk smartly on the ground, a current of air, hitherto retained, being sharply emitted through the trunk, as from a valve, at the moment of impact. The sound made resembles that of a large sheet of tin rapidly doubled. It has been erroneously ascribed by some writers to the animals beating their sides with their trunks.

The ranges of wild elephants are very extensive, and are traversed with considerable regularity. In the dry months—that is, from January to April, when no rain falls—the herds seek the neighbourhood of considerable streams and shady forests. About June, after the first showers, they emerge to roam and feed on the young grass. By July or August this grass in hill tracts becomes long and coarse, and probably bitter, as tame elephants do not relish it. The elephants then descend now and again to the lower jungles, where the grass is not so far advanced. They here visit salt-licks and eat the earth—strongly impregnated with natron or soda—in common with most wild animals: also a fruit which grows at certain seasons on a dwarfed tree in the low country. I have been unable to ascertain its botanical name with certainty. It is said by natives to produce intoxication in elephants, under the influence of which they break surrounding trees, &c. I have never seen any signs of this myself, but the notion is widely spread amongst jungle-people.

Another reason for their leaving the hills during continued rain is the annoyance caused by the flies and mosquitoes which then become very troublesome. The elephant-fly is always less numerous in the low-country jungles. This truly formidable pest appears in the rains; it lives mostly in long grass, and attacks bison and sambur as well as elephants. When the grass becomes very wet, these flies collect on any passing animals, and so great is the irritation they cause, that elephants and bison are always found about the outskirts of the jungle at this time. The elephant-fly is dark grey in colour, about the size of a small bee, and has a most formidable proboscis; it is very soft, and the slightest blow kills it.

Whilst in the low-country jungles a few elephants, chiefly males, occasionally stray into cultivation; the mothers with calves keep aloof from the vicinity of man's dwellings. About December, when the jungles become dry, and fodder is scarce, all the herds leave the low country, and are seldom seen out of the hills or heavy forests until the next rains.

Whilst in open country the herds move about a good deal during the day in cloudy, showery weather. On very stormy and inclement days they keep to bamboo cover which is close and warm. During breaks, when the sun shines for a few hours, they come out eagerly to warm their huge bodies. They are then fond of standing on the sheet rock so common in the Mysore country about hill-ranges. The young calves and staid mothers, in small groups, half dozing as they bask, form tranquil family pictures at such times. Elephants are partial to rocky places at all seasons.

Whilst marching from one tract of forest to another, elephants usually travel in strict Indian file. They seldom stay more than one or two days at the same halting-place, as the fodder becomes exhausted. They rest during the middle hours of the night, as well as during the day. Some lie down, and they usually dispose themselves in small distinct squads of animals which seem to have an affection for each other. (Tame elephants frequently display a particular liking for one or other of their fellows.) About three o'clock they rise to feed or march, and by ten o'clock in the day they are again collected, and rest till afternoon; at eleven at night they again rest. In showery cool weather elephants are frequently on the move all day long.

Elephants generally drink after sunrise and before sunset. They seldom bathe after the sun is down, except in very warm weather. Whilst fording water on cold nights, tame elephants curl up their trunks and tails to keep them out of it; and if taken at a late hour to be washed after their day's work, frequently show their dislike to the unseasonable bath.

Though a few calves are born at other seasons, the largest number make their appearance about September, October, and November. In a herd of fifty-five captured in June 1874, in Mysore, there was only one calf under six months of age, whilst seven were from eight to nine months. Amongst the females captured, eight calved between September and November. In eighty-five elephants captured in Chittagong, in January 1876, the bulk of the calves were from one to three months of age. I observed in Mysore that the herd invariably left heavy jungle about October for more open and dry country, on account of the wet and discomfort to the calving females and their offspring.

When a calf is born the herd remains with the mother two days; the calf is then capable of marching. Even at this tender age calves are no encumbrance to the herd's movements; the youngest climb hills and cross rivers assisted by their dams. In swimming, very young calves are supported by their mothers' trunks, and held in front of them. When they are a few months old they scramble on to their mothers' shoulders, helping themselves by holding on with their legs, or, they swim alone. Young calves sent across rivers in charge of our tame elephants often did this, though they could swim by themselves if necessary.

Full-grown elephants swim perhaps better than any other land animals. A batch of seventy-nine that I despatched from Dacca to Barrackpur, near Calcutta, in November 1875, had the Ganges and several of its large tidal branches to cross. In the longest swim they were six hours without touching the bottom; after a rest on a sand-bank, they completed the swim in three more; not one was lost. I have heard of more remarkable swims than this.

Much misconception exists on the subject of rogue, or solitary elephants. The usually accepted belief that these elephants are turned out of the herds by their companions or rivals is not correct. Most of the so-called solitary elephants are the lords of some herds near. They leave their companions at times to roam by themselves, usually to visit cultivation or open country, whither less bold animals, and the females encumbered with calves, hesitate to follow. Sometimes, again, they make the expedition merely for the sake of solitude. They, however, keep more or less to the jungle where their herd is, and follow its movements. Single elephants are also very frequently young, not old, males—animals not yet able to assert a position for themselves in the herd, and debarred from much intimate association with it by stronger rivals. They wander by themselves on the outskirts of the herd, or two or three such are found together, so that solitary is rather a misleading appellation. A really solitary elephant is, in my experience, and according to native hunters, an animal rarely met with. I do not believe in any male elephant being *driven* from its herd. If unable to cope with some stronger rival, it has merely to keep on the outskirts and give way, and it avoids molestation. I have seen this constantly;

and where elephants are really solitary I believe the life is quite of their own choosing. Young males are only biding their time until they are able to meet all comers in a herd.

I once met with a remarkable instance of a young male elephant, about two years old, which had lived a solitary life for three or four months. Its mother had probably fallen into one of the numerous old elephant-pits on the Billiga-rungun hills, and the calf must have remained near after the herd left the vicinity. It subsequently took up its quarters in the low country, and though one herd visited the locality, the young one was refused admission, and it remained in the same place after the herd left. I captured it soon afterwards.

Single male elephants spend their nights, and sometimes days, in predatory excursions into rice and other fields in the immediate vicinity of villages. They become disabused of many of the terrors which render ordinary elephants timid and needlessly cautious. These elephants are by no means always evilly disposed. A solitary elephant I knew intimately at Morley was a most inoffensive animal, and, although bold in his wanderings, never injured anyone. Some male elephants, however, as much wandering herd tuskers as really solitary animals, are dangerous when suddenly come upon, but rarely wantonly malicious.

Of cases recorded of really vicious animals perhaps the most notable is that of the Mandla[1] elephant, an elephant supposed to have been mad, and which killed an immense number of persons about five years ago. It is said to have eaten portions of some of its victims, but it probably only held their limbs in its mouth whilst it tore them to pieces. The Mandla elephant was shot, after a short but bloody career, by two officers.[2]

I have only known one instance of two full-grown male elephants, unconnected with herds, constantly associating together. These were a tusker and *muckna* (or tuskless male), in the Kákan-koté forests. They were inseparable companions in their night wanderings, but always remained a mile or two apart during the day. I knew the pair well in 1870–2; in the latter year I shot the tusker, as he had become dangerous, and had been proscribed by Government for killing people. ...

[1]Near Jubbulpore, Central Provinces.
[2]See A. Bloomfield in Section II.

The large area of rice-fields within the bed of the Honganoor lake was assessed long ago at one-third the usual rates on account of the depredations of elephants. The actual damage caused to crops by wild elephants is much less than is popularly supposed. The chief evil of their presence is the bar they oppose to any advance in certain localities. Agricultural progress in India is always on a very small scale. One cultivator secures an acre or two of land, and opens it up in rough style, but as he possesses little capital to withstand a bad season, he generally abandons his land if his first crop be eaten up by elephants or other animals. Reclamation in jungle-localities only succeeds where several ryots open land together. In Mysore every facility is given by Government in granting jungle-land free of rent for some years, and on a reduced rental for a further term; but the country bordering jungle-tracts is seldom sufficiently populous to necessitate any extensive incursions upon the surrounding jungles. When the necessity arises elephants can be easily driven back.

The usually received notions of the height which elephants attain are much in excess of fact. Out of some hundreds of tame and newly-caught elephants which I have seen in the south of India and in Bengal, also from Burmah and different parts of India, and of which I have carefully measured all the largest individuals, I have not seen one 10 feet in vertical height at the shoulder. The largest was an elephant in the Madras Commissariat stud at Hoonsoor, which measured 9 feet 10 inches. The next largest are two tuskers belonging to his Highness the Maharajah of Mysore, each 9 feet 8 inches, captured in Mysore some forty years ago, and still alive.

Of females, the largest I have measured—two leggy animals in the stud at Dacca—were respectively 8 feet 5 inches and 8 feet 3 inches. As illustrating how exceptional this height is in females, I may say that, out of 140 elephants captured by me in kheddahs in Mysore and Bengal, in 1874 and 1876, the tallest females were just 8 feet. The above are vertical measurements at the shoulder.

In India elephants are often measured by throwing a tape over the shoulders, or even back, the ends being brought to the ground on each side, and half the length taken as the animal's height.[3] Even the same elephant varies with its condition when measured

[3]This accounts for the 11- or 12-foot elephants we sometimes hear of.

in this way. An 8-feet elephant, in fair condition, gives a height of 8 feet 9 inches by this method.

There is little doubt that there is not an elephant 10 feet at the shoulder in India. As bearing on this subject, I many quote the following from the *English Cyclopaedia*. The Mr Corse referred to therein was a gentleman evidently thoroughly conversant with elephants, probably in charge of the Government animals in Bengal. His paper on the elephant was read before the Royal Society in 1799.

> During the war with Tippoo Sultan, of the 150 elephants under the management of Captain Sandys, not one was 10 feet high, and only a few males 9½ feet high. Mr Corse was very particular in ascertaining the height of the elephants used at Madras, and with the army under Marquis Cornwallis, where there were both Bengal and Ceylon elephants, and he was assured that those of Ceylon were neither higher nor superior to those of Bengal.

The age to which the elephant lives is, as must ever be the case with denizens of the jungle, uncertain. The general opinion of experienced natives is that it attains 120 years in exceptional cases, but more generally to about 80 years. This view, however, is based on observations of elephants in captivity; under the more favourable conditions of a natural life the elephant must attain a greater age than when confined. My own opinion is that the elephant attains at least to 150 years.

One of the best instances I have seen from which to form conclusions is the case of a female elephant, Bheemruttee, belonging to his Highness the Maharajah of Mysore. This elephant was captured in Coorg in 1805, and was then a calf of three years of age. She is still, at 76, in good working condition, and does not present the appearance of a particularly aged elephant, which is always shown in the lean and rugged head, prominent bones, deeply-sunk temples, and general appearance of decay. Bheemruttee is, however, past her prime.

In captivity she has lived under much less favourable conditions than a wild elephant, in being exposed to heat, often underfed, and subjected to irregularities of all kinds. Amongst newly-caught elephants I have seen many females evidently older than Bheemruttee with young calves at heel. Mahouts believe that female elephants breed up to about 80 years of age.

Morlay Hall, Sanderson's Elephant-Catching Camp in Mysore (Karnataka).

One of the most remarkable facts in connection with elephants is the extreme rarity of any remains of dead ones being found in the jungles. This circumstance is so marked as to have given rise to the notion amongst the Sholagas of the Billiga-rungun hills that elephants never die; whilst the Kurrabas of Kakankote believe that there is a place, unseen by human eye, to which they retire to end their days. In my own wanderings for some years through elephant-jungles I have only seen the remains of one female (that we knew had died in calving), and one drowned elephant brought down by a mountain torrent. Not only have I never myself seen the remains of any elephant that had died a natural death, but I have never met anyone amongst the jungle-tribes, or professional elephant-hunters, who had seen a carcass, except at a time when murrain visited the Chittagong and Kakankote forests. Bones would not decay for some years, and teeth and tusks would survive for some time, yet not a single pair of ivories has ever, as far as I know, been found in the Mysore jungles during the time I have known them. In Chittagong, in January 1876, I found a portion of a large tusk in a morass, much eaten by exposure; it weighed 33 lb. Another was found in Tipperah, almost fossilized, weighing 36 lb.; there were no other remains in either case.

The fact of remains of bison, deer, and other wild animals seldom being found is equally singular. Their bones would be sooner disposed of than those of elephants; still it is strange that, except in cases of epidemics amongst these animals, they are hardly ever seen. Certain classes of wild animals may possibly retreat to quiet localities when they find their powers failing them, as places where alarms and necessity for flight are unlikely to overtake them. But this is not the case with such gregarious animals as elephants. It may be supposed that in thick forests vultures do not attract attention to their carcasses, and monsoon rains and jungle-fires soon dispose of them. Still one would think that some carcasses at least would be found, whereas they never are; and though it is certain the animals do die, I know of no reasonable explanation of what becomes of them. ...

This belief of a universal sepulchre is, however, quite untenable as regards Mysore, as there is no spot in its jungles that is not penetrated at times by the Sholagas or Kurrabas. Nor is the idea defensible on other grounds.

There is an epidemic disease, corresponding to murrain in cattle, from which wild and tame elephants suffer at long intervals. It attacked the elephants in the Government stud at Dacca, in Bengal, about thirty years ago, and carried off nearly fifty per cent of a total of upwards of three hundred. It lasted, with varying virulence, for more than ten years. The animals in best condition suffered most; only two, both in poor condition, are recorded as having recovered after seizure. The symptoms were, breakings-out and gatherings on the throat and legs, spots on the tongue, and running from the eyes. With the cessation of the flow from the eyes the animals died, usually on the second day after attack. In 1862 a similar epidemic carried off large numbers of elephants in the Chittagong forests. A few years later the herds in the Kákankoté jungles in Mysore were attacked; but the mortality was not great, and the disease soon left. On this occasion the fact of the elephants dying was well known to the Kurrabas.

The period of gestation in the elephant is said by experienced natives to vary as the calf is male or female, being twenty-two months in the case of the former, and eighteen in the latter. I cannot of my own observation afford conclusive proof that such is the case, though I believe there is some truth in the statement. I have known elephants to calve twenty months after capture, the young always being males when eighteen months were exceeded, and it was not known how long the mothers had been in calf before capture. The female elephant receives the male again about eight or ten months after calving.

Male elephants of mature age are subject to periodical paroxysms, supposed to be of a sexual nature. They are said to be *must*, or mad, when under their influence. Fits of *must* differ in duration in different animals; in some they last for a few weeks, in others for even four or five months. Elephants are not always violent or untractable under their influence, being frequently only drowsy and lethargic. The approach of the period of *must* is indicated by the commencement of a flow of oily matter from the small hole in the temple on each side of the head, which orifice is found in all elephants, male and female. The temples also swell. The elephant frequently acts somewhat strangely, and is dull and not so obedient as usual. In the advanced stages the oily exudation trickles freely down from the temples, which are then much swollen.

On the first indications the elephant is strongly secured. If he becomes dangerous his food is thrown to him, and water supplied in a trough pushed within his reach. Fatal accidents are of common occurrence in cases of *must* elephants getting loose. They usually attack man or any of their own species near, and the society of a female does not appear always to appease them. I once saw one of our tuskers, which was then only under suspicion of an approaching fit, break away from the control of his mahout as he was being ridden to water, and, despite severe punishment, attacked and knocked down a female at her picket near; and, had his tusks not been cut, he would without doubt have killed her on the spot. He was at last driven off by spears thrown at his trunk and head, when he stalked across the open plain with his mahout on his neck, fury in his eye, master of all he surveyed, and evidently courting battle with any created being. The men had a difficult and dangerous task to secure him. His hind-legs were at last tied from behind the trunk of a tree near which he stood, and the mahout having drawn up a chain by a cord, and secured it round his neck, he was moored fore and aft. I shall never forget the mahout's fervent ejaculation of 'Allah! Allah!' as he slipped over the elephant's tail when he was made fast.

The flow of *must* occasionally, but very seldom, occurs in female elephants. I have seen it twice in newly-caught females in the prime of life, and in very full condition. It never occurs, I believe, in tame female elephants.

Mahouts can usually tell the age of elephants tolerably correctly. A young animal, though of full size, or a very old one, cannot be mistaken, but it requires much experience to estimate those of middle age. I have known even experienced men differ about the same animal to the extent of fifteen years. The general appearance of the animal suffices in some cases. A very old elephant is usually in poor condition, and the skin looks shiny and shrivelled. The head is lean and rugged, the skull appearing to have little but skin upon it; the temples and eyes are sunken; and the fore-legs, instead of bulging out above the knee with muscle, are almost of the same girth throughout. Instead of walking firmly and planting the feet flat, an aged elephant brings the feet to the ground somewhat in the manner of a plantigrade animal, touching with the heels first. But all the above symptoms may be present in a greater or less degree in debilitated, middle-aged animals, and are consequently not conclusive; but the appearance of the elephant's ear will probably settle the question. The ear is relied upon in ageing elephants as the teeth are in a horse. In very young elephants—up to six or seven years—the top of the ear is not turned over (as in man); but with advancing years it laps over, in old elephants very much so, and the ear is ragged and torn along the lower edge.

The elephant is full grown, but not fully mature, at about twenty-five years of age. At this period it may be compared to a human being at eighteen; and it is not in full vigour and strength till about thirty-five. Female elephants usually give birth to their first calf at sixteen years of age, sometimes at thirteen or fourteen, but are then palpably immature themselves. I have heard of what appears to be a well-authenticated case of a female elephant having two calves at a birth. Many wild female elephants are accompanied by two, sometimes three, calves of different ages.

Elephants breed about once in two and a half years. Two calves are usually sucking at the same time; and I have even seen the eldest of three, a young elephant five and a half feet high, and about five years old, that had to stoop to reach its mother, suck occasionally. I need hardly say that the young elephant sucks with its mouth, not its trunk.

Calves usually stand exactly three feet high at the shoulder when born; the trunk is then only ten inches long, and possesses little flexibility. The average weight of several calves I have weighed on the second day after birth has been 200 lb. They live entirely upon milk till six months old, when they eat a little tender grass; their chief support, however, is still milk for some months.

The elephant very rarely breeds in confinement, but this is owing to the segregation of the sexes, and also to the physical causes of insufficient food or hard work. It would not answer from an economic point of view to breed elephants in India, as, before they were of a useful age—fifteen years—they would have cost more than would suffice to capture a number of mature wild ones, ready for work. It is said that they are bred in a semi-wild state, and with little expense, in parts of Burmah and Siam. The females there are shackled and left at large in the forests during the non-working months, where wild males have access to them. But in Burmah fodder is plentiful, and the young stock cost nothing till taken up for sale.

The female elephant evinces no peculiar attachment to her offspring. The statement of Knox, quoted by Sir Emerson Tennent, that 'the shees are alike tender of any one's young ones as of their own' is incorrect. Much exclusiveness is shown by elephants in the detailed arrangements amongst themselves in a herd, and if the mothers and young ones be closely watched, it will be seen that the latter are very rarely allowed familiarities by other females, nor, indeed, do they seek them. I have seen many cases in the kheddahs where young elephants, after losing their mothers by death or other causes, have been refused assistance by the other females, and have been buffeted about as outcasts. I have only known one instance of a very gentle, motherly elephant in captivity allowing a motherless calf to suck along with her own young one.

Sir Emerson Tennent mentions the belief that if a wild female elephant happen to be separated from her young for only two days, though giving suck, she never after recognizes or acknowledges it. I apprehend that this idea arose from the fact that amongst newly-captured elephants, through the anxiety and exhaustion attending the mother's efforts to escape, her milk is invariably dried up for the time being. I have then seen elephants repel their calves, whose importunities annoyed them. But with the return of milk after a few days' rest and cooling food they have suckled them as before. In captivity the female is by no means jealous of her young being handled, and strangers may approach and fondle her calf immediately after its birth without incurring her resentment.

It is exceedingly entertaining to note the gravity of young calves, and the way in which they keep close to their bulky mothers. The extreme gentleness of elephants, the care they take never to push against, or step upon, their attendants, doubtless arises from an instinctive feeling designed for the protection of their young, which a rough, though unintentional, push or blow with the legs of such huge animals would at once kill. Amongst all created creatures the elephant stands unrivalled in gentleness. The most intelligent horse cannot be depended upon not to tread on his master's toes, and if terrified makes no hesitation in dashing away, even should he upset anyone in so doing. But elephants, even huge tuskers whose heads are high in the air, and whose keepers are mere pigmies beside them, are so cautious that accidents very seldom occur through carelessness on their part. In the kheddahs, though elephants are excited by struggling, they never overlook the men on foot engaged in securing the captives; and though there would seem to be great danger in being amidst the forest of huge legs and bulky bodies of the tame elephants, they evince such wonderful instinct in avoiding injuring the men that I have never seen an accident occur through them.

When an alarm occurs in a herd the young ones immediately vanish under their mothers, and are then seldom seen again. A herd containing a large number of calves would be supposed under these circumstances by the uninitiated to consist entirely of full-grown elephants. I have only known two young elephants disabled in many rushes and crushes of large herds that I have witnessed. The mothers help their offspring up steep places with a push behind, and manage to get them through or over every difficulty with great ingenuity.

The tusks of the Asiatic elephant are much smaller than those of the African. The largest tusks of any elephant that I have myself shot measured respectively 4 feet 11 inches and 5 feet in length, outside curve; 16½ inches in circumference at the gum; and weighed 74½ lb. the pair. An elephant with one enormous tusk, and one diseased and broken, was shot in the Billiga-rungun hills in 1863 by Sir Victor Brooke and Colonel Douglas Hamilton. An account from the pen of the former gentleman of their adventures with this elephant appears in Chap. XVII; and the following dimensions and weight of both tusks, from the same source, may be relied upon:

RIGHT TUSK.

	Feet.	Inches.
Total length, outside curve,	8	0
Length of part outside socket or nasal bones, outside curve,	5	9
Length of part inside socket, outside curve,	2	3
Greatest circumference,	1	4.9
Weight,	90 lb.	

LEFT TUSK.[4]

	Feet.	Inches.
Total length, outside curve,	3	3
Outside socket, do.,	1	2
Inside, do. do.,	2	1
Greatest circumference,	1	8
Weight,	49 lb.	

Tusks are firmly embedded in sockets or cylinders of bone which run up to the forehead and end at a line drawn from eye to eye. Tusks, except those of very aged elephants, are only solid for a portion of their length; the hollow is filled with a firm, bloody pulp. In young animals the tusks are only solid for a portion of their length even outside the gum, and are hollow throughout the embedded portion. With age the pulp cavity decreases in depth, till, in very old animals, it becomes almost obliterated. In the large tusk referred to above, the pulp hollow extends from the base through half the embedded portion (about 13½ inches). In a pair of tusks belonging to Colonel Douglas Hamilton it is 10½ inches

[4]Sir Victor Brooke says: 'The diseased (left) tusk is a very remarkable example from a pathological point of view. The pulp cavity is entirely obliterated, a mass of excessively dense nodular dentine being formed in its place. As far as I can judge, the tusk has been broken off short, after attaining large dimensions, and in the rupture a deep longitudinal rent extended backwards into the pulp cavity, giving rise to diseased condition of the pulp. The stench from the tusk when extracted was horrible.'

in an embedded length of 25. As a rule, tusks show barely one half of their total length outside the jaw of the living animal. The length within and without the nasal bones is generally exact, but the lip or gum hides a few inches of the projecting half. As the sockets or nasal bones of a large elephant are from 1 foot 6 inches to a foot 9 inches in length, this admits of an elephant's having a tusk 3½ feet long, of which only 1½ foot (the gum hides about 4 inches) is visible. This rule holds pretty closely for all elephants until they become aged, when, if the tusks grow abnormally long, which is not always the case, the exposed portion becomes longer than the embedded, as the latter is limited to the length which the nasal bones attain, viz., about 1¾ foot in the largest skulls.

The points are usually cut from the tusks of tame elephants, and the extremity is encircled with a brass or iron ring to prevent the tusk splitting, and for show. In cases where too much has been cut from the tusk and the hollow portion entered, dreadful mischief ensues. I have seen a tusker, one of whose tusks had rotted away from this cause, with the socket far into the head filled with maggots. Tusks if once lost are never renewed.

Sir Emerson Tennent considers at some length the use for which the tusks of male elephants can be designed. He says:

> But here there arises a further and very curious inquiry as to the specific objects in the economy of the elephant to which its tusks are conducive. Placed as it is in Ceylon, in the midst of the most luxuriant profusion of its favourite food, and with no natural enemies against whom to protect itself, it is difficult to conjecture any probable utility which it can derive from such appendages. Their absence is unaccompanied by any inconvenience to the individuals in whom they are wanting; and as regards the few who possess them, the only operations in which I am aware of their tusks being employed is to assist in ripping open the stems of the joggery palms and young palmirahs to extract the farinaceous core; and in splitting up the juicy shaft of the plantain.
>
> If the tusks were designed to be employed offensively, some alertness would naturally be exhibited in using them. So peaceable and harmless is the life of the elephant, that nature appears to have left it unprovided with any special weapon of offence; and although in an emergency it may push or gore with its tusks' their almost vertical position, added to the difficulty of raising its head above the level of the shoulder, is inconsistent with the idea of their being designed for attack, since it is impossible for the animal to deliver

an effectual blow, or to wield its tusks as the deer and the buffalo can wield their horns.

Among elephants, jealousy and other causes of irritation frequently occasion contentions between individuals of the same herd; but on such occasions their general habit is to strike with their trunks, and to bear down their opponents with their heads. It is doubtless correct that an elephant, when prostrated by the force or fury of an antagonist of its own species, is often wounded by the downward pressure of the tusks, which in any other position it would be almost impossible to use offensively.

Before treating on this question I must refer to Sir Emerson Tennent's work, *The Wild Elephant*, published originally in 1859, and again in 1866. This is, I believe, the most recent work on the elephant, and has been serviceable in removing some of the grossest misapprehensions regarding it; but it is full of the errors which are unavoidable when a man writes on a subject with which he has no practical acquaintance, and musters information without having sufficient knowledge to enable him to choose the good and reject the evil. The book is written in such a fascinating and earnest style that it is difficult to believe that the author is mostly romancing, and before I knew anything of elephants I revelled in his descriptions. But when on even short personal acquaintance with the noble animal I found that, amongst his numerous accomplishments, the power to take all four feet off the ground at the same moment was not one, I was obliged to conclude that the elephant, in the case quoted by Sir Emerson as having cleared a barricade 15 feet high, only carrying away the top bar, could not have accomplished the feat; and though Sir Emerson subsequently wrote to the person from whom *he* had the information, who wrote to the Cutchery Modliar of Kornegalle who had told *him*, who sent a *native* to measure the place again, who said he found the elephant had only made a clear jump of 9 feet, because he had climbed on to a white-ants' hill from which he sprang, I found myself unable to place further belief in the author. More extended acquaintance with elephants entirely dissipated my faith in the wild elephant of Sir Emerson Tennent's imagination and of my inexperienced days. Sir Emerson Tennent has, in many places in his work, substituted theory and fancy for fact.

In the above matter of tusks he has indulged in pure theory. In his account of the two or three captures of elephants he witnessed (the largest number caught at one time being apparently nine), he does not mention any tuskers having been taken, though the artist in the illustrations to his work (which are excellent and lifelike pictures) has thrown in a tusker amongst the captives. Sir Emerson Tennent being confessedly no sportsman probably never saw a wild tusker. In Ceylon tuskers are few and far between, and no one but a sportsman who constantly followed elephants would be likely to fall in with them.

Far from tusks being useless appendages to elephants, and of little service for offence, they are amongst the most formidable of any weapons with which Nature has furnished her creatures, and none are used with more address. They are not placed almost vertically, as stated by Sir Emerson Tennent, and they can be used at almost any angle. In a herd of elephants the tuskers maintain the height of discipline. Every individual gives way before them, and in serious fights amongst themselves one or other is frequently killed outright. So great is the dread entertained by all elephants of a tusker, that our stanchest tame females shrank if any of the tame tuskers turned suddenly in their direction. Superiority in a herd appears to attach to the different tuskers in proportion to the size of their tusks; no tusker thinks of serious rivalry with one of heavier calibre than himself. In the kheddahs in Mysore we found the services of tuskers invaluable; we had two, amongst others, that were taller and with longer tusks than any wild ones we captured, and their presence was always sufficient to awe the most obstreperous wild male whilst the men were securing it. Our tame elephants' tusks were cut and blunt, but we had steel glaives to slip on if necessary, with which they could have killed any elephant in a very short time.

Tusks are not used to assist the elephant in procuring food. Small trees are overturned by pushing with the curled trunk, or feet if necessary; and to get at the core of a palm-tree, or break up the plantain, the pressure of his feet alone is used.

On the continent of India *mucknas*, or male elephants *born* without tusks, are decidedly rare. The word *muckna* is derived from *mookh*, the mouth or face. Mucknas can hardly be distinguished from females at the first glance, but if they are full-grown animals their superior size shows their sex. Their tusks or prongs are generally a little longer and thicker than those of female elephants. It is a common belief that mucknas are larger as a rule than tuskers. This is not the case, but they are generally stouter and more vigorous animals. Their good development is sought to be accounted for by their being said to be allowed by their mothers to suck after young tuskers have been driven off, when their sharp little tusks hurt their mothers; but this, though an ingenious explanation, is not a correct one, as the young tusker can suck without its tusk touching its mother, and I have always seen them suckled as long as the female calves are.

A common belief that mucknas are usually vicious animals is also groundless. They are generally much ill-treated by the tuskers of the herd, upon whom they are powerless to retaliate, and I have seen one or two decidedly timid in consequence. A timid elephant is always less safe than one of better courage, but I have not found mucknas to be naturally ill-tempered. The absence of tusks appears to be a merely accidental circumstance, as the want of beard or whiskers in a man. Mucknas breed in the herds, and the peculiarity is not hereditary nor transmitted. This is a known fact, and is demonstrated by the occasional occurrence of tuskers, doubtless from tuskless sires, in Ceylon herds.

In Ceylon a male elephant with tusks is a *rara avis*: Sir Samuel Baker says that not more than one in 300 is provided with them. Out of 140 elephants, of which 51 were males, which I captured in Mysore and Bengal in 1874–76, only 5 were mucknas.

It is difficult to imagine what can cause the vital difference of tusks and no tusks between the male elephant of continental India and Ceylon. The climate may be said to be the same, as also their food; and I have not seen any theory advanced that seems at all well founded to account for their absence in the Ceylon elephant. There is a somewhat similar case in the common antelope (*Antilope bazoarctica*) of Southern India's having inferior horns to those of Central India, an 18-inch black buck being a decided rarity in Mysore, and 14 inches being the average, whilst in other parts of India they attain to 26 or 27 inches. Sambur (*Rusa aristotelis*) in the Chittagong and other forests to the east of the Bay of Bengal have inferior horns to those of the Neilgherries and other parts of India.

Elephants occasionally lose one tusk, sometimes both, in accidents in the jungle, and some have only one tusk from birth. The latter are known as 'Gunésh' (the name of the Hindoo god of wisdom) by Hindoos, and are reverenced by them if the tusk retained be the right-hand one.

The tusks of the male elephant-calf show almost from birth. I believe that they are never renewed, and that the first tusks are permanent. In many works on the elephant it is stated that the first tusks are shed before the second year, but I believe this to be an error—one that has gained ground through so many writers deriving their information from a common source. I have made this a point of particular inquiry amongst experienced elephant-attendants, and have found them unanimous in dissenting from the idea of any such process of renewal. It is impossible that such an important matter could have escaped their notice (natives are keen observers), and I apprehend that the error—as it undoubtedly is—has arisen through some *savant's* diagnosis of the elephant's dentition, based on analogy, or confounding the teeth and the tusks, as the same word is used to denote either in several native languages. Jerdon has given his support to the statement as far as adopting it goes, but this is a case in which a deservedly trusted writer could hardly have had the information from his own observation. I have had many young elephants in my charge, and never noticed anything of the change alluded to.

The Indian female elephant is always born with *tushes* or short downward prongs in the upper jaw, rarely more than four inches in length out of the gum: these, whilst present, are used for stripping bark off trees, &c.; but they are seldom retained long, being generally broken off early in life, and they do not appear to be at all necessary to the elephant. Female elephants use them amongst themselves in striking each other, raising their trunks in doing so, and bearing downwards with their tushes. These tushes are never renewed. A young female which I had, in trying to overturn a tree, broke both her *tushes* one after the other.

The only pace of the elephant is the walk, capable of being increased to a fast shuffle of about fifteen miles an hour for a very short distance. It can neither trot, canter, nor gallop. It does not move with the legs on the same side together, but nearly so. A very good runner might keep out of an elephant's way on a smooth piece of turf; but in the ground in which they are generally met, any attempt to escape by flight, unless supplemented by concealment, would be unavailing.

As before stated, an elephant cannot jump, and, though very clever in surmounting obstacles, can never have all four feet off the ground together. Whether it is the peculiar formation of the hind-legs, with knees instead of hocks, or the weight and bulk of the animal that incapacitates him, I cannot say, but he is physically incapable of making the smallest spring, either in vertical height or horizontal distance. Thus a trench seven feet wide is impassable to an elephant, though the step of a large one in full stride is about six and a half feet.

The idea that wild elephants have decreased of late years is not uncommon in India. It appears to have arisen from the fact of orders having been issued of late years by the Supreme and Local Governments for their protection; also from their undoubted decrease in Ceylon. But the case of that island is hardly analogous to that of the continent. In Ceylon elephants have always been made a peculiar object of pursuit by large numbers of sportsmen and paid native hunters, whilst their range is not without its limits. In continental India the actual numbers shot by European sportsmen has always been very small, and it was only for a few years that natives were induced to turn their attention to killing them by a reward given for their destruction in the Madras Presidency. This was soon withdrawn, when the natives' interest in their pursuit ceased; and the representations of humane officials having further led to the curtailment of the wasteful methods of trapping them practised by native hunters, the wild elephant now enjoys perfect immunity throughout the Western Ghats, and those boundless jungles extending for hundreds of miles along the foot of the Himalayas into Burmah and Siam. The number annually caught by the Government establishments is comparatively very small; and there is no doubt that all the forest ground that can be legitimately allowed to the wild elephant is as fully occupied at present as is desirable. I have examined the elephant-catching records of the past forty-five years in Bengal, and the present rate of capture attests the fact that there is no diminution in the numbers now obtainable; whilst in Southern India elephants have become so numerous of late years that the rifle will have to be again called into requisition to protect the ryots from their depredations, unless more systematic measures for their capture and utilization than are at present in vogue be maintained. It cannot but be a matter of hearty congratulation to all interested in so fine and harmless an animal that there is no chance of the sad fate that is pursuing his African congener, and leading to his rapid extinction, affecting the Asiatic elephant.

G.P. SANDERSON

The Elephant in Captivity

The opinion is generally held by those who have had the best opportunities of observing the elephant, that the popular estimate of its intelligence is a greatly exaggerated one; that, instead of being the exceptionally wise animal it is believed to be, its sagacity is of a very mediocre description. Of the truth of this opinion no one who has lived amongst elephants can entertain any doubt. It is a significant fact that the natives of India never speak of the elephant as a peculiarly intelligent animal; and it does not figure in their ancient literature for its wisdom, as do the fox, the crow, and the monkey.

The elephant's size and staid appearance, its gentleness, and the ease with which it performs various services with its trunk, have probably given rise to the exalted idea of its intellect amongst those not intimately acquainted with it. And its being but little known in Europe, whilst what is known of it justly makes it a general favourite, leads to tales of its intelligence being not only accepted without investigation, but welcomed with pleasure. Many of the stories about it are intended for the edification of little folks, and as such are well enough; but in a sober inquiry into the mental capacity of the animal they must be duly examined.

One of the strongest features in the domesticated elephant's

From *Thirteen Years Among the Wild Beasts in India*, 1878.

character is its obedience. It may also be readily taught, as it has a large share of the ordinary cultivable intelligence common in a greater or less degree to all animals. But its reasoning faculties are undoubtedly far below those of the dog, and possibly of other animals; and in matters beyond the range of its daily experience it evinces no special discernment. Whilst quick at comprehending anything sought to be taught to it, the elephant is decidedly wanting in originality. ...

Let us consider whether the elephant displays more intelligence in its wild state than other animals. Though possessed of a proboscis which is capable of guarding it against such dangers, it readily falls into pits dug for catching it, and only covered with a few sticks and leaves. Its fellows make no effort to assist the fallen one, as they might easily do by kicking in the earth around the pit, but flee in terror. It commonly happens that a young elephant falls into a pit, near which the mother will remain until the hunters come, without doing anything to assist it, not even feeding it by throwing in a few branches. This, I have no doubt, is more difficult of belief to most people than if they were told that the mother supplied it with grass, brought water in her trunk, or filled up the pit with fagots, and effected her young one's release. Whole herds of elephants are driven into ill-concealed enclosures which no other wild animals could be got to enter, and single ones are caught by their legs being tied together by men under cover of a couple of tame elephants. Elephants which happen to effect their escape are caught again without trouble; even experience does not bring them wisdom. These facts are certainly against the conclusion that the elephant is an extraordinarily shrewd animal, much less one possessed of the power of abstract thought to the extent with which he is commonly credited. I do not think I traduce the elephant when I say it is in many things, a stupid animal; and I can assert with confidence that all the stories I have heard of it, except those relating to feats of strength or docility performed under its keeper's direction, are beyond its intellectual power, and are mere pleasant fictions.

It often happens that persons who do not understand elephants give them credit for performing actions which are suggested to them and in which they are directed, by the mahout on their necks. There is no secret so close as that between a horse and his rider, or between an elephant and his mahout. One of the chief characteristics in the domestic elephant's temperament is, as before stated, its obedience, and it does many things at the slightest hint from its mahout, whose directions are not perceived by an onlooker unacquainted with the craft of elephant-guidance. This has led to such mistakes as Sir Emerson Tennent makes[1] in describing the conduct of tame elephants while engaged in capturing wild ones in Ceylon, when he says: 'The tame ones displayed the most perfect conception of every movement, both of the object to be attained and the means to accomplish it. They saw intuitively a difficulty or a danger, and addressed themselves *unbidden* to remove it.' Another writer on a capture of elephants in Travancore says:

> It may be interesting to mention a trait of one of the trained elephants, which shows such a degree of intelligence and forethought that it is to be placed on record. While the animals were being driven towards the enclosure, one of the trained elephants, a large tusker, was observed to pick up stones from the ground with his trunk, and hand them up to his keeper on his neck. He did it in such a deliberate and matter-of-fact manner, that it was plain he comprehended perfectly the reason for which stones were required.

Such are the notions with which those with superficial acquaintance with elephants fly away. I have seen the cream of trained elephants at work in the catching establishments in Mysore and Bengal; I have managed them myself, under all circumstances; and I can say that I have never seen one show any aptitude in dealing, undirected, with an unforeseen emergency. I have a young riding-elephant at present, Soondargowry, often my only shooting companion, which kneels, trumpets, hands up anything from the ground, raises her trunk to break a branch, or passes under one in silence, stops, backs, and does other things at understood hints as I sit on her pad; but no uninitiated looker-on would perceive that any intimation of what is required passes between us. The driver's knees are placed behind an elephant's ears as he sits on it, and it is by means of a push, pressure, and other motions, that his wishes are communicated, as with the pressure of the leg with trained horses in a circus. As well might performing dogs which spell out replies to questions be credited with knowing what they are saying, as elephants with appreciating the objects to be gained by much which they do under the direction of the rider.

[1] *The Wild Elephant*, by Sir J. Emerson Tennent.

So much for the intelligence of the elephant. Let us now consider its temperament in captivity. I think all who have had to deal with elephants will agree in saying that their good qualities cannot be exaggerated, and that their vices are few, and only occur in exceptional animals. The not uncommon idea that elephants are treacherous and retentive of an injury is a groundless one. Male elephants are subject to periodical fits of *must*, of the approach of which, however, due warning is given, and during the continuance of which care is necessary in dealing with them, as they are quite irresponsible for their actions. But at all other times the male elephant is generally perfectly safe, rarely suddenly changeable in temper. Female elephants are at all times the most perfect-tempered creatures in the world. Amongst some hundreds which I have known, only two have had any tricks. Of these, one would not allow herself to be ridden by a strange mahout; the other had a great aversion to any natives but her own two attendants approaching her. She was, however, perfectly friendly with Europeans, as I used to feed and pet her; and when engaged at the kheddahs in Mysore, she was frequently fed by the ladies present.

The elephant's chief good qualities are obedience, gentleness, and patience. In none of these is he excelled by any domestic animal, and under circumstances of the greatest discomfort, such as exposure to the sun, painful surgical operations, &c., he seldom evinces any irritation. He never refuses to do what he is required, if he understands the nature of the demand, unless it be something of which he is afraid. The elephant is excessively timid, both in its wild and domestic state, and its fears are easily excited by anything strange. But many have a good stock of courage, which only requires developing; the conduct of some elephants used in tiger-hunting demonstrates this.

Much misapprehension prevails regarding the uses and power of the elephant's trunk. This organ is chiefly used by the animal to procure its food, and to convey it, and water, to its mouth; also to warn it of danger by the senses of smell and touch. It is a delicate and sensitive organ, and never used for rough work. In any dangerous situation the elephant at once secures it by curling it up. The idea that he can use it for any purpose, from picking up a needle to dragging a piece of ordnance from a bog, is, like many others, founded entirely on imagination. An elephant might manage the former feat, though I doubt it; the latter he would not attempt.

Elephants engaged in such work as dragging timber invariably take the rope between their teeth; they never attempt to pull a heavy weight with the trunk. In carrying a light log they hold it in the mouth as a dog does a stick, receiving some little assistance in balancing it from the trunk. Tuskers generally use their tusks for this and similar purposes, and are more valuable than females for work. An elephant is powerful enough to extricate a cannon from a difficult situation, but he does it by pushing with his head or feet, or in harness—never by lifting or drawing with his trunk. The story . . . of the elephant lifting the wheel over the prostrate gunner, is a physically impossible one. Elephants do not push with their foreheads, or the region *above* the eyes, but with the base of the trunk, or snout, about one foot below the eyes.

An elephant rarely uses its trunk for striking other elephants or man. Newly-caught ones seldom attempt even to seize anyone coming within their reach with their trunks; they curl them up and rush at the intruder. Should any accident happen to an elephant's trunk to prevent it conveying water to its mouth, it drinks by wading into deep water and immersing the mouth in the manner common to most quadrupeds. In drinking, only about fifteen inches of the end of the trunk are filled with water at a time; the trunk is then curled backwards so as to reach the mouth, and the water is blown into it. Wild elephants' trunks are occasionally cut by the sharp edges of split bamboos whilst feeding. One which I saw had more than a foot of the outer cuticle stripped off the trunk; another, a healed gash penetrating to one of the nostrils of the trunk from the outside.

The elephant is essentially a native's animal. Natives alone have fully studied his peculiarities and classified him into castes; his capture, training and keeping, are in native hands, as well as the trade; and the native standard of merit regulates the market. . . .

Elephants are divided by natives into three castes or breeds, distinguished by their physical conformation; these are termed in Bengal *Koomeriah*, *Dwasala*, and *Meerga*, which terms may be considered to signify thoroughbred, half-bred, and third-rates. The term *Koomeriah* signifies royal or princely. *Meerga* is probably a corruption of the Sanskrit *mriga*, a deer; the light build and length of leg of this class of elephants suggest the comparison. *Dwasala* in Persian means two things or originals, and in reference to the elephant, signifies the blending of the first and third castes into the intermediate one. . . .

The elephant is said to be subject to albinism. I have never myself seen a really white one, nor have any of the experienced native hunters whom I have met. There is at present in his Highness the Maharajah of Mysore's stables a young tusker, captured twelve years ago, which is of a somewhat light colour, both as to his skin and hair, and his eyes are light blue. Amongst those I captured in Mysore, in 1874, was a calf of a very light shade, somewhat of a dirty cream colour; ordinary calves are quite black. Regarding the white elephants of which we read as forming the most cherished possessions of the King of Ava, I am unable to give any information. I have never heard of any trustworthy European writer's having seen them.

Real vice in any elephant is a thing almost unknown. Natives attach less importance than we do to the temper of elephants; all can be managed by some means, and the possession of an unruly animal, if of good figure, is sometimes regarded as rather desirable than otherwise.

No male elephant can reach high merit without good tusks; the longer and heavier they are the more is their possessor valued; but they must be of good shape, curving upwards like the runners of a cradle, and diverging gracefully from each other. Tuskers are far more valuable for work than females, not only from their greater strength, but from the good use they make of their tusks in turning and carrying logs, &c. A tusker, if given the end of a rope to pull, puts it over one tusk, and holding the end between his teeth, can move a weight with this purchase which a female with only the hold with her teeth would be unable to manage. Tusks usually require cutting once a year: the elephant is made to lie down in water, and the portion to be removed is then sawn off. This gives him no pain, and is necessary to prevent elephants injuring each other, not as a precaution for the safety of their attendants. The rule for cutting an elephant's tusk is as follows: Measure from the eye to the insertion of the tusk in the lip; this length measured from the latter point along the tusk will give the spot where it should be cut. In young animals a little more should be allowed, as the above measurement may approach too nearly the medullary pulp of the tusk.

Elephants are used by Government for the transport of troops, for provisioning outpost stations which are not connected by roads, &c. The progressing development of roads and railways in India may be expected to do away with the necessity for the services of some in the most accessible localities, but it will always be necessary to keep a certain number in case of movements in rough and uncivilized countries. Elephants were indispensable in the Abyssinian, Looshai, and other petty wars and expeditions in recent years, and similar services may be required at any moment.

The merely useful elephant, whose employment is to assist the movement of troops, to transport timber from the forests to river-banks, for shooting purposes, &c., is usually of the Dwasala or Meerga class. Amongst these the tuskers cost much more than the females. For work males are more powerful; their tusks enable them to perform a variety of services which the female renders less efficiently; and for shooting their superior courage is indisputable. A male elephant bears about the same relation in appearance and power to the female as a domestic bull does to a cow. From females being more generally employed in shooting, being more readily procurable, males seldom have the opportunity of showing their natural superiority in courage and strength; but where they are employed they are immeasurably superior.

For draught, elephants are very valuable, as logs can be brought by their aid from localities where they would otherwise be inaccessible. The elephant's power is most advantageously employed where a great exertion is required for a short distance, through a limited space of time. When elephants are harnessed, the dragging-rope is either attached to a collar round the neck or to a girth behind the shoulders. The latter plan is the better of the two, as it gives more bearing surface, and there is less liability to gall. To pull from the girth, the elephant's pad is first put on, to prevent the girth-rope from galling the back. The girth, a strong rope ninety feet in length, is then passed tightly several times round the elephant behind the shoulders, and a small breast-rope is attached to prevent it slipping backwards. The pulling-rope or chain is then fastened to the girth, half-way up the elephant's side. Native attendants are very careless, and pulling-ropes are constantly breaking, which makes elephants that have once been frightened in this way cautious about throwing themselves into the collar. But an elephant with confidence in his gear will make the most extraordinary exertions, leaning forward far beyond his centre of gravity, or kneeling and almost resting on his forehead, in his attempts to move the load. In dragging light timber a rope about three feet long is generally fastened round one end of a log. The elephant takes the rope in its teeth, and thus raising one end clear of the ground, half drags, half carries it away. An elephant can be harnessed to a cart in the same way as a horse. In Dacca two elephant-wagons were employed for carrying away the litter from the elephant-lines.

As a beast of burden the elephant can scarcely be considered satisfactory in all respects, chiefly from his liability to gall under such heavy weights as he is otherwise able to carry. This difficulty can be avoided with great care, but it requires constant attention from more heedful and humane masters than ordinary elephant-attendants. Some of these do not attempt to prevent a sore back—rather the reverse—when elephants are on long and arduous service. A sore back once established, the elephant cannot be used for weeks, often months, and its attendants escape work, even the bringing its fodder. The best preventive has been found to be putting everyone connected with the elephant on half-pay till the animal has recovered. An elephant well packed will carry an immense bulk and weight; and in difficult country, especially hilly or swampy districts, their place cannot be taken by any other means of carriage. For transporting light guns in mountain warfare they are invaluable. An elephant's gear consists of a thick, soft-padded cloth, covering the whole of the back from the nape of the neck to the croup, and hanging half way down the animal's sides. Over this comes a saddle, which consists of two pads or flat bags of stout sacking, each six feet long and two and a half broad. These are stuffed to one foot in thickness with dried grass or coconut fibre, and are attached by cross-pieces, so that one lies on each side of the elephant's backbone, which is thus protected from pressure. Upon the first pair of pads is another large single pad. On this the load is placed. Thus all the weight should rest on the upper part of the animal's ribs, without touching the spine, as in a horse with a well-fitted saddle.

Half a ton is a good load for an elephant for continuous marching. In hilly country seven hundredweights is as much as he should carry. I have known a large female carry a pile of thirty bags of rice, weighing 82 lb. each, or one ton and two hundredweights, from one storeroom to another, three hundred yards distant, several times in a morning. By the Bengal Commissariat code elephants are expected to carry 1640 lb., exclusive of attendants and chain, for which 300 lb. extra may be added; but this is too great a weight for continued marching. The weight of one of his Excellency the Viceroy's silver State howdahs and trappings is a little over half a ton, as below:

	Cwts.	qrs.	lb.
Howdah,	6	1	22
Gold cloth,	1	0	14
Punkahs, &c.,	0	2	25
Ropes and gear,	1	5	15
	10	2	20

Elephants are kept by natives of rank in India solely for the purposes of display, and in this sphere the animal is more at home than in any other. The pompous pace of a procession suits his naturally sedate disposition, and the attentions lavished upon him please his vanity. Only male elephants are valued for this purpose, and tuskers are preferred to mucknas. Every inch of height adds immensely to an elephant's value after nine feet at the shoulder has been passed. I have already said in the last chapter that ten feet at the shoulder is probably the extreme height of the Asiatic elephant. One or more elephants are attached to most temples of note in India, and take part in the religious processions connected with them.

Government elephants are often used for riding by the European officers who have charge of the departments in which they are employed, and they are of much use in country where horses cannot be taken. Though an elephant is but a poor means of progression on a highroad, in jungly or hilly country he is most useful, as guides and gun-bearers are always in attendance in such places, and the elephant can move as quickly as the party would be able to proceed without him. A light elephant, trained for *sowari*, or riding, if active and free, is a very pleasant mount. Half-grown ones are the best. As a rule, long-legged, lanky animals of the Meerga caste are the most active walkers. Calves are always quick movers. I have used them as small as thirteen hands at the shoulder, with a soft pad and stirrups, bestriding them as a pony. They are wonderful little creatures for getting up or down any difficult place; they give no trouble; and will keep up with a man running at any pace before them.

Elephants very rarely stumble; should they even do so they never fall from that cause, as they can go down on one or both knees—an easy position for an elephant. I have sometimes, but rarely, known them fall flat on their sides in slippery soil during wet weather.

Elephants can always be guided, except when frightened, by the slightest tap with a small stick on either side of the head, the pressure of the knee, or even by a word; but if alarmed, they have to be controlled or urged forward by the driving-goad. An elephant is as much afraid of this implement as a horse is of the curb, and can be restrained by it as well. When under the influence of fear, of course the elephant may run away, as a horse does, regardless of punishment. It is a terrible thing to be bolted with in jungle by an elephant; the rider is fortunate if he escapes with whole bones. I have felt on the one or two occasions on which it has happened to me as a man might if bestriding a runaway locomotive, and hooking the funnel with the crook of his walking-stick to hold it in!

It is very difficult to cure a confirmed bolter, as the habit has its origin in fear, and the animal is always liable to be startled by unexpected sounds or sight, chiefly the former. It is a rare trick, however, and I have only known two elephants subject to it. One was a fine baggage animal, but almost useless for jungle-work from this trick. . . .

Four miles an hour is a good pace for an elephant, but long-legged ones will swing along at five or upwards for a moderate distance, say ten miles. I have known thirty-nine miles done at a stretch at a moderate pace. Single wild elephants that have been wounded or much frightened will often travel as far as this in a few hours without a halt.

The elephant's use in tiger-shooting is well known, and speaks volumes for the tractability of an animal naturally so timid and disinclined for such work. Female elephants are more commonly used than males for tiger-shooting, being more easily procurable. But a well-trained male elephant is infinitely superior to any female, from his greater courage and strength. Unless they are well disciplined, however, there is danger of some male elephants attacking the tiger when they see him, which is a dangerous habit, as the occupants of the howdah may be shaken out during the animal's endeavours to crush the tiger.

A case of this kind occurred at Dacca in May 1876, whilst I was there. A lady and her husband, Mr and Mrs I—, were at a tiger-hunt in a howdah on a female elephant, when a tigress charged across the open ground where they were stationed, not so much at the elephant as to get into a piece of cover behind it. The elephant rushed to meet the tigress, in this case more from excitement and terror than real courage. I— fired and rolled the tigress over in front of the elephant, which kicked at her. The tigress grasped one of the elephant's hind-legs with teeth and claws, and pulled, or fell, down on to her. I— was thrown out, his rifle going off in the shock of his fall, but fortunately without doing any harm. He helped Mrs I— from the howdah, and they ran to the protection of another elephant at some distance. The tigress was killed on the spot by the fall of the elephant upon her. In this case, had the elephant stood her ground, I— would probably have killed the tigress before she got to close quarters.

As elephants are not bred in captivity, the demand for them from the forest is unwavering. Kabul merchants are the chief agents for the supply of high-class animals. These energetic traders frequently attach themselves to Courts where liberal prices are given, and in their service penetrate the remote tracts of Burmah and Siam. Here they purchase tuskers for figures seldom exceeding £100 on the spot, and march them, perhaps occupying more than a year on the road, to India. Their outlay is considerable in feeding them highly and in marching them slowly. I have heard of a case where a tusker, which had cost the merchant much money and labour, died almost at the gate of the city of the rajah for whom he was designed; who, when the merchant appeared with the elephant's trappings and tusks, bewailing his misfortune, ordered, with true Eastern munificence, that he should be paid the full value of the animal!

The chief marts for the supply of elephants to India hitherto have been Ceylon, Burmah, Siam, and a few of the forests of continental India; but from several causes the number brought into the market is now smaller than formerly, and prices are rising accordingly. The following statistics have been obligingly furnished me by the Secretary to the Government of Ceylon, of elephants exported from the island during the years 1863–76. The sudden decrease in 1870 is due to the imposition in that year of an export duty of £20 per head, and lately the export has been entirely closed as a temporary measure, as it was feared that under the then existing rules for their capture and destruction, the practical extinction of elephants in the island might be expected at no distant date.

ELEPHANTS EXPORTED FROM CEYLON FROM 1863 TO 1876.

Year.	Number.	Year.	Number.
1863, ...	173	1870, ...	30
1864, ...	188	1871, ...	63
1865, ...	270	1872, ...	51
1866, ...	202	1873, ...	83
1867, ...	148	1874, ...	77
1868, ...	163	1875, ...	7
1869, ...	199	1876, ...	3

The great annual fair held at Sonepoor, on the Ganges, is the chief mart in India for the sale of elephants. It is held on the occasion of the gathering of thousands of pilgrims to worship at a noted shrine of Shiva, and bathe in the Ganges, at the full moon of the month of October–November. Thousands of horses and hundreds of elephants are collected there, and for this point all dealers in elephants make. Such elephants as they do not then dispose of are taken about amongst rajahs and native princes. Traders in elephants are, as to character, pretty much on a par with dealers in horses all the world over. I once met a humorous old Kabul merchant at Dacca. He and some fellow-dealers came to the *peelkhana* (elephant-stables) day after day, and importuned me to sell some of the newly-caught elephants from Chittagong. It is not uncommon to dispose of such as, from some cause, may be unfit for Government service; but on this occasion all were required for filling up vacancies in the Commissariat Department. There was one very old female, however, that I knew would never be fit for work, whilst being handsome, and in good condition, she might suit a native for show. I therefore offered her to the dealers, for 400 rupees (£40), a very low figure. We proceeded to her picket, where the head dealer, a patriarchal-looking old fellow, examined her with attention for some time, and then turned away with a sigh. I asked him if the price was too high. 'No,' he said, 'it is not that. The sight of the elephant makes me think of my poor old grandmother. She died when I was a lad. What an elephant that would have been for her!'

The price of elephants throughout India has increased enormously of late years. A considerable number were formerly purchased at Sonepoor and elsewhere by the Bengal Government, but of late years prices have become almost prohibitory. In 1835 the price of elephants was £45 per head; in 1855 about £75; in 1874, twenty were purchased at Sonepoor for the Bengal Government at £132, 15s. each; in 1875, seventy were required at Sonepoor, for which £140 per head was sanctioned, but not one was procurable at that figure. £150 is now the lowest rate for which young animals, chiefly females, and not fully grown, can be obtained. The price of good females of the working class is at present from £200 to £300. The value of tuskers is very capricious; it depends mainly upon the nearness of approach of their points to those of the Koomeriah. The best are only found in the possession of those who can pay fancy prices, but all male elephants are in high demand for the retinues of rajahs and temple purposes. Scarcely any limit can be placed on the price of a really perfect Koomeriah; £2000 is not an unknown figure. Tuskers of any pretensions at all command from £800 to £1500. Two newly-caught tuskers of no particular merit were sold out of the Dacca stud, in 1875, for £1600 the pair.

The elephants required for the service of Government in Bengal are mostly captured by the Government Kheddah (or elephant-catching) Establishment, the headquarters of which are at Dacca, in Eastern Bengal. This establishment is under a European officer, and contains a large number of trained elephants and native hunters, and yearly in December penetrates some of the forests of Assam, Chittagong, or other tracts, and captures elephants, which are marched to Dacca before the rains commence in May. Here they are trained for service, and about November are despatched to Barrackpoor, near Calcutta, whence they are allotted to different Commissariat stations. The average annual number of elephants captured by the Dacca Establishment during the seven years prior to 1875–76 was fifty-nine.

The Superintendent of Kheddahs at Dacca is also empowered to grant licences to natives of capital to capture elephants upon certain terms, by which Government secures a further annual supply. These lessees work in forests where the Government kheddahs are not working, and the terms usually are that half of the elephants measuring over six feet, and below eight and a half feet, at the shoulder, are to be handed over as Government rent; whilst all below six feet, and over eight and a half feet in height, are the exclusive property of the lessee. Government is further at liberty to purchase any or all of the lessee's share of the elephants between six and eight and a half feet at £5 per foot of height at shoulder (for instance, £40 for an eight-feet elephant), which is very much below the usual price of newly-caught elephants.

This system is advantageous both to the Government and the lessee. Should the hunt be unsuccessful the former is not saddled with a money payment, whilst any really valuable tuskers, over eight and a half feet high, fall to his share. On the Government's part, the entire expenses of the kheddah are borne by the lessee, so no loss can be sustained. Should Government give any assistance in tame elephants for securing the captives when impounded, ten per cent of the latter are taken as remuneration.

The supply of elephants to Government must always be kept up by kheddahs and the licence system. The figure for which they are now captured need probably never be exceeded. The outer market is not likely to become easier, as, though the demand will decrease to some extent as the less wealthy native notables, and a few Europeans who keep elephants for sport, must curtail their studs to the ability of their pockets, the supply has decreased in a disproportionate degree owing to restrictions in hunting. An elephant which costs Government £40 to capture would cost at least £150 in the market.

The Madras Government is entirely dependent for its supply of elephants on Burmah, as there is no Government catching-establishment in the Presidency, as in Bengal, and the immense number of elephants roaming the Madras forests is turned to no account. The elephants are shipped from Moulmein to Coconada in vessels specially chartered for the purpose. A batch of about 60, imported eight years ago, cost £176 each when landed. Prices have risen since. The Collector of Coimbatore, a district of Madras, commenced elephant-catching in 1874, upon the plan adopted in Mysore, and between 1874 and 1877 captured 76 elephants, but the cost has been so great (about £13,000), and so many have died, that the scheme has been a financial failure. The idea, however, is a move in the right direction. The experiment has necessarily cost proportionately more than further operations need cost. It is evidently inexpedient that a distant market should be trusted to, in which prices are rising fast, and must continue to rise, whilst the jungles of the Madras Presidency abound with elephants. A catching-establishment cannot be got into order in a day, nor by the isolated efforts of one officer. The Dacca establishment has been working in one form or other since the beginning of the century. If the Madras Government is convinced of the necessity of keeping up its present stud of elephants—a matter admitting of much consideration, now that good roads, railways, and the settled state of the country have modified the former military requirements—it would seem to be a matter deserving of consideration whether the Commissariat requirements in elephants cannot be met from local sources. A fallacious idea that the Madras elephants are less hardy than those of Burmah has sprung out of the fact that many die before they are fit for service. But this is the case everywhere. Those imported from Burmah have been already seasoned, and consequently the mortality amongst them is lighter.

The Breeding of Elephants

The question has sometimes been raised whether it is the male or female elephant which comes into season. I have heard the opinion advanced that it is the former; but it is an erroneous one, probably founded on the fact of most male elephants in captivity having periodical paroxysms of *must*. Some male elephants never, or only at long intervals, have these fits; in others they are of tolerably regular occurrence. They occur also in wild individuals, chiefly in the cold weather from November to February. The temples swell, and an oily matter exudes from them, as in tame elephants, but the wild elephant, I believe, shows no violence whilst under their influence. The occurrence of *must* in tame elephants is connected with their condition, and rarely appears in animals much below par. It does not appear in animals under about thirty years of age, though tuskers breed from the age of twenty.

There is ample proof that it is not the male elephant that comes into season. In following single males with a view to capturing them with trained females, they may always be relied upon to make advances to the females, usually to some particular one, and the efforts of the mahouts are frequently necessary to keep her out of the male's reach.

The period of heat is not marked by any particular signs in the female, which has probably helped to strengthen the erroneous opinion spoken of. In approaching a male elephant, a female desirous of his attentions utters certain sounds, and courts his society; but only those conversant with elephants would notice this. It has frequently happened that the tame females of the kheddah parties have been found in calf after work in the jungles, where wild males have had access to them, though no indications of their being prepared to receive the male were observed even by their keepers.

It has been a disputed point as to the manner in which the connection between the two sexes takes place. Some have supposed that the female kneels or lies down to receive the male, but this is not the case. I have myself, on four different occasions, witnessed the act—once, by two animals belonging to a wild herd in the jungles; on the others, by animals which had just been caught, and which were at large within the kheddah enclosures. On each, the female elephant stood to receive the male in the manner common to all quadrupeds. The opposite opinion may have arisen from the fact that it is possible for a heavy male to bear down to her knees a female much smaller than himself. On none of these occasions did the male elephant exhibit signs of *must*; which shows that it is not only when under its influence that male elephants court the society of the females.

SAMUEL BAKER

A Temperamental Elephant

It is well known that the entire males of many domestic animals are naturally savage. The horse, bull, boar, and the park-fed stag are all uncertain in their tempers and may be pronounced unsafe; but the male elephant, although dangerous to a stranger and treacherous to his attendants, combines an extraordinary degree of cowardice with his natural ferocity. A few months ago I witnessed a curious example of this combination in the elephant's character. A magnificent specimen had been lent to me by the Commissariat Department at Jubbulpur; this was a high caste bull elephant named Bisgaum that was well known as bad-tempered, but was supposed to be courageous. He had somewhat tarnished his reputation during the last season by turning tail upon a tiger that rushed out of dense bush and killed a coolie within a few yards of his trunk; but this momentary panic was excused, and the blame was thrown upon the mahout. The man was dismissed and a first-rate Punjaubi driver was appointed in his stead. This man assured me that the elephant was dependable; I accordingly accepted him, and he was ordered to carry the howdah throughout the expedition.

In a very short experience we discovered the necessity of giving Bisgaum a wide berth, as he would fling out his trunk with extreme

From *Wild Beasts and Their Ways*, 1890.

quickness to strike person within his reach, and he would kick out sharply with his hind leg whenever a native ventured to approach his rear. He took a fancy to me, as I fed him daily with sugar-canes, jaggery, and native chupatties (cakes), which quickly established an understanding between us; but I always took the precaution of standing by his side instead of in his front, and of resting my left hand upon his tusk while I fed him with the right. Every morning at daylight he was brought to the tent with Demoiselle (the female elephant), and they both received from my own hands the choice bits which gained their confidence.

My suspicions were first aroused by his peculiar behaviour upon an occasion when we had killed two tigers; these were young animals, and although large, there was no difficulty in arranging them upon the pad, upon which they were secured by ropes, when the elephant kneeling down was carefully loaded. Hardly had Bisgaum risen to his feet, when, conscious of the character of the animals upon his back, and, I suppose, not quite certain that life was actually extinct, he trumpeted a shrill scream, and shook his immense carcass like a wet dog that has just landed from the water. This effect was so violent that one tiger was thrown some yards to the right, while the other fell to the ground on the left, and without a moment's warning, the elephant charged the lifeless body, sent it flying by a quick kick with his fore foot, and immediately proceeded to dance a war-dance, kicking with his hind legs to so great a height that he could have reached a tall man's hat. A vigorous application of the driving-hook by the mahout, who was a powerful man, at length changed the scene, and the elephant at once desisted from his attack upon the dead tiger, and rushed madly upon one side, where he stood nervously looking at the enemy as though he expected it would show signs of life.

This did not look promising for an encounter with a live tiger, as it would have been absolutely impossible to shoot from that elephant's back.

A short time after this occurrence, when upon my usual reconnaissance through the jungles in the neighbourhood of the camp, I came upon the fresh tracks of a large tiger close to the banks of the Bearmi river, and I gave instructions that a buffalo should be tied up as a bait that same evening.

Early on the following morning the news was brought by the

shikaris that the buffalo had been killed, and dragged into a neighbouring ravine. As the river was close by, there could be no doubt that the tiger would have drunk water after feasting on the carcasses, and would be lying asleep somewhere in the immediate neighbourhood.

The mucharns (platforms in trees) had already been prepared in positions where the tiger was expected to pass when driven, as he would make for the forest-covered hills which rose within half a mile of the river.

The spot was within twenty minutes of the camp; the elephants were both ready, with simple pads, as the howdah was ill-adapted for a forest; and we quickly started.

Three mucharns had been prepared: these were about 100 yards apart in a direct line which guarded a narrow glade between the jungle upon the river's bank and the main body of the forest at the foot of a range of red sandstone hills; these were covered to the summit with trees already leafless from the drought.

The mucharn which fell to my share was that upon the right flank when facing the beat; this was in the open glade opposite a projecting corner of the jungle. On the left, about 70 yards distant, was a narrow strip of bush connected with the jungle, about 4 yards wide, which terminated in a copse about 30 yards in diameter; beyond this was open glade for about 40 yards width until it bounded the main forest at the foot of the hill-range.

We took our places, and I was assured by the shikaris that the tiger would probably break covert exactly in my front.

It is most uncomfortable for a European to remain squatted in a mucharn for any length of time; the limbs become stiffened and the cramped position renders good shooting anything but certain. I have a simple wooden turnstool, which enables me to shoot in any required direction; this is most comfortable.

I had adjusted my stool upon a thick mat to prevent it from slipping, and having settled myself firmly, I began to examine the position to form an opinion concerning the most likely spot for the tiger to emerge from the jungle.

The beat had commenced, and the shouts and yells of a long line of 150 men were gradually becoming more distinct. Several peacocks ran across the open glade: these birds are always the forerunners of other animals, as they are the first to retreat.

Presently I heard a rustle in the jungle, and I observed the legs of a sambur deer, which, having neared the edge, now halted to listen to the beaters before venturing to break from the dense covert. The beaters drew nearer, and a large doe sambur, instead of rushing quickly forward, walked slowly into the open, and stood within 10 yards of me upon the glade. She waited there for several minutes and then, as if some suspicion had suddenly crossed her mind, gave two or three convulsive bounds and dashed back to the same covert from which she had approached.

It struck me that the sambur had got the wind of an enemy, otherwise she would not have rushed back in such sudden haste; she could not have scented me, as I was 10 or 12 feet above the ground, and the breeze was aslant. . . . Then, if a tiger were in the jungle, why should she dash back into the same covert?

I was reflecting upon these subjects, and looking out sharp towards my left and front, when I gently turned upon my stool to the right; there was the tiger himself who had already broken from the jungle about 75 yards from my position. He was slowly jogging along as though just disturbed (possibly by the sambur), keeping close to the narrow belt of bushes already described. There was a footpath from the open glade which pierced the belt; I therefore waited until he should cross this favourable spot. I fired with the .577 rifle just as he was passing across the dusty track. I saw the dust fly from the ground upon the other side as the hardened bullet passed like lightning through his flank, but I felt that I was a little too far behind his shoulder, as his response to the shot was a bound at full gallop forwards into the small clump of jungle that projected into the grassy open. My turnstool was handy, and I quickly turned to the right, waiting with the left-hand barrel ready for his reappearance upon the grass-land in the interval between the main jungle and the narrow patch. There was no time to lose, for the tiger appeared in a few seconds, dashing out of the jungle, and flying over the open at tremendous speed. This was about 110 yards distant; aiming about 18 inches in his front, I fired. A short spasmodic roar and a sudden convulsive twist of his body showed plainly that he was well hit, but with unabated speed he gained the main forest, which was not more than 40 yards distant. If that had been a soft leaden bullet he would have rolled over to the shot, but I had seen the dust start from the ground when I fired, and I knew that the hard bullet had passed through without delivering the shock required.

The beaters and shikaris now arrived, and having explained the incident, we examined the ground for tracks and quickly found the claw-marks, which were deeply indented in the parched surface of fine sward. We followed these tracks cautiously into the jungle. Our party consisted of Colonel Lugard, the Hon. D. Leigh, myself and two experienced shikaris. Tiger-shooting is always an engrossing sport, but the lively excitement is increased when you follow a wounded tiger upon foot. We now slowly advanced upon the track, which faintly showed the sharp claws where the tiger had alighted in every bound. The jungle was fairly open, as the surface was stony, and the trees for want of moisture in a rocky soil had lost their leaves; we could thus see a considerable distance upon all sides. In this manner we advanced about 100 yards without finding a trace of blood, and I could see that some of my people doubted the fact of the tiger being wounded. I felt certain that he was mortally hit, and I explained to my men that the hard bullet would make so clean a hole through his body that he would not bleed externally until his inside should be nearly full of blood. Suddenly a man cried 'koon' (blood) and he held up a large dried leaf of the teak-tree upon which was a considerable red splash: almost immediately after this we not only came upon a continuous line of blood, but we halted at a place where the animal had lain down; this was a pool of blood, proving that the tiger would not be far distant.

I now sent for the elephants, as I would not permit the shikaris to advance further upon foot. The big tusker Bisgaum arrived, and giving my Paradox gun to my trustworthy shikari Kerim Bux, he mounted the pad of that excitable beast to carry out my orders, 'to follow the blood until he should find the tiger after which he was to return to us'. We were now on the top of a small hill within an extensive forest range, and directly in front the ground suddenly dipped, forming a V-shaped dell, which in the wet season was the bed of a considerable torrent. It struck me that if the tiger were still alive he would steal away along the bottom of the rocky watercourse; therefore, before the elephant should advance, and perhaps disturb him, we should take up a position on the right to protect the nullah or torrent-bed; this plan was accordingly carried out.

We had not been long in our respective positions when a shot from the direction taken by the elephant, followed instantly by a short roar, proved that the tiger had been discovered and that he was still alive. My female elephant Demoiselle, upon hearing the sound, trembled beneath me with intense excitement, while the other female would have bolted had she not been sharply reminded by the heavy driving-hook. Several shots were now fired in succession, and after vainly endeavouring to discover the whereabouts of the tiger, I sent Demoiselle to obtain the news while we kept guard over the ravine. No tiger having appeared, I stationed natives in trees to watch the nullah while we ascended the hill on foot, directing our course through the forest to the place from whence the shots had been fired. We had hardly advanced 80 yards before we found both the elephants on the top of the steep shoulder of the hill, where several of our men were upon the boughs of surrounding trees. Bisgaum was in a state of wild excitement, and Kerim Bux explained that it was impossible to shoot from his back, as he could not be kept quiet. Where was the tiger? that was the question. 'Close to us, Sahib!' was the reply; but on foot we could see nothing, owing to high withered grass and bush. I clambered upon the back of the refractory Bisgaum, momentarily expecting him to bolt away like a locomotive engine, and from that elevated position I was supposed to see the tiger, which was lying in the bottom of the ravine about 100 yards distant. There were so many small bushes and tufts of yellow grass that I could not distinguish the form for some minutes; at length my eyes caught the object. I had been looking for orange and black stripes, therefore I had not noticed black and white, the belly being uppermost as the animal was lying upon its back, evidently dying.

The side of the rocky hill was so steep and slippery that the elephants could not descend; I therefore changed my steed and mounted Demoiselle, from the back of which I fired several shots at the tiger until life appeared to be extinct. The ground was so unfavourable that I would not permit any native to approach near enough to prove that the animal was quite dead. I therefore instructed Bisgaum's mahout to make a detour to the right until he could descend with his elephant into the flat bottom of the watercourse, he was then to advance cautiously until near enough to see whether the tiger breathed. At the same time I rode Demoiselle carefully as near as we could safely descend among the rocks to a distance of about 40 yards; it was so steep that the elephant was impossible to turn. From this point of vantage I soon perceived Bisgaum's bulky form advancing up the dry torrent-bed. The rocks were a perfectly flat red sandstone, which in many places resembled artificial pavement; this was throughout the district a peculiar geological feature, the surface of the stone being covered with ripple-marks, and upon this easy path Bisgaum now approached the body of the tiger, which lay apparently dead exactly in his front.

Suddenly the elephant halted when about 15 yards from the object, which had never moved. I have seen wild savages frenzied by the exciting war-dance, but I never witnessed such an instance of hysterical fury as that exhibited by Bisgaum. It is impossible to describe the elephantine antics of this frantic animal; he kicked right and left with his hind legs alternately, with the rapidity of a horse; trumpeting and screaming, he threw his trunk in the air, twisting it about, and shaking his immense head, until, having lashed himself into a sufficient rage, he made a desperate charge at the supposed defunct enemy, with the intention of treating the body in a similar manner to that a few days previous. But the tiger was not quite dead; and although he could not move to get away, he seized with teeth and claws the hind leg of the maddened elephant, who had clumsily overrun him in the high excitement, instead of kicking the body with a fore foot as he advanced.

The scene was now most interesting. We were close spectators looking down upon the exhibition as though upon an arena. I never saw such fury in an elephant; the air was full of stones and dust, as he kicked with such force that the tiger for the moment was lost to view in the tremendous struggle, and being kicked away from his hold, with one of his long fangs broken short off to the gum, he lay helpless before his huge antagonist, who, turning quickly round, drove his long tusks between the tiger's shoulders, and crushed the last spark of life from his tenacious adversary.

This was a grand scene, and I began to think there was some real pluck in Bisgaum after all, although there was a total want of discipline; but just as I felt inclined to applaud, the victorious elephant was seized with a sudden panic, and turning tail he rushed along the bottom of the watercourse at the rate of 20 miles an hour, and disappeared in the thorny jungle below at a desperate pace that threatened immediate destruction to his staunch mahout. Leaving my men to arrange a litter with poles and cross-bars to carry the tiger home, I followed the course of Bisgaum upon Demoiselle; expecting every minute to see the body of his mahout stretched upon the ground. At length, after about half a mile passed in anxiety, we discovered Bisgaum and his mahout both safe upon an open plain: the latter torn and bleeding from countless scratches while rushing through the thorny jungle.

On the following day the elephant's leg was much swollen although the wounds appeared to be very slight. It is probable that a portion of the broken tooth remained in the flesh as the leg festered, and became so bad that the elephant could not travel for nearly a fortnight afterwards. The mahouts are very obstinate, and insist upon native medicines, their famous lotion being a decoction of Mhowa blossoms, which in my opinion aggravated the inflammation of the wound.

I returned Bisgaum to the Commissariat stables at Jubbulpur directly that he could march, as he was too uncontrollable for sporting purposes. Had any person been upon his back during his stampede he would have been swept off by the branches and killed; the mahout, sitting low upon his neck, could accommodate his body to avoid the boughs.

DOUGLAS HAMILTON

Elephants

At one time during my service I had a good deal to do with the Indian elephant, both wild and in captivity. I was in charge of one of the large teak forests in Southern India—the Annamullies—where the wild elephant roamed at will. I had a number of tame elephants employed to drag timber to the stacks. In those days before iron had taken the place of wood, a great deal of teak wood was used in ship building, and this I had to supply to the Bombay Dock Yard. The teak wood is cut into large beams or planks as they are called in the forest, averaging about twenty-six feet in length, and from twelve to fourteen inches square throughout—not a very heavy load for an elephant to drag. A hole is cut at one end of the beam and a thick drag rope is tied to it; this the elephant takes in his mouth, dragging the beam alongside; occasionally, a fallen tree lies across the path, and I have often watched with astonishment the wonderful sagacity and intelligence of the animal when such a thing as this occurs. The elephant, the instant the beam touches the obstacle, does not put a particle of pressure on, but calmly steps back, lifts the end on to the fallen tree with his trunk, and then pulls it gently over.[1] Besides dragging

From *Records of Sports in Southern India*. Ed. Edward Hamilton. London: R.H. Porter, 1892.

[1]The Author evidently does not share the views of Sanderson and others as to the intelligence of this animal. . . . Blandford takes the same view; he says, 'I

the beams to the stack yard the elephants also pile them one over the other with the utmost regularity; no man could do it better. When the logs have been brought to the stack where they are to be piled, the drag rope has to be untied, and it is necessary that a man should accompany the elephant for this purpose, but I had a clever little elephant who untied the drag rope herself, and thus saved the wages of one man the whole time I was in the forest.

An elephant is generally guided and kept in order by a Mahout or keeper, armed with an iron hook and spike which acts as both rein and spear; but in the very damp climate of the Annamullies, the slight scratches and punctures made by this instrument had a tendency to fester, so we only allowed a light bamboo cane to be used, not thicker than one's little finger, and this answered perfectly. Few people are aware that the elephant with a skin nearly an inch in thickness is one of the most sensitive of animals, and will be as much annoyed or even more so by the sting of a mosquito than by a prod from the Mahout. A blow from a bamboo switch will make an elephant roar out much louder than a school boy does when he has to hold out his hand for punishment. Now by this little bamboo switch the elephants were maintained in perfect order. The Mahout if he had to leave the elephant for a time in the forest would take the animal up to a fallen tree and make him put one forefoot on it, and the bamboo stick would then be balanced on that foot. I have often passed an elephant standing perfectly still with one foot on a fallen tree balancing the stick, and half an hour after found him still in the same position, though the jungle around was teeming with all kinds of elephant luxuries—a wonderful instance of obedience and docility quite apart from their intelligence.

Some of the best working elephants I had were those that had been captured when full grown, yet these, and in fact all tame elephants, have a great dread of the wild ones. On Sundays we used to let all the tame elephants loose, and they had a day to themselves in the forest. They were quite unfettered except by a chain attached to one of the hind legs, and they have often come

---

quite agree with Sanderson in believing that the intelligence of elephants has been greatly overrated; they are singularly docile and obedient; no other animal is known to be capable of domestication when adult to nearly the same extent, and docility in animals is generally, I think, confounded with intelligence.' —Ed.

rushing into the station alarmed by the presence of wild ones in the neighbourhood. There was no fear of their running away; what with their dread of the wild ones and their attachment to, I was going to say, their keepers, but I ought to say their rice puddings, they were sure to come in at nightfall. These rice puddings were the greatest luxury the elephant could have: a mass of boiled rice about four or five times the size of an ordinary pudding was prepared for each elephant every evening. The cook having carefully rounded the pudding would dig his fist deep down into the top of it, leaving a sort of hollow cup; this was filled with a sweet kind of oil. The elephants were then drawn up in line, and the puddings being ready, at a given signal each one threw up his trunk and opened wide his mouth, when the Mahouts popped the luscious morsel with its oily accompaniment into the mouth, and no alderman could have eaten with more gusto the green fat of the turtle than the elephants did their rice puddings.

One Sunday they did not come in for their puddings, and early on Monday morning a messenger came up quite breathless to me (my hut being about four miles from the station) to say that the tame elephants were surrounded by a herd of wild ones, that the keepers dare not go in to rescue them, begging me to come at once, as the wild ones were killing our tame ones. I lost no time in collecting my rifles and hastened down. I can hardly describe the scene I witnessed when I arrived. The forest usually so silent was now resounding in every direction with the screaming and trumpeting of the animals, and the crashing and breaking of bamboos. In fact the turmoil was quite appalling, and I had visions of my finest elephants being killed or maimed. I knew that the best thing to be done was to shoot one of the wild beasts, as that would at once disperse the herd; now as a rule, one can always distinguish the tame from the wild elephant, for the former being regularly groomed and washed is as black as a piece of India rubber, while the wild animal covers itself with mud and sand to keep off the mosquitoes and flies of all kinds, so I crept up very cautiously and soon spied two very dirty-looking elephants standing under a tree. I got up to about seventeen yards of them, and taking aim at the brain of the nearest one, was actually pressing the trigger of my rifle, when I heard the clink of a chain just in time to save its life. I firmly believe that these two elephants had covered themselves with mud and sand so as not to be recognized and attacked by the wild herd around them.

There were about sixteen of the wild ones, all females with young ones, which accounted for their being so troublesome. I had great difficulty in getting up to them, and in my first attempt failed to kill one; I had to run some distance to intercept them as they were now thoroughly alarmed, and rushing through the grass which in some places was so high that I could only see the tops of their backs; suddenly an old female either saw or smelt me, and came charging through the grass right at me; to run would have been dangerous, as there were no trees to get behind, so I waited till I could see her eyes; on she came, and when she was not more than eight yards from me I let drive and planted a ball exactly between her eyes; but to my horror she did not fall; there was a stream behind me, and the hop step and a jump I made over that stream would, I think, have won me a prize at any of the athletic games of modern times. Nothing like an enraged elephant at one's back to make a long jump. As I jumped I looked over my shoulder, thinking the beast was upon me, and I saw that she had fallen dead. I immediately recrossed the stream, and with my other barrel knocked over another which was trying to pass its fallen companion; the rest of the herd rapidly dispersed, and I was glad to find that none of my tame ones had received any injury.

Elephants when in captivity are liable to become very delicate in their constitution, and are often ailing; I used to be a good deal troubled at times to know whether an elephant was ill or not, and I was obliged to depend upon the report of the head keeper as to whether the patient should have a bucket, or half a bucket of castor oil, or an opium pill strong enough to kill a dozen men. On one occasion I paid dear for interfering; a teak beam had been put down with its number underneath, and as I wanted particularly to ascertain what the number was, and there were no men available, I ordered the keeper of a fine male elephant to bring him up and make him turn over the plank. The Mahout said that the elephant was not very well and could not do it; now making an elephant turn over one of these planks would be about the same as asking a railway porter to turn over a tolerable sized portmanteau; I thought the man was humbugging me, so I insisted that my order should be obeyed. When the elephant was brought up he was very reluctant to touch the plank, and it was only after some trouble we got him to turn it over; this was all he had to do; the next morning he was dead, and I made up my mind never again to attempt to force a sick elephant to do any work. These tame elephants become much attached to their keeper and his belongings; it is touching to see how gentle they are with children. I have often watched the little children of the keeper playing about between the legs of a big brute, the animal standing perfectly quiet for fear of treading upon them.

'The Knowing Old Engineer.'

The elephant in his wild state is quite a different animal to the elephant in captivity; when roaming about the hills they are cunning and cautious to a degree, and the bulls as a rule, but not always, take the precaution to send their wives and children in advance. The old tuskers always come last in the single file in which they move when on the foray. Their olfactory organs are extremely sensitive and when stalking them the direction of the wind must be most carefully considered. You may come up to within a few yards of them if care is taken in this respect. The pace they go when disturbed is marvellous, particularly when one sees the shuffling sort of movement they have. The paths they make over the ranges of hills they frequent are quite wonderful examples of engineering, and one cannot help being struck with the skill with which they are traced; the gradients are truly wonderful, avoiding every steep and difficult ascent by regular zigzags, and I could not help thinking what a knowing old engineer the first marker of the track must have been.

Wild elephants generally go in herds of from fifteen upwards; the largest herd I ever saw was on the Annamullies, it numbered at least sixty animals and was a wonderful sight. The size of the wild elephant has been often greatly exaggerated; anything over nine feet is very large, one of ten feet is a monster. Sanderson says 'there is little doubt that there is not an elephant ten feet at the shoulder in India'; the account of the exciting encounter with the large tusker shot by Sir Victor Brooke, proves that at times they do exceed ten feet but it is a most rare occurrence.

Sanderson gives such an excellent and accurate description of the habits of this animal in its wild state that I need not further dwell upon the subject and will confine myself to a few examples of sport on the Neilgherries, and Annamullies.

A.J.O. POLLOCK

The Elephant

The haunts of the wild elephant in southern India comprise the virgin forests of Coorg, Canara, the Wynaad, Coimbatore, Mysore, and Travancore, and their hill ranges, together with the fringes of lesser jungle which abut on the cultivated lowlands in those districts. They are, in fact, identical with those inhabited by the bison. In the forests near the Godavery the wild elephant is also found, and when tiger shooting in those districts, news was occasionally brought to camp of their presence in the vicinity.

Since the ukase issued by the Madras Government in 1871 against the killing of wild elephants, and the subsequent cessation of kheddah operations, these animals have increased enormously in the forests of Southern India, and the outcry of the ryots cultivating lands adjoining these tracts has become louder in proportion to the enhanced damage sustained by their crops each successive year. A small herd of a dozen elephants will destroy many acres of rice or jowari* fields during a nocturnal raid lasting but a few hours, not only by eating it, but by tramping it down, for, although when in the jungle they are much addicted to travelling in single file, directly they debouch into arable land they extend on a broad front, a formation better suited for foraging, as otherwise the leaders of

From *Sporting Days in Southern India*. London: Horace Cox, 1894.

*Same as cholum—a species of millet.

the herd would annex all the tit-bits. These visits will almost to a certainty be repeated by succeeding herds, which have a habit of following the same routes as their predecessors, and which are adhered to from year to year. A few years previous to the veto against the shooting of elephants, a Government reward of seventy rupees was actually paid for every elephant killed, and great numbers were destroyed by native shikaries with huge guns, fired from a tripod by slow match. As one elephant per annum was sufficient to keep the man living in comparative luxury for the whole of that time, some of the junglewallahs made a good thing of it, especially as they also used pitfalls, which were dug in the routes by which the elephants proceeded during the rains on their annual visit to the bamboo jungles, in search of the young shoots, of which they are very fond. These still exist in some jungles, and are twelve feet long, eight broad, and fifteen feet deep. A stick is placed across the pit to break the fall of the elephant when it is intended to catch him alive, but the depth is so great that the unfortunate animals generally succumb to internal injuries or broken limbs. I have a dim recollection of seeing some pits in the Annamullays, in which a pointed stake had been driven to kill the animal, which, if a tusker, occasionally escaped by digging down the sides of the pits, and gradually filling them with the earth thus displaced. The pits were arranged in groups of four or five, two usually being in front, and one on each flank to intercept those that bolted on the collapse of the leading elephant. Bison and sambur were not unfrequently victimized by these contrivances. The Mysore Government also prohibited the killing of elephants in the same year (1871), and since then have only sanctioned enterprises against 'rogues', which are solitary male elephants addicted to infesting the vicinity of roads, where they interrupt the traffic and frequently kill any human being they may meet. A few of these brutes were on the warpath almost every year in the Mysore jungles. One was a well-known muckna (tuskless male), and lorded it over the natives in the Karkancottah jungles. Several men had been killed by him. It was stated that he had been wounded by a sahib, and that this had the effect of making him an implacable enemy to all mankind. Mucknas are credited with being far more dangerous than the ordinary tusker, and it was one of these brutes that killed Wedderburn in the old muzzle-loading days, in the Wynaad jungle near Tippicado.

F.T. POLLOK

Big Game of Lower Burma

Naturalists acknowledge but two species of elephants, the African and the Asiatic—in which they are undoubtedly correct; but why they assert that the muckna or hine is identical with the goondas I do not know. Mr Sanderson—for whom I have the greatest respect as a sportsman and observer—remarked in his *Thirteen Years Among Wild Beasts*, that the having tusks or not was merely accidental, like whiskers in a man; but I maintain that the two beasts are varieties, though of the same species. Any good mahout, whether Indian or Burmese, laughs at such a theory. There are marked differences, not only amongst the males, but those differences extend to the females. In Ceylon they are almost all mucknas, also in Sumatra; in Burma there are more hines than goondas. In Assam goondas predominate, but there are plenty of mucknas too. In India the latter are decidedly in the minority, and, I think, if further search be made, it will be acknowledged that Mr Sanderson made a mistake in saying they were identical. The goondas, male and female, have a broader expanse across the forehead; the bump between the eyes and the root of the trunk is more prominent, but the hollow between the eye and ear, commonly called the temple, is less marked. Its countenance is

From Col. F.T. Pollok and W.S. Thom, *Wild Sports of Burma and Assam*. London: Hurst and Blackett, 1900.

more pleasing, its eyes brighter and kinder-looking; it seldom grows to the height of the Muckna. The males have large tusks, the females rudimentary ones.

The Muckna, called 'Hine' in Burma, has the head much longer and narrower, the temple very much depressed; the trunk is longer, more ponderous, possessing immense strength, as if to compensate the beast for the want of the formidable tusks possessed by its rival. Both males and females have rudimentary tushes only, longer and thicker in the male than in the female; the eyes are small and sleepy-looking, and its general appearance morose; and even when quite young it has an old look. In size, they grow taller and are more leggy than the goondas. The two varieties herd apart, but interbreed at times, the males often fighting for possession of the females, and the result of the cross-breed is that you get large males with very poor tusks, but still tusks, as distinct from tushes, which adorn the Mucknas.

In Ceylon there is not above one tusker to three hundred Mucknas. I doubt if there would be that number even, had not tuskers been imported from the mainland for work in the timber yards, as only tuskers can carry and stack the heavy squared logs. Some of these in days gone by have probably got loose or have had intercourse with the female elephants of the country, and a throw back is now and then the result. But from long association with both varieties I am convinced, in my own mind, that they are varieties, and not identical.

If Nature has not given intellect to these animals, it has given them an instinct next thing to it. One has only to hunt them in their wilds to learn how wonderfully Providence has taught them to choose the most favourable ground, whether for feeding or encamping, and to resort to jungles, where their ponderous bodies so resemble rocks or the dark foliage by which they are surrounded that it is most difficult for the hunter to distinguish them from surrounding objects; while their feet are so made, that not only can they trample over any kind of ground, whether hard or soft, thorny or smooth, but without emitting a sound. Some of their encamping grounds are models of ingenuity, surrounded on three sides by a tortuous river, impassable for ordinary mortals by reason either of the depth of water, its precipitate banks, quicksands or entangling weeds in its beds, whilst the fourth side would be protected by a tangled thicket or quagmire. In such a place (as I have found them in) the elephants are in perfect safety, as it is impossible to get at them without making sufficient noise to put them on the alert. Their mode of getting within such an enclosure is also most ingenious. They will scramble down the bank where the water is deepest, and then, either wading or swimming up or down stream, ascend the opposite bank a good half-mile or more from the place they descended, thereby increasing the difficulty of following them. I was over an hour once endeavouring to get into such a fastness as I have attempted to describe, in which some twenty or more elephants were assembled, within a space nowhere more than four hundred yards square, but so well were all the approaches protected, that when at last I did succeed in getting over the preliminary difficulties, the noise we made was sufficient to have awakened the seven sleepers, to say nothing of disturbing a herd of elephants always more or less on the *qui vive*, that I had the pleasure of seeing them make their exit one way as I entered that on the opposite, and I never even got a shot, for such was the intricate nature of the country, it was useless—indeed all but impossible—to follow them with any chance of getting within range. They prefer forests by day and open ground by night, and feed on bamboos, wild cardamum, plantains, null, branches of certain trees, the ficus preferred, or long grass, which is abundant in all the plains; but if there be any cultivation within reach of their stronghold they will go for it and do more harm by trampling it down than by devouring it, which is not inconsiderable either. It is marvellous too how they remember the seasons when certain fruits are ripe. I have noticed this more in Africa than in India, but it is true of both. Before this fruit or vegetable appears there will not be an elephant within fifty miles of the locality; directly it ripens, down come the lordly beasts and hover about till the season is past or the succulent morsels devoured.

To hunt these animals successfully on foot is very hard work, and requires a man to be not only in good training, sound of wind and limb, but also to be possessed of determination, undaunted pluck, a quick eye, and very sharp ears; he must also have learnt the art of walking over ground covered with fallen timber and debris, and through dense jungles and forests without emitting the slightest sound.

Huge as are these beasts, none are easier to kill if the hunter comes across one whilst on foot at sufficiently close quarters, and if he knows the right spot to aim at and hit, and the angle to fire. A knowledge of the two must be combined; one without the other is useless. Although I have lately read in Mr Chandler's *Through Jungle and Desert* that with the Mannlicher .256 rifle, his comrade Von Hohnel killed elephants at 300 to 400 yards, I need not say such would be impossible in India, because you would never see them at such distances. The golden rule is to get as close as possible—the distance should not exceed 20 yards, better if it be some ten paces closer. General Michael, the great elephant shot of Southern India, lays down certain rules for shooting them in the *Encyclopaedia of Sport*. They differ very slightly from mine already published in *Sport in Burma*, and *Fifty Years' Reminiscences of India*. ...

Although the trumpeting of elephants at night leads one to suppose that they are close at hand, yet this noise is very deceptive. They wander about so silently, and, as a rule, they go to such immense distances, that a stern chase is, with them, the proverbially long one. ... Elephants are at all times a wandering race; they consume so much, and waste so much more, that no single forest could long support them, hence their roving propensities. During the rains they are very destructive to the paddy crops; when the harvest has been gathered, they retire to their hill fastnesses; it is best to follow them there, but somehow—with a few exceptions—sportsmen nowadays fear discomforts and fever more than a generation or two back. There is no royal road to sport—risks must be run, if you wish to be successful and are at heart a *shikarie*. You must first learn to shoot quickly and accurately; then study the habits of the beasts you wish to follow, and the right way to circumvent them, and then to rough it.

Elephants have a very keen sense of smell and of hearing,[1] and so they must be approached up wind; and in the dry season, owing to the number of fallen twigs and leaves, it is almost impossible to come close enough to a herd to be able to kill one. If they hear the slightest noise, off they go, but after the jungles have been burnt and a shower or two has fallen, particularly when they are feeding

[1]Their sense of hearing or sight is dull, in my opinion, compared with their sense of smell.—W.S. Thom.

on bamboos, they are easier to get at. A friend of mine once got so close to a tusker's quarters, that he gave him a pat to make him turn out, which he did, only to fall dead instantly.

The tree leeches,[2] so plentiful in forests inhabited by beasts in Lower Burma, are a sad drawback to the pleasures of sport—as I never found anything which could keep them out for long. I tried the crude petroleum as obtainable in Burma; that did for a while, but directly it got washed off by the dew, in they got. The best—though by no means an absolute—preventative, is wearing first thick worsted stockings, and over them drawing on a pair of closely knitted cotton or silk stockings, and saturating them with either petrol or a thick decoction of salt and very little water. But then if they can't get at your legs or feet, they will crawl down your back, or get in anywhere, where a loophole is left. They not only deplete one, but the bites very often fester. In fact they, ticks, and mosquitoes, are the plagues of a sportsman's life, and cause him frequently, I fear, to use many and often big, big D's. ...

The following is an extract from the *South of India Observer*, by 'Hawkeye'—General R. Hamilton, I believe; a brother of that famous draughtsman and *shikarie*, General Douglas Hamilton, better known as 'Velvet Foot' of the old sporting magazines.

> On another occasion I was *blown* by a wild elephant, who threw her trunk out from behind the jungle lining the narrow path along which we were running to intercept the herd, and blew her nose so suddenly in the chest and face of the leading man, that he fell back right upon me. We had cut this elephant off from her companions and having a young calf to take care of, she had loitered behind the herd. In this case we noticed what I have before alluded to—the wonderful and extraordinarily quiet manner in which these gigantic animals noiselessly move through the forest when trying to avoid observation or danger.

The height of an elephant is all but twice the circumference of the front foot as it rests on the ground. This is not quite exact, but near enough for all purposes. ... I do not think that elephants grow to the same size as they used, for one of 10 feet is now very rare, and a taller all but unknown; but there is the skeleton of one in the Calcutta Museum of Natural History which measures 11 feet, 2 or 3 inches in height, and must have been, when living, close on

[2]None in Upper Burma.—W.S. Thom. He has found plenty lately in the Arrakan Yomahs.—F.T.P.

12 feet. The tallest elephants I have ever seen, wild or tame, were Mucknas. There was one in the Commissariat, a very old decrepit one, 10½ feet, but 9 feet for a male is a fair size—rather over than under, and 8 feet for a female. For Lower Burma elephants are a *sine qua non* for hunting. There are places where game can be followed on foot, when you get there, but to reach the localities you must have these giants to take you there.

I have never known an elephant that could be invariably depended upon for dangerous shooting; they are like women—'Uncertain, coy and difficult to please.' I have had them as staunch as possible one trip; perhaps the very next—without the slightest cause—they would run from a deer and even from a hare!—whilst if a peafowl or partridge got up with a whirr under their trunks, they would quake with fear and hesitate to advance. One of my elephants, a very massive, powerful female Koonkie, did not care two pins for a tiger, but if she saw a pony coming towards her at a canter she would run for her life, and nothing could stop her. ...

A good mahout will instil pluck into a cowardly elephant, whilst a coward will cause the pluckiest animal to run away. We all know what influence a man has on a horse—it is doubly so on an elephant, which is a far more impressionable beast, and with not half the spirit of a thoroughbred horse. The behaviour of the animal is but a reflex of that of his rider. ...

Elephants differ greatly in make and size; and a really good mahout will tell pretty accurately whence the animal came by merely looking him over. Elephants utter peculiar sounds to denote certain meanings. A whistling noise produced by the trunk indicates satisfaction; when they trumpet or utter a hoarse, sharp scream it is a sign of rage; a noise made by the mouth like 'pr-rut-pr-rut' is a sign of alarm, so is the striking of the trunk on the ground accompanied by a pitiful cry, whilst a noise like 'urmp-urmp' denotes impatience or dissatisfaction. Elephants are never still, their bodies are always swaying to and fro, the ears and tail are constantly flapping or brushing off flies, the trunk is in incessant use, the legs are constantly rubbed one against the other; but if the same animal, so full of restlessness, becomes suspicious, he becomes for the moment as rigid as a rock, with his trunk raised and ears cocked forward, using his olfactory and acute hearing to the utmost. I do not think their eyesight is very good, they trust more to the two senses I have just mentioned, but if an elephant runs away and all other means fail to stop his flight, try blindfolding him. I have known it succeed several times.

Elephants when asleep often snore: they are very human-like in many of their ways; for instance, I have seen them use a foot as a pillow on which to rest their head. They get a piece of wood and use it as a toothpick, they will plug a wound with clay, they scratch themselves with the tip of their trunk, or if they cannot reach the irritable part with that, they take up a branch and use it. An elephant often thrusts his trunk into his mouth and extracts a quantity of water which he squirts over his body, and often over his riders. ...

An elephant is naturally very gentle and would not hurt a worm, but they can be taught anything. Never allow your beast to make a football of a dead beast between his legs; he will do it at first with reluctance, and only when forced, but it teaches him bad habits, and if frightened he might do it to his own master. No elephant will tread upon anything if he can avoid it; they are wonderfully sure-footed, and will go up and down the steepest places which to any other beast would be impossible. The way they slide down the steep side of a nullah with fore-legs stretched out in advance and the hind doubled backwards dragging them along, or ascend an equally steep place by bending the fore-legs and walking as it were on their knees, has to be seen to be believed.

I would rather be on an elephant that runs away than on one given to charging. I have been run away with dozens of times, and have had some narrow squeaks. Unfortunately, if an elephant gets into a panic, and he sees a forest anywhere near, he will make for it straight across country as hard as he can amble along, for they cannot canter or gallop; but it is astonishing how fast they can go at their shamble. A good runner might have a chance on a smooth sward, but he would have none over rough ground. An elephant cannot jump—a deep ditch of over 7 feet is to him impassable unless he can go down and up it.

As a rule, they are frightened at seeing fire, but an elephant of the battery in Debrooghur in Assam would help to put out a fire, and she would do what I never saw any other elephant do, and that was—after a fallen buffalo's throat had been cut through to the vertebrae, she would, when told, put her foot on the neck, twist her trunk round the horns, and wrench the head off and hand it up to the mahout. Some few elephants will pick up birds after being shot and hand them up, but not as a rule. ...

The period of gestation in an elephant and the age it lives to, have been accepted on very meagre grounds, which are not, in my opinion, conclusive, or even likely. Mr Sanderson says the average age of an elephant may be reckoned at 150 years. Mr Nuttall, Mr Sanderson's predecessor for thirty years in the Government keddahs, held a different opinion. Writing to the late Frank Buckland he said:

> When the British captured Ceylon, a memorandum was found left by Colonel Robertson, who was in command of the island in 1799, which stated that the elephant attached to the establishment at Matura had served under the Dutch for upwards of 140 years, during the entire period of the occupation from the expulsion of the Portuguese in 1656, and found by them in the stables when they took possession of the island.

Even if this were the case, as one swallow does not make a summer, it does not follow that because there was one Methuselah amongst elephants, all should live to the same period. But as Mr Nuttall continues:

> The stories of elephants living to an immense age in India I put no trust in, because with any favourite elephant in former days (when the jemadar had the naming of them) they had special names for these animals, and as their vocabulary of names was but limited, they used to give three or four elephants the same name, as, for instance, Pobun Peary, No. I, Pobun Peary, No. II, and so on. 'Pobun' means 'the wind', and an elephant in the depot possessing swift and easy paces would go by the name of Pobun, and when Pobun I died, Pobun II became I, and so on. These names appeared in the office books, while the casualty rolls were kept merely on fly-sheets, and were after a while disposed of as waste-paper, and therefore no check was possible to the true identification of an elephant, and as no trace could be found except in the office books, which simply showed the same names of elephants running on continually year after year, it appeared as if the elephants reached an extraordinary age. But all this has now been altered, and the books better kept. I consider an elephant to be at its prime about thirty-five or forty, and capable of working up to seventy or eighty years of age. An elephant's life may extend rather longer than a human being's, but not by much; but I do not believe in animals (except a very occasional one) living up to 150 years. There are mahouts whose fathers,

grandfathers, and great-great-grandfathers were all mahouts, and my opinion is founded on theirs, supplemented by my own observations of the past thirty years.

One of the reasons given for believing that an elephant's age extends to 150 years is that the gestation takes from twenty to twenty-four months. When I pointed out that although the mare took eleven months, and the human race only nine months in gestation, and that there could be no comparison in the ages attained by man and horse respectively, Mr Cameron says this comparison is inadmissible, because cattle and mankind respectively belong to different natural orders. Cattle are born in a condition to take care of themselves, while mankind are born helpless, like naked birds in a nest, and pass, so to speak, through a period of extra-uterine gestation; which, if we are to compare them with cattle, must be added to the intra-uterine period.

If so, add a year or a year and a half, by which time a child is about as capable of taking care of itself as a calf or a colt at birth, and we should get a far longer period of gestation for man than even the elephant, and if so, why should not men's days be 150 years instead of three-score years and ten?—but I am not learned enough to argue on such subjects. About 1890, when I was at Bangalore, an officer there showed me some photos of a male elephant *in coitu* with a female. He had served several, and several photos had been taken. This is a most unusual occurrence, and as the elephants belonged to the Government stud, the Commissariat officer doubtless made a note of the date, and should be now in a position to state how long gestation took place; and if the young ones brought forth from this connection live, the generation living about 2136 or thereabouts should be able to settle as to the longevity or otherwise of these most useful beasts.

There is, or was, a saying that no one had ever seen in England a dead donkey or a postboy. Many sportsmen who have spent a lifetime in jungles infested with these pachyderms wonder what becomes of the remains of elephants who die a natural death. Sanderson, Sir S. Baker, and others, all assert that they have never come across a dead elephant. ... This may apply to sportsmen solely, but in my own case it is different. I was not only a sportsman but an engineer employed in opening out countries little known; for this purpose I had hundreds of men employed in cutting traces through the enormous savannahs of Assam and Burma—countries where wild elephants are probably more numerous than in Ceylon or Southern India. I had to traverse these at all seasons, even in the rains; if I could not go by elephants I had to go by boat. I had to burn these jungles yearly—in all for over twenty-one years. Yet I have never come across the body of an elephant that died a natural death, though I have seen hundreds of carcases of deer, gaur, gayal, buffalo, and tsine lying dead—and also the remains of elephants killed by either myself or others.

In Somaliland there are numerous hyenas, in Assam and Burma not one. I cannot credit deer and cattle demolishing the enormous head and pelvis of an elephant. I instance the case of a large Muckna shot by Herbert Bainbridge in Assam, which was in evidence for about eight years, although shot in a vast plain, far away from all civilization and subject yearly to inundation in the rains and to fire in the dry weather. Why should not deer, of which there were plenty about, and buffaloes which roam about in herds, have demolished those remains like the tame cattle and koodoos are supposed to have done in Somaliland? If the bones are eaten, what becomes of the tusks? these would be a tough morsel, and could not be demolished at a sitting. Why has not a gnawed one ever been found? The truth is, we are all in the dark on these subjects, and theories are founded on conjectures. ...

Some elephants are vicious by nature—those born in a state of captivity more than those caught wild; the former, whilst losing their dread of man, get treacherous and almost useless for sport or for ordinary traffic, owing to their fears of all wild beasts, which those caught have been used to. When D'Oyly and I lived together at Tongho, he used to hire elephants in preference to indenting on the Commissariat for them, for his jungle trips. One beast he hired was particularly vicious; he had killed several mahouts, and at last ran away into the jungles, became quite wild, and did a great deal of damage to the crops, so a reward was offered for his death.

As he haunted the jungles in the vicinity of Tongho many officers went for him, but though he was frequently wounded, no one succeeded in producing his tail; but he suddenly disappeared, and every one who had fired at him claimed having killed him. Nothing was heard of him for a good six months, and the ryots had peace, and supposed that he had either died in the remoter jungles or had wandered away elsewhere. After the epidemic, placards were posted at the Cutcherie that all elephants brought in and passed—if moderately cheap—would be purchased: so good, bad, and indifferent were brought in for sale. I was always looking at them, taking an interest in all animals, and elephants in particular. Amongst those for sale was a sleepy-looking brute with lumps about his head which looked suspiciously like embedded bullets, and he moreover reminded me of the one D'Oyly used to hire (He, poor fellow, was no more.) I spoke to Mackellar, advising him to have nothing to do with the brute in question, but he did not know one beast from another, and moreover was completely under the thumb of his head Gomashta, a Madrassie, a very able man, who had all the Burmese in that part of Burma in the palm of his hand, and said he would cause inquiries to be made. Armagum, the Gomashta in question, said I was altogether mistaken, the elephant was well known, very quiet (too quiet, I thought) and ridiculously cheap. So he was bought and taken off to the Pheel Khanah. In a few days he began to show signs of vice, and one day when being taken for his charah, he threw his mahout and prodded at him with his long sharp tusks; by wriggling on one side, the man just escaped, and the brute impaled his own trunk right through. The alarm was quickly given, and he was soon recaptured by the other elephants, and after being securely tethered, his trunk was released, but mortification set in and he died, and on examination numerous bullets were found embedded in him. The truth then came out. I was right in my conjecture—it was D'Oyly's old beast. A knowing Burman had watched the brute, and noticed that he followed certain paths going to and from the cultivation, so he threw down goor well impregnated with opium in the paths. The elephant ate thereof, and became partially stupefied; he was caught and taken here and there, far away, for sale, being always under the influence of opium, but everybody fought shy of him, and as nobody would purchase him, the man was about to turn him loose when he heard that the Government wanted elephants, so first drugging him well, and doubtless by means of palm-oil, he succeeded in selling him and got clear away with the money—some Rs 1500.

Elephants take strange antipathies; here is a case in point, from the *Oriental Sporting Magazine:*

A female elephant which I had lately bought had, partly from not having been long caught, and partly by bad management by the mahout, so great a dislike to Europeans that she was with much difficulty approached by them, even to mount her; and when feeding, she would start off if any European came near her. It was supposed it was their dress which alarmed her, and the plan proposed was to dress her attendants like Europeans. To test this, a native, calling himself a Portuguese, was sent towards her. To the surprise of everybody she allowed him to approach and caress her without any signs of dislike, though he was dressed in European clothes. It was evident it was not the dress, but the colour of the face which alarmed her. A friend and myself now approached her slowly, with black crape tied over our faces, and no signs of dislike were shown. While patting and talking to her I slowly drew back the crape so as to uncover my face. The first effect of this was the quick wrinkling of the muscles of the face, the foot half raised, and the body swung back as if for a start; but she came back slowly to the 'stand at ease', with the peculiar grumbling which they make when satisfied with anything. This singular experiment was made several times, and always with the same result, and in one instance a red handkerchief was used.

Nothing was given to her that evening by us, but the next day she came without any trouble to the verandah and when called forward, came up and took fruit from our hands with her mouth, as all well-trained elephants do. There is something very much resembling reason in this change in the animal's behaviour; she got over her fright as soon as she discovered that white and black faces could be made to appear at pleasure.

When a male makes up to a female and she does not chime in at once with his wishes, he often seizes her by the tail and wrenches it off. I have seen several instances of this.

Considering that elephants and rhinoceros and buffaloes herd and feed almost together, why the first should have—when domesticated—such a dread of the second, I cannot think, but it is a fact. They dislike the smell, but the grunting noise made by these thick-skinned beasts they dread far more. I have known an elephant's leg cut to the bone by the tush of a rhinoceros, and also one knocked over by a buffalo. But the *shikar* elephants in Burma and Assam do not dread the bubali so much, as the tame ones are nearly as large as the feral, and equally savage, but whilst going for Europeans, they take no notice of elephants or of the native children who herd them.

I have known of a female suckling her own calf and that of

another cow that had died. Some say the females are vicious to the calves; it may be the case with old maids, but I have never seen it in the case of a female who had had young of her own. An old bull elephant will at times knock over a presuming hobbledehoy who annoys him, but generally they are very sociable and peaceable amongst themselves. Full-grown males cannot, however, be trusted to live in amity; thus for greater security, the tips of Government elephants' tusks are sawn off.

Chumpa's Roll, 'Elephants are usually very sure-footed.'

V.M. STOCKLEY

Asiatic Elephant

My experience with wild elephant has been confined to Upper Burma. A full-grown Asiatic male elephant stands between 8½ ft and 10 ft in height (*straight* measure) at the shoulder, but the average height, according to the best authorities, is about 9 ft, and that of females rather less than 8 ft. Sanderson—a great (if not the greatest) authority—expressed his belief that there was not a 10 ft elephant in India. He used to travel to any part of the country to inspect exceptionally large elephants he had heard of, and under the cold truth of his measurements the reputed 12 ft to 15 ft elephants always shrank to under 10 ft. Major Evans, however, in his book *Big Game Shooting in Upper Burma*, records that he shot an enormous elephant in that country, each of whose forefeet measured (by a steel tape) within a fraction of an inch 5 ft 4 in. in circumference. Twice the circumference of an elephant's forefoot, when resting on the ground and enlarged by pressure, gives roughly its height at the shoulder, therefore this elephant, whose foot was measured after death and consequently off the ground must have been at least 10 ft 8 in. high. He fell in such a position that the body measurement could not be taken. The tusks were—the right, length, 6 ft 4½ in.; circumference at gum, 16¼ in.; and the weight, 57½ lb. The left, 4 ft 6½ in.—

From *Big Game Shooting in India, Burma, and Somaliland.* London: Horace Cox, 1913.

16½ in.—42 lb. The length of a tusk is measured along the outer curve.

Sanderson shot a good number of elephants in India. His largest pair of tusks measured 5 ft and 4 ft 11 in. in length; were 16½ in. in circumference at gum, and weighed 74½ lb. the pair.

The record tusk for India, shot by Sir Victor Brooke in 1863, was 8 ft long, 20.9 in. at the greatest circumference and weighed 90 lb. This was the right tusk. The left was diseased and broken.

The record pair for Burma, shot by Mr Clough of the Burma Police, in 1896, measured: the right 7 ft, 9¾ in. long and 21 in. at the greatest circumference. The weight was stated to be 138 lb. The left, 8 ft 5½ in.—20½ in.—142 lb.

The great difference in the weights recorded for tusks of about the same size (Sir Victor Brooke's right tusk and either of Mr Clough's) would indicate some mistake in the weighing of one or the other.

Sanderson writes:

> As a rule, tusks show barely one half of their total length outside the jaw of the living animal. The length within and without the nasal bones is generally exact, but the lip or gum hides a few inches of the projecting half. As the sockets or nasal bones of a large elephant are from 1 ft 6 in. to 1 ft 9 in. in length, this admits of an elephant's having a tusk 3½ ft long, of which only 1½ ft (the gum hides about 4 in.) is visible. This rule holds pretty closely for all elephants until they become aged, when, if the tusks grow abnormally long, which is not always the case, the exposed portion becomes longer than the embedded, as the latter is limited to the length which the nasal bones attain—viz., about 1¾ ft in the largest skulls.

If this is so, then it is evident the length of tusks in a full-grown elephant does not as a rule exceed 3½ ft, unless he is old or of very exceptional size. The only elephant whose tusks I measured outside the gum agreed exactly with this view. The tusks were 4 ft 3 in. and 4 ft 2 in. long and the elephant a big one, rather past his prime, though in no way aged. The Shans with me estimated his age eighty to ninety years. Sanderson considers an elephant attains its full strength and vigour at thirty-five and (in a wild state) lives to at least 150 years. The 4 ft 3 in. tusk measured 2 ft 2 in. outside the gum: then adding (in accordance with Sanderson) four inches for the part hidden by the gum, there remained just 1 ft 9 in. for the portion within the bony socket.

On the other hand, I have shot an elephant with tusks quite 4 ft long, which, though a full-grown animal was certainly not old—in fact, could only have just reached his prime; and another with tusks 3 ft 7½ in. and 3 ft 6 in. in length, which had not attained his full size, being but 8 ft 3 in. in height at the shoulder, and the circumference of the tusks at gum only 9 in.

Females have tusks protruding several inches from the gum. A big female (over 8 ft. high) I once was obliged to shoot had tusks coming 5 in. to 6 in. out of the gum.

Tusks are not shed or renewed, and show almost from birth.

A male elephant without tusks is called a 'muckna'.[1] They are said to be generally larger than tuskers. In India and Burma nearly all the males have tusks. Sanderson states that out of fifty-one males he captured in Mysore or Bengal, only five were mucknas. The same authority says that mucknas are ill-treated by the tuskers of a herd; upon whom, they cannot retaliate owing to the absence of tusks. Regarding the use of tusks, he writes:

> In a herd of elephants the tuskers maintain the height of discipline. Every individual gives way before them, and in serious fights amongst themselves one or other is frequently killed outright. So great is the dread entertained by all elephants of a tusker, that our staunchest tame females shrank if any of the tame tuskers turned suddenly in their direction. Superiority in a herd appears to attach to the different tuskers in proportion to the size of their tusks: no tusker thinks of serious rivalry with one of heavier calibre than himself.

That tuskers are given way to in a herd I can bear out by my own experience. I heard elephants one forenoon about eleven o'clock in some dense jungle. They were evidently resting during the heat of the day, under which circumstances it is very difficult to approach them in thick cover successfully. The month was April. A Burmese local shikari with me said he knew a pool not far off where they would probably come to drink in the afternoon. So we went there and waited. About three o'clock we heard the elephants moving. A man on the look out up a tree reported that they were making for the water. About four o'clock a small tusker appeared in the opposite side of the pool, which was some sixty yards across. He walked into the water and drank. After a time more came, females, calves, and a few tuskers, but no big ones.

[1]Also 'hine' in Burma.

Soon they were all drinking, rolling, and splashing about, and occasionally trumpeting. A jungle scene that lives in the memory. There seemed about thirty elephants altogether. I noticed the manner the tuskers bullied the females, pushing them out of their path, and how the females always gave way at once. I did not get a chance for some time at a tusker that looked worth firing at, but at last one came down into the pool about sixty yards from us, and thrusting aside a couple of females, immersed half his head in the water. He appeared to be the biggest tusker of the lot, and, as some of the elephants were now moving off, I fired at him, aiming between eye and ear, judging for the brain as he was half facing me. The bullet did not hit the brain, but it confused and partially stunned the elephant, as he floundered about in the water, allowing me to put five more bullets into him from a couple of double-barrelled eight-bore rifles I was using, and bring him down as he was clambering up the bank. The tusks were poor.

These elephants drank, some by carrying water to their mouths with their trunks, and others by plunging their heads into it.

The wild elephant is generally distributed over Burma, both in the hill tracts and the low country along parts of the Irrawaddi and the larger rivers.

Their food consists of grass, leaves, bamboo shoots, and wild fruits. Tuskers and females unhampered by calves, also raid rice and other cultivation, and are fond of getting into a banana garden when the opportunity offers.

Elephants waste and destroy so much in their feeding, besides what they actually eat (tame elephants require 800 lb. of green fodder daily), that a herd of any size cannot remain long in one place—say an area of ten square miles. Nevertheless there are many tracts in Burma of 100 to 200 square miles which always contain elephants—sometimes a large number, and at other times a few. When at Maymyo—the hill station of Upper Burma—I established a hunting headquarter in the Northern Shan State of Mong Long, by building good huts for myself and followers and shelters for my ponies and other animals, near a small village on the border of a considerable jungle tract, of which an area of at least 200 square miles to the north contained no human habitation; and to all sides the forests were extensive and sparsely inhabited. Mong Long State was administered by its Native Chief, and had no European living in it either officially or non-officially.

The village near which I established myself had only been in existence a year, and neither it nor the tract of country I hunted had (according to the villagers) ever been previously visited by a white man.

I finished building the huts by the middle of March and from that time to the end of August made several trips of a few weeks' duration to them from Maymyo. My camp equipment, a good deal of my stores, and other necessaries, were kept in the huts, so that I could travel backwards and forwards between them and Maymyo marching 'light'. As far as the huts I could transport things in bullock carts, but beyond them to the north I was obliged to use carriers, the heavy jungles traversed only by game paths, being generally impassable for even loaded pack animals. It was very hilly, in fact mountainous in parts. My huts must have been at an elevation of not less than 4000 feet, and some of the hilltops about were certainly 1500 feet higher. A small river, formed by two head streams that joined three or four miles to the north of the village, flowed through the tract from south to north. The beauty of the scenery along its banks cannot be rendered in words. The bed was generally stony and rocky, the rocks often showing above the water, which in the rapid parts seethed against them. Deep, quiet pools occurred in the winding river, surrounded by a tangle of luxurious vegetation, and overshadowed by giant trees through whose branches showed the forest-clad hills around. It was Nature at her wildest—the forest as it had existed from remote ages.

The only paths were made by wild animals—the elephant chiefly. These elephant paths when going up and down the steep hillsides, zigzagged as scientifically as if their course had been planned by engineers. Old traces of elephant were frequently met with—devastated and broken bamboo clumps,[2] torn branches, masses of dung, the deep circular holes made by their great feet in muddy bottoms and since caked hard: occasionally fresher tracks with the holes still soft or filled with water, freshly broken bamboos, and fresh dung. Or perhaps elephants would be heard—their trumpeting and their crashing through the jungle, the breaking of branches, and the snapping of the bamboos sounding like pistol shots as they fed.

A common sound in these forests was the curious cry of the Gibbon monkey, sounding over the hills and valleys something

[2]I have seen areas of several square miles in extent so devastated.

like 'hoo-oo! hoo-oo! hoo-oo!' kept up for half a minute or more by a number of monkeys together.

Bison tracks would occasionally be found, but none of the animals seen unless specially followed up. It was strange how seldom deer of any kind were seen or heard. The most likely animals to come upon, in fact, were elephants. Following them in this country was pretty hard work. Apart from steep, heavily forested hill sides to get up and down, the river or its branch streams had often to be crossed. The rocky parts of their beds were sometimes too difficult for a ridden pony, and had to be waded at a fordable point, perhaps through waist-deep water. There were also muddy bottoms to cross, impossible to ride over, in parts of which you might sink knee-deep at every step, with generally the added impediment of thick, high grass to struggle with. Or an old muddy stretch might be come upon, dried up but full of deep holes caused by elephants having passed over it when it was soft, and offering an obstacle to progress like military *tuns-de-loup*.

In the several visits I made to my huts I invariably found elephants in the neighbourhood, perhaps not during the first day's hunting, nor the second, but always after persevering for a few days. They would often, however, be only small tuskers and females. Sometimes I came on tracks of the night within two miles of the huts. I shot a few tuskers during the five months in which I made my shooting excursions, though only one good one, a fine solitary elephant. But, as I have said, elephants were always somewhere about in this particular tract I hunted, and the villagers (amongst whom I obtained my trackers and shooting-carriers) told me that they were to be found within ten miles in one direction or another pretty well throughout the year.

Elephants rest, as a rule, in some thick cover during the day, from about ten o'clock to three. They then get on the move again, making their way slowly to water for their afternoon drink and continue to feed and wander, with occasional spells of rest, through the night. When day breaks they make for water and then head slowly for the cover wherein they intend to pass the heat of the day, which they do standing and dozing, or lying down on their side and sleeping.

These movements during the twenty-four hours are those followed generally by all the heavy game, such as elephant, rhinoceros, bison, and buffalo. The only difference in their general habits is that elephant and (less often) buffalo may be found near villages, and raiding cultivation at night, which bison and rhinoceros practically never do, both shunning the vicinity of man and all his works. ...

Herds of elephants number usually from twenty to fifty, but I have heard of much larger ones from sportsmen who have seen them. A herd of any size breaks up into detachments while feeding, but on an alarm, closes up, and then moves rapidly off. The alarm is said by most hunters to be communicated by a short trumpet, and no doubt often is so, but though I have frequently alarmed a herd, either by their hearing or winding me, I have rarely heard a trumpet on those occasions. They have generally moved off, either silently without my knowing it till I discovered it by their absence and their tracks, or with a sudden stampede and loud crashing through the jungle, but without trumpeting. Even when their first warning of danger has been the report of my rifle, I have not known them trumpet, nor even then invariably stampede. They have usually first collected in rather a deliberate manner (some of the herd perhaps scenting round with elevated trunks to catch the enemy's wind), and then made off in a body at a quick walk. They seem at times not to be able to locate the sound of the shot, as I have known them after assembling to come in a direction rather towards me than away from me, with the wounded one, if able to travel, surrounded by the others, thereby protecting it from further fire. Burmans have told me they have seen wounded elephants being actually helped along by others on either side. I once saw a small herd of about a dozen, that was passing me with a wounded tusker in the middle, stop and remain by him when he dropped, for a minute or so, and then not being able to move him, proceed on their way, all except a female which stayed with him, and which I ultimately was obliged to shoot.

On one occasion I killed a tusker early in the morning that was a few hundred yards from a herd. At the shot the latter stampeded noisily through the thick 'kaing' grass in which they were. After examining the slain one I had returned to the village (about three miles distant) where I was staying, and sent men to cut out the tusks. They were accompanied by most of the inhabitants to bring away the meat, which is always a windfall for the neighbourhood generally. They did not return till late that night, and informed me they had not been able to go up to the dead elephant for a long time, owing to a female which mounted guard over it, and would not be driven away till they had fired the grass around.

A herd when changing its ground (that is, travelling without feeding) moves in single file, headed by a female. The larger tuskers, though keeping in the vicinity of a herd, are often to be found singly at some distance from it, and during movements may take a line of their own. If with the herd, they will be generally in the rear of it. On becoming aged, they usually live a solitary life; and these are the ones which will give the hunter the finest tusks.

Sanderson states that detachments of a large herd may be very widely separated during feeding, and that they keep touch with the movements of the main body by their wonderful sense of smell, which enables them to wind each other at considerable distances. This authority on elephants states that he has known his tame elephants wind wild ones at a distance of three miles, when the wind was favourable. This seems extraordinary, but doubtless their sense of smell is very highly developed. I have seen a wild elephant come up to a path on which my party had been walking ten minutes before, stop dead on reaching it, wheel round, and rush back trumpeting. The wind was favourable with regard to ourselves, so the elephant could not have winded us, but only our scent in the path on which we had been walking. Major Evans is of opinion that an elephant will wind a man at a distance of at least half a mile.

Their hearing is fairly good. I have more than once known a herd put on the alert by hearing my movements in thick, dry jungle, where it is impossible to move noiselessly, however carefully you may go.

Their sight is poor. A man may approach them closely when in their line of view, if he moves slowly, especially, it is said, if he can manage to approach an elephant directly from its front, the animal not being able to see an object so placed as well as in an oblique line. Any quick movement or action will, however, be instantly observed. Several such cases have occurred to me. I will relate two of them.

I was watching some female elephants that had filed past me and were feeding within thirty yards, in hopes of a tusker following. Jaggat Singh (previously mentioned in my tiger shooting) carried my second rifle. We were only partially concealed by a small tree and some thin bushes. A tusker hove in sight, but he was not big, and I wanted to wait in case a better one came up. Jaggat Singh supposed I had not noticed the tusker and pointed towards it with a sudden movement of his hand. Two females that were half facing us about twenty yards off, caught the movement, raised their trunks in our direction and advanced a few steps towards us. The wind being right they could not scent us, but were evidently bent on further investigation; so, seeing we must be discovered in a few moments, and not wishing to let the females come too close to us, I fired at the tusker, which otherwise I should not have done, as he was not favourably placed for a shot and I was waiting in hopes of a larger one appearing. On my firing all the elephants bolted. We followed up the tusker for hours until the blood trail ceased and we lost the tracks on hard ground.

Another time, again with Jaggat Singh as second gun-carrier, I was quite close to some elephants we had been following for a long way. Several of them, amongst which was a tusker, were moving very slowly less than twenty yards from me, but in thick jungle, and I could make out nothing to fire at with any certainty of an effective result. In a few yards, if continuing their course, they would have come out into thinner jungle where I might have put in a good shot. I was waiting for this, standing stock still, in the rather open bed of a small nullah. Jaggat Singh, instead of following my example and remaining motionless, stopped to obtain a view of the elephants. His movement attracted their attention, for they all stood quite still at once, and after a few moments turned and walked noiselessly away. The alarm was communicated in some manner to the herd, which was feeding in scattered detachments, as we found afterwards that every elephant had gone. We came up to the herd some hours later, but never saw the tusker again.

Now, in acting as he did, Jaggat Singh broke a well-recognized rule of big game shooting, that I had often tried to instil into him, viz., to copy your leader's movements exactly—crouching when he crouches, remaining motionless (whatever the position) when he does, and in short acting in every way the same. Jaggat Singh though, as I have said, a very good tiger-shikari, was quite unsuited by his temperament to be a gun-carrier in heavy game shooting. He could not control himself, and was constantly fidgeting to point out something he thought you did not see, or to get some special view for himself. But really the best of gun-carriers often give you away, or put you out, and though I have generally approached game with one so as to have a second rifle handy (and with an orderly gun-carrier to get my empty rifle loaded at the same time), I question if it would not be better to discard gun-bearers on arriving within reach of game and approach it alone, accepting the disadvantage of having only one rifle. This would be partly remedied by using a magazine rifle, if you considered the increased number of shots without reloading compensated for its disadvantages as compared with a double.

Where the gun-carrier may undoubtedly come in useful, if a trusty man, is when following up wounded animals.

The track of the forefoot of a full-grown elephant forms a rough circle with a general diameter of fourteen to twenty inches, according to the sex of the animal. A male's will be generally from sixteen to twenty and a female's from fourteen to sixteen. I say *general* diameter because (not being a perfect circle) measurements taken over the centre of the track from different points of its edge will vary slightly. Anything over eighteen inches, measured across the *width* of the track, indicates a big elephant, and if the impression of the two front toes is distinct it indicates heavy tusks. Usually, however, the toe impressions are scarcely observable, even of big tuskers.

The fore foot is larger and rounder than the hind, whose form is more an oval than a circle.

Elephants are considered to live to about 150 years. Sanderson states that females usually give birth to their first calf at sixteen, when they are palpably immature themselves, and that mahouts believe they breed up to eighty years of age. Also that when a calf is born the herd remains with the mother two days, after which time the newcomer is capable of marching.

A calf is able to walk a little distance within a few hours of its birth. When out after elephants one day in the month of June, I heard the stomachic rumbling they often make, and guided by it approached to within seventy yards of two females. My gun-bearer, who climbed up a tree, said there was quite a small calf with them. While watching them the wind changed, and other elephants that we had not seen went off. The two females and the young one moved away very slowly and came to a halt again a few hundred yards further on with—my man said—the calf between them. I could not make out the calf, and did not like to approach very near, as that would have been certain to provoke a charge, when I should have been obliged to shoot in self-defence. Going to the place where they had been standing when we first saw them, we found the ground splashed with blood and other signs of the birth of the calf, which must have taken place that morning. One female had stayed to help the mother, and even after they had winded us, and the rest of the herd had gone away in alarm, would not desert her. Nor would the mother leave her little one. It was a case of real devotion and staunch friendship, as elephants are more alarmed by winding human beings than by seeing them. The herd to which these two females belonged had evidently been thoroughly put out, for we followed their trail from midday till four o'clock, probably covering six or seven miles, without coming up to them (the herd taking a straight line without stopping to feed anywhere), when we gave it up in order to reach home by night.

The period of gestation is said to be twenty to twenty-two months. One calf is born at a birth, and several calves of different ages may be seen with their mother.

It has been noted as a curious fact, for which no reasonable explanation can be given, that remains of elephant which die a natural death are very rarely found in the jungles.

Sir Emerson Tennent, in his work *The Wild Elephant*, gives evidence to the same effect—from both European and native opinion.

I once came across a few bones (plainly those of an elephant) in the Mong Long jungles. The men with me knew, or pretended to know, nothing concerning the cause of its death.

The pace of the elephant is a walk which may be increased to a fast shuffle. It moves least easily down hill, so if a man is pursued his best chance is to run or dodge down hill if possible; but the kind of ground on which elephants are generally found makes running hopeless.

They cannot trot or gallop, neither can they jump nor make any kind of spring, though they are able to scramble up and down steep slopes and in and out of most nullahs. A steep cut ditch or trench 8 ft wide is said to be beyond an elephant's stride, and therefore impassable for it. Trenches of this kind from 10 ft to 12 ft wide may be seen round lonely rest houses in forest reserves, built for the convenience of forest officers, since elephants are mischievous and destructive animals, and would damage or even break them down unless they were so protected. This destructive and aggressive disposition leads elephants at times to tear down telegraph lines and posts along railways, fences, and huts, strike terror into small villages, and even make matters uncomfortable in the camps of the sportsman or official. In parts where they are numerous, travellers by jungle roads, both European and native, have occasional startling experiences. Stories without number might be told of roads 'held up' for days, all traffic stopped and men and animals killed by rogue elephants as they are termed. But as a matter of fact most big tuskers are more or less rogues, in the respect that it would be at all times unsafe for an unarmed man to meet them. And herds, even when engaged in the peaceable occupation of feeding, are given a wide berth by travellers of every description.

An elephant kills a man (or an animal) by treading or kneeling on him with his forelegs, and by driving his tusks into him. Sometimes he will tear his enemy to pieces by grasping each limb in succession with his trunk or his mouth and tearing it off, while he keeps the body fixed firmly under his heavy foot or knee. Not long ago, an elephant was seen to tear a native girl to pieces by means of his trunk and fore foot; and the dismembered bodies of men have been recovered on several occasions of late years by rescue parties called to the scene by companions who escaped. An elephant in the Mandla District of the Central Provinces (in the seventies) which killed a great number of people before it was shot, sometimes tore its victims to pieces with its mouth and ate portions of their flesh, according to eye witnesses who had taken refuge in trees.

The sufferers have generally been villagers (men, women, and children) attacked without provocation as they proceeded along a forest road, or were engaged in some work in the jungle.

It is not often that high officials or other personages have narrow escapes from elephants, the unpleasant experiences, injuries, and loss to life and property falling on humbler folk: otherwise the ardour displayed in the preservation of these animals might be cooled. But such a case occurred a few years ago, when one of the principal officials in Southern India was riding on tour with his staff along a forest track in Coorg. From what I could gather from the accounts in the Indian press the circumstances were as follows.

An elephant was heard proceeding parallel with the party. The Commissioner sent one of his companions (a police officer) forward a short distance to where the path turned, to see if the road was clear. The officer on arriving at the turning was immediately charged by a tusker, which was standing on the path. He wheeled his pony about and galloped back with the elephant trumpeting in hot pursuit! Seeing this sudden apparition bearing down on them, the rest of the party did the same as the policeman—went about and rode for their lives. Unluckily for the Commissioner he became the hindmost of the fugitives, and, finding the elephant close upon him, turned his pony off the track into an opening in the jungle, in hopes of shaking off his pursuer. But the tusker turned after him, and the clearing was soon closed up by the jungle, which impeded his pony's progress; so, seeing himself on the point of being overtaken, the rider, with great skill and resource, threw himself off into the thickening cover and managed to hide in it, while the elephant went on after the pony. The hero of this adventure—fortunately unhurt by his feat—got as quickly as possible behind the nearest tree of sufficient size, and might well have considered his troubles over. But no—back came the persistent enemy in less than a minute, having apparently discovered the adroit trick played on him, and wanting the man and not the pony, for he searched about, quartering the ground and feeling the wind in all directions with his trunk, without, mercifully, catching the taint he sought, and at length made off to what must have been the intense relief of the hidden Commissioner, who had meanwhile been shifting his position according to the movements of the elephant so as to keep the tree between himself and his would-be destroyer. To such straits had a high official been reduced! On his companions returning to 'pick up the pieces', they were met instead by their chief—whole and sound, who 'turned up smiling'.

When I was shooting in the Katha District in Burma in 1898 (which was before the act for the preservation of elephants in that country had been passed) the locality I hunted was terrorized by elephants. They used to come close to the villages at night (I have seen their tracks within fifty yards of houses), and inflict immense damage on the cultivation. The people were afraid to enter the jungle or to travel from one village to another except in large parties. I killed several tuskers in a short time and relieved the neighbourhood temporarily of its incubus, besides supplying it with plenty of meat (much appreciated by the inhabitants), the elephants clearing out in a week or so from that locality—by which I mean an area of about 100 square miles. I should have done much better than I did if I had had any previous experience in elephant shooting.

Ten years later, when in the Mandalay District, Forest Officers told me that wild elephants were a pest in the reserved forests, interfering with operations therein by worrying the tame ones, and making the forests unsafe for the Department's employees. At the suggestion of a Forest Officer, who hoped I should be allowed to shoot some of the elephants troubling his own forest, I applied to the Commissioner for leave to shoot a tusker or two, mentioning the opinion of the officer on the subject, but was refused with the information that it was against the Government's policy to allow elephants to be shot. I then had to seek for territory not administered by British officials in order to shoot elephants:

Complaints are now constantly made in Southern India to the authorities, by the planters and other cultivators, of the depredations of elephants, and the advisability urged of making the restrictions on shooting them less stringent.

There is some extraordinary sentiment regarding elephants that causes them to be thus strictly preserved, when their numbers are so increasing as to make them a plague and a danger to the inhabitants of the country. Government does not require for its tame establishment one in a hundred of these numerous wild elephants. Nor do the Native States, such as Travancore, whose ruler turns a deaf ear to the petitions of European planters to have some measures introduced to diminish the numbers of the wild herds.

Previous to the preservation enactment in the seventies, a reward was given in Southern India by the local governments for each elephant killed. This was no doubt wrong, and led to a great decrease in the numbers of elephants through natives making the killing of them a means of livelihood. But in abolishing the reward Government went to the other extreme, and introduced the strictest preservation. Burma followed this example by bringing in a Preservation Act a good many years later (in 1900 I think), though, as I have stated, elephants were a plague in some parts of the country. This plague will now continue to increase until some revision of the Preservation Acts will become absolutely necessary.

F.W. CHAMPION

Elephants

In most places in India and Burma, elephants are protected by Government, under a special Elephant Act, and it is only when an elephant becomes dangerous to human life or property that he is declared a 'rogue' and permission is given for him to be shot. Many 'rogues' are declared on insufficient evidence, in that the elephant in question may only be in musth temporarily, or may have been annoyed consciously or unconsciously in some way or other. Forest and Civil officers have always to be very careful in this matter of declaring elephants as 'rogues', as there are unscrupulous persons in India who are not above working up an agitation against some particular elephant in the hope of getting an opportunity to shoot him. In addition, a genuine 'rogue' elephant is very dangerous and few people are willing to go sufficiently close to be able to give the accurate description of the elephant, which is necessary for his proclamation as a 'rogue'. To the man who has had little experience of elephants, all elephants look much the same, particularly as they nearly always remain more or less concealed in the jungle; and a good many innocent elephants are shot on the plea, genuine or otherwise, of their having been proclaimed as rogues. A real 'rogue' is usually an elephant which has become injured in some way or other, often at the hands of poachers, and naturally feels that he has a grudge against mankind, in which

From *With a Camera in Tigerland,* 1927.

feeling he has the hearty sympathy of genuine animal lovers. A beautifully written story of such a 'rogue' elephant appeared under the title of 'Swe Leing—The Story of an Elephant' in the issue of *Fighting Forces* for September 1925.

Elephants have been domesticated in India for an extremely long time. ... They were at one time used in the Indian Army for transport work and for dragging guns; but they are not suited to modern conditions, and are now no longer used for military purposes. The Afghans, however, used a few in the 3rd Afghan War of 1919, when I personally saw seven, through field-glasses, on the Afghan front. These were probably State elephants, which were brought out to the front in order to give 'morale' to the troops, and their actual usefulness against modern machine guns, aeroplanes, etc., must have been negligible. Elephants are still used in considerable numbers in Burma and Southern India for piling timber and transport, but in most places they are kept nowadays only for show and shooting purposes, by Indian potentates, and by Government for the use of those officials whose work takes them into jungly parts. They cost at least Rs 100 per month to keep, when all incidental expenses, such as pay of mahawats, uniform, trappings, etc. are included and when the daily ration of 600 lb. of green food comes from Government forests. If this enormous quantity of green food has to be purchased, the cost is more than doubled. It may be remarked that a determined effort is again being made to domesticate African elephants in the Belgian Congo, and an interesting article on the subject appeared in the *Illustrated London News* of June 6th, 1925. The attempt started in 1899, by order of King Leopold, who obtained a few domesticated elephants and mahawats from India. After a number of reverses and interruptions, the station at Api contained, in 1925, 42 African elephants, many of which were well trained and docile. These trained elephants have been found to be very useful for transport purposes, and the number of training stations is being increased, so that the domestication of the African elephant may now definitely be said to be an established fact.

It is sometimes stated that elephants will not breed in captivity, but this is not the case, and there have been numerous cases of captive elephants giving birth to calves. Several instances of this have been recorded in the *Indian Forester*, of which the following are examples. In 1921 it was recorded that a Forest Department elephant, in Madras, first produced a calf when only 13 years old. She has since had four more calves at the ages of 19, 22, 26 and 30, and there is every hope that she will produce more. In 1924, a record was published of a wild tusker crossing the female elephant 'Daisy', of the Deputy Commissioner of the Chittagong Hill Tracts, on 5.1.22. She gave birth to twin calves—a male and a female—on 5.11.23, so that the period of gestation was 22 months.

It has long been a mystery as to what happens to elephants when they die, and many fanciful tales have been written, based on the supposition that elephants all go to some hidden place to die when they feel death coming upon them. Indeed, one or two expeditions have, I believe, been made in Africa, purely with the object of searching for such treasure troves of hidden ivory. The point has never been solved, and it is certainly remarkable that so few traces are ever found of wild elephants which have died a natural death. In this connection it is interesting to note that there are four records of elephants having been found dead, within recent years, in the sub-montane forests of the United Provinces. ...

I would suggest that the tradition of wild elephants collecting in some secret place to die has little foundation in fact, and that the hidden treasure troves of ivory exist only in imagination. Elephants live in very sparsely-populated districts in tropical forests and their life-span is very long. Deaths are therefore not common and may occur anywhere within immense tracts of forest. In tropical countries, carcasses are attacked by innumerable scavenging creatures, such as vultures, crows, hyenas, jackals, pigs and porcupines, whereas their work is soon supplemented by that of ants, termites and fungi. Following upon these agents comes the annual monsoon, which produces grass and other rank vegetative growth, twenty or more feet high, in a few months, so that a single season may easily remove the entire body and much of the skeleton of an animal even as large as an elephant. The tusks may easily be covered with vegetation and they are certainly largely gnawed by porcupines; they must also be old, worn and broken by the time an elephant dies of old age, so that they might easily disappear after a few years' exposure to a tropical climate and its attendant decomposing influences. However, records of wild elephants which have died of old age are extremely scanty and one is not justified in arguing from a particular case.

F.W. CHAMPION

Photographing Wild Elephants

Although wild elephants are still common in South India, Ceylon, Burma, and Siam, their numbers are, unfortunately, very limited in the sub-montane forests of the United Provinces, to which my photographic expeditions have been confined. They were, at one time, fairly common in these forests, but their numbers were sadly depleted during the earlier part of the last century, and it was only the protection afforded by the Government 'Elephant Preservation Act' which saved them from complete annihilation. They now number only from 100 to 150 individuals, divided up into several small herds, with a large number of semi-solitary bulls and maknas; and the photographs reproduced in this book consist mostly of these latter, which wander about singly, or in parties of two or three. Solitary elephants are usually reputed to be bad-tempered, but, as a general rule, I have not found this to be the case on the numerous occasions on which I have approached them for the purpose of taking photographs. This is remarkable when one considers the way these elephants were harried before they were afforded protection by Government, and the fact that many of them must bear scars of old wounds to this day. In a well-known book on big-game shooting, published some time ago, the writer describes how, in these very forests, he scored

From *With a Camera in Tigerland*, 1927.

25 hits on 10 elephants, of which 3 were cows, and his total bag was only 1 makna, which naturally did not even provide him with tusks as trophies! Admitted that elephant shooting is not easy, this still remains one of the most dreadful stories of callous shooting that I have ever read. The writer appeared to creep up to an elephant, fire at it with an enormous rifle, wound it, and then make no real effort to follow the poor creature up; but passed on to repeat the performance on some other wretched beast. Nothing whatever would induce me to attempt to destroy one of these magnificent creatures, and, considering the treatment they have received in the past at the hands of that much-vaunted creature, *Homo sapiens,* it is marvellous that they do not bear him a greater grudge than they appear to do. A real 'rogue' should, of course, be destroyed—although he often has my sympathy—and in places elephants are so numerous, and do so much damage to crops, that their numbers must be reduced by captures; but even some of India's greatest shikaris have not derived any great pleasure from bagging this—perhaps the finest of God's wild creatures. The extracts quoted below amply bear out this statement. Major-General Nigel Woodyatt, in his *Sporting Memories*, writes:

> I have never shot an elephant; nor, except going twice after a 'rogue', have I ever tried to shoot one. The huge monster is such a magnificent beast, such a mountain of growth, so human, and so fascinating in its captivity. The idea of trying to lay low one of its species, for the sake of a pair of problematically-decent tusks, is positively repugnant to me. There is also the question of gratitude. I owe so much to the assistance of the shikar elephant. It has given me hundreds of days of good sport; and though, just like the wild ones, it has given me also moments of anxiety, still I love it.

Again Sanderson, when a young man and a desperately keen shikari, in describing the bagging of his first elephant, writes:

> After the momentary exultation had passed, I thought regretfully of the noble life, which I had sacrificed in order to afford myself the pleasure of a few hours' mad excitement. The beast to whom Nature had given so noble a life; which had roamed these grand solitudes for probably not less than a hundred years; which may have visited the spot on which it now died half a century before Waterloo was fought; and which, but for me, might have lived for half a century more—lay bleeding and quivering before me, deprived of its harmless existence to gratify the passion for sport of a youth hardly out of his teens. Nor had

> it had a fair chance. I had not faced it boldly, and killed it in open fight. It had not even seen its enemy, nor had it had a chance of retaliation. Trackers, from whom escape was as impossible as from blood-hounds, had been urged in pursuit; the most powerful weapons which science could place in the hands of a sportsman, against which any other animal of creation would have gone down at once, had been used for its destruction. Could I congratulate myself greatly on my achievement? The forest around was indescribably grand. No sounds but those of Nature fell on the ear. The trees were of immense proportions, and to their huge stems and branches numbers of ferns and orchids of different kinds clung. Their trunks were moss-grown and weather-beaten. The undergrowth consisted of ferns up to our shoulders. Truly an elephant must have a noble nature, and one may almost believe that he delights in the wild places he inhabits, as much for their beauty as for the safety they afford. He wanders from stream to hill-top, rubs his tough hide against the mighty forest-giants, and lives without fear except of man, his only enemy. What a bloodthirsty creature the self-constituted lord of creation is! Though impressed with the wild beauty of the creations of Nature around him, how his heart jumps at the sound of the game which he has doomed to destruction! and, with Nature only as a witness, how fearlessly he raises his impious hand against her creatures.

I well remember my attempt at photographing the first wild elephant I ever saw. I was marching one day, in the early morning, from one forest rest house to another, mounted on Balmati, my faithful friend and ally. As we were going quietly along, we were suddenly startled by a loud report, which came from the dense *sal*[1] forest near the forest-road along which we were marching. The report sounded just like the crack of a rifle, and, although it was an unlikely place for poachers, it seemed as though the noise must have been caused by someone illicitly shooting deer. Balmati's mahawat, Karim Baksh, however, who has spent his life among tame elephants, assured me that it was caused by a wild elephant pushing over a young *sal* tree, in order to feed on the fresh juicy green bark, which, much to the forest officer's sorrow and annoyance, wild elephants regard as a special tit-bit. I was naturally greatly excited, as I had never seen a wild elephant before, and I was only too anxious to try my reflex on this, my first chance. Unlike most Indian mahawats, Karim Baksh is not frightened of wild elephants, and Balmati is staunch with all wild animals, so it was agreed that

[1]*Shorea robusta.*

we should creep quietly into the jungle, in the direction from which the sound had come, and if possible make some exposures. After some ten minutes of very slow and careful progress, we came suddenly upon the wild elephant, a makna, who was standing quietly over the *sal* tree which he had knocked over, watching to see—if he did not already know from the scent—what manner of beast was creeping up to him so stealthily. Unfortunately the light was poor, so that I was at a loss as to how to set about taking photographs. It was useless to attempt to go any closer, so, against the advice of Karim Baksh, I foolishly stood upright on Balmati's back and managed to make two very shaky exposures from my extremely unsteady, and, as I have since realized, dangerous position. One can never foresee what a wild elephant will do, and it is this uncertainty that makes photographing wild elephants such a fascinating pursuit. Had he made himself objectionable, or had Balmati been nervous, I must have fallen, in which case I was certain to have smashed my camera, and to have hurt myself, more or less, in the fall, even if the makna had not taken it into his head to add to my discomfiture. However, beginner's luck is proverbial, and, although my two exposures were so blurred and under-exposed as to be quite useless, no accident happened and at least I gained a certain amount of experience, without being any the worse for my foolishness. After I had made these two exposures, the makna, who had been watching my antics steadily all the time, decided that he did not care for company, and, turning suddenly, went off at a sharp walk into the dense forest behind. We attempted to follow, but he went much faster than we could do and we lost sight of him altogether after a few minutes' futile effort to keep pace with him. I shall never forget my astonishment at the extraordinary way that huge beast—going away fast but without any flurry—seemed to melt away, in absolute silence, through the dense forest. It seemed almost impossible for so huge an animal to make so little noise, and I was left with the impression as of some weird grey phantom balloon floating away through the gloom of the dark jungle.

Later the same year I came across bull elephants, singly or in parties of two or three, on several occasions, and made a number of exposures with varying success, although none of the resultant pictures of that year were good enough. These elephants were generally located by the noise they made when breaking down

'The enraged lord of the herd lifted his fore-leg and charged at us.' Note the dark *musth* discharge from the orifice between the eye and ear.

bamboos, as they fed from the twisted bamboo-clumps, but the lighting conditions were very rarely satisfactory—as is nearly always the case in the dark Indian jungles, where absence of sufficient light for daylight-photography is the greatest difficulty with which one has to compete. Sometimes these elephants got my wind from a distance and disappeared forthwith; but more often they stood still and allowed me to make one or two exposures at about 20 yards' range, before turning to depart rapidly to some distant place. In these latter cases I soon found that it is utterly useless to attempt to follow, as a wild elephant, once he thinks he is being pursued, will go for miles, without stopping, over the most appallingly difficult and mountainous country, in which any attempt to come within photographic distance a second time is foredoomed to failure.

When I again went on tour the following season, I had—for better or worse!—embarked upon matrimony, and was naturally anxious to show my newly-wed wife one of the most interesting sights of these jungles—a wild elephant in its native haunts. We had not been out in camp very long before a report came in that a tusker was chasing the local staff in a certain piece of bamboo forest not far away. Thinking this story to be somewhat exaggerated, as is usually the case in India, we decided to go out on foot to see if my wife could be lucky enough to get a glimpse of her first wild elephant. Directly we reached the spot, we heard the crashing of trees and bamboos, and, on going closer, saw the enormous head of an obviously angry elephant quite near to us. He was clearly in a bad temper and I was just beginning to regret having brought my wife to be introduced to such a nasty-looking individual when he stepped quickly in our direction and knocked a biggish tree over with a crash. We were standing behind a large fig-tree at the time, and, remembering that a tusker of similar appearance in the next Division had recently been declared by Government to be a 'rogue', I decided that the introduction had already been effected, and conveniently called to mind that I wanted to inspect a piece of jungle some distance away. We therefore retreated under the cover of the fig-tree and went on to do this inspection. Some little time later we had to return past the same place, and, on approaching somewhat nervously, we found, to our relief, that the elephant had departed, having knocked over two or three more trees—including a *rohini,* which elephants never eat—on his way. When we reached camp we heard from Karim Baksh that this animal was probably the 'rogue' in question and that he was emitting the smell peculiar to elephants in musth, which must surely have accounted for such surly behaviour on being introduced to his local Forest Officer's wife!

We had another encounter with a wild elephant a few weeks after the above incident, and this time I succeeded at last in obtaining some moderately satisfactory pictures. We were out on Balmati looking for photographic adventures one morning, and, as we were proceeding along a river-bed, with dense forest on either side, we once more heard the familiar cracking sound made by a wild elephant feeding on bamboos. My reflex was all ready, so we cautiously advanced towards the spot, and soon came upon a fine young tusker enjoying his morning meal in what, for an Indian jungle, was a very good light. I made one or two exposures at once, while the tusker was watching us closely in the usual wild elephant fashion. After a minute or two he decided to come nearer to investigate, and I continued to expose plates as, gradually, he approached closer and closer, until, finally, his image covered the whole of the focusing-screen of my camera. By this time we were beginning to get a little nervous, so I told the mahawat to fire a shot with a small rifle over the beast's head. This he did, with the result that the tusker, a little startled, retreated a few yards and then stood, broadside on, sucking his trunk in perplexity. I made one last exposure on him in this position—the resultant picture was unfortunately slightly blurred—before we finally retreated, to be followed a short distance as he watched us going away down the steep hill side.

The following day we went out again in order to try to make a second series of pictures, and ultimately found this same tusker once more; but, on this occasion, he was accompanied by another tusker, whose tusks had been broken off and sharpened up again. This time I left my wife, with my orderly, in a safe position in the river-bed, and advanced towards the two tuskers alone. I managed, under cover, to get very close, before the second tusker's head appeared within a few yards from behind a tree trunk. I had time for only one exposure ... before both tuskers, suddenly deciding to flee, rushed away, straight down into the river-bed, where my wife was waiting. She was luckily more or less concealed and the elephants, failing to see her, hurried down the open river-bed in single file, to disappear for good in a dense patch of bamboo forest on the other side.

Our next exciting adventure with wild elephants occurred the following year, and provided us with, possibly, the greatest thrill we have yet experienced in our photographic adventures among the wild beasts of these forests. We were having what in India is known as a 'Europe morning' (which means that one does not get up with the sun) when we were awakened at about 7 a.m., by a knock at the door, followed by a deep voice announcing that a herd of wild elephants was feeding in a patch of open forest nearby. We had been longing for an opportunity to photograph a herd of elephants, and in particular a baby elephant, but somehow or other we had always managed just to miss the herd, so we jumped out of bed, and were soon mounted on Balmati and on our way to the scene of action. We soon came upon signs of the herd, in the shape of numerous footprints of all sizes, with debris of smashed bamboos and trees scattered all over the place; and, shortly afterwards, we saw a rather indifferent bull, who was obviously hanging about on the outskirts of the herd. We decided to leave him alone as unworthy of our attention and hurried on to where we thought the herd would be. In a very short time we saw several elephants, standing in a half-dried pool, throwing dirt and muddy water over themselves and enjoying their morning bathe. As we were watching these elephants we suddenly realized that a massive bull, accompanied by a large cow and a delightful little calf, some 3½ ft high, was feeding on the bamboo clumps a short distance in front. Karim immediately announced that the bull was musth, but, nothing daunted, we pushed Balmati forward in such a way as to intercept the line in which these three elephants were slowly advancing as they fed. As we were doing this, the calf arrived at a piece of extremely dense shade, to be followed shortly by the bull, who stood just behind his baby and gently caressed him with his trunk. The great trunk made a curious rasping noise as it gradually slid down. The comparatively diminutive back, and the whole formed a most fascinating scene, which would have made an ideal picture; but—as so frequently happens—the shade was so dense that it seemed quite impossible to obtain a fully exposed plate, and we were reluctantly forced to wait, in the hope that the elephants would emerge from the shade in due course. This they did, the cow and baby leading, to be followed by the bull, who ambled leisurely on to a bamboo-clump, some distance ahead, where he proceeded to make a meal as I pushed Balmati a little closer and started to bring my camera into action. I made a number of exposures on him in this position, when, suddenly realizing that something was wrong, he turned, and, seeing us, his whole body gave a start, his ears went back, his trunk started to curl, and we realized that we were really in for trouble this time. There seemed nothing else to do, so I continued to make exposures as hard as I could, while Karim, on the spur of the moment, and probably as the result of a lifetime spent among tame elephants, shouted to him in Hindustani to go back. This was, of course, the worst possible thing to do, as, the moment the great beast heard a human voice, his worst suspicions were confirmed, and he knew for certain that hated creature, man, had come to interfere with him and his family. Karim, however, soon covered his initial mistake by doing the right thing, and fired a shot with a gun, just as the enraged lord of the herd lifted his foreleg and charged at us, looking for all the world like a great lumbering motor-omnibus bearing down upon us. It appeared that nothing could save us, and, armed with no more than a camera and feeling guilty about my wife, who should not have accompanied me, I was just holding my breath for the shock of the impact when Karim providentially fired his second barrel, right over the monster's face, thereby causing him to swerve with a crash past one side of a small *rohini* tree, just as Balmati turned and fled on the other. We departed, fully routed, at Balmati's best pace of some 8 miles an hour, expecting the great brute to follow; but, after we had gone about 100 yards, we realized that we had made good our escape, more than a little shaken, but none the worse, except for the loss of my sun-helmet, and the valuable lens out of my reflex camera. Directly we stopped, we heard a shrill trumpeting as the whole herd foregathered, preparatory to departing at a rapid pace to some distant jungle, far away from the possibility of further interference from man.

We retraced our steps as soon as the herd had gone and had the good fortune to recover the lens, quite uninjured, from the dense grass into which it had fallen. We then returned at once to camp, vowing, as we went, never to try to photograph musth elephants again. I wonder how long that vow will be kept! The photographs obtained on this occasion are of great interest, showing, as they do, the dark patch on the cheek caused by the oily musth discharge—referred to in the last chapter—which emerges from an orifice midway between the eye and the ear hole. One of the beast's tusks was broken and the head and trunk were covered with the scars of old wounds, presumably as the result of a fight for the mastery of the herd, which took place during the previous monsoon. This fight is said by local villagers to have lasted for three days, and this tusker, although ultimately victorious, must have suffered considerably in the fray. A similar fight, in which both combatants were killed, was recently recorded, from Orissa, in the Bombay Natural History Society's Journal. Another point of interest is that the trunk of the elephant was never coiled up like a watch-spring, as is usually related to be the case in stories of charging elephants. The ears were tightly pressed back against the sides of the head, in the fashion of most animals when in a bad temper, and were not pushed forward, as is described in more than one book that I have read. Lastly, this experience shows that a musth elephant sometimes retains affection for his young, despite his notoriously bad temper at the time of this little-understood functional derangement.

The incident related above had rather an amusing sequel. One of my Indian rangers is an exceedingly hard-working and intelligent assistant, with a taste for natural history, but unfortunately he somewhat lacking in a sense of humour. I related the story of this charge to him, and, telling him that I would like to make some more observations on the position of the trunk and ears in a charging elephant, suggested jokingly that he should make a series of experiments for me on the numerous wild elephants in his range. He took me quite seriously, and replying at once, 'Very good, sir, I will make some experiments by means of my forest guards', he went off, leaving me to wonder how much compensation I should have to pay to the widows of the poor unfortunates who were to be used in the experiments. I assured him as he was going away that I was only joking, but later I received a most amusingly worded report—which unfortunately I had mislaid—to the effect that he had now had three men charged, and in each case the elephant's ears were laid back. Did I require the experiments to be carried on any more, because if so, he would, 'no doubt', be able to make some more observations, even though his Forest Guards were not very enthusiastic in the matter! But I had already come to the conclusion that the joke had been carried much too far as it was and ordered him to drop the matter at once. I was only too thankful that no accident had occurred, and wondered when I should receive an official censure from Government for using Forest Guards in a manner not provided for in the Civil Service Regulations!

One of the great difficulties with which one is faced, when taking photographs of wild elephants from the back of a tame one, is that the latter is often—for some unaccountable reason—extremely frightened of its wild cousins. Balmati, my favourite tame elephant, was caught some twenty or more years ago in the last *khedah* in these very forests, and, although she is perfectly staunch on all occasions, her heart often beats so violently when close to a wild elephant that the camera shakes with the very vibrations, thus spoiling many a good picture. One often wonders what thoughts are running through her mind on these occasions, and whether her agitation is caused by suppressed fear or by her recognition of what may possibly be one of her own blood relatives.

Another difficulty is the mahawat, who, nine times out of ten, has such an instinctive terror of wild elephants that nothing will induce him to go anywhere near one, if he can possibly avoid doing so. Karim Baksh, Balmati's mahawat, is above reproach in this respect, but his assistant and adopted son, Ishmael, whom I have tried to train in the difficult art of mahawat to a tame elephant used for elephant photography, used positively to shake with terror at the mention of wild elephants. One day, just as I was approaching my camp about midday after a very long and unsuccessful morning, we suddenly came upon [a] young elephant. One does not expect to see wild elephants in the hot midday sun, and I was somewhat taken by surprise, but, seeing the beast in the distance, I at once decided to force the boy to go up to it, in the hope that, the ice once broken, he would perhaps realize that wild elephants are not so much to be feared after all. With extreme reluctance, and only because he was afraid of my anger if he refused, he finally took Balmati up to within 25 yards of where the young tusker was digging mineral earth out of the bank of a dry water-course—evidently to cure himself of some internal trouble. The elephant turned at once, and, facing us, gave me the opportunity to take a picture, on plate while the boy's face grew more and more livid as he sat on Balmati's neck, facing for the first time in his life, that ogre of his imagination—a wild tusker at close quarters. As I have frequently emphasized in this book, none can anticipate the actions of a wild elephant, and, although I was more or less prepared for anything myself, I devoutly prayed that nothing would go wrong on this occasion, or my hope of curing the boy of his inborn fear would be hopelessly frustrated for ever. My lucky star was, however, in the ascendant, and, after the usual intent stare, the beast turned and went off down the water-course at his best pace, giving me the chance to produce one last picture. ... Finding that nothing happened to him, the boy, extremely pleased with himself, returned with us to camp, where he became quite a hero among the staff for many a long day afterwards. Since then, he has gone up to wild elephants with me on quite a number of occasions, and he is now quite a satisfactory mahawat for the purpose, although he still has to learn to use a gun in emergencies before he can be entirely reliable.

There is one very fine tusker, known locally as the 'Palakdanta' (curved tusker), which frequents these forests, but which I have not had the good fortune to meet. I will conclude this chapter with a few verbatim extracts from vernacular reports on this elephant, as translated into English by a junior clerk in my office.

> Sir,
>
> On the 31.8.26, while coming to Shampur from Laldhang, at about 3 p.m. with my servant and 3 Forest Guards of Chandi Range, I saw an elephant, whose face was turned towards us, standing at a distance of about 200 fathoms from the road. I was on horse and therefore could see the elephant first. I called out to my men that an elephant is standing. As soon as I uttered these words he turned towards us and began to pace fast; my companions ran away, scattered into the forest, and I made my horse run as fast as I could along the road, but the elephant too followed the horse speedily for about a furlong. The elephant, when there was distance of about 50 fathoms between I and him, gave loud shriek, from which my horse got alarmed and I fell down.
>
> Taking speed of elephant in view I concluded at the time of my falling down from horse that the elephant's foot would be on me and I therefore resolved to save my life by running on foot and the same I did as soon as I fall from horse. I could see nothing while running, the cause of which was the serious hurt on my head. I could not see elephant after falling from my horse.
>
> Gopal Dutt, who was running on ahead, asked me not to run and feel frightened as elephant had stopped. I then felt somewhat soothing but due to hurt I was feeling giddy and sat on ground.
>
> Gopal Dutt, etc., came out to me and they pressed me on with their hands. After 15 minutes I came to my senses opened eyes and could see around. I have got hurt in my right hand and over head. I feel that my mind has been affected by hurt on head as I am still feeling giddy to the time of my making this report on 1st at 5 p.m.
>
> On reaching Laldhang I was informed by one Ram Sarup that same elephant made him fled a week ago; besides this the elephant has also run behind some Gujars who with very difficulty save their lives.
>
> I am very much astonished at being alive. I have at least on 50 occasions faced the elephants in forests in my service but have never seen such a rogue and fast runner.
>
> It is very difficult to save one's life from such elephant's attack unless the help of God is with him.
>
> Last year too this elephant attacked the Gujars so much that a Gujri breathed her last in Nalonwala block.
>
> From these occurrences it appears that this elephant is getting more habituated to oppress people day by day, which would become danger for general public in future. If after inquiries it is proved that same

elephant has been attacking the people arrangements must be made to put end to this danger in interest of public welfare.

Identification marks of elephant:

(1) Tall stature
(2) Both tusks long enough and fat.
(3) White spots on head and near neck and ears.

The 'Palakdanta' is a rare and precious elephant. He deserves special protection from Government. In case he proves dangerous in future and commits number of crimes an officer of the same capacity may be given an opportunity for this trophy!

JOHN SYMINGTON

Dev Raj and Chota Hathi

As a routine I made a circuit of the district every ten days for the purpose of supervising the work in general—fighting epidemics of tropical and other diseases, seeing especially serious cases, and advising as to the line of treatment. Between my routine visits, I went out on urgent calls in any or every direction—wherever my services seemed to be most required. It was necessary to use an elephant in this work, in order to reach certain sections lying to the west, because of the heavy rainfall, which averaged 180 inches a year, the greater part falling in the space of five or six months during what is called the rainy season. In Britain and in many of the States of America, the average rainfall is between 30 and 50 inches, and this is more or less generally scattered throughout the whole year. When a rainfall of 180 inches takes place in six months, or less than half a year, it gives double the concentration that it does when the same amount is distributed throughout the whole year. This means that the earth becomes soaked with water, that great floods take place, and that dry beds of rivers are filled 'labalab', or to the top of the banks with water, and that large rivers overflow. The whole countryside becomes more or less of a quagmire, and water pools and overflowing streams

From *In a Bengal Jungle: Stories of Life on the Tea Gardens of Northern India*. Chapel Hill: University of North Carolina Press, 1935.

seem to be everywhere. This extensive overflowing of streams, with inundations of once hard and dry land, is certainly caused to a great extent by the heavy rainfall, though it is greatly augmented by the melting snow coming down from the eternally snow-capped Himalaya Mountains.

The district lay on the plains touching at some places the base of the foothills of these great mountains, which rise abruptly from the edge of the plains. From the foot of the hills there is a very gentle slope to the sea about four hundred miles away. So gentle is the descent that it seems almost flat, and we were only five hundred feet above sea level.

Through the middle of the district flows the Rydak river—a large and beautiful tributary of the Brahmaputra. The Rydak is the second fastest flowing river in India—the Sutlej, a branch of the Indus, being the fastest. After emerging from a gap in the foothills of the Himalayas, it divides into three branches, which again flow into each other from eight to twelve miles further south, these affluents and effluents thus forming two large islands, which are again traversed and dissected by other streams into smaller islands. In the main river bed great boulders are rolled along by the force of the swift current, having lost their grip on the mountainside many miles higher up the river. Hundreds of the larger boulders lie strewn for miles at the junction of the mountains and the plains, and thousands of smaller size are carried in the river bed miles further down into the plains. Some of these stones are about as round as a football because of the friction they have received on their way from the mountains down. The stony river beds in the dry season are a strong contrast to the general surface of the earth, for scarcely a stone is to be found in the whole distance from the mountains to the sea, the earth being composed of rich alluvial soil. When the river beds are filled with water and the river is flowing with speed and power, the bottom is sometimes a mass of grinding, moving boulders, making a very insecure footing for an elephant or any other animal attempting to ford at such a time. The roar of the water over its stony bed can be heard for a mile or two away.

In the dry season, extending from the end of September to May, one or two of these large affluents dry up or become shallow enough to be crossed on horseback. Across the third a temporary bridge is usually thrown, though it may be necessary to bridge two and sometimes all three. At the beginning of the rains, when the rivers swell again, these bridges are carried away, for nothing except heavy permanent structures can withstand the force of the waters; and even a permanent and expensive bridge might be left high and dry when the channel further up becomes blocked with boulders and trees brought down from the mountains, and the river, overflowing, burrows out a new bed for itself. To train this river into one broad and deep channel, over which a strong, permanent bridge could be built, would be an engineering feat, and the expense is considered prohibitive at present. Hard surface roads, however, are being built in the district, and one can picture a bridge or three bridges spanning the affluents of the Rydak River in the future.

All these factors—changing courses, which prohibited the building of permanent bridges, the deepness of the water and its swiftness, which made it impossible for a horse to cross, and the washing away of all temporary bridges—compelled us to use an elephant as the only method of negotiating those parts of the district lying between the river beds, a distance of some four miles straight across and six miles going at an angle, in order to reach another division further to the south. Between the rivers is forest and tall jungle grass, and this forest extends all along the plains at the foot of the Himalayas to the west of the rivers and is cut into here and there by tea gardens—the Duars, the Terai, and Dehra Dun joining together to form a stretch of territory at the foot of the hills extending from Assam halfway across India. There are other rivers which intersect these districts as do the Rydak and the Jainti, the Toorsa and several others having been spanned by strong permanent bridges.

My routine circuits of the district meant crossing these awful rivers every ten days at least, both going and returning, and often more frequently. Unless the streams were very deep, they were not necessarily dangerous—barring accidents; but, unfortunately, it often happened that when the time came to cross, heavy rains had taken place in the hills the day before, and I would arrive at the river to find it swollen 'labalab' and to realize that this meant a prolonged and continuous struggle on the part of the elephant to cross safely, for it was during the rainy season that the only method of negotiating these rivers was on the back of an elephant. The

Debraj, Height 10ft. 4in photographed in Cooch Behar Pilkhana. 'I could never understand why Cooch Behar Raj decided to sell this magnificent animal to a tea Company'.

temporary bridges erected for use in the dry season had been washed away; the rivers were now too deep to be forded on horseback; the current had become too strong and dangerous for a ferry, so that neither horse nor motor car could be crossed over. Thus it was necessary to use an elephant for the purpose.

There were two elephants kept on our side of the river, one of which, during the rainy season, was usually at the command of the medical officer. One was a large male tusker, said to measure about ten feet six inches in height and ranked as one of the largest elephants in captivity in India. He had been bought from the Maharaja of Cooch Behar, and in his youth had roamed the forests where now he was driven or guided by the hand of the mahout. He was named Dev Raj after the 'King of the Gods'—in this case the elephant gods—and it often happened that as we rode along on this great beast one Indian and another would step forward, stand in reverence, and salaam the elephant as we passed. These were elephant worshippers. Dev Raj was a powerful elephant as well as a big one, and in this lay at once his safety and his danger, for he would enter the river with an over-assurance of his strength and greatness, seeming to say to himself, 'Am not I Dev Raj, and is there any river a match for me?' On this account it was sometimes not long before he got himself into difficulties and was compelled to return to the bank to make another start, while we on his back felt thankful and relieved that he had not been carried away by the current.

The other elephant was a female and without tusks. Though small in comparison to Dev Raj she was of a fair size and a hefty creature. She was very clever in the rivers and could often cross where other elephants of her size would fail. She was also, in some respects, a safer elephant than Dev Raj, because she seemed to know her strength and ability and would never allow herself to be driven beyond her depth, except sometimes when the greater part of the river had been crossed and she found that the remainder was beyond her strength and too deep to ford. She would then give herself a strong shove in the direction of the bank and, launching out at an angle downstream, would reach the opposite side in a last great effort, by swimming, but in an almost submerged condition. As a rule, she knew before going very far into the river whether or not she would be able to cross. In this lay her safety, and no mahout could make her cross when once she decided that she could not.

Sometimes it would be necessary for both elephants to cross at the same time, and then Chota Hathi ('little elephant'), as the smaller elephant was called, would keep carefully to the lee side of Dev Raj. Indeed, there were times when the only way it was possible for Chota Hathi to cross was by keeping carefully and closely by the sheltered side of the big elephant. The latter would walk with his head at an angle upstream and take away the force and weight of the water from the little elephant. This method was not without danger, for sometimes, owing to the slippery and often moving stones and bowlders at the bottom of the river, the feet of Dev Raj would slip and a collision would be only narrowly averted. The force of the waters in their rapid flow as they came against the elephant made a noise like that of a steamer at sea plowing through the water, and as we emerged on the opposite bank there would be a noticeable silence when the swishing sound of the river beating against his body suddenly ceased.

The little elephant, when crossing the river by herself, and when it was just a question of whether she would be able to do it, owing to the depth and force of the water, usually turned her head upstream and side-walked it across. One could scarcely perceive her movements and sometimes came to the conclusion that she was just standing still there in the middle of the river. But she was moving inch by inch or foot by foot sideways. Her hind legs would be partly outstretched and acted as two great props against the force and weight of the water, and she seemed to use the bulk and weight of her body against the force of the current by leaning slightly forward and directly upstream, her face and the root of her trunk cutting the water like the prow of a ship. At these times, when the river was so dangerous, she would feel along the bottom with her trunk for a secure place to plant one or two of her feet before letting go her hold and taking another step. Having taken a step—of maybe only a few inches—up would come her trunk for a breath of air and then down again it would plunge to the bottom of the river. In this manner she would gradually but steadily move across, the progress very slow and the process very tiresome. It was tiring for all concerned—for the elephant, the mahout, and myself.

One morning we had mounted the small elephant and

commenced to cross the river. Chota Hathi had decided to cross at one place, the mahout at another. She wished to go at an angle downstream, the mahout wanted to drive upstream, and there ensued a battle royal. She kept on moving downstream and all the efforts of the mahout to get her to move upwards against the current seemed of no avail. He had used, up to now, words of command, his hands and his toes and a hard-wood stick, but all proved useless. Seizing his iron elephant goad, he hoisted it in the air and with both hands brought it down with all his might, striking the elephant a heavy blow on the forehead. This enraged the animal, and she immediately ducked her head under water, so that the mahout, sitting astride on her neck, was submerged up to his armpits. It seemed that she had not only dipped her head under water but had gone down on her knees, for I found myself occupying the only dry spot on her back, which was about a yard in diameter, and I felt that it had an awkward sloping angle forward. Up came her head from below the surface, and with a twisting motion she attempted to throw the mahout from her neck and to get rid of everything on her back. It seemed from her efforts and contortions that the rope girths binding on the pad would snap, and that we should be thrown into the raging torrent. As her head came into view again, it received an awful stab from the sharp end of the heavy iron goad. This caused her to duck under water a second time, and the mahout, losing his seat on her neck, nearly fell into the river. He caught hold of the ropes in his hands, however, and managed to regain his seat, and gradually, after many blows, shoutings, and stabs on the part of the mahout, and twistings, trumpetings, and divings on the part of the elephant, the latter was brought under control and the fight ended. It seemed to have ended in a compromise, for the elephant proceeded at an angle neither downstream nor upstream, but she commenced to go straight across the river, walking sideways with her head pointing straight upstream and continued to do so until the opposite bank was safely reached.

FRANK NICHOLLS

Tame Elephants

For forty years I used elephants for *shikar*, and in fact for over twenty-two years I had two of my own. On occasions, when entertaining friends in camp during the cold weather season, I had as many as five at once, three being hired ones.

The individual characters of elephants are, in my opinion, more distinctive than in the case of any other animal. Indeed, one can say that there are no two elephants alike. Being with them and watching their different ways over long periods one realizes how fascinating some are, whilst others can become most treacherous and dangerous.

One elephant I hired had a horrible habit of swinging its tail if you passed too near, which resulted in a grass cutter, who was not used to this, losing his front teeth in a second! I knew of another two which appeared quite docile but would occasionally try to squeeze their mahouts to death when passing the trunks of trees. One large tusker I had many years ago in lower Assam was absolutely staunch when following up dangerous animals and was usually a very likeable animal. However, if an elephant ever suffered from a bad liver at times, I am sure that this one did!

At the northern end of the estate on which I worked in those days there was a long protection drain, running along the boundary a few yards beyond the tea. This drain was six feet deep and four

From *Assam Shikar*. New Zealand: Tonson Publishing House, 1970.

feet wide at the top. The land sloped slightly from the Bhutan Hills towards the tea area and this drain was there to catch the surface rain water which washed down. On some Sunday mornings, when I went out for shikar, the tusker would take that drain in its stride. On another Sunday, however, it would refuse to cross over that drain. It would stand there trumpeting loudly, rolling from side to side, trying to get me off. The more it did this the more the mahout applied the ankus to its head. Then it would roll so much that the mahout would say 'no good sahib!'

The mahout would take me to a tree and I would step off on to a branch, while he took the elephant away for another try. But again, on reaching the drain, it would refuse to go over. Then the fun would begin! The mahout, not having me to think of, would let the elephant really have it with his iron prong. The elephant would behave like a small boat in a rough sea but after five minutes or so of bedlam, with wild screams and trumpetings, over the drain it would go. After recrossing a few times to be certain that it would not play up again that day, the mahout would bring it to the tree and I would step on to the saddle and we would cross the drain without further trouble! That elephant would take bananas gently out of my pocket at lunch time but occasionally and after a few weeks had passed, it would play up again and we would go through the same procedure.

The Miri who was employed to cut grass for the elephant to eat at night was, for some reason, not at all popular with that particular elephant and he was very careful to keep just out of reach of its trunk. I suggested to the grasscutter that he should look for employment elsewhere and he left to work for another elephant owner. Shortly afterwards I was transferred. Some three years later, this man was re-engaged by the new manager and I learned afterwards that the elephant had taken him unawares one day and had killed him!

On one occasion I hired another elephant which intensely loathed crossing deep pools, especially those very deep ones where all that could be seen was its trunk looking like a submarine's periscope above the water. Although other elephants with it used to cross willingly enough, this elephant went through every possible antic in an endeavour not to swim those pools. On one occasion it tried to rub the mahout against a projecting rock. I learned from the owner afterwards that some twenty years before, soon after being captured and while still only a five foot high baby, it had been roped to a fully grown elephant and made to swim the very wide Brahmaputra. It had probably swallowed a lot of water during that trip and had never forgotten that unhappy experience.

At the same camp, I had a female elephant with an eighteen months' old calf. The calf was full of mischief, mostly brought about by native boys playing and wrestling with it. The mother was the most lovely elephant, Motimali by name, that I have ever hired. She had no vices whatsoever. She died of old age a few years ago. One bitterly cold morning in January, the male guests in this camp were standing on the river bank, busily preparing their fishing rods and tackle for the day's fishing. Motimali and four other elephants were tethered to trees about fifty yards away. My guests were facing the river and a cold wind from the gorge was blowing. I noticed that the baby elephant, with mischief in its eyes, was circling around in the trees behind us. I had a shrewd idea as to what the baby elephant's intentions were. As it was working its way nearer and nearer to us, my friend Freeman was saying that he thought preparing one's rods, lines and flies for the day's fishing was nearly as enjoyable as the actual fishing. He had just finished the sentence when the young elephant, which was about four and a half feet high, came like a charging bull and put him straight into the river below us and then bolted back to join its mother!

My friend's language was blue and so was he, by the time he had clambered up some fifty yards downstream! The bank at that spot was four or five feet high and precipitous. After the rest of us had stopped laughing, we saw the young elephant against its mother and standing partly behind a tree, with just its head sticking out, watching the result of its early morning effort. A number of elephants born in captivity, as this one was, eventually become too nervous for shooting purposes, especially when they have to approach dangerous game. They have not the nerves of elephants which have roamed the forests for some years prior to being captured. Furthermore, animals born in captivity cannot be trusted and often become dangerous as they grow up. This is because they become too familiar with human beings from the time of their birth.

Many of these so-called trained and staunch elephants that one is offered by native owners, when an extra elephant or two is required for camp, can be very dangerous. It is also a most nerve-racking experience to be on a bolting elephant, weighing some three tons, crashing through the low branches of trees festooned with spiked creepers, many of which have barbs like fish-hooks strong enough to pull a man off. It is difficult to describe the feeling of being on a bolting elephant, but imagine yourself perched on the top of an express engine with a hooked stick round the funnel, trying to pull it to a standstill while it rocks from side to side and dashes under very low bridges. A good friend of mine, who was a very powerfully built person, would, on these occasions, spring up on to a branch of a tree for safety. However, it is quite possible to drop and damage one's rifle when doing this trick.

During my years in the jungle, I had three such experiences, and wish for no more! Providing that no wild elephants, buffaloes, bears, tigers, or leopards were following close behind, I would look for a soft place to jump down to as soon as possible. It would be easy to break one's neck by getting caught under the jaw by one of these very strong creepers, some being even strong enough to hold an elephant. Moreover, if pulled off unexpectedly, one is liable to come down under the elephant's back feet. These incidents usually occur in very thick and dense jungle, as these are the places where one sometimes disturbs a sleeping tiger or bear, and the resulting noise is quite enough to frighten some elephants.

Most mahouts, when they find they cannot hold their elephant with the sharp hook of their ankus, just lie as flat as they can behind the elephant's head for protection and hope for the best. If they are swept off, the elephant is often lost for days. I remember an occasion when two tame elephants took fright together. One bolted upon the sudden closing of a car door and the other followed sympathetically. They both kept together and went fully five miles before they became more or less exhausted and the mahouts managed to pull them up. I saw the mahouts the next day and they looked a very disfigured couple with many deep scars on their faces and legs. They certainly were a brave pair and were suitably rewarded for not losing their charges.

Not far from an estate which I was on many years ago, a rhinoceros had gone berserk and had killed some natives. It had made its home in *a bheel* or large muddy pond, surrounded by high grass, from where it rampaged through the surrounding villages. The local planters decided to destroy it and as many of even the staunchest of elephants are really terrified of rhinoceros, no less than seven shikar elephants were collected together. They advanced towards the bheel where the rhinoceros had taken up its residence, when out came the animal and with a terrific snort and bubbling sound it made towards one of the elephants and the whole seven turned and fled for their lives. Fortunately, it was open grassy country so no one was hurt but not one of those elephants pulled up under three miles.

I was on an elephant once which I knew to be staunch as far as wild elephants, buffaloes and tigers were concerned. While proceeding over some open country, we came upon the dung of a rhinoceros. The elephant turned and bolted and the mahout was not able to stop it for about half a mile. The rhinoceros was somewhere about and that was quite sufficient for that elephant!

My mahout's father, who had spent all his life with elephants and who must have been seventy when I first knew him in 1927, was one of the most interesting old men I have ever met. He has been dead many years now but up to his death, although too feeble to work, the old fellow still loved being on an elephant with his son, my mahout, roaming through the jungle. Before I employed him the old man had been in charge of twelve elephants which belonged to a European and had been used by him for catching wild elephants in the Assam forests. He once told me of a terrifying experience he had once had, deep in the wilds, with his employer. They were moving camp and had two elephants, one carrying the pots and pans, glasses, crockery and other utensils in a large box, in addition to carrying his employer's personal servant. Another servant was following behind carrying two empty kerosene tins, which had been used for carrying water from the river for the camp.

They had just entered the forest, when the man behind dropped the two empty kerosene tins, just behind the elephant's hind legs. The elephant immediately bolted. Some pots and pans soon dropped off and this further noise caused the elephant to accelerate. These were followed by the box containing the glasses and dishes crashing to the ground, with the result that the elephant increased its speed still further! The servant was brushed off but the mahout managed to cling on and he pulled up a mile or so further on, just as darkness was setting in. As elephants do not realize that when passing under low branches in the blackness of the forest the mahout can be easily swept off, it is no fun riding on an elephant in the jungle at night! Therefore, after calling out for some time and obtaining no reply from the servant the mahout hurried on to get out of the forest before darkness finally closed in. Although the European had seven elephants out early the next morning and searched daily for a week, the poor servant was never found. They came to the conclusion that he had tried to cross the winding river of the Dikal in the darkness and been swept away and drowned. This river was partly in flood at the time as it was the end of the cold season and there had been a lot of rain in the nearby hills. I know the area well where they were in camp and the surrounding forests contain many hundreds of wild elephants, tigers and bears.

I know of a gentleman and his wife who were out shooting one day on the north bank of the Brahmaputra River. They had two elephants. Husband and wife were on one elephant and the other was for carrying their lunch and any game that might be shot. This latter elephant was rather nervous and very likely to bolt if a gun was fired too near. She was therefore kept a couple of hundred yards or more away. After a barking deer was shot, the mahout brought her along and after loading the deer, went away again to a good distance from the other elephant.

Unfortunately, there were some bottles of soda water in the luncheon basket and owing to the heat and movement of the elephant one of these exploded. Off bolted the elephant, the mahout unable to stop her. More soda bottles popped, up went her speed and she eventually shed her mahout! She then swam the Brahmaputra River, possibly a mile wide at the site where she crossed, and reached her home, with the barking deer and luncheon basket, some three weeks later. I guess that the deer must have exploded too during that time and might have helped accelerate her journey home!

Elephants can be fitted with howdahs, or platforms with seats, but these are quite unsuitable for thick jungle and would get pulled off immediately and my elephants were fitted with saddles. With the ordinary saddle the feet of the riders simply hung down and this could become very tiring, so I designed a new kind of saddle with running boards on either side of the elephant on which the riders' feet could be rested. I gave this style of saddle to the Kaziranga Game Reserve which had several elephants for visitors who went to see the animals there, for these elephants had only the ordinary saddle. Strange to relate, the first person to use it was Mr Pandit Nehru, Prime Minister of India, and Mr E. P. Gee, whom I knew, took a photograph of him seated on the saddle which I had invented!

While writing this book, I received word from the owner of Motimali's death. For twenty-six years I had hired her whenever necessary. Of all the elephants I have known, including my own two, she stood out above them all as the most human and intelligent. She had no vices and was lovable and adorable at all times. She was the mother of at least six calves, one of which was the young male which very cleverly put my friend Freeman into the cold river early one morning. From her back, I shot over twenty rogue elephants and also many tigers and bears.

She would pick up the smallest of things dropped by anyone riding on her back—often without being told. Many topees and hats and even a cartridge did she carefully pick up in her sensitive trunk. These she handed to the mahout gently, and did not just throw them up, as many elephants do. Once a very thin rope, thinner than one's little finger and about eighteen inches long, came adrift from the iron ring at the back of the saddle. Without any instructions, she stopped suddenly, turned completely round and picked this very thin short rope out of the grass and handed it up.

I think the most intelligent thing she did and one which saved me from a very embarrassing position, was when going into camp with my sister-in-law and nephew. We had crossed a river and were just coming to a bank some five feet high, which we had to climb. Motimali stopped dead and absolutely refused to move another step in spite of the mahout's efforts. He then suggested that perhaps she was standing on a snake, hence her refusal to move for a few minutes. However, eventually he had to dismount. Imagine our surprise when the mahout announced that the girth securing the saddle was broken! Imagine the chaos which would have ensued if the saddle had slipped off when we were halfway up that bank, the three of us falling over backwards for quite ten feet. I would have landed on the top of my sister-in-law, a terrible thing, as I then weighed 14 stone 8 lbs! I offered up a silent prayer of thanks.

One day in 1955, Motimali was feeding peacefully under some

tenga trees just behind the camp. Tengas are large apple-like fruit, very acid but loved by most wild animals, particularly elephants. Hence the name 'elephant apple'. She was hobbled by her front feet so she would not stray too far. My mahout had just handed over his duties to a new man and was leaving for his home that afternoon. At noon, two wild tuskers came out of the jungle and had a terrific battle in the river-bed some two hundred yards below camp. After some time they stopped and separated, each taking one side of the river. Seeing these two tuskers facing each other, my mahout asked to be taken safely past the trouble. I took my rifle and with the new mahout, escorted my man some way along the jungle path leading out of the jungle. On seeing us, the tuskers casually walked away in opposite directions, the one which was on my camp side of the river, going up the bank and entering the forest. Little did I realize at the time that he would make for my female elephant Motimali.

Imagine my surprise to find, on my return, that the tusker had taken Motimali away to a herd some two hundred yards from my camp, to add her to his harem. The new mahout and myself followed the tracks towards the herd but the tusker kept coming at us, while Motimali retreated further towards the centre of the herd. I did not want to shoot the tusker and as the whole herd was gradually moving further and further away from us, we were compelled to give up the chase. We knew that the rope which tied Motimali's front feet loosely together would wear through in two weeks or so and that she would eventually go back home. By the time I had hired other elephants to try to intercept her, four days had passed and she was many miles off in a dense wild area.

Six weeks later she arrived back at the home of her owner, some sixty miles away, very fat and in good condition. A few years before this episode, she had absconded from a place where she was on timber work about eighty-six miles away and had reached home safely some two months later.

Not all runaway elephants will make for home like Motimali. Many years ago, in some very wild country, I came upon a herd of bison. Most of the magnificent creatures were lying down but immediately behind them stood a large female elephant with two calves, one about six feet in height and the other about two years of age. The bison got up and cleared off but the female elephant, with her ears wide, allowed us to get within about twenty yards of her before moving off. The mahout and I could see clearly that she had a perfectly round hole in her ear, about the size of a golf ball. She was undoubtedly an escaped animal. Later my mahout spoke to his old father about it, and the old man knew all about this elephant, having seen her previously with her owner and with the hole through her ear.

She had been captured when young and escaped six years later and had since then been wandering in the jungle for the last fifteen years. Her two calves were the progeny of a wild male. The old mahout said that as a rule elephants that had been in captivity remained alone in the forest.

It was in 1960 when the manager of a tea estate, some 10 miles from my camp site, asked me if I could possibly go and shoot an elephant that was causing damage to tea nurseries and shade trees. It also visited the assistant's compound some nights and ate his banana trees and damaged his vegetable garden.

I searched for that elephant for a day and a half without finding it. On the second afternoon, about 3 p.m. I told the mahout to have his tea and proceed back to camp with the elephant. Apparently, on his way back, he took something very much stronger than the 'cup that cheers'! He then proceeded for about two miles and near some labourers' houses at the Rungaghur Tea Estate he parted company with the elephant, falling against her front feet, and fortunately near where some labourers were standing.

The elephant, Mohonmalla by name, was a most intelligent and docile animal. She stopped immediately after the mahout fell and did her part, as she thought, by more or less throwing the man back on to her neck! Down went the mahout, up he went again, down again, up again and finally and mercifully, down. By this time a man who was witnessing this performance, with ready wit cut down one of his own banana trees from nearby and gave it to the elephant, after which she stopped trying to replace the mahout on her neck to eat the banana stem. The mahout's son, who resided a quarter of a mile or so away, was sent for and he took charge of the elephant and rode her back to camp.

The mahout was carried to his house for the night, with blood coming from his nose. He turned up at camp the next afternoon, and appeared to treat the whole thing as a joke. He said that after leaving me, a friend had given him too much drink and on an empty stomach and in the hot sun, his head started to spin. He had no recollection of the elephant's attempts to lift him and he did not remember anything until the next morning!

Two weeks after this, I broke camp, and returned the elephant to the owner in North Lakhimpur some forty miles away. There was very little natural fodder where the owner resided, so the elephant lived more or less for six months on banana trees until she returned to my care again, where she became very fat.

After being back with her owner for about two months or so, she absconded one night, and proceeded in the direction of my late camp, some forty miles distant. Probably she was remembering that large area, and the most wonderful time she had there with all kinds of luxuriant fodder, not least of all the sugar cane that she was given by me twice daily and for which she always showed her thanks by purring. She had only about four miles to go to reach her old camp area, when her owner, who was on her heels tracking her, caught up with her and compelled her to return. He told me later that she greatly resented being captured and trumpeted to show her disgust at having to return home!

I was once upon a huge tusker and roaming through a patch of jungle which had been burnt off a few weeks before. All of a sudden the elephant stumbled and almost came down but recovered itself and stopped, holding up its front foot. The mahout dismounted, realizing that something had entered the animal's foot and I also got down. On telling the elephant to lie down, it went down very quietly, on its side. The head of a small stake was to be seen embedded in the sole and broken off flush with the rough surface. The mahout soon got his penknife out and after cutting away a small piece of the pad of the foot round the end of the stake, he cut a niche round the head of it. He then tied a strand of jute from one of his ropes to the stake and we both took a pull and extracted it. It was four inches long and one and a half inches in diameter! The elephant remained perfectly still throughout the proceedings. When we got home we cleaned the wound thoroughly with hot water and applied Stockholm tar and after a week of rest the elephant was no longer lame.

A horse or cow would have been very much more difficult to treat under similar circumstances, but from the beginning the elephant seemed to realize that we were helping it.

I have read many articles in this connection which have always interested me and I have been asked many times whether there is any truth in the widely held belief that old elephants proceed to a communal burial place.

During my many journeys into the forests, I came across only three dead mature elephants in a reasonable state of preservation. Two of these three were very, very old females and without a doubt had died of old age. One I found a few yards from a salt lick but the other female was lying dead in a very remote area where there was no water. The third elephant, a male, was also found in similar country but not very far from a river.

I, for one, do not believe that elephants make for any particular spot before they die, any more than do other wild animals. What I often saw, however, was that most elephants died in ravines or gorges in the foothills many miles from human habitation. Both my mahouts, whom I had for years, shared the same belief. Many a time, when wandering up the river-beds near the foothills, I saw old elephant bones amongst the boulders near an entrance to a ravine and on searching around, often found other bones also. These bones were washed down out of the ravines and gorges in the rainy season.

It stands to reason that an old or sick elephant will not remain in open forest where gad-flies and leeches will worry it. They naturally make for the narrow, cool gorges, far up some mountain stream, where there is perennial water and their favourite, lush grasses and creepers.

I have come upon a number of old elephants, usually on their own, their skins withered and many of them deaf. Some have been so old and infirm that they could just move their trunks to smell my elephant and I have even patted some of them as we passed by.

I have the greatest admiration and love for elephants.

Two years after selling my big makhna elephant, which I had had for twenty-two years, to the Government of Assam, I received a visit from a Government official who was riding it. I had not seen that elephant for two years and he made quite a loud gurgling sound as if greeting me.

They often do this when they meet a person they like or if they are pleased to see one and even do so among themselves.

On the guest leaving, I walked down the path about ten yards behind the elephant to see him off. I said goodbye to my visitor and went towards my late elephant to pat it. It turned and came half way to meet me, pushed its face into mine, almost pushing me backwards and gurgled away for quite a few seconds. The mahout was quite taken aback, as he was unaware up to that time that the elephant had belonged to me.

An elephant never forgets!

II
The Most Dangerous Game: Indian Elephants

J.G. ELLIOTT

Shikar as a Part of Life

On 15th August 1947 the Dominions of India and Pakistan, as they were then styled, came into being and the exodus of Britons began in real earnest. Civil servants of all grades, officers and men of the three services, pensioners, who had planned to end their days in the India they had served, arrived in Bombay by mail train and military special in a steady stream. And all their worldly goods came with them. The stacks of luggage mounted on the platforms and were spirited away to the docks under the watchful eye of the old Parsee shipping clerk in the high, shiny hat. There was little, except the labels, by which even their owners could tell one pile from another: neatly patched bedrolls, uniform cases, the names in white paint worn faint by miles of travel, and of course, the gun cases. Canvas-clad and stained with oil they were the poor relations of the portmanteaux in opulent hide to be seen on the platforms of Euston or King's Cross on the eve of The Twelfth. And the guns inside, though reckoned singly and not in pair, had to their credit bags which made up in variety what they may have lacked in numbers. They were all marked 'Not Wanted on Voyage': some of them would never be wanted again in the hands of those who then owned them. They were part of a way of life, symbols of a passing era.

From *Field Sports in India*. London: Gentry Books, 1973.

The troops of the Honourable East India Company, fighting their way against the Mahrattas north west from Calcutta to the frontier on the Jumna, found a countryside where the cultivation surrounding the villages was interspersed with areas of thick jungle, tall trees growing out of dense undergrowth and extensive thickets laced with briers. And through this plentiful cover swarmed tiger, pig, deer, peacock, partridge, quail, snipe and duck. Small wonder that the officers of those days turned to sport for relaxation, setting a fashion that persisted to the end. By the start of the nineteenth century field sports were everywhere recognized as part and parcel of the life of the British community. In 1804 the Marquess of Wellesley addressed a cogent minute to the Court of Directors advocating the establishment of a zoo worthy of the teeming fauna of the country. In anticipation of sanction he set up the Barrackpore Menagerie, but the Court, who took a realistic view of the objects on which the Company's money could properly be spent, would have none of it; resisting even the blandishment of a series of paintings of animals and birds, by Dr Buchanan Hamilton and Indian artists working under him, which the Marquess sent home to lend colour to his proposal. These sketches are still on view in the India Office Library.

In 1807 Ormes of Bond Street published Williamson and Howitt's *Oriental Field Sports.* Family album size, the clarity of the text and the charm and vigour of the plates are eloquent testimony to the place that field sports had established for themselves. The plates are titled in French as well as English. There is further evidence in the diary of Lieutenant John Pester for the years 1802–6, *War and Sport in India,* which covers a period of fighting the Mahrattas in the triangle Delhi–Bareilly–Gwalior. John Pester did nothing by halves. On hearing that war with the Mahrattas was inevitable he notes:

> If an officer should wish to get forward he should pray for opportunities to distinguish himself and let none escape that offer. To be first and foremost in danger should be his object. If he falls, he falls gallant and respected, and it is a thousand to one if he is not rewarded should he succeed in doing his duty in the style of a soldier.

And he welcomes the appointment to command his brigade of one Colonel Whyte, who by his gallantry had earned the name of the God of War. When not fighting, Pester was out in search of game, preferably under conditions that involved some risk to life and limb. It was clear that in time of war an officer should not study comfort, but he saw no point in hardship for its own sake. Be as comfortable as you can. 'Packed ten dozen of Madeira and four dozen of port with some beer in grass for the march.' 'Our guns, elephants, servants with a good store of claret, madeira, fowls, hams etc. etc. left cantonments today.'

The officers of those days were born and bred in the English countryside and a love of sport was in the blood. There was game to be ridden, hunted or shot by anyone who took the trouble to ride a mile or two out of camp or cantonment. 'We had agreed to fire at nothing but tiger, and in consequence the deer and hogs, which we found in greater abundance than I could have believed, all escaped.'

Those halcyon days did not last for ever but the next seventy-five years were the era of the great shikaris: Williamson, Shakespeare, Burton, Kinloch, Forsyth, Gordon, Cumming, Sanderson, Baker, Pollock, to name but a few of them. Game was everywhere plentiful and there was little limit or restriction imposed on what they shot, or where. In fact it was a matter of government policy to clear whole areas of game to open up fresh tracts for cultivation. About 1880 it began to dawn on the early conservationists that things had gone far enough. Soil erosion, following in the footsteps of the sacred cow, was stripping the countryside bare up to the boundaries of the government forests. And inside those forests some control became necessary over what might be shot. The early game laws date from then. Responsibility for giving effect to these laws rested with the officers of the Indian Forest Service, men who spent the months from November to March in the jungle, 'wise in more than woodlore alone', and they made a good job of it.

With the tradition of the English hunting field behind them the early sportsmen very soon took pigsticking to their hearts. Using its own distinctive weapon pigsticking has always remained in a class of its own. ...

At the time of the First World War field sports were still firmly established in favour and, the if one can believe the evidence of an India Office letter circulated in 1916, they were within the reach of everyone. At that time the Indian Army had suffered heavy casualties in France and Mesopotamia and there was an urgent need for men with battle experience to officer the wartime battalions that were being raised. The obvious recruiting ground was among officers of the British Army who had fought in France. Deciding that if it was to be done it must be done well, an offer was made of permanent commissions in the post-war army. No pains were spared to paint the prospects in glowing terms. The task was given to one Colonel Ramsay Gordon and it is clear that he wrote from the heart. The letter which bears his signature earned the flippant sub-title of 'Tigers at the bottom of the Compound'. It began with a few sordid details about pay and pensions, and had a word to say for the attraction for the serious soldier of small wars on the frontier, but after that, the ink warm and flowing freely, the writer really gets down to it. The rest of the letter is required reading for every travel agent. 'Apart from soldiering, India offers attractions in the way of games and sport which cannot be beaten anywhere. Big and small game shooting such as, in Europe, is open only to the very rich, in India is within reach of all.' 'Pigsticking, of which India has practically a monopoly, is the King of sports, but not the sport of Kings, as the most impecunious subaltern can join in.' 'Fishing for mahseer affords splendid sport. The rivers, with very few exceptions, are open to everyone and fish up to 50 and 60 lb. are frequently to be caught, amidst surroundings and scenery which make Scotland seem tame.' 'The summer heat is no doubt unpleasant but, on the other hand, most of the fishing and big game shooting occurs during the hot weather.' 'Kashmir, which is now only a few hours by motor from the Plains, provides fishing and big game shooting of a very high order and thus adds considerably to the possibilities of sport and pleasure, in a delightful climate during the summer months.' 'For the keen soldier India is a land of many opportunities, and for the keen sportsman, of moderate means, a paradise.'

Between three and four hundred officers took the fly floated so skilfully over their noses.

And what of the Promised Land? Did it live up to expectations? The letter was a bit overdrawn, but substantially there was a lot of truth in it. Sport was there for those with a mind to look for it, and many of those coming out to India to the I.C.S., the Police and the Army were so minded.

Except for those who hobnobbed with princes and governors,

and they had to do little more than take their places in the battle and discharge their firearms at the appropriate moment, the charm of sport in India lay in the depth of the background. From start to finish it was your show. You were pitting your wits against a wild animal and if you were successful satisfaction came not from having shot it but from the knowledge that you had outwitted it. If you failed it was probably your fault, and you did not make the same mistake again. You had to be very fit and, to cap it all, there could be the spice of danger, that slight tautening of the nerves, the knowledge that when you came to fire you could not afford to miss.

Babur, when he invaded India, had to penetrate no deeper than the banks of the Indus to indulge his favourite sport of hunting rhinoceros. Four hundred years later the soldier in the Punjab or on the North West Frontier in search of big game had to travel to the government forests of the United Provinces or Central Provinces, or even further to the jungles south of Belgaum or down to the Mysore ditch below the Nilgiris. But he got two months leave every year, and that was long enough even to march a hundred miles or more into the mountains behind Kashmir and still have four weeks left for shooting.

The trips taken on long leave are unforgettable. You booked your forest block weeks, even months, ahead, wrote to the Survey of India for large scale maps, and pored over them in anticipation till you felt you knew every corner of them. Then the day came and you were away, away from the heat and dust of the plains, away from the monotony of an individual training programme that decreed that on the first of April each year the trained soldier once more became a recruit, away to the cool and peace of the jungle where you could not walk a hundred yards without seeing a track or hearing a sound that excited your curiosity and tested your jungle lore. Or if your fancy took you into the hills, you marched for a week or ten days through scenery which in truth 'made even Scotland seem tame'. Cold sparkling air; perhaps by the side of the road a tiny waterfall pouring down over a cliff, the rocks tinged with rust, the water, ice cold, tasting faintly of iron; the camp fire outside the tent in the evening. You stalked barasingh, or ibex or markhor at a height of over 15,000 feet across ground so precipitous you began to wonder why you had ever been fool enough to leave the flat. If you went back empty handed, though you seldom did, you had a host of memories to console you in your disappointment.

If your regiment was stationed in central India, Cawnpore, Jubbulpore, Mhow, Belgaum, the jungle was at your doorstep and if you had your scouts out, and an indulgent colonel who asked no questions if you disappeared for a couple of nights, you might bring back a panther or even a tiger.

But there were few stations where there was not bird shooting and perhaps fishing to be had within a radius of twenty-five miles. When a battalion was due for a change of station and the day drew near for the publication of the Indian Army Order promulgating the moves for the next trooping season, keen students of form would be busy with their forecasts. Coloured largely by the preference of the individual, they were usually wrong. One commanding officer fell heavily in the popularity stakes when word went round that he had been pulling strings in Simla to secure a move to Hyderabad, Sind. Whatever the merits of a hot, dry climate in the eyes of one who was later to be crippled with rheumatism, Hyderabad was a one-battalion station, a hundred miles from anywhere, and with an evil reputation for the longest and harshest hot weather in the land. His rating improved slightly, at any rate among the bachelors, when someone pointed out that there was, within easy reach, some of the best duck shooting in the world. As it turned out the battalion was sent to Waziristan, which shows that it does not pay to pull strings.

A great feature was that it was always considered quite natural that you should combine business with pleasure. It was not that duty was neglected, far from it, but if the path of duty led where you might expect to find something to shoot, it was foolish not to go prepared to spend such spare time as there might be as agreeably as possible. It is likely that this custom dates back to the days when all regiments and batteries moving in relief went by march route along the Grand Trunk Road, which had been built for that purpose. When, in 1862, Major Francis of the Bengal Horse Artillery took his battery from Delhi to Hazaribag, two hundred miles north west of Calcutta, they were fifty-six days on the road. This was a large slice out of life, so he took his wife with him. ...

Camping grounds were seldom more than fourteen miles apart,

so by noon tents would have been pitched, horses and men watered and fed and in the afternoon 'we contrived to get some shooting'. ...

It would be quite wrong to suppose that these diversions were the preserve of the martial classes: very much the reverse. District officers of the Indian Civil Service in the cold weather spent weeks, if not months, in camp and if they were so inclined they had remarkable opportunities for combining sport with duty, the one in no way distracting from the proper discharge of the other. There was one commissioner for the Kumaon who took his whole establishment with him into the jungle and arranged his day's work to suit the habits of the tiger, with the result that he did his office work between three and five in the morning, much to the disgust of his clerks who were nothing if not family men. Lady Lawrence in *Indian Embers* gives a picture of her husband, commissioner of Belgaum 'in shabby shikar clothes at the door of his ten', interviewing village officials and petitioners whose troubles he probably sorted out in ten minutes when he visited the spot the following day. It was the same Henry Lawrence who found himself in the awkward predicament of having to follow up and shoot a wounded tiger in time to catch a train to take him to a meeting of the Legislative Council in Bombay. Luckily the mail train was two hours late, but even so it was a close thing. A far cry from the cloistered calm of Whitehall, black coats and pinstripe trousers, where the worst dilemma to vex a man in a twelve-month might be to double date himself on a brace of committees. ...

There was a commanding officer who saw fit to write in the confidential report of one of his company commanders: 'If he took as much interst in his profession as he does in shikar he would be a good officer.' The victim of course took this as a tremendous compliment.

The Mighty Nimrods

There are three well-defined though overlapping periods in the story of the sport of the British in India: up to about 1840, for forty years to 1880, and from then to 1947. There was little finesse about it to start with. Few knew or cared much about jungle lore; they were fearless, hard hitting, straightforward Nimrods, ready to ride down with spear or rifle anything they came across. They set the fashion and laid the foundations for those who came after them, but over the next seventy-five years the whole pattern of life changed so much that it is worth a couple of chapters to take a look at what went on in those early carefree days. ...

To consider in rather more detail how they set to work, the operative word to describe their activities was not shooting: they hunted. In England it was the heyday of fox hunting and most of the officers coming out to join the Presidency Armies, and many of the civilians, arrived with that background behind them. When they got to India they were agreeably surprised to find that wherever they went there was something for them to shoot or hunt: in particular the pig, an altogether more formidable opponent than the fox, but just as plentiful as rabbits in the English countryside they had left behind them. ...

Game swarmed over the countryside and village life over large areas was disrupted by man-eaters. When the new military road was built from Calcutta to Benares to cut the distance of the old route along the Ganges, a belt of jungle had to be kept clear for a hundred yards on either side; otherwise tigers would have taken such toll of the travellers that only formed bodies of troops could have used the road. The evolutions of a battalion at drill might be thrown into disorder by a stag seeking refuge from a tiger lurking in the jungle that bordered the parade ground. And when the day's work was over three or four officers would make up a party and go questing after tiger, pig, deer or whatever the countryside offered, much as their successors a hundred years later would go out after partridge or peacock from battalion camp.

The sportsmen of the early days were not above bird shooting for the pot, but they did not have a very high opinion of it as sport. ...

When game was everywhere so plentiful it is not surprising to read of bags that far exceed in numbers anything that a sportsman of later days would have felt justified in shooting. In *Sport in Bengal*, Baker tells how from his camp, without using his binoculars, he could distinguish 'at least three score wild buffaloes and between two and three hundred spotted deer feeding in the open'.

There were in those days 'two giant Nimrods', one of them Colonel S—d, who shot eleven black buck in a day, the other 'Gunga' Brown who over and over again shot seventy brace and upwards of painted partridge. A party of three guns returned from a ten day shoot with a bag of four tigers, two bears, seven sambhur, two cheetal, one four horned antelope, one hyena, four black buck, four chinkara, two boar, a total of twenty-seven head. This was described as 'very fair sport'.

Before condemning these figures out of hand as sheer butchery it is well to remember the standards of the days in which these men lived. There was still a gallows at Tyburn, and no doubt the grandfathers of the men who campaigned for the abolition of çapital punishment joined the crowd that went along to see the fun when a notorious malefactor was to be hanged. In 1814 a man was executed for cutting down a tree, and cock fighting was still a popular sport in England. ...

When the Mahratta wars were over, about 1810, the countryside began to settle down, troops were collected in cantonments and game became scarce in the immediate vicinity of military stations, but elsewhere it was still plentiful, and there were no game laws. You might have to travel forty or fifty miles to find something to shoot but there was no difficulty about that: parties of two or three would go into camp for a fortnight or even longer. With some semblance of law and order prevailing, the government, the East India Company as it still was, turned its attention to exploring the resources of what was really virgin forest. It was the day of Sanderson among the elephants in Mysore, Forsyth and Sterndale in the Central Provinces, men seconded for duty for the purpose. Their books mark the first serious attempt to record the natural history of the country, the customs of the people and the habits of the animals they shot. ...

Nimrods in Action

A popular vote would probably rate the tiger as providing the finest sport of all the Indian game animals. The more knowledgeable would qualify this by adding that much depends on how you set about it. Sanderson, on the other hand, awards the palm without hesitation to elephant shooting.

> It is difficult to define the exact elements which make elephant shooting the supremely exciting sport it is; but its danger and the necessity for the exercise of the sportsman's personal qualities of perseverance, endurance

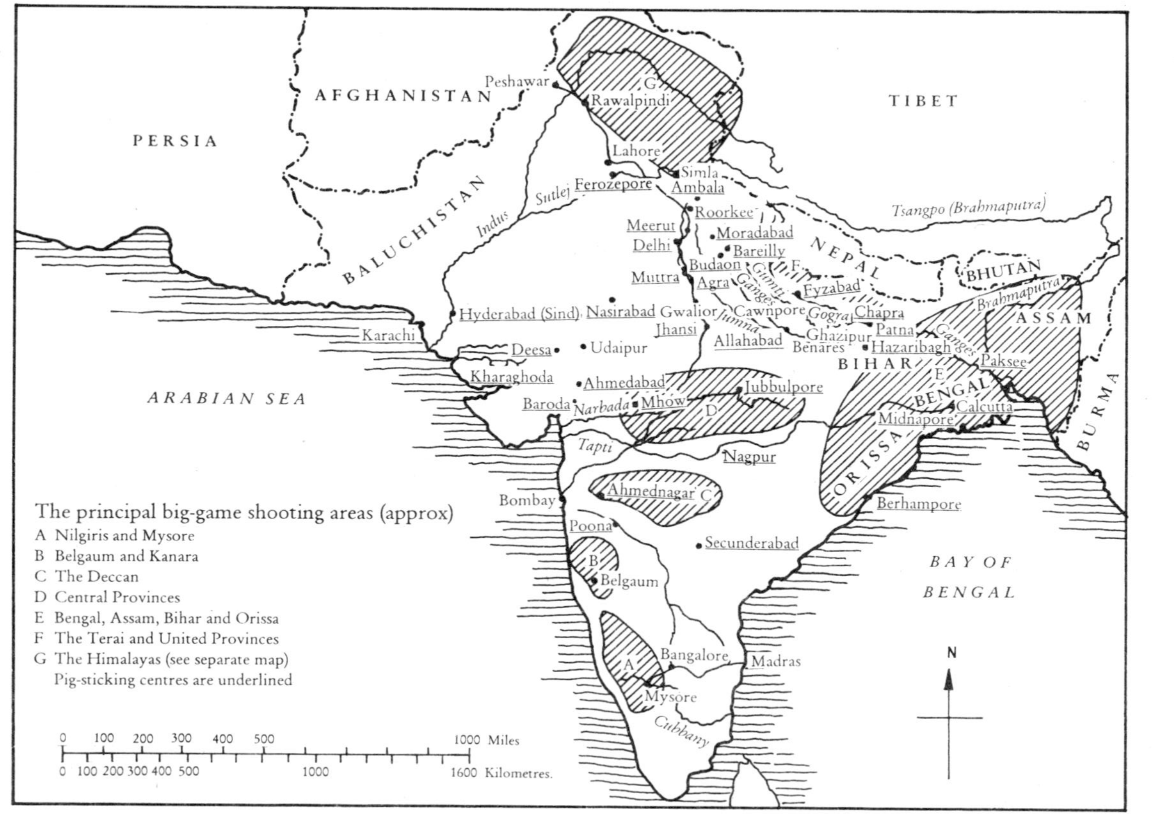

The Principal Big-Game Shooting Areas Upto 1947.

> and nerve, are prominent ones. The best trackers can only bring their master up to the game, when everything depends on himself. The size of the noble beast; the fine line of country through which the chase always leads; and the fair stand-up nature of the encounter when the game is met—all tend to elevate elephant shooting above all sports with the rifle.

Elephant shooting in India was never practised on anything like the same scale as was general in Africa. His home is in thick jungle among the foothills and in the early trigger-happy days the sportsman did not penetrate into these more remote areas. The comparative ease with which he could be caught and tamed, and his use for ceremonial occasions, for sport, forestry and heavy construction work led to restrictions being placed on elephant shooting many years before it was thought necessary to pass game laws for the protection of other game animals. He was more valuable alive than dead.

In areas where the numbers were not kept down by capture, elephants could become a menace to cultivation, and even when restrictions were in force they might be lifted to deal with the occasional rogue which was threatening the lives of the villagers in jungle tracts. On the authority of 'the greatest of ancient or modern Nimrods', Sir Samuel Baker, elephant shooting ranks as the most dangerous of all sports if fairly followed for a length of time.

> The wild elephant's attack is one of the noblest sights of the chase. The cocked ears and broad forehead present an immense frontage; the head is held high, with the trunk curled between the tusks to be uncoiled at the moment of attack; the massive forelegs come down with the force and regularity of ponderous machinery; the whole figure is rapidly foreshortened, and appears to double in size with each advancing stride.

An elephant may admittedly be shot without the sportsman being in any great peril; by coolness and good shooting it is possible to settle the matter with a single shot, but if he does charge the moment is one of supreme danger. The crux of the matter is that although it is as easy to hit an elephant as a haystack, the vital target is very small. The weight of bone, tissue and muscle virtually rules out the shot at the shoulder, and there remains only the brain, which even in a large animal measures no more than twelve inches by six. Located between the eye and the ear, it presents a constant target from the flank, but from the front allowance must be made for the rapidly changing angle of head and trunk; and in the heat of the moment it is by no means easy to pick the spot at which to fire. ...

Elephant and buffalo might have their champions, but when all was said and done there was something distinctive about shooting a tiger; something the griffin, the young man fresh out from England, could quite literally write home about. ...

Apart from all that there was a practical aspect to it. In the very early days in Bengal tigers were so numerous as to be a real threat to the community. They might be seen in twos and threes along the public highway, and every year they were responsible for the deaths of hundreds of villagers. In 1782 Paul, a noted German shikari who lived in Calcutta, shot twenty-three in a week. They were comparatively plentiful till a much later date, and in the 1850s a district officer in the Central Provinces, who should have known better, shot sixty in two years before handing over his district on promotion.

The elephant as an animal you shot from, not at, is the key figure in nearly all the tiger-shooting stories of the early days. The sportsman on the back of the elephant was faced with a problem familiar enough to gunnery officers of the Royal Navy and tank crews of the Royal Armoured Corps: how to shoot from a moving platform. It was, moreover, a platform that apart from the eccentricities of pitch and roll might without warning change direction by 180°.

To be able to take a snap shot from the back of a moving beast was the outcome of much practice, but it was something the sportsman had to learn to do. He could hardly expect to win the confidence of the mahout unless he could demonstrate his ability to shoot fast, shoot straight and keep on shooting in an emergency.

A good elephant was the sportsman's best friend, and simplified tasks that would otherwise have been difficult or extremely dangerous. A bad elephant was a danger to life and limb. If he took fright and bolted those on his back ran the risk of being swept off by overhanging branches. In the words of one who had experience in the matter: 'You might as well try to halt a bolting elephant as stop a railway engine by hooking a walking stick round the funnel.' There is a story of an elephant which was slightly mauled before the tiger that attacked it was shot dead at its feet. It disgraced itself by bolting, the howdah and its occupants being swept off as it passed under a low overhanging branch. That evening the elephant was rubbed down with the fat of the tiger and its staunchness was never again in question. ...

Forsyth's view was that the finest way of tiger shooting, the *crème de la crème* of the sport, was for a man to shoot on his own, in the fierce hot months before the monsoon when cover was less dense, setting out after breakfast on a single elephant, in search of a known tiger over a well-reconnoitred piece of ground. Both elephant and mahout had to be trained for this sort of work. If they were, then the elephant was very much more than just a mount to carry you through the jungle. He would take an active and intelligent interest in the proceedings, and could almost learn to talk. His vocabulary was limited, consisting of a single word, but it could never be misunderstood. An elephant on the scent strikes the end of his trunk on the ground, producing a sound like the tap of a drum. He never makes this sound except when he is close on a tiger. A writer in the *Oriental Sporting Magazine* describes a famous animal named Hyder Guj.

> He was one of the best in India. I have seen him discover a tiger with as much ease as a pointer would a partridge. He makes the sound above described and points with his trunk in the direction in which the tiger is lying; the mahout has no occasion to guide him for he will carry you straight up to the tiger's lair or tear away the bushes which conceal him. When the tiger is discovered, Hyder stands as steady as a rock until you have fired, and if the tiger is only wounded will follow with apparently as much eagerness as the sportsman in the howdah; if killed, will put up his trunk for his well-earned *seer* of *gur* (two pounds of rough brown sugar).

Considering again the comparative stopping power of the rifles in use in those days it is not surprising to find a number of stories where things went wrong and a tiger managed to establish a foothold on the elephant before it was killed. Fatal accidents were more common than in recent times. ...

They had strange ideas about diseases generally. It was universally accepted that malaria, or jungle fever, was contracted through breathing the unwholesome air that arose from damp ground. Various preventative measures were suggested. One man had a half circle of fires kept burning up wind of his camp so that the warm air wafted the poisonous vapours over his head. Another thought they could be dispelled by smoking cheroots.

The early Nimrods were the founders of a great tradition. Life in civil station or cantonment might be petty and boring, but there was no lack of excitement for those who chose to go in search of it. It could never be boring, it might be dangerous: it would seldom be easy, you won success in the sweat of your brow. And they were men with a tremendous zest for the good things of life. When the hero of *Seonee* got back to breakfast after a start before dawn he expected to find ready for his repast 'omelettes and kitchree, dry curries, a round of cold corned beef, potted wild duck, eggs, toast and chupattis'. At the end of the day he and his young friend gathered round a roaring fire after 'a hearty dinner of soup, sanwal fish from the lake, a roast haunch of black buck, pintail duck and blue bull marrow bones, with a bottle of good Burgundy'.

Forsyth was firmly of the opinion that although every sensible man in India spends his Christmas in the jungle he need not forgo the traditional fare.

> We spent a Christmas of considerable joviality in that remote wilderness, dinner consisting of a peacock and sambar tongue, supported by roast haunch of red deer venison, as *pièces de résistance* with cheetal cutlets and fillets of nilgai veal as *entrées*, followed up by boiled quails and roasted teal, and concluded by the orthodox plum-pudding and mince pies out of tins. Sundry glasses of whiskey toddy, imbibed round a rattling bonfire in front of the tents, were fully justified by the really severe cold after sunset.

No one went into the jungle without a good supply of claret, and it is by no means uncommon to read of an exceptional day's sport being celebrated by cracking a couple of bottles of well-iced champagne. ...

A. BLOOMFIELD

The Mad Elephant of Mandla

(Thirty years ago Col. RW. Burton obtained and passed on to the Society a manuscript copy of Col. A. Bloomfield's 1871 pamphlet on the shooting of the rogue elephant of Madhya Pradesh, celebrated by Rudyard Kipling as the mad elephant of Mandla in the Second Jungle Book. We are serializing a condensed version.—Eds of *Hornbill*.)

In one of the many disturbances that took place during the troublous times that prevailed in Berar between 1830 and 1840, a male Elephant escaped from his master at Ellichpur and made off in a northerly direction into the jungle and forests that clothe the range of hills that extend thence across the Central Provinces to the Eastern Ghats overlooking the Bay of Bengal. He was there, a veritable 'needle in a haystack' and it is not wonderful that those who went in search failed to find him.

Thence he roamed the forest-clad hills into the Chindwara district, in the dominions of the Rajah of Nagpur. The Rajah sent off detachments of Infantry and Cavalry to effect his capture. The pursuit was continued for months, every known device being tried to secure him, until at last, the elephant leaving the Chindwara hills, passed south not far from Nagpur city and thence turning to the North-East, found his way into the Balaghat hills forming the

From A. Bloomfield (1871), 'The Mad Elephant of Mandla'. Condensed version of MS copy published in *Hornbill* 1981(3), 1981(4), and 1982(1).

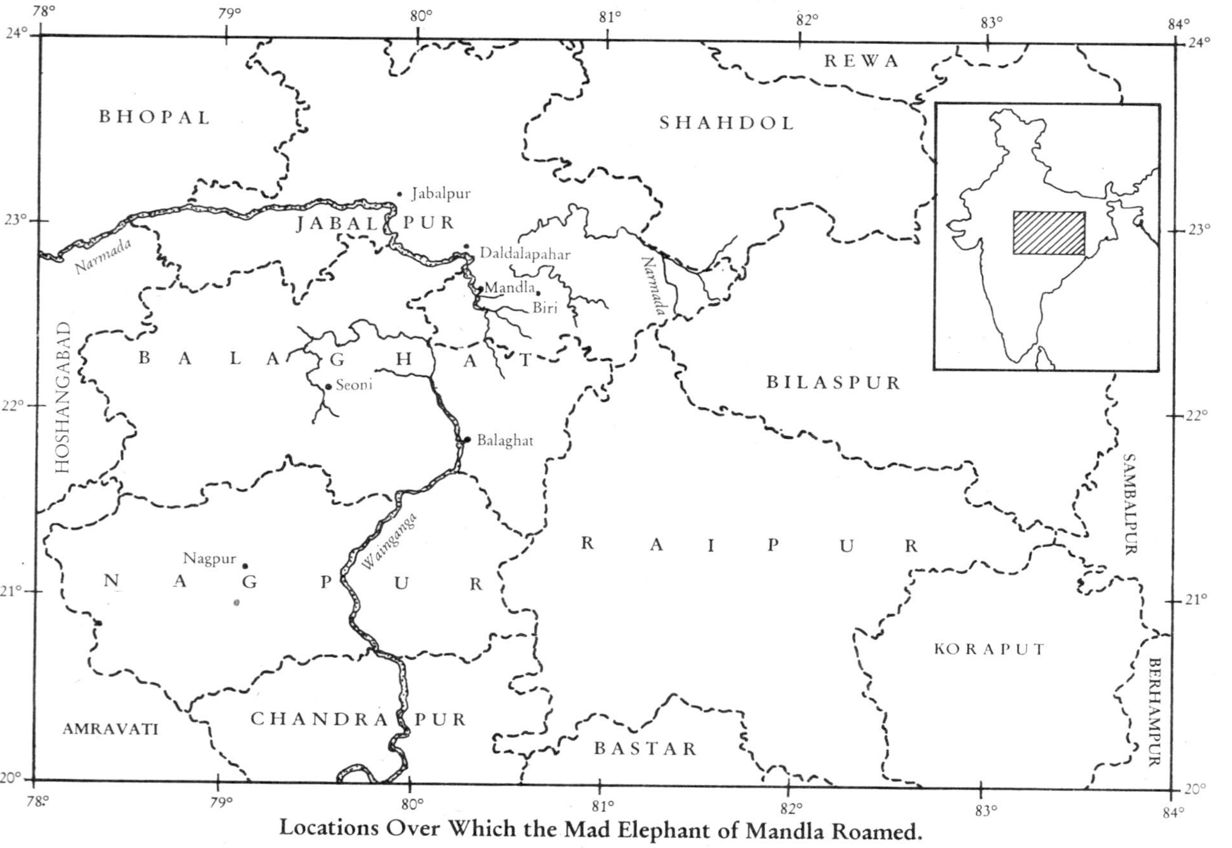

Locations Over Which the Mad Elephant of Mandla Roamed.

North-Eastern boundary of the Nagpur plain country. These hills are from 1700 to 2800 feet above the level of the sea, and for about 20 to 30 miles from the scarp are covered with dense forests of bamboos and various kinds of trees; and quite uninhabited except by a very few widely scattered villages of the aboriginal tribes of Gonds and Baigas. Here, too, his pursuers followed and tried by pitfalls (still to be seen), and other devices to capture him, but without avail.

Here in these beautiful hills and forests he remained and roamed about wherever he liked. Everywhere he found abundance of food in the fruits, foliage and roots. He was seldom disturbed or even seen by any human being and never damaged or even visited the few scattered patches of rough cultivation within his reach. When in 1868 I joined the Balaghat district as Deputy Commissioner, he was in the pathless forests further North in the Bhaisanghat range and on the borders of the Mandla district. He was on rare occasions seen by the wild forest tribes, but it was only in the rainy season that he sometimes visited the semi-cultivated tracts in the neighbourhood of Bhimlat, where he was said sometimes to have amused himself by playing with the ploughs left in the fields and carrying them from one village to another. Apparently he did not much damage the crops, for no complaints were made about him.

There are in the Central Provinces no wild elephant anywhere except the Matin and Uprora Zamindaries of the Bilaspur district, some 250 miles from these jungles. This elephant therefore, hard pressed for companions, was said to pass most of his time with two wild buffaloes, which sometimes, so the rumours were, he used to chastise in his displeasure.

On several occasions, when passing through the forests, I used to come upon his huge foot prints, several months old, made during the preceding wet season. I used to enquire about him, but my time was too much occupied with my official duties to admit of my entertaining any idea of following him up.

Moreover I was not satisfied that it would be right to kill a harmless animal, which if by any chance captured would prove both useful and valuable. It would have been quite a wild-goose chase to have followed him without obtaining certain information and fresh tracks.

It was not until the cold weather of 1870–1 this elephant brought himself conspicuously to the notice of the public by entering the Mandla district and killing several people.

Having no personal knowledge of his exploits in that district, I cannot perhaps do better than copy some official papers that were published at the time in the Local Official Gazette.

The Elephant is reported to have killed 21 persons (6 men, 8 women and 7 children) between 27 January and 17 February.

According to the reports made by the Police, the Elephant made his appearance in the night of 26th–27th January in the Saliwara circle (in the East of the district) at the village of Tar̀raj, about 9 miles south of the station house. The villagers first took refuge on the roofs of the houses, but a woman and child attempted to escape by running away and thus attracted the brute's attention. He pursued and killed them close to the village.

On the night of the 30th January he killed a woman at Barbaspur, 9 miles west of Kukramat outpost, in the Ramgarh circle tearing her limb from limb; and on the night of the first February he killed a man and a woman at Kamria, a village near Barbaspur; on his next approaching Dongria the villagers tried to escape by flight, but he overtook and killed 2 old women tearing them to pieces. The villagers declared, he actually devoured these women. One woman at this place had a narrow escape with her life, the elephant having placed his foot on her chest.

From here he appears to have gone to Manori, 12 miles south of Ramgarh at night, and killed a woman and two children whose bodies were not recovered. The report of this did not reach the station house till some 20 days after the occurrence. It was made by the Kotwar (village watchman) who stated he was an eye witness of the tragedy.

Passing on, he came on the morning of the 5th February to Karbeli, 9 miles south of Ramgarh and twice entered and left the village, killing a baby which he snatched from its mother's arms; and the same evening he killed a man at Katholi Dadar, an adjacent village. This victim he is said to have devoured. Thence at 8 p.m. that night, going to Nighari in the same neighbourhood, he killed and is said to have devoured an old woman 80 years of age.

On the night of the 7th February, he came past the Ramgarh Tahsil and station house into the adjacent village of Umrerpur—the Police turned out to the number of 12 or 14 and fired at him.

He retreated towards Bijori, a mile to the east and killed a man and a boy on the banks of the nala.

The next night he surprised on some hills three or four miles west of Ramgarh, some people of Nanda, who had, through fear, deserted their village and taken refuge in the jungle. He took a baby out of its mother's arms and destroyed it.

From Ramgarh the elephant turned off towards Shahpura to the north, and surprising some travellers of Shahpura, killed one of them.

He killed, seemingly on the succeeding night, a man at Beljara, some 6 miles east of Belgaon. Thence he seems to have gone off to Salaya, a village near the Mheswani outpost, without doing further mischief on the way. Salaya I should say must be 25 to 30 miles from Belgara. At Salaya, which he reached on the 14th February, the villagers all escaped in time, save one boy, who was rolled about and apparently played with by the elephant, which left him without killing him, and then went into the village and pulled down several houses.

The next report states that on the 15th February the elephant wounded a man and a woman at Matiari, 12 miles west of Mheswani outpost, rolling them about on the ground and inflicting various injuries but not killing them. He also destroyed a house in the village.

The next report is from the Narainganj station house dated 19th February stating that the elephant had, on the night of the 17th killed one man and wounded another at Bistaria 21 miles north of the station house, and that on the 21st the Chief Constable started with a party in pursuit.

Soon after the first reports were received, the Deputy Commissioner in my absence from the station, directed a re-inforcement of 6 police to be sent to Ramgarh station house. These men took up the pursuit of the elephant and followed him across the Narbada river near Mheswani into the Narainganj circle where they were joined by the Chief Constable of that station house. The elephant re-crossed the Narbada near Shringarpur in the Mandla circle towards the end of February. I arrived at Shringarpur the day after he had come there. From the traces found, there seems no doubt that he took refuge in a large hill called Daldalli pahar, which is covered with thick jungle. I think that there is little doubt that the

Constable's pursuit of the brute rendered him timid and disinclined to attack human beings as recklessly as before. He appears also to have been wounded.

He is a fine large animal with tusks said to be three or four feet in length. He no doubt commenced this series of attacks being in a state of 'must'! and the cessation of his bloodthirstiness may be also imputed partly to the cessation of his 'must'. I am not sufficiently acquainted with elephants to say how long they remain in that state.

In 1868 and also in the following years, a wild elephant, possibly this one, appeared in the district but did no mischief to life and little to property.

This is the plain official report of the Superintendent of Police of the Mandla district of the performances of the elephant in that district in the early part of 1871. During the seven months of hot weather and rainy season, nothing was either heard or seen of the animal, but with the approach of the cold weather again he became 'must' and distinguished himself as shown in the following narrative.

On the afternoon of the 2nd of November 1871, I had just completed the trial of a heavy criminal case and was sitting in the small court room in the wonderful building that in those days accommodated everybody and everything representing the Government in the district, when in walked F.A. Naylor, the officer-in-charge (i.e. District Superintendent) of Police and said—'That man-eating elephant that killed so many people in the Mandla district in the beginning of the year, has appeared in this district and killed and partly devoured a man near Behir,' the headquarters of the tahsildar (sub-divisional officer) of that part of the district. I said 'All right, we must stop his fun and will start as soon as possible.'

That evening when our work was done we prepared our batteries and ammunition. It may interest some to know of what they consisted. Mine were 2 twelve-bore breach loaders recently made to order through Mr G.W. Bales, of Ipswich. The rifle weighed 12 lbs with 28 inch barrels, grooved after Forsyth's (high-initial-velocity) principle and carrying spherical-faced solid lead conical bullets weighing 6½ to the pound (about 1077 grains) each. Ordinarily with these I used 4½ to 5 drams of gun-powder, but for this special business I loaded with nearer 6 than 5 drams—my second weapon was a rather heavy smooth-bore with 4 drams of powder and spherical bullets. Naylor had a rather heavy No. 12 single-barrelled rifle and a No. 12 smooth-bore.

This being the time of the year when Civil Officers are expected to be often out in the district under canvas, all our equipage with buffaloes for carriage was ready.

Without loss of time we started. Naylor had to go due north considerably out of his way to attend to a police case at Mau in the upper Wainganga Valley, promising to join me with the least possible delay at Behir, and thence take up the trail together. I went by the direct route via the Warri (windy) pass up the hills 700 feet high towards Behir. Fortunately during the three years I had held charge of the district, I had caused the Baigas, the wildest of the wild aboriginal tribes of the Central Provinces, to become my great friends. When I first knew them in 1868 they left their villages and disappeared in the jungles whenever any Government Official or stranger approached, but by this time they had become very friendly, and not only joined my camp whenever I marched anywhere near their villages, but also occasionally paid me flying visits in the plains below. They are a chip of the block of aborigines who from time to time had been severed and pushed back by the various tribes that have invaded India. They, and those like them, are now to be found in only a few remote places. They live in as wildly natural and primitive a state as any people in the world. The whole worldly possessions of one of their families consist [of] vessels worth altogether about one shilling. Their houses are made of sticks, bamboos, grass and leaves, without even a thought of nail, saw or hammer, or any other tool save their ordinary axe.

The clothing of the men consists of a strip of cloth a few inches wide round the loins and a smaller and more ragged piece round the head. The women generally possess a piece sufficient to cover them from their arm-pits to their knees.

As I passed under the frowning forest-clad cliffs of the Khandaparh hill I did not forget a very snug little village of Narotia Baigas that was safely hidden from view in the secluded nook far up near the summit. Anticipating that some tracking would have to be done I sent word to the Baigas to join my camp.

That afternoon (3rd November 1871) I reached Jatta, a small village about 8 miles south of Behir. There I found encamped, Mr Hankin, District Superintendent of the Mandla Police. He told me that he had pursued the elephant from the Mandla district but could not get near it. He said the more he pressed it and the harder he worked to get near it the further it seemed to get away from him.

He was a keen sportsman and I was much disappointed when he told me he could not possibly stay and help me, but must return the next morning to his own district.

On enquiry I found that on the 27th October, the elephant had invaded Singhbagh-tola (*Tola*—clusters of houses detached from the main part of the village) a small hamlet of Behir about 15 miles from the Mandla border. At this time of the year, when the crops sown in June, the beginning of the rainy season, are well advanced towards harvest, the cultivators whose lands are within reach of wild animals, erect machans (platforms on poles 10–12 feet high and covered over with an arch of bamboo matting) in their fields, from which to watch their crops and drive away wild animals such as deer of all kinds and wild pigs.

Where these abound tigers, panthers, and bears are occasional visitors and therefore it is necessary to have the platforms a considerable height from the ground.

Though sometimes, as in the case of the celebrated man-eating panther of Asola of the Wardha district, panthers that have acquired a taste for human blood, mount the machans and drag down the occupants. Hence in jungly places the practice is for two persons to occupy one machan, one sleeps while the other watches. A fire is frequently kept burning near the foot of the machan.

That night at Singhbagh-tola, an old Gond and his son were thus watching their crops. In the middle of the night when the cold in these uplands keeps all the thinly-clad natives in as warm places as they find, the son heard approaching the heavy footsteps of some animal that never before had visited his fields. No tiger, no panther or other small animal could make noises such as now fell upon his ears with ever increasing distinctness. At last when it had come quite near, he realized that it was an elephant, and as there were no elephants, tame or wild within at least 50 miles, he knew it must be the dread animal that a few months before had destroyed so many human beings in the Mandla district. He immediately awoke his father and hurrying down from the machan and calling for his father to run for his life, he ran off to the village as far as his legs could carry him. His father endeavoured to follow him but was too late; the huge brute was upon him and quickly smashed him up into the shapeless mass he was found by his family when the next day they came to search for him.

Whither the elephant went on the 28th October no one knows, but on Sunday night the 29th he appeared in the fields north of the village of Jatta. There he entered the rice fields of a Gond, who with his wife was in a machan keeping watch. The wife, a mere child, was on the alert, for she had heard of the doings of the elephant two nights before.

As soon as she became aware of his approach she roused her husband and remembering that two boys were in a machan in the next field, rushed down and calling the boys, fled with them to the village. Here as in other places all the houses belonging to a village are clustered close together. Her husband apparently did not believe her when she first gave the alarm and was not so quick in his movements as he might have been. The elephant pursued and killed him. The next day his scattered remains were found, the head nearly severed from the body, the lower part of the body with the right leg attached was some distance away and the left leg had been torn off and thrown several yards further.

Not being able to find any more victims in the fields on the north of the village, the elephant wandered round to the south. The watchers scattered about the fields became aware of his approach and fled to the village. But one poor old Gond, who certainly was not capable of much running, told me that as the others fled he necessarily fell behind. He ran for dear life as fast as he possibly could but behind him the heavy crashing of the elephant through the standing rice came nearer and nearer. At last in his frantic efforts to get away he turned completely over and fell on his back and before he could get up the elephant was upon him and thrust his two huge tusks deep into the ground on either side of his body. 'I thought,' the old man told me, 'that I should be immediately killed, so I placed my hands one on each of the tusks and called to our God Ganesji and immediately the elephant left me and went away.' This was certainly a most extraordinary escape and I questioned the old man with a view to ascertain how much he had drawn upon his imagination, but he consistently maintained his story, and was quite sure he had his hands on the elephant's tusks.

The elephant next went to a small hamlet Telitola to the south-west of the village of Bhanderi. There he amused himself by pushing in and pulling down the walls and roofs of six houses and helping himself to the grain he found stored therein.

The houses of the Gonds are but flimsy structures quite unable to resist anything approaching such a ponderous attack. The walls are merely coarse bamboo mats plastered within and without with mud. The roofs are made with rafters about the size of one's arm, laid and tied on with strips of bark without anything approaching a nail. Much of the inside of the houses of the poorer classes is occupied by large square dolhas (receptacles) of bamboo matting, made air-tight by being plastered with mud inside and outside. At the gathering in of the harvest these are filled with grain for the use of the household. The elephant went from house to house lifting up the thatch, knocking in the gable ends and inserting his huge trunk pulled down the grain dolhas and broke the earthen vessels and devoured and scattered everything he could reach. Had he eaten what he wanted and left the remainder alone he would have done comparatively little damage, but he seemed to delight in scattering about and destroying everything he could touch.

As the inmates of each house he attacked fled, he pursued them but when they escaped from him, he returned to their houses and completed his work of destruction. Many of the people thus frightened, collected in the house of the local pujari, the person who performs all religious ceremonies, and pretends to cast out devils, decide boundaries, shut tigers' mouths and so forth. But the elephant had no regard for all these things and came to the pujari's house. This was a fine opportunity for the pujari to display his priestly powers. This he attempted to do, for, when the elephant began to pull his house to pieces he took up a position inside the doorway and said 'Oh Ganesh Maharaj, spare me this time, I have many children in the house, and I am a poor man!' The elephant then shook his head, being evidently deaf to all his prayers and turning round went out off the enclosure to commence to tear down the back of the house. This was too much for the terror-stricken people huddled together inside; they all, headed by the pujari, fled to the village of Bhanderi and remained there two days.

This was the state of affairs when I arrived with my camp at Jatta on the morning of the 3rd November (1871). The elephant had disappeared and no one could give me any clue as to the direction he had taken. The small piece of partially cleared country in which Behir and Jatta are situated is surrounded on all sides by hills as much as 1000 feet above, covered and embedded in thick pathless tree and bamboo jungles, and shoots of the vast forest tracts that stretch in the north through the Mandla district to Rewa; on the east to the hills bordering the west and north of the Chatisgarh plain round to Amarkantak; south to the wilds of Bustar; and west to the range overhanging the Wanganga valley. Mr Hankin had sent out scouts but they had not returned and nothing could be learnt about the monster further than that he had been seen going south, after pulling down the houses in Telitola, and was probably hidden in the jungles hard by. In short the elephant would have proved a veritable needle in the haystack of the surrounding forests, had not my good friends the Baigas from Khandaparh been at hand ready to assist.

I advanced them a few rupees to supply themselves with food and sent them off to the south to extend east and west as they went, and to send back at once and report as soon as they struck any certain or likely trail.

Having thus made my dispositions, I could do nothing but wait for information. Without it, to move at all might take me in the wrong direction.

I had not to wait long, for in the afternoon some of the Baigas of Deodongar Hill brought a message from my detachment of Baigas I had sent south, that 3 days before, the elephant had passed through the Baiga village of Jagla 9 miles south of Jatta.

Later in the day another report from the same direction came to the effect that the elephant had passed through the Baiga village of Limoti; and the following day had killed two men in the villages of Kudapahar and Mandar, 14 miles further south. This information was most satisfactory, for it left no doubt as to the direction the elephant had taken.

The next morning, early when the first sign of daylight appeared, I started in pursuit. The track we had to follow lay through the wildest country, rugged, stony hills covered with occasionally a small open valley that marked the site, where after the forest had been cut down by the Baigas, Gonds had settled and by their plough cultivation had broken up the land and prevented the forest from recovering itself. However the overhanging trees had not prevented the lower growth of vegetation, the rank grass and reeds were about 7 feet high and were so wet from the heavy dews that always prevail at that time of the year, that although I was riding a fourteen-hand Arab I had not gone far before my clothes were wet through up to my waist. And as for my attendants who were on foot, the heavy grass that overhung our path drenched them from head to foot. I selected for this work the Bay Arab, Mozart, a horse that a few years before had carried off everything on the Kampti race course and was perfect in courage and steadiness, even though a gun were fired off between his ears.

All the way we followed the tracks of the huge monster. Wherever the ground was soft his foot prints were perfect, and ever and anon some one of my attendants would stop, and measuring the prints, enlarge upon the probably huge dimensions of the enemy. Eight or nine *(hath)* cubits (12 to 14 ft) was the least they put him at for, had not the people of the villages he had already attacked, told he was as tall as the ridges of their houses, with tusks equal to a man's height in length.

On the way we learned that during Monday (30th October) and Tuesday (31st Oct.) the elephant had been in the Barwahi jungles, and then following on his way the little huts which the Baigas had erected on their clearings as watch houses and with one solitary exception had eaten all the grain in them.

Jagla was situated on the very highest point of a hill, about 2700 feet above the level of the sea. Rising abruptly some 800 feet from the expanse of almost trackless and impenetrable forest, it was itself densely covered with bamboo and tree forest except in a few places where the huge boulders of granite, piled one above another, defied the efforts of the hardiest shrub to obtain a footing.

As we approached no road or well-marked path showed that any human habitation was near, and no voice of man or animal, domesticated or otherwise, broke the stillness of the vast solitude. Our Baiga guide steadily followed the narrow track the elephant had followed. It appeared to be no more than a wild animal's track marked by the blazes on the trees that the Baigas always make to show the way to their newly formed settlement.

The top of the hill, not an acre in extent, had been cleared of all trees and undergrowth, and, in the middle of it stood the small square of Baiga houses, closed all round, with merely a narrow passage between two of the houses in the northwest corner. In the centre was the usual 'Mandwa', and close to it a stout-pole about 10 feet high, surrounded by a bunch of peacock's feathers, and below this bunch, stuck into it, a small axe with a head only 3½ inches long by 1¼ inches wide, and a hair rope and iron whip hung over it. The small axe is dedicated to Bhimsen, and the Gurz (iron whip) to Gansham Deo. These things showed that the pujari of the village was a professed medicine man, who when possessed by his Deo could while flogging himself unharmed with the iron whip, effect miraculous cures of all ailments.

But his miraculous powers availed him nothing, when on that Tuesday (31st October) midnight the sleeping village was suddenly aroused by the lifting up of the roof and the crashing in of the gable end on the northeast of the square. The fame of the destroyer had come before him, so that even if the brilliant tropical moon had not rendered the elephant clearly visible, they would all have known the meaning of the crashing, tearing sound. So rapidly did he break into the first house, that the Baiga and his wife had barely time to make their escape into the pujari's house on the south of the square, where the other inhabitants quickly collected in the hope that the holiest and strongest of the houses would escape or resist all attacks.

The elephant not finding anything in the first house, partly broke down and explored several others, and then walking into the middle of the square examined the pole and the things on it. All this time the trembling shivering Baigas, crowded into the pujari's house, watched through the many crevices in the walls, the movements of the monster; and when they saw him leave the houses and go to the standard, they thought he had finished his work of destruction. But, to their horror he turned towards the pujari's house and began tearing ('Torrtarr' as they called it) and lifting up the roof of the house. The Baigas described to me the terrible state of fear they were in, as they crouched shivering at one end of the gradually crumpling hut. They fortunately uttered not a sound and as they described it 'ceasing to breathe, their bodies dried up'. Had they made any noise, the blood-thirsty brute would certainly have forced his way in and smashed up some of them. Certainly some of the people that had interviewed this elephant did seem literally dried up, for, as they told me their stories a few hours afterwards, they seemed absolutely terror-stricken and, with their hands clasped before them, shrank as if still overshadowed by the elephant. Their brown skins prevented their faces from looking pale, but their colour changed to a livid hue as if half way to death.

Just as the poor Baigas began almost to feel the breath of the elephant as he moved his trunk about inside the house, the brute suddenly stopped his work of destruction, and turning out of the village stood on the edge of the plateau leisurely swinging about his trunk, tail, and one or other of his legs with that restlessness so universal with healthy elephants.

After standing in this way a few minutes, the elephant turned, and going in a southerly direction, disappeared in the forest. I have never ceased to wonder why, after 40 years of wildlife in the hills and forest in the north, this wonderful creature deliberately turned to the south and made his way towards those plains where he had spent his early days in captivity. Was it instinct or was it fate that thus led him back to his destruction?

A few hours after leaving Jagla, the elephant appeared at Limoti, another Baiga village a few miles further south; another small inhabited spot in this vast ocean of forest. There, three wayfaring Gonds were sleeping in the open 'mandwa' in the village square. They were awakened by the approach of the elephant and immediately jumped in, fled in different directions into the jungle—one was pursued by the elephant, but escaped among the rocks and bushes. Before the elephant could return to the village, the Baigas had all collected together and with all their drums etc. made such a clamour that the brute turned off into the jungle. I reached Limoti that evening, my men and animals thoroughly tired out by their scramble through rocks and forest tangle.

Here I held a consultation with all my Baiga friends among whom were some fine grey-bearded pujaris who could read the jungles and the signs thereof better than most people. They all agreed that it was most probable that the elephant when he reached the plains in the south, would feel out of his element and turn again north into the hills. I therefore sent out two strong detachments of Baigas, one to the east and the other to the west to prevent the elephant from doubling back north without my being aware of his movements. They were instructed to spread themselves in a long line through the forest so that he could not possibly pass north unnoticed.

On the morning of the 5th November, leaving behind all needless impediments and taking only a small 'Sholdari' tent and other things that could be carried on men's shoulders, I moved on 23 miles via Kurajuri, Kudapahar, and Goderi, below the Ghats to Suswa in the plains of the Hutta Pegana. The first 18 miles were chiefly through absolutely trackless forest. The Baigas alone could possibly have guided me through. In many places there was absolutely no track or path but the trail of the elephant which the Baigas were following without a check kept us in the right direction. Sometimes piles of granite rock through which it was impossible to pass a horse blocked the way and long detours had to be made to get round them. How the elephant managed to get through or over is a mystery. Soon after I started I met some men from the plains below and was not a little surprised to learn from them that the elephant had left the hills and killed two persons at the village of Goderi in the plains.

Up to this I had felt almost sure that the elephant would turn back as soon as he reached the passes leading into the plains and I expected soon to meet him.

At Kurajuri six miles south of Nimboti, some Gonds returning from their fields carrying a large round earthen vessel full of Kutki *(Panicum malicum)* suddenly caught sight of the elephant coming towards them. In an instant they had put down the vessel and disappeared in the long grass and undergrowth. The elephant heard the noise and looking round failed to see the fugitives. But perceiving the vessel which stood on the track the Gonds were following, he came to it and knocking it to pieces with his forefoot, ate as much as he liked and scattered the remainder. He must have eaten very little, for, when we passed by we found the grain scattered over a large surface and pieces of the vessel thrown to a considerable distance. Kurajuri was a village in name only, for it consisted of nothing but a few small huts scattered among tall forest trees that had been left when the land was cleared. The lowest branches must have been some 30 feet from the ground, and the huts in consequence appeared unusually small. The whole scene reminded me of pictures of Central Africa.

Leaving the small clearing around Kurajuri we tracked the elephant through thick bamboo jungle with but few large forest trees. This showed that the country had not many years before been cleared by the Baigas and wilder classes of Gonds. Sufficient time had not elapsed for the forest trees to recover themselves, but the quick growing bamboos had quickly taken possession and covered the whole surface. Viewed from the top of some of the huge piles of granite that were met with in several places, the jungle appeared like a softly rippled surface covered with soft emerald green velvet. All the way we passed through beautiful bamboo arches of every shape and size. Where the soil was thin and stony they were so low that my men on foot could scarcely pass under and I had to dismount and by dent [sic.] of cutting away in places, managed to get my horse through. But where the alluvial soil lay rich and thick, the large bamboos, commonly called 'Kattango' (pronounced kutung) rose up to more than 90 feet in height.

After going about 4 miles we came to the small Gond village of Kudapahar.

Destruction. Wednesday 1st November, the elephant visited this place at night and killed a cowherd who was warming himself by a fire. He jumped up and ran into the jungle where the elephant followed him and found and killed him.

The same night visited Mandar village, knocked over a machan in the fields and trampled underfoot the Gond who was sleeping in it.

Leaving Kudapahar I soon came to a pass leading about 1000 feet down into the plains below. I did not follow the elephant's track, but having reliable information as to his movements I took the shortest route—the so-called pass was only fit for 'Gonds and monkeys'. There was nothing but a winding track over and between the boulders of granite of every shape and size. It was absolutely impossible to ride down and with great difficulty I was able to lead my horse down literally crawling, slipping, and stumbling about without doing himself any serious damage.

Immediately at the foot of the hills I came to the village of Bhanpur, a small Gond village nearly hidden in the bamboos close to the foot of the hills. Here and there amongst the houses were a few large tamarind trees spreading their huge arms around like large pollarded oaks. These were no longer the abode of flying foxes and birds, but bore a plentiful crop of large platforms made of branches and leaves. The people told me that when the news of the invasion of Kudapahar by the mad elephant reached them, they at once made these machans for places of refuge at night or on the arrival of the elephant, and since then they had ceased to occupy their houses at night but always before darkness came on, mounted up into these places. Many civilized beings would have been unable to do so, for a single bamboo with its branches cut off short was the only possible way up, and a very rickety and shaky way it was too.

The elephant did not, however, visit this village having evidently descended the hills further south, near village of Goderi.

Destruction at Goderi. He first came to the tola of Goderi and knocked down two houses. Killed a Marar girl 10 years old after chasing her mother and several other people who managed to hide in a deep water course while the rest fled to the jungle.

After that the elephant turned towards the village (i.e. the main collection of houses) of Goderi, where many of the people had made their abode high up the trees. After tearing down part of a bamboo enclosure he turned towards the centre of the village, where the cowherd, who with his cattle had fled from Kudapahar was encamped under a large Kadam tree *(Nandea orientalis)* but, suddenly turning off went in an easterly direction towards the Deo river that flows under the scarp of the hills.

There on the dry sand in the river bed eight men, who had come from the neighbouring village of Bargaon for bamboos, were sleeping and a few paces from them were five (Dhimars) fishermen and a boy named Fogal. The moon was shining but these people being close under the hills, they were in comparative darkness. This boy happened to be awake. Hearing a noise he looked up and saw something coming towards them. At first he thought it was a tiger, but by the time he had awakened the others, the huge outline of the elephant was within a few yards of them. They all immediately jumped up and with the exception, one, Marar, fled into the thick jungle up the side of the overhanging hill. The elephant pursued them, but by separating in the thick scrub they prevented him from coming with them. He then turned to the bed of the river. The Marar had run about 400 yards down the right bank and slipping down the bank, hid in some thick tamarisk bushes.

The footprints showed that the brute had traced this man step by step, and when he came to where he was hidden he put his forefeet together and slipped down the bank until he was within reach of the man who must have been completely hidden from view. He however pulled him out and smashed him to pieces. When I arrived I found the remains still lying there. The arms and legs looked as if there were no bones in them, for they pointed in all directions and the body and head besides being flattened, had been disfigured by jackals.

That morning, I had started before sunrise when there was barely sufficient light for the Baigas to take up the trail; and although I could not have come more than 18 miles it was 2 o'clock (afternoon) when I arrived at Goderi. While my men were resting and obtaining food, I rode round making enquiries. All around was thick jungle and no one had ventured into them since the elephant came. Owing to the hills, the south and west were the only directions in which the elephant could have gone. As no one could give me any definite information of where the elephant was, I caused the Goderi headman to send out two search parties of four each, to get information with instructions to return as soon as possible. At 4 p.m. no news had arrived and nothing had been heard of the search parties. I could wait no longer. I had several miles of jungle to pass through, and the evenings being very short at that time of the year, I had but little time to do it in. The people all said that the elephant was not far off, so shouldering my rifle loaded ready for action, I marched off preceded by 2 of my Baigas and followed by the remainder of my party. Rumour had it, that the elephant had killed several men in Mate and 7 in Suswa. So I followed the road west to the latter village. I had not proceeded a mile into the jungle, when I met all together the 8 men who had been sent out as scouts, 4 to the west and 4 to the south. I called out to them, 'Where is the elephant?' expecting to hear they had marked him down near by. 'Where he is, we don't know! You had better be quick through the jungle, or you will meet him on the road.' On we went, keeping a sharp look out, and a few minutes after darkness had come on, we arrived in Suswa in the open country beyond.

This night I pitched my tent and accommodated all my people inside a closed courtyard belonging to the village headman. My poor naked Baigas felt the cold much, so I arranged for them an outhouse with a good wood fire in the middle; there with all the food they wanted, the doors closed and the place full of smoke, they were perfectly happy.

The Suswa people told me that the elephant had killed 10 men at the next village Mate, and gone on in an easterly direction to Kinhi.

I learnt that after killing the people at Goderi he had gone to the neighbouring jungles of Batkari, where he was seen by several people the next day.

At 4 p.m. that afternoon he walked into the little village of Mandora and began pulling down the houses. The inhabitants fled into the jungles on the north, except one old man who rushed down south towards the Deo river followed by the elephant. Before he reached the water the elephant had seized him and lifting him up in his trunk smashed him to pieces against his uplifted foot until the other people, amongst them his son, who were looking on from the high ground on the other side of the village, saw only a 'Tempa' (splinter) left in the brute's trunk. At 7 p.m. that evening we returned to this village and then went towards Mate.

Leaving Suswa early in the morning (of 6th November) I came to Mate village. The whole village turned out to meet me, and as I rode through their fields, they told me the destruction the elephant had caused, and that to propitiate him they had held grand ceremonies in honour of their God Ganesh and had freshly covered with brilliant vermilion paint all images of him. Since the elephant's visit they had all slept inside the village in the strongest houses.

Destruction at Mate. About 11 p.m. Friday 3rd November 1871 before the moon had risen the elephant was seen in the village coming towards a group who were warming themselves beside a fire. Knocked down a machan in which were Ramu Marar and his nephew, and the nephew was killed while Ramu remained quiet when he fell.

After this the elephant left Mate and turned west towards Kesa.

Destruction. Moonlight night. A man and a woman killed.

Thence (from Kesa) the elephant turned again westward towards Dhatta, another small village in the plain and entered the fields in the early hours of Saturday, the 4th November 1871 and killed one man and a girl 6 years old.

TOTAL PEOPLE KILLED

Nandar village	1
Markapahar	1
Mate	4
Kesa	2
Dhatta	1
Dhaidi	1
Total	10
Wounded at Mate	2
	12

Thus in one night, the 3rd November Friday and Saturday, the 4th November 1871 did this unequalled savage brute kill and pound to pieces ten human beings and wounded 2 others. A piece of butchery that has never before been anywhere approached by any man-eating tiger or any other brute. A record that is not likely to be surpassed or even equalled. It is a most extraordinary fact that though none of these villages were 10 miles away from Goderi, where 2 persons were killed the night before, yet no one had heard that he had killed some people at Kudapahar and Mandhar in the jungles above the hills but they could not believe that the brute would leave the forests and venture out into the open plain.

Note. During the whole of the forenoon of Saturday the 4th November 1871 the elephant was in a scrub jungle between the village of Sale and the Deo river. Hundreds of people collected on the high ground on either side and, from a good safe distance, watched the brute feeding on the bamboos in the ravines, and enjoying himself in the water (Deo river).

That day, there was the ordinary weekly market day (bazaar) in Dhaidi. About 3 p.m. some 14 or 15 people of Mate, headed by Ganpat Singh, the tall and stalwart Rajput, headman, and armed with 2 guns, swords, etc. etc. determined to make an effort to reach the Dhaidi market. They arranged that they would first reconnoitre from the high bank of the river, and then, if necessary, having fired off a shot or two at him, to pass over to the market.

Accordingly they all walked down to a place where the river bank was very high and perpendicular with a large deep pool of water below. There 8 of them were standing all in a row vainly looking for their enemy, when suddenly one of those who had lagged behind, rushed up shouting 'Run, run, the elephant has come.' They turned round and there sure enough was the elephant with his ears up close upon them, entirely cutting off their escape by land. A moment's delay meant certain destruction to one or more of them. So sudden and terrifying was the surprise, that no one thought of their weapons, but dropping them into the water beneath, they all jumped in after them, and holding on to the long grass growing out of the bank, they hung there with only their heads above water. Looking up, they saw the elephant's head above them and his huge trunk moving backwards and forwards trying to reach them. The last man to take to the water was Faizu Pinjara, who almost felt the elephant's breath, as he dropped out of reach. He was so thoroughly terrified that the sight of the huge trunk stretching from above towards him, was too much for him. He let go the grass he was holding, and swam towards the opposite bank. Immediately, the elephant saw him he rushed along down stream until he came to a place where the bank was a little sloping, and there, putting his forefeet together and going down on his hind knees, slid down into the water making two huge furrows as he went. Faizu saw this, just as he reached the sand on the other side.

Across this he rushed and scrambled up a perpendicular bank about 5 feet high, caused by the silt in a dry water course being cut away by the falling flood in the river. He had barely got up this and climbed a few feet into a tree, when the elephant breasted it and stretched out his trunk to seize him. 'How far was his trunk from you then, Faizu?' I asked when I came up, and he with his face still showing his fear and his eyes staring from their sockets, held up his left arm and grasping it at the elbow with his right arm he replied (*itna bucha*) 'so much'. Not reaching his victim the elephant pulled down several boughs off the tree, but not being able to get up the steep bank, he turned down stream, found a way up the bank and came back to the tree. The tree was not large, and again the elephant failing to reach the man, broke down all the boughs he could reach all around the tree and then after waiting for some time moved slowly away and disappeared.

Darkness had come on before Faizu ventured to go home, where his pursuit and destruction by the elephant had been duly reported by his companions, who had lost no time in getting out of the river and running home as soon as the elephant followed Faizu.

Their arms were in the river when I arrived on the 6th November, Monday.

When I heard of this performance of this elephant I began to think he was a more formidable adversary than I had anticipated. I had comforted myself that although he might be bold and pursue people at night he would not show much fight in daylight, but I could no longer doubt that his courage was as good by day as it was at night, and when we did meet, the fight would not be one sided.

Ganpat Singh of Mate afterwards told me that when I passed through his village it was commonly said: 'There goes the Sahib; he looks cheerful and grand now but wait till he meets the elephant; the like of the brute was never seen and no earthy bullet can touch him. He will eat up the Sahib horse and all.'

Ganpat Singh added: 'He has so frightened me that the bare sight of your tame elephant makes me tremble.'

The news, that the elephant had tried to kill Faizu and was coming, reached the people assembled at the Dhaidi market. A general panic and stampede ensued, and everyone skeldered with as much as their own and other people's things as they could lay hands on leaving not a little scattered about the ground.

About sunset, the elephant was seen passing through the fields to the north of Sale and breaking down all the machans as he went (why?); he turned round the hills towards Kinhi.

The people of Sale were well satisfied with themselves. The elephant had for a considerable time been quite near to their village, but had never once invaded it nor hurt any of the inhabitants. They particularly impressed this upon me; and their headman, as I passed through, repeatedly assured me that frequent prayers (pooja) to the God Ganesh, and the many ceremonies performed in his honour, had caused the elephant to spare their lives and property.

The people of Kanhi had no idea of the impending danger. They had heard that an elephant had killed several people above the hills, but had not heard of the havoc he had caused at Mate and the neighbourhood.

Destruction. A man and a woman killed.

The elephant then went off to the village of Kandra about 2 miles north, and after he had partly demolished a house, disappeared in the jungle.

He then went to Kadoburra and demolished a house.

Thence he passed on to Kakori about 5 miles south and there threw over a man in his machan and stamped upon the fleshy part of his leg, but he marvellously escaped without any further injury.

Following up this trail of destruction from the early morning at Saswa, I arrived about 3 p.m. at a place called Junawanitola. There all I could learn was that in the early morning of 6th November 1871 he had crashed through some of the outer enclosures of the village and gone off in an easterly direction. Where he had gone to no one knew. None had left the village during the day lest the monster should appear from the heavy jungle not a quarter of a mile away, and, for the same reason no one had ventured to come from elsewhere.

The continued trudge through the heat of two consecutive days had nearly worn us all out. There had been no halt since the morning, nothing to eat, but plenty of water as opportunity offered.

I therefore collected them under a large tree just outside the village, and having arranged for food to be supplied to them, I mounted 'Mozart' and rode off to find the trail. Outside Pipalgaon I came upon it. A man named Misr Konbi, in charge of the headman's threshing floor, had, as the day broke, seen the elephant approaching.

Having thus struck the trail I deputed several of the villagers to follow it up and returned to Junawanitola to prepare my people for a fresh start. While I was doing this a report came up that, as the day was breaking the elephant had passed through Joditola and had been seen in the jungles not far off.

When we were nearly ready to move on, I was not a little pleased to see my friend Naylor ride up. I knew then that I had with me a companion on whom I could implicitly rely to stand with me against any charge the elephant might make or anything else he might do. I believed that Manohar Singh my spare gun bearer, would stand fire, though I felt some misgiving on the subject. Soon we were ready to start without spare gun carriers and some of the Baigas. At the edge of the jungle two of the villagers I had sent forward offered to show us the trail. Leaving our horses outside we entered the thick scrub and soon came upon the fresh tracks. It was not long, however, before we perceived that our village friends were showing the white feather, and, instead of following the best trail, were fooling us by taking up the older ones.

We at once sent them to the rear and putting on Bakt and

Garour, the two best Baigas, before we had gone a mile came upon tracks so fresh that we expected every moment to see our enemy rush out. But we were disappointed for just then we heard loud shoutings outside the jungle that the elephant had appeared. At first we thought the frightened villagers had made a mistake and had seen the tame elephant we had with us. But louder and louder grew the shouts and no room was left for doubt. We rushed out of the jungle to our horses and mounting, rifles in hand, galloped back to Kakori where the brute was said to be. Close by Kakori village we rounded a corner of the jungle and there about a quarter of a mile ahead we saw the huge black monster going away just outside the scrub. We galloped after him,but before we could get within shot he disappeared into the jungle. It was then nearly dark and nothing more could be done.

It appears that he had coolly strolled out of the jungle towards Kakori and amused himself by knocking over the machans and kicking down the banks of the rice fields without deigning to notice some 20 or 30 men, who from a safe distance were watching his operations.

Darkness had come on before we reached Junawanitola, where I had ordered our tent to be pitched. I had previously cautioned my people, since we had commenced the chase, that it was most important to pass the night in secure places that all might sleep undisturbed. What then was my disgust to find, that notwithstanding we had sighted the enemy and knew that he must be in the jungle near by, our people had located themselves in an exposed position, well away from the village.

On a mound close to the jungle stood a square of large mango trees, planted at regular intervals, except in one place on the jungle side; by this gap had they pitched our little tent. A large fire was burning in the middle of the square and round this were clustered our native attendants. There was nothing to prevent the elephant attacking us whenever he liked, and if he had come he must have first come on our tent. But, not wishing to show any anxiety, we made the best dispositions we could for the night. It being certain death to dogs to leave them outside exposed in these jungles we fastened them to pegs round the inside of our tent, that they might give the alarm on anything unusual approaching. Then, between our two beds of straw, we placed a chair with matches and a candle on it, and weapons heavily loaded leaning against it, well within our reach, in fact we quite filled the tent. All ought to have been asleep by 9 o'clock. We slept lightly, but whenever we awoke we heard the incessant subdued chatter of the natives sitting round the fires and it was quite certain they were not getting much sleep.

About 2 o'clock in the morning I was awake and I heard a servant say 'A-re Manohar Singh, did you hear that?'

Manohar Singh 'No, what is it?'

Servant 'Listen!—*tarr; torr, tarr*;—there is the elephant breaking down something.'

Immediately afterwards a servant rushed to our tent and exclaimed 'Sahib, Sahib, the elephant is coming!'

In a moment we were up, and rifles in hand, were standing in the dark outside our tent, ready for action. A distant '*torr, tarr*' certainly could be heard and there could be no doubt that it was the destroyer at work. Exactly what was being broken it was impossible to tell, though in the stillness of the dark night no other sound could be heard, no human voice or cry of any kind. All in our camp was still as death, not a move anywhere; the *torr, tarr* gradually ceased and all was again quiet. But we remained standing there fully expecting that we should have our turn.

But, about ten minutes after the noise had ceased, the Kotwal (village watchman) of Lorangi crept quietly into our camp and trembling and shaking from fear, told us the elephant had passed through their village; smashing down houses right and left as he went. Whither the brute had gone they had no idea. Nothing of course, could be done in the darkness, so cautioning some of our men to be on the look out, we again returned to our tent and fell asleep.

After this, all remained quiet and we were not disturbed until just as the false dawn began to lighten the eastern horizon, when one of our servants rushing up to the tent, and shaking us both in short of suppressed terror-stricken voice said 'Sahib, Sahib, here comes the elephant!,' evidently meaning he was close upon us. In an instant, we were up and out, barefooted and in our night suits (commonly in England called pyjama) and took our positions outside the tent, facing the east. 'There he is,' 'There he is,' whispered our servant, and there sure enough was the huge outline, clear against the dimly-lighted sky, of a dark mass slowly moving towards us. What will he do? I thought. Will he come for us or go for the tame she elephant we had brought with us? But, where was the tame one? She was nowhere visible in the dim light, almost darkness under the trees surrounding our camp! So I shouted out. 'Where is the camp elephant?' A voice from the people on the trees replied, 'No one knows. When the alarm was given at midnight the mahout let her loose and got up one of the trees where he is now.' I immediately turned to Naylor and said, 'Don't fire. That may be the tame one.'

We stood quite still and allowed the monster to approach. When it came within about 20 yards without showing any signs of attack, we knew that it was the friend, and not the enemy. The mahout was called down from his lofty perch where he had secured himself with some of his elephant ropes and gear.

As soon as it was fairly daylight we sent out men to bring in information of the evening's movements and leaving our men to break their fast and prepare for another day's hard work, we walked over to Lorangi to see what damage had been done. Destruction more wholesale than I had yet seen met our eyes. The brute had literally walked straight through the village, not along the roads and paths, but through gardens and enclosures, breaking down houses and fences as he went.

We had not finished our inspection of Lorangi when our scouts brought in word that about daybreak the elephant had disappeared into the jungles of Kosmara, about 4 miles to the east, after having chased several people of that place.

It appears he had passed near Kosamdehi where he chased the village watchman.

Destruction, knocking down houses, chasing people and destroying their store of corn. And thus matters stood when we arrived at Kosmara about 10 a.m. All the inhabitants of that village turned out to receive us, but of the other villages we had passed through that morning not a single man accompanied us. All was intense excitement. The wrecked houses, the partially burnt log and the unthreshed corn that the elephant had scattered about were all shown to us, and many came forward to tell us of the perils they had escaped.

We had no time to listen to their stories, for, the time had arrived for real action. The fact that the elephant generally had begun his work about 4 to 5 p.m. and not retired into the jungles, until 6 to 7 a.m., forced upon me the conclusion that about the middle of the day he must be asleep or bathing or otherwise recruiting himself.

Many ways of destroying him had been suggested to me, e.g. sitting upon a tree over the tied up she-elephant; beating him out with much noise of drums, horns, firearms, etc.; following up on horseback, etc. But I had determined that should opportunity offer we would walk him up in dead silence in the middle of the day, and if possible see him before he could see us. Now was the opportunity. We had come upon his last track in the very nick of time, so that we might probably come up with him about noon, the time most likely for him to be in his deepest sleep. There in front of us was pointed out on the opposite side of the nala (water course) into which he had chased Rupra, his huge footsteps up the bank and his wide track through the long grass and scrub above. Our arrangements were quickly made. First the tame she-elephant was divested of all her trappings and one of her heavy ropes was fastened round her body and neck and under the tail, to enable the driver to stick on or step down in any direction necessary. We determined to take her to attract the wild one, and thereby give the chance of an extra shot in the event of a dangerous charge.

Leaving behind at the houses, our horses and everything else we did not want, we formed our line of an advance. The two best Baigas—Bakt and Garour—armed with spears led the way followed by me; Naylor, Manohar Singh with my smooth bore, Suklal Singh with Naylor's second gun, a policeman with police musket, two Baigas, 2 men leading my 5 dogs taken ready to be slipped and create a diversion in case we were hard pressed, then the tame she-elephant and last 2 more Baigas.

All expressed their readiness to accompany us except the elephant driver who was in so manifest a state of fright that we had to assure him we would shoot him if he lagged behind. All were cautioned to make no more noise than was necessary, and that no one was to speak under any pretence whatever, except on a sudden attack by our enemy. Rupra volunteered to show us the way, but when we descended into the nala and approached the track, he would come no further, having seen enough of the elephant. All three sets of Baigas were cautioned to keep a sharp look out, for with the grass and scrub above our heads it was impossible to say from which direction the attack might come. He might double back near to his track and attack us in rear.

In this order we entered the track. The undergrowth of grass and scrub was above our heads, so thick that we could not see more than 5 to 6 yards through it. Slowly and without a sound we steadily, for more than a mile, followed the trail, the leading Baigas pausing occasionally closely to examine the trail and communicate the result by sundry movements of the hands.

On a high piece of ground overlooking a low place full of long reeds and grass, Bakt suddenly stopped. Starting out with excitement, and pointing forward with his right hand, he said in almost a whisper, or rather hissed out, '*Wuhhai*' 'There he is', and drew back behind me. And there he was sure enough, only 35 paces off, lying sound asleep in the long grass.

He was evidently lying flat on his side with his back towards us, for we could see only the huge arch of his ribs and some of his spine, no parts of his head, neck or tail, were visible. It would have been worse than useless, if indeed not absolutely foolish, to have fired at what I could see. So, I began to creep forward and give him two good shots in the head at close quarters. But just as I began to move, Naylor touched me on the shoulder and signalled for me to move to the left. I had not taken three steps in that direction when I disturbed some dry leaves and twigs. This aroused the elephant and he immediately raised himself on his forefeet as if to listen for more certain sounds. Now was the time his right ear was clearly visible. I fired straight at his ear entrance and immediately afterwards a shot from Naylor followed. The brute disappeared for a moment and thinking to myself 'now comes the charge', I re-loaded the barrel I had fired. I had barely done so when I saw the huge back of the brute going up the opposite bank. Again I fired and hit him in the back. A cane pushed into the wound when he was dead entered nearly three feet. Again loading we gave chase as fast as we could, some of our followers after their manner calling out (*khub laga,* etc.) 'he is hard hit, he can't go far'. The grass was very thick and high and I could barely see ten yards ahead. But exclaiming to Naylor, 'He must be kept going! We must keep the pot boiling and not give him time to get himself together for a charge', we plunged along the track, not knowing the moment we might blunder up against him.

About 200 or 300 yards on we sighted him about 40 yards ahead under a large tree, with his tail towards us, with a small piece of his right check visible. I immediately fired and on he went against at a pace that seemed that we should see him no more. There was no elephantine gallop or long trot that we sometimes see depicted, but after him we rushed and again came suddenly upon him. This time also his tail was towards us, but I could just see behind his left ear, over which he was looking out for us. I got a good shot and planted a bullet behind his ear.

In this way we went on for nearly a mile, pegging into him whenever we got a chance. At last, as we descended into a dry nala we saw our enemy on the top of a high sloping bank opposite. He had chosen an admirable position and was apparently in the act of wheeling round for a charge. But his whole left broadside was exposed, which Naylor immediately took advantage of and planted a bullet in the left side of his head. On this he spun round exposing his right side and I emptied both barrels into the region of his right ear. With a shrill trumpet, he fell on his side, burying one of his tusks deep into the earth. Immediately the she-elephant, coming up behind, probably recognizing the death cry of her race, wheeled round and bolted to the rear, doubtless encouraged therein by her timid rider.

As we rushed up, two police muskets were fired into the fallen monster but there was no movement except a few slow stretchings out of his trunk. The two leading Baigas sprang forward and balancing their spears above their heads and shouting that they must put their spears into the (*badmash adamkhor*) (scoundrel, man-eater) plunged them in with all their might, though with microscopic effect.

At first, we could hardly believe our eyes. There lay the monster, the terror of the country for many miles, that for about a week had been the object of our every movement and the subject of our every thought. The effect on our nerves was most peculiar. A heavy weight seemed lifted up and innumerable tightly compressed springs unloosed. Our success had been complete. We threw our helmets into the air and cheering as if we should never cheer again, patted our Baigas on the backs and congratulated each other all round.

He was in perfect conditions. His skin was glossy black, not the sickly brown of some poor elephants in confinement. Under the skin was a thick coating of fat, and so round was the body as the natives expressed it, as he lay on the ground 'a man standing on one side could not see the man standing on the other side of it'.

The place where he fell was not far from the edge of the jungle, so that the smoke of our last shots had hardly cleared away, when the people from the villages outside began to stream in to gaze on the monster that many looked upon as the incarnation of one of their deities. Until darkness came on and for two or three days afterwards the people crowded in to see the wonder. Even as we marched away we met many still going to see what remained.

Our first thought was how to secure so grand a trophy and we decided to preserve as much as possible. How to sever the head from the body was a puzzle. Among the spectators was a native gentleman armed with sword and daggers. We said to him 'Now is your chance to test your weapons.' But in vain he tried for his sword though fairly sharp, made hardly a visible scratch. Certainly the skin was very tough. We could not cut it at all until with a sharp pointed leather cutters's tool called a 'rapi' we had pierced it and made way for the insertion of a sharp knife. We wished to take off the head and take it to our camp lest the hyaenas and jackals should spoil it during the night.

At last we severed it from the body, but what was our astonishment, when we found that all the men we could crowd round it and all the power we could apply were not sufficient to lift it on to the back of the tame elephant. Nothing could be done but leave it where it was, until by removing the skin and the flesh, we could lighten and make it moveable. We however took the precaution to cut a few boughs and place them on both the head and the body, having learnt from our jungle experiences that no wild animal would come near them, knowing full well that wild animals do not sleep with boughs on them, and recognizing the presence of some human strangers would give it a wide berth.

In the crowd that stood around when the huge head and the four feet were being cut off, were many low caste people who eat meat of any kind when they can get it, and that, but at very long intervals; some even feasting on carcases of animals that have died from any disease. For the benefit of these we called out that they had now a chance of a good meal all round. But all declined and explained that their fathers and grandfathers before them had never eaten anything of the kind. They were in no way moved when we told them that we intended to eat some. That evening we had a piece from one of the feet cooked, but it was so tough, like a steak from a huge it was s tough, like a steak from a huge ship's cable cut crosswise, that we could get through but very little. Flavour, it had none. Perhaps it required keeping! Even the next day when all knew what we had done no one followed our example. 'Oh, no, Sahiblog (Europeans) are unaccountable people and will do anything, but we have a caste to care for and preserve its native purity!'

We probed all the wounds we could find. Besides that quite through the head and the deep one into the loins we found one near the right ear and another near the left that went deep into the skull. The balls from the police muskets had only pierced the skin and appeared like the swellings of incipient boils. There was no trace of any former wounds.

That night we gave an ample feast, both solid and liquid (too much of the latter perhaps) to our Baigas and all our people. Until a very late hour that night the loud noises of merriment were a strange contrast with the usual quiet and repose of our camp.

The next day, the government reward of Rs 200 offered for the destruction of the elephant was paid to the Baigas in attendance. A huge windfall for them, for ordinarily their money earnings, when anything at all, are not more than Rs 2 per month (say one shilling per week). Some soon spent all, but Bakt and others bought bullocks and started as tillers of the soil, a calling quite new to them, but alas! that is another and long story.

The whole of this day was occupied in skinning and cleaning the elephant's head and skinning the body. In the latter, there was a serious difficulty. That part which lay upwards was easily managed, but how about that part between the carcase and the ground? Ten times the power at our command would not have raised that huge mass from the ground. We rolled the skin up close to the carcase, and in vain the tame elephant and about 100 men pulled at the ropes tied on the upper legs and tried to turn it over. Such was the height of the body that the pull was as hard as possible and the rigid mass refused to move.

At last, we devised a series of levers. With long forked pieces of wood in the shape of a leaning W (pieces of young trees 15 ft long), passing the ropes over these, we at last succeeded in pulling over the carcase with a crash that threatened to burst it altogether.

But even when the skin was altogether separated, it was so thick and heavy that any number of men could not lift it. This skin was so lined with fat that it defied drying and rotted except tail and feet. We cut it into four pieces and then got it on to the tame elephant.

Thus ended the career of what, Sir Samuel Baker, of African fame told me, was the worst rogue elephant he has ever heard of. I certainly think I may claim for him the proud position of being 'the record monster' whose atrocities have been or will be seldom or ever equalled.

Private letters and copious notes written at the time have enabled me now to write this fairly complete narrative.

G.P. SANDERSON

The Narrowest Escape

The narrowest escape I ever had in elephant-shooting happened more than a thousand miles from the scene of the above adventures (in South India). It occurred in the Garrow hills, whilst I was in temporary charge of the Elephant Kheddah Establishment in Bengal in 1875–6. Before relating it I will venture to give a short account of these hills, as they are practically a *terra incognita,* even to Europeans in India, not a hundred of whom have ever visited them. The duty which led me into the hills was a prospecting expedition for the elephant-catching establishment. I had with me nine elephants for travelling. The large number in the stud at Dacca enabled me to select good ones, with which I was able to move comfortably and fast.

The Garrow hills are situated on the north-eastern frontier of Bengal and are bounded by Nepaul on the north, and Assam on the east. They are some 4000 square miles in extent, or four times the area of the Neilgherries. They have only been subject to British rule since 1868; prior to this they were independent and unexplored territory. The lawlessness of the Garrows, who made raids into the low country of Bengal from time to time, eventually necessitated their being placed under supervision. For this purpose an armed police force entered the hills in 1868, and established the present

From *Elephant Hunting in India*, 1878. The title is not in the original.

small hill-station of Tura. The hills are now under the Chief Commissioner of Assam. A deputy commissioner, police officer, and surgeon reside at Tura, which boasts of three wooden bungalows, a rough-and-ready style of jail for peccant Garrows, and a compact block of police huts. It has water 'laid on' from the hills above, and neatly-cut walks and rides through the woods near.

Until 1870 this distant abode of the British Lion was defended by a stockade, the palisades bristling with sharp fire-hardened bamboos, whilst the neighbourhood was pleasantly *panjied*. The uninitiated may imagine that this *panjieing* is some ornamental arrangement of the grounds, so I must explain that *panjies* are not a device for the attraction, but for the discouragement, of visitors. They consist of bamboo spikes driven into the ground, almost level with the surface, the earth being scraped away round each so as to form a cup. Hundreds of these are laid in every direction; grass, falling leaves, &c., soon hide them; and if trodden upon they inflict fearful wounds. A place strongly *panjied* is quite safe against night attack or general assault, and can only be approached by a person knowing the locality, or after the *panjies* shall have been disposed of in detail.

The Garrow people are not tall, but are well built, and both men and women have open good-natured countenances. They are warlike and constantly at variance amongst themselves, feuds between different villages being kept up for many years. They have a passion for human heads, and are in the habit of decapitating their enemies. When a village has possessed itself of the head of a member of another, there is no peace between the two communities until the loss has been adjusted by a head from the original offenders. Open fighting is not resorted to so much as stealth. For this reason Garrows seldom venture abroad but in well-armed parties. They believe that a decapitated person cannot be at peace in the next world until they have got another head for him from amongst his murderers. Consequently a sacred obligation rests upon his friends to procure him one. It may be soon, or not for years, but it must be got in the end. When a long interval of time intervenes, they are accustomed to say that their friend in the next world will have a 'very long neck!' Much has been done by the British government since taking over the hills to put a stop to this practice, and it is now only in vogue in villages distant from Tura, and which are still little influenced by British power. I learnt from Captain

Williamson, the Deputy Commissioner at Tura, that if the skulls collected by contending villagers be destroyed, the feud must, by the Garrows' usages, cease, and that he had had an immense number burnt at Tura in presence of the parties interested, though there was no doubt they were but a small portion of the heads still in the possession of the Garrows. ...

The jungles in the Garrow hills differ widely in character from anything to be seen in the south of India. There is a scarcity of heavy timber, owing to immemorial *joom* or *dhaya* cultivation (the felling of heavy forest and sowing for one or two seasons); consequently, in the absence of shade, grass fifteen to twenty feet high, creepers, canes, and undergrowth of all kinds, flourish apace. There is a large amount of bamboo in the hills, but it is of an inferior kind. There are few places where anything like stalking can be done; consequently, though game is plentiful, it is not a desirable hunting-ground. The game comprises wild elephants, a few rhinoceros, buffalo in the lower valleys, bison, bears, sambur, barking-deer, two kinds of pheasants, jungle-fowl (*Gallus ferrugineus*; the common grey jungle-fowl of Southern India—*Gallus sonneratii*—is here unknown); the hullook, or tailless black monkey (and at least two other species); and a few minor animals.

The hills are well suited for elephant-catching; the herds are large, numerous, and undisturbed, and the supply of water and fodder unlimited. There would be some little difficulty about labour at first, as the low-country people fear entering the hills, evil spirits and fevers being supposed to be somewhat prevalent. I therefore decided on this occasion not to commence kheddahs in this locality, but it will probably be one of the most important elephant-fields for the supply of the Bengal Commissariat hereafter.

Having made all the inquiries I desired, I commenced my return-march to the plains of Bengal. This was in October 1875. During the first day's march I passed two large herds of elephants; one probably contained eighty individuals. Next morning I was walking in advance of the baggage-elephants when we heard elephants feeding in a valley to our right. The jungle was tolerably feasible here, so I determined to have a look at them to form an idea of their general stamp, and what fodder they were most intent upon, and other particulars. My gun-bearer, Jaffer, who had accompanied me to Bengal from Mysore, and an experienced mahout to examine

'The Narrowest Escape.'

the elephants, accompanied me, with a heavy rifle in case of accidents. The herd consisted of about fifty individuals, and after examining them for nearly an hour at close quarters, merely keeping the wind, we turned to rejoin the pad-elephant on the path.

Just then a shrill trumpeting and crashing of bamboos about two hundred yards to our left broke the stillness, and from the noise we knew it was a tusker-fight. We ran towards the place where the sounds of combat were increasing every moment: a deep ravine at last only separated us from the combatants, and we could see the tops of the bamboos bowing as the monsters bore each other backwards and forwards with a crashing noise in their tremendous struggles. As we ran along the bank of the nullah to find a crossing, one elephant uttered a deep roar of pain, and crossed the nullah some forty yards in advance of us, to our side. Here he commenced to destroy a bamboo-clump (the bamboos in these hills have a very large hollow, and are weak and comparatively worthless) in sheer fury, grumbling deeply the while with rage and pain. Blood was streaming from a deep stab in his left side, high up. He was a very large elephant, with long and fairly thick tusks, and with much white about the forehead; the left tusk was some inches shorter than the right.

The opponent of this Goliath must have been a monster indeed to have worsted him. An elephant-fight, if the combatants are well matched, frequently lasts for a day or more, a round being fought every now and then. The beaten elephant retreats temporarily, followed leisurely by the other, until by mutual consent they meet again. The more powerful elephant occasionally keeps his foe in view till he perhaps kills him; otherwise, the beaten elephant betakes himself off for good on finding he has the worst of it. Tails are frequently bitten off in these encounters. This mutilation is common amongst rogue-elephants, and amongst the females in a herd; in the latter case it is generally the result of rivalry amongst themselves.

The wounded tusker was evidently the temporarily-beaten combatant of the occasion, and I have seldom seen such a picture of power and rage as he presented, mowing the bamboos down with trunk and tusks, and bearing the thickest part over with his forefeet. Suddenly his whole demeanour changed. He backed from the clump and stood like a statue. Not a sound broke the sudden stillness for an instant. His antagonist was silent, wherever he was.

Now the tip of his trunk came slowly round in our direction, and I saw that we were discovered to his fine sense of smell. We had been standing silently behind a thin bamboo-clump, watching him, and when I first saw that he had winded us, I imagined he might take himself off. But his frenzy quite overcame all fear for the moment; forward went his ears and up went his tail, in a way which no one who has once seen the signal in a wild elephant can mistake the significance of, and in the same instant he wheeled round with astonishing quickness, getting at once into full speed, and bore straight down upon us. The bamboos by which we were partly hidden were useless as cover, and would have prevented a clear shot, so I stepped out into open ground the instant the elephant commenced his charge. I gave a shout in the hope of stopping him, which failed. I had my No. 4 double smooth-bore loaded with 10 drams in hand.

I fired when the elephant was about nine paces distant, aiming into his curled trunk about one foot below the fatal bump between the eyes, as his head was held very high, and this allowance had to be made for its elevation. I felt confident of the shot, but made a grand mistake in not giving him both barrels; it was useless to reserve the left as I did at such close quarters, and I deserved more than what followed for doing so. The smoke from the 10 drams obscured the elephant, and I stooped quickly to see where he lay. Good heavens! he had not been even checked, and was upon me! There was no time to step right or left. His tusks came through the smoke (his head being now held low) like the cow-catchers of a locomotive, and I had just time to fall flat to avoid being hurled along in front of him. I fell a little to the right; the next instant down came his ponderous fore-foot within a few inches of my left thigh, and I should have been trodden on had I not been quick enough, when I saw the fore-foot coming, to draw my leg from the sprawling position in which I fell. As the elephant rushed over me he shrieked shrilly, which showed his trunk was uncoiled; and his head also being held low instead of in charging position, I inferred rightly that he was in full fight. Had he stopped I should have been caught, but the heavy bullet had taken all the fighting out of him. Jaffer had been disposed of by a recoiling bamboo, and was now lying almost in the elephant's line; fortunately, however, the brute held on. I was covered with blood from the wound inflicted by his late antagonist in his left side; even my hair was matted together when the blood became dry. The mahout had jumped into the deep and precipitous nullah to our left at the commencement of hostilities.

How it was that I did not bag the elephant I cannot tell. Probably I went a trifle high, but even then the shock should have stopped him. He was, I believe unable to pull up, being on a gentle incline and at full speed, though doubtless all hostile intentions were knocked out of him by the severe visitation upon his knowledge-box. Had I done anything but what I did at the critical moment there is no doubt I should have been caught. I felt as collected through it all as possible. The deadly coolness which sportsmen often experience is in proportion in its intensity to the increase of danger and necessity for nerve.

Jaffer and I picked ourselves up and pursued the retreating tusker. He was now going slowly and wearily, and we were up with him in two hundred yards from the scene of our discomfiture, but in such thick cover that it would have been folly to have closed with him there; so, as we had the wind, we kept about thirty yards behind him. Unfortunately the bamboo-cover was extensive, and in about a quarter of a mile he joined the herd without once emerging into the open, as we had hoped he would, and afford us another chance. The herd had only gone about two hundred yards at the shot, and were feeding again; and as I feared that following the tusker would only bring us into collision with other elephants, we abandoned the chase and returned to the pad-elephant. Had I only had my Mysore Sholaga of Kurraba trackers with me we should no doubt have recovered the elephant.

A.A.A. KINLOCH

The Asiatic Elephant

I have often heard people talk of Elephant-shooting as cruel and unsportsmanlike; for what reason I cannot imagine. I do not think that anyone who has stood the charge of a wild elephant could describe the sport as tame! I certainly think it is a great shame to slaughter numbers of female Elephants which might be caught and made useful, and which have no tusks to make them worth the shooting; but if the sportsman confines himself to old males he will not do much harm, while he will enjoy one of the most exciting sports in the world. Unfortunately there are few parts of India where Elephant-shooting is now permitted.

I have been singularly unlucky in Elephant-shooting and am still unable to account for not having bagged several fine tuskers; but there is a certain knowledge of angles which one must acquire before one can be successful, and I am not the only man who, though otherwise a fair shot, has failed in his early attempts at Elephant-shooting. The brain is the deadly spot in which to hit the Elephant, but in order to do this the aim must be taken according to the position of the head, and this is what requires great experience. In order to succeed, it is necessary to get as close to the Elephant as possible, anything over fifteen yards being considered a long shot. In approaching an Elephant, the direction of the wind is of paramount importance; no animal has a more delicate sense of smell, though its sight is by no means so acute.

From A.A.A. Kinloch (1892) (3rd rev. edn). *Large Game Shooting in Tibet, Himalayas, Northern and Central India.*

I know few more exciting sensations than that of tracking an Elephant among high grass and jungle, when one expects every moment to come upon him. I know I have felt my heart beat pretty quickly while doing so, and have felt it 'come into my mouth' when a Chital has uttered its sharp bark, or rushed through the jungle within a few yards of me! But as soon as the mighty game is viewed, excitement gives place to perfect coolness. A short account of my own adventures with Elephants, unsuccessful though they have generally been, may give some idea of the sport.

I first saw wild Elephants in 1863. On the 2nd of June I was encamped in the Andera kohl (dark glen), near the Mohan pass through the Siwalikh hills. I had come to the '*kohl*' on purpose to look for a herd of elephants which I had heard had lately arrived there. In the evening I went up to the head of the '*kohl*,' directing my camp to follow me. I had not hunted very long before I discovered a herd of about fifteen Elephants standing on an open sort of table-land. I lay down and watched them, but could see no tusker. I had intended to fire at no tuskless Elephant, but I found the temptation too strong and attempted the stalk. On reaching the place I found that the Elephants had moved off, and had entered some thick jungle. I ran round to head them, and soon saw the backs of several above the high grass. They were moving away, and I thought they were the last of the herd. I went after them, and as I was climbing up a bank I heard a noise behind me, and on turning round saw eight or ten Elephants going away at full speed, and not more than twenty yards off. I had walked nearly under their trunks without seeing them. I ran as hard as I could in pursuit of the herd and as they stopped to have a look I could not resist firing at the side of the head of the largest, though nearly seventy yards off. The bullet (a steel-tipped one) cracked loudly on her head, and she staggered a little, but went off with the remainder of the herd right down the stony watercourse which formed the bed of the '*kohl*'. I followed, half expecting to find my camels, &c., smashed by the retreating Elephants, but they left the watercourse, and I met my camels about a mile back. I now chose a spot for my tent, and while I was assisting to pitch it sent out my gun-carrier to look after the Elephants.

He came back again directly, having found some of the herd close by. I at once went out, and found seven elephants, four large and three small, standing on the summit of a low hill which was nearly surrounded by a rather deep ravine. I went round to leeward, but could not get nearer than about ninety yards on account of the ravine. I lay watching them until they at length moved, and were passing along the opposite bank within sixty yards of me. I took steady aim at the head of one and fired. She merely shook her head, and I don't know where my second bullet struck. The Elephants then hurried across the ravine to my left and halted in a slight hollow about thirty yards below me, where they stood with their trunks up, uncertain which way to go. I was standing on the open hill-side with no tree to get behind, and only a little low jungle about fifty yards off to retreat to in case of a charge. I loaded as fast as I could, but could only find one rifle bullet, and had to put a small gun bullet in the left barrel. My gun-carrier stood by me well, and, just as I put the caps on, the Elephants wheeled round came straight towards me. I picked out the nearest and largest, and gave her both barrels in the head: she staggered and seemed quite bewildered, and as she moved slowly off with the rest of the herd I fired a heavy single rifle and struck her again. The herd made for the bed of the stream and rushed down the bank within thirty yards of my tent, frightening my servants considerably. They reported that the wounded Elephant was a long way behind the others, and appeared very sick. There was lots of blood on her track, so I hoped to find her in the morning.

I had returned to camp about half an hour, when down came an Elephant into the watercourse within two hundred yards. I jumped up and loaded my rifles and had a large fire lit, but the beast would not go away, but occasionally startled us with a crash and we could sometimes hear him chewing within one hundred yards. In the middle of the night I was awoke by a cry of '*Hathi ata hai*'. Jumping out of bed and seizing my rifle, I saw ten Elephants come down the bank within forty yards. One or two of them stopped, and I could easily have hit them in the head, as it was bright moonlight, but I thought that if I merely wounded one it might bring the herd down on us, when, in the dim light, there might have been a catastrophe; so I did not fire. One of them seemed inclined to have a long look at us, until a hill dog of mine went at her and drove her away screaming.

Next day I tracked the herd for many miles, but could not come up with them. I hunted without success for several days, until I became so lame from a boil on the leg that I had to return to Delhi.

Early in September of the same year, I disregarded all warnings about jungle fever, and set out to have another try for Elephants in the Siwalikhs. I took the precaution of swallowing a glass of sherry with a good dose of quinine every morning when I got out of bed, and I never had a touch of fever. The grass was tremendously high and thick, and the heat in the narrow '*sots*' very oppressive. It was generally impossible to move through the jungle except by following the Elephant tracks.

On the night of the 6th of September, soon after I had gone to bed (I was encamped at the village of Rasulpur, about sixteen miles from Rurki), a man came to say that an Elephant was feeding in a field not far off. At daylight next morning I started and went to look for the tracks; the man who had brought the news soon joined me and pointed out the field in which the Elephant had been feeding. The crop was Indian corn, and it was half eaten and trampled down by the brute, whose footmarks showed him to be a very large one. Taking up the track where it left the field we followed it towards the Siwalikhs, and after going a couple of miles found ourselves in thick jungle, where the tracking, which had been sometimes rather difficult, now became easy enough. We reached the place where he had drunk, and from which he had returned to the jungle. Farther on we came to a place where he had evidently stood for a long time; and still farther on, to where he had again drunk. I had several times heard deer bolt through the jungle, but soon after leaving the water I heard a rush which I felt sure must be that of the Elephant and on following the track a little farther we found that I was right. After a time I again heard him, but the jungle consisted of thick trees and creepers, and I could not see five yards. About a mile farther on, I once more heard the Elephant in front of us, and the jungle being more open I exchanged the double gun I was carrying for a heavy single rifle, and ran forward for a shot. Immediately there was a crash and a trumpet, and back charged an immense Elephant. My men at once concealed themselves; I was a few paces in front and saw no available cover. Two stems, not thicker than my leg, were on my left, and I stepped behind these and placed my rifle to my shoulder. The Elephant charged up to within ten paces and then stood still with his trunk raised, his ears cocked, and his vicious little eyes searching in every direction. He was not, although so close, in a favourable position for a deadly shot, so I waited with the rifle to my shoulder for fully half a minute, hoping that he would turn his head a little. He would not do so however, and as I expected him to discover me every moment, I thought it best to fire, and therefore aimed as I best could for the brain and pressed the trigger. Under cover of the smoke I ran back to the nearest tree. The elephant stood apparently stupefied for a moment, and then turning, rushed into dense reed jungle, where, as I had only a single barrel, I thought it unadvisable to follow him.

Next day I moved camp a few miles and hunted several *'sots'* without success. Towards evening I met some woodcutters, who informed me that they had seen a tusker in Golni Kohl. On going to the place we found the recent track of a large Elephant, and selecting a likely spot near some water sat down to listen. After about half an hour a loud crack, as of a breaking branch, disturbed the silence, but the sound was not repeated. After a time I went towards the place whence the sound had proceeded, and found the perfectly fresh footmarks of an Elephant which had passed since we came up. Following the track, I found that the Elephant had entered a long belt of high grass on the margin of the watercourse, so I went down to the end to wait for his appearance. Taking up a good position, I sent my gun-carrier up the high bank above me to look out; he presently saw the Elephant cross the *rao* and enter the jungle on the opposite bank. I soon got across to him and found him feeding on some bamboos. Getting in his path I waited for him to feed up to me, and got a steady shot within fifteen yards between eye and ear, which I felt certain must prove fatal. To my disappointment, however, after blundering about some time in such a cloud of dust that I could not see to fire again, he made off, and as it was becoming dusk I had to leave him till next morning, when I took up the track.

I followed it for many miles, and at last lost it among those of a herd of Elephants which I found in another *'kohl'*. I had a look at a number of them, but as they were all females and young ones, I would not fire at them.

For several days I hunted in vain for a tusker, but saw females and small ones nearly every day. I sometimes lay for hours watching their habits with great interest. Their extraordinary faculty of scent was one of their most observable characteristics. I noticed that whenever an Elephant went to leeward of me, though at many hundred yards' distance, up went her trunk, the signal of alarm was given, and the herd collected together, betraying the greatest uneasiness. On one occasion I had a peculiarly good opportunity of watching them, as I was lying on a high rock overlooking a level valley in which the herd had taken up their station.

Finding no tuskers, I left the Siwalikhs and went down to the open country below Hardwar. Here I was told some tuskers resorted, and I had only been three nights in the village of Bhurpar when three Elephants came at night to the fields close to the village.

Next morning I followed the tracks which showed that they were all large ones, and one, judging from the height of the mud marks on the trees, must have been an enormous one. They had however, gone straight down wind; it was impossible to move through the dense jungle except in their path, and when I at length came up with them and heard them chewing under a tree forty yards ahead of me, they had already scented me, and at once made off. As they went down wind, pursuit was unsuccessful. That night they again visited the gardens, but my leave was up and I was obliged to return.

In May 1865, I again visited the Dun and Siwalikhs, determined to do my best against the Elephants. I had a most powerful battery, which I felt confident would enable me to give a good account of any Elephants I might come across. The result shows how useless the heaviest guns are unless used scientifically.

My battery consisted of a single-barrelled two-grooved 5-bore rifle, weighing sixteen pounds, carrying a spherical belted ball (hardened with quicksilver), and a charge of *one ounce* of powder; and two double-barrelled 10-bore rifles, fourteen pounds in weight, carrying hardened spherical bullets with nine drams of powder. My friend F. accompanied me, and I lent him one of the double rifles; he had also a single-barrelled Whitworth.

We began hunting at Purduni, about five miles above Hardwar. The first two days we found fresh tracks, but no Elephants; on the third day we were more fortunate. After in vain attempting to follow up the fresh track of an Elephant which we soon lost on stony ground, we suddenly came upon him as we were descending a small valley. He was unconscious of our presence, so we stalked behind a bamboo bush and waited for him to pass us. As he was leisurely passing within fifteen yards I made a slight noise to attract his attention, and as he cocked his ears to listen I took a steady aim at his temple. To my disgust the cap snapped! The elephant at once turned and made off. I ran after him, but could not get a fair shot, so I let him go, so as to give him time to get over his alarm. We now went to some water which he was in the habit of frequenting, and sent a man on his track with orders to watch him and bring us word if he stopped. After an hour or two the man rejoined us at the water with the news that the Elephant had halted under a shady tree. We at once set out after him, and on approaching the place soon heard him. Going carefully towards the sound we discovered that he was lying on his side. Creeping quietly round we got within fifteen yards of his head, the ground was quite open with the exception of a few bare stems. I now wished to walk up and shoot him in the head, while F. covered my retreat from behind a tree in case I did not kill the beast. F., however, wished to accompany me, which I did not think safe, and during the momentary hesitation the opportunity was lost and the Elephant began to rise. As he straightened his forelegs I fired at his forehead with the heavy rifle; F. gave him right and left about the ear, and I gave him one from the double barrel as he went off. After going a few yards he fell on his knees, but recovered himself directly; I fired the remaining barrel in hopes of making him bleed and thus assist in tracking him. We followed him as hard as we could for several miles, but had at last to give up the chase as hopeless.

Next day we were unable to track him, so we shifted our ground, and crossing the Siwalikhs by Khansrao, went to Rasulpur, and from thence hunted the various '*kohls*' in the neighbourhood. For four or five days we could meet with no Elephants. But on the 13th we heard of some in Andera Kohl.

Taking the man who had seen the Elephants with us, we started early and went up the '*kohl*'. We could find no tracks in it, so we ascended the hills between the Andera and Binj '*raos*' to the place where the Elephants had been last seen. Taking up the tracks, we followed them through all sorts of extraordinary places, across Binj and another '*rao*'. In the latter we saw an Elephant with one small tusk, and got down to within twenty-five yards of him, but he was very wary, and either heard or winded us, and made off without giving us a chance. He went up the very path we had come down, passing close to some men whom we had left there.

We returned on his track for a short distance, but gave it up, and had just sat down to rest when we heard a crash on the other side of the valley, and on looking up saw a magnificent old tusker forcing his way through the trees. We at once set out after him, but on reaching the place he had gone, and we could see nothing of him. After some time we discovered that he had crossed to Bulawala, whither we followed him, but lost his tracks in the stony '*rao*'.

Returning to Binj we met some woodcutters, who informed us that they had seen an Elephant go into Amsot. We went to the place and found plenty of tracks, among others a large fresh one which led along a path which went up the *'sot'*. I followed it for some time, but at last reached a spot where it appeared that the Elephant had been going the other way, so I turned round. I had hardly done so when I heard a noise, and on looking round, saw a tusker about forty yards off. Had I gone a few paces forward I should have come right on him; as it was, he heard or saw us and made a rush. I ran as hard as I could to get a shot, but he would not give me a very good one, and I had to fire hurriedly behind his ear at about twenty-five yards. He reeled to the shot, and F. gave him one with one of my heavy double barrels. I took the other, and gave him a second shot behind the ear. He seemed quite stupefied; but on F.'s hitting him again he trumpeted and went down the *'sot'*. I gave him my last barrel behind the right ear, but away he went, slowly, and bleeding a good deal. We followed for some distance, and then gave up, as it was becoming dark, but left directions with the woodcutters to keep a sharp lookout, promising a reward if they found him.

Next day we sent several men out to look for tracks, but none having returned by two o'clock, we went up Binj and explored various curious dark *'sots'*, but without success. On the 15th, we had no better luck, and F.'s leave being up on the 16th, we parted, and I marched for Riki Khes, in the north-east corner of the Dun, where the Ganges leaves the hills. Arriving there on the 19th, I spent two days in searching for a rogue elephant, who was said to be in the neighbourhood, but I was unable to find him.

On the 22nd, I crossed the Ganges, and encamped at a village called Kaṇkar. Here I obtained news of Elephants. I was out early on the morning of the 23rd, and soon found fresh tracks, which I followed in an easterly direction for several miles; they then turned and brought us back nearly to the place where we first found them, a large jungle of *'nal'* and *'baru'* reeds extending in a belt along the foot of the hills. Ascending a low hill above this, I sent a man up a tree to look out, and he soon saw an Elephant not far off. I went round to the place, and found five Elephants standing in some thick jungle at the foot of the hill. I crept carefully down to within twenty yards, and watched them for some time. There were an old tusker with a good pair of tusks, another with one tusk, two *'maknas'* or females, and a young tusker. The single tusker was nearest me, and I carefully studied his head to make out where the brain lay, and waited for him to turn it in a good position. At length he turned straight towards me, and taking a most careful and steady aim, I fired. I made certain of bagging him, but, whether from being above him or some other cause, I must have miscalculated the angle, for he merely staggered, and went off with the rest of the herd without giving me the chance of another shot.

I returned much disgusted to Kankar, and in the afternoon sent my camp to Kunar, while I again went along the foot of the hills to the *'nal'* and *'baru'* jungle. About half way along this I heard an elephant in it, and went in after him. I got within twenty-five yards, but the reeds were so high and thick that I could hardly see him, and I think he must have heard me, for he put up his trunk, and, after looking uneasy for some time moved off into the thickest reeds without giving me a chance; he had one large tusk. As I was stalking him a Tiger roared in the reeds not far off.

Next morning I hunted along the foot of the hills without seeing anything. During some showers of rain I rested in a *'Banjara's'* hut opposite the centre of the *'nal'*. As I was preparing to start again, an Elephant made his appearance at the edge of the reeds. I at once went after him, but he moved into the jungle where it was so thick that I could not get at him, and after following him a short distance I came out again and went round to the other side, sending men up trees to watch him.

Not seeing anything of him for some time, I went back to where I had first seen him, and found that he had taken up his old position at the edge of the reeds. Outside was a level plain covered with short grass, and no tree or shelter of any kind near; however, I resolved to go up to him, trusting to my heavy rifle. Under cover of a slight angle in the reeds I walked close up to him (I could have touched him with a fishing rod!) and stood for a minute waiting for him to turn his head, and as he did so, fired between the eye and ear. He staggered at the shot, and went blundering about, sinking down on his hind knees. As he turned round, I aimed behind his ear with the double barrel, which was quickly put into my hands, but the cap snapped, and he was too much turned away when I gave him the second barrel. He then disappeared in the reeds, and having reloaded I inquired from the men in the trees where he had gone to. They informed me that he was moving off very slowly, so I ran on, and turning down an open ride in the '*nal*', headed him. I heard him coming up very slowly, and as he halted in the ride I fired at the orifice of his ear from a distance of about fifteen paces. He seemed completely stupefied, and stood stock still; my double rifle was handed to me, but as I was raising it a brute of a gun-carrier fired from behind me and struck the Elephant somewhere about the ear. Round he came, and attempted to charge, but he was too much shaken, and rolled over with a heavy crash. Up went his legs in the air and I shouted Whoo-Whoop! and ran up to him. But I was too soon; his great head rose above the reeds, and I had just time to give him a shot in the forehead as he regained his legs and charged. I dodged behind a tree, and the Elephant went on. I reloaded and followed him with difficulty through a tremendous thicket of reeds of various sorts, where it was impossible to move except in the path which he had made, and which few animals but an Elephant could have forced their way through. At length I again heard him in front of me, and on emerging from the cover and ascending a slight rising ground I saw him moving slowly about among the reeds not a hundred yards off. I could of course have easily hit him, but I would not fire, as I expected him every minute to come out and give me a fair shot. There was no way of getting at him in the impenetrable reeds, and at last, as it became dusk, I reluctantly left him, though feeling sure of being able to track him in the morning. He had one fine tusk, and was the same Elephant I saw on the previous evening.

It rained in torrents all night, so that tracking was out of the question. In the morning I went out without my guns, but though I hunted all that day and the succeeding one I never found a trace of the wounded tusker. He must have died, as he had two 5-bore bullets propelled by sixteen drams of powder, and three 10-bore bullets with nine drams behind them, in his head; all fired from the distance of a few paces only.

On the 28th, I had returned to Riki Khes, and was sitting at breakfast, when a man came in a state of breathless excitement with the news that the *'Khuni hathi'* was by the roadside not a *'kos'* off, having just stopped his bullock cart.

Having finished breakfast and looked to the caps of my rifles, I accompanied the man, and had not gone much more than a mile when I saw a huge pair of hind quarters and a swinging tail through a vista in the trees. The wind was in the wrong direction, so I sent my guide up a tree, and making a long detour, regained the road on the other side of the Elephant. Here I found two men with the bullock cart, in an abject state of terror. Telling them to keep quiet, I went after the Elephant, and soon came in sight of him again. He moved towards some thick jungle, so I ran on and placed myself in the direction which he seemed most likely to take. He came straight on to within twenty yards, but the branches and high reeds prevented me from getting a clear view of his head, so I would not fire. He passed me and went round to leeward, so, fearing that he would scent me, I determined to try the effect of laming him, and accordingly fired the heavy single barrel at his shoulder from a distance of about forty yards. He turned round and bolted.

Finding plenty of blood, I followed as fast as I could, and had tracked for perhaps half a mile, when I heard an Elephant a little to my left. Going in the direction of the sound, I saw him standing under a thick *'maljan'* creeper. I fired at his off shoulder, thinking that as he had stopped so soon for one bullet, he would not go far with both shoulders lamed. He made off, and I had to wait a short time for bullets. On taking up the track I found blood on the right side, and plenty of it.

I had gone but a short distance when I again heard an Elephant in front of me, and soon saw him standing under a tree among thick undergrowth, where I could not well get at him. I therefore watched him for some time from a distance of about thirty yards. I could only see the top of his head and his ear, so I could just make out what position he was in. At length he turned straight towards me; and kneeling down, I took a steady shot at the centre of his forehead. I heard one crack, as the sound of the rifle died away, and then all was still. Walking up to the place, I found the huge beast lying stone dead, my bullet having struck him just above the bump on the forehead. To my great disgust he was a '*makna*' (tuskless male). I had been unable to see whether he had tusks or not, on account of the very thick jungle, but had taken it for granted that he had, and my gun-carrier Moti had declared that he saw one large tusk. Blood was oozing from under his left shoulder, on which side he had fallen, but to my astonishment there was no wound on the right shoulder. I could not at first make this out, but soon came to the conclusion—which was of course correct—that I must have fired at *two* Elephants.

Going back to where I had left the track of the second Elephant on (as I thought) seeing him, I found that it turned off in another direction. I followed it at best pace for several miles, but at last gave it up, as the Elephant seemed to have no idea of stopping.

Returning to the dead one, I cut off his tail and forefoot, and took his measurements very carefully. He stood ten feet one inch at the shoulder, and his forefoot was exactly five feet and half-an-inch in circumference. The rule that twice round an Elephant's forefoot gives his height is more accurate than might be supposed. It will generally be found correct within an inch or two.

I also set men to work to cut out his grinders, and it was after completing this work on the following day that poor Moti was killed by a Tiger, as elsewhere related.

After in vain endeavouring to avenge Moti's death, I gave up shooting in the Dun, and walked from Riki Khes to Dera on the 30th of May—a long and hot walk.

DOUGLAS HAMILTON

Records of Sport in South India

The first elephant I ever killed was on the 12th September, 1854, when at Bundipore. I started about 3.30 to the hill nearly south of the bungalow, saw a peacock airing himself and shamefully missed him. Just before this I had heard a very loud report not far off, and as I was loading, two native shikaries came up. I looked upon them with no friendly eye, but to my astonishment they told Francis, my shikarie, that there was an elephant close by at which they had fired and wounded and that it was still in the ravine; in a very short time we arrived at its edge and one of the men pointed down. It was a very deep thickly wooded place and I could see nothing: the next instant the bushes moved and I heard a kind of grunt and the great brown back of an elephant came in sight; on creeping up I saw another, but when I was about forty yards from them they both quietly walked away; a little further on we found them standing in a small open space where a third had joined them. I crept up to some bushes and on looking through saw one of them facing me, another nearly broadside on and the third a little way behind them. Not being quite certain where to hit the one facing me, I took the one which was broadside on, aiming at the hollow over the eye, or rather between the eye and ear; at the shot down she went, to my intense

From *Records of Sport in Southern India,* London: R.H. Porter, 1892.

satisfaction. The others stood for an instant and then dashed away crashing through the jungle; had I been an experienced hand I might have had a crack at one of them before they bolted, but fearing that the fallen one might get up again, I reserved my shot. The two native shikaries had bolted at the very first crash. The fallen elephant, however, remained quite still, but seeing its eyes moving I went close up and put a bullet through the back of its head and afterwards a third into the hollow above the base of the trunk, but the first shot had killed her. A fine female; we cut off her tail and went our way highly delighted.

In shooting wild elephants care should always be taken that there is a tree handy to get behind in case you fail to kill and the animal charges, and every one who goes in for this sport ought to know the precise position of the brain and where to place the bullet. ...

On the 6th of September, 1855, when on the Annamullies I killed my first tusker, I had breakfasted very early, and took my whole battery with me all loaded for elephants. The head karder joined us, making five karders with me.[1] Within a short distance they struck off an elephant track made the night before, it led us up hill and down dale across the river and over a high ridge of the mountain down into swamps which would be impenetrable but for the elephant paths through them. At one place we saw where the tusker had rammed his tusks into the side of the hill. The holes looked like rabbit burrows. I put my arm to above my elbow into one of them. We afterwards got into an immensely thick swamp with reeds far above my head and bushes covered with thick creepers. I sincerely hoped we should not meet with the elephant in such a place, as if he charged and I did not drop him there would be no getting out of his way.

The scent was now becoming warm, and the excitement proportionately great, but on holding up my hand I found I was perfectly steady, it did not shake a bit. The tusker had crossed and recrossed the swamp several times—at one place he had evidently remained for some time, at another he had taken his bath; presently, Atley, the shikarie, heard him ahead, we hurried to get round him, but before we could overtake him he had passed out of the thick jungle

[1] The karders are the native inhabitants of these hills and are excellent trackers.

at the head of the swamp on to some rising ground clear of the jungle; we pushed on, for there was no time to be lost as it was nearly five o'clock. Presently, Atley saw him, and in an intense state of excitement pointed to some reeds in a small swamp, and I caught sight of his great brown back above them; we crept up close till I could see his head, but he was still over thirty paces from me. I wanted to get nearer but they told me to fire, so I aimed to hit him between the eye and ear. At the shot down he went, but my exultation was short-lived, for he kicked up a tremendous dust, evidently trying to get on his legs again, and before I could get down my side of the ravine he was going up the other as if nothing had happened. I fired at him again, with a projectile, aiming behind the ear; it stopped and staggered him, but he held on, going very slowly. We managed by running quickly to get in front of him; and as we came to a bit of open forest posted ourselves behind a large tree. We heard him below us crashing through a thick clump of bamboo; presently he appeared right in front of us going up the hill, head low, and looking very groggy. I advanced a pace or two from the tree, knelt down so as to get low enough for the shot between the eyes, took a steady aim and sent a projectile into his brain; he fell dead on his side without a struggle. Vyapooree, the head karder, made me fire a couple more shots to make sure, which I did, although I felt certain he was quite dead. The karders were highly delighted. I measured him round the forefoot and from the foot to the shoulder; twice the circumference of the former exactly corresponded with the latter, viz., nine feet eight inches; his tusk at the thickest part was sixteen and a half inches in circumference—one four feet nine and the other four feet eight in length. It was just five o'clock when I killed him, and we were a long way from home. We lost the path in the dark, and had to grope our way through the jungle to the river, and it was no easy work crossing; I was once or twice nearly down amongst the rocks and stones; but the karders brought me home safely.

On Friday, November 9th, 1855, I had a most exciting adventure with a tusker. After an early breakfast, I started at six o' clock a.m. to look for elephants with my battery of four guns, and after some time we hit upon a last night's track; it got mixed up with others on the banks of a stream, and the karders did not seem to be carrying it on satisfactorily to themselves, when one of them suddenly struck upon a fresh track with the droppings not cold in the centre. We had not proceeded very far when the leading karder (a Takedy man) suddenly retreated upon me; I expected he had come on the elephant, but on stepping forward saw in a small open space a bear grubbing for food. After effectually accounting for him and another, we carried on the spoor of the elephant, and shortly came to signs that he was not far ahead; we soon heard him, and then saw his great body through the bamboos. I ran on with the big rifle and waited for him on the other side of a clump, some fifteen yards or so from me, and on his head appearing, I saw he was a tusker; I took a steady aim between the eye and ear and down he went, but from the way he fell I knew he was not killed. I ran up to him and put a couple of projectiles behind his ear as he got on his legs again, but they failed to drop him, and then after firing another apparently well-placed shot which had not the slightest effect upon him, I became so excited and so afraid of losing him, that I fired one or two shots at random, and on attempting to reload found to my intense disgust that I had no more powder. I had foolishly brought out with me my small powder horn, forgetting that the large charges for elephants would soon empty it.

I had now only one charge left. The elephant was so badly wounded that he could not go out of a slow walk, and I saw that one eye was closed, so I ran up on his blind side and getting a little forward fired my last shot between the eye and ear; down he fell and I thought the victory was mine, but no, to my astonishment I saw him slowly rise again and walk off. From the way he ran against trees and bamboos I made certain he was quite blind; he crossed the stream again and went a short way up the opposite side. I stole near him and then plainly saw that my surmise was correct. It was then about ten o'clock, so I determined to stand guard over him all day, and an extraordinary day's guard it was. I found he was without a tail, every particle of which had been eaten away by disease, and this tailless behind of his appeared to give him much trouble, as he several times calmly scratched it against a tree. It was a sight to see him come against a good sized tree and knock it down, but the bamboo clumps bothered him extremely; he pushed up against them with all his force; they cracked and split and bent, but he could not force his way through them; his rage at times was very great, he would knock a tree down, trample it under foot and

'We Held on Like "Grim Death." '

'The Tables Turned.'

'Help! Help!!'

'We Secure Him At Last.'

kick it backwards and forwards. I tried to induce him to move towards Takedy by occasionally throwing a stone at him, but this only made him still more furious, so finding we could do no more with him in the way of driving him I left him alone, and as it was near five o'clock and he was evidently getting weaker and could not go far we returned home. The next morning I went out to look for him and found him dead a few yards beyond where we had left him on the previous evening. I made him by measurement nine feet two inches at the shoulder, and his tusks one foot five and a half and one foot five in circumference, five feet four and a half inches and four feet nine inches respectively in length.

On the 20th September, 1856, I started for a day at Perevai-Colum, my principal object being to try if I could kill a buck cheetul. As the elephant keepers wanted meat I took two of them with me, but just beyond the first nullah Atley pulled up at the fresh track of a herd of elephants; I sent the Mussulmen back, and away we went after the Hutties. Early in the chase we came upon two bull bison feeding together; they were both fine, but one of them was particularly handsome with fine wide-spreading horns; what a snort he gave as he stood broadside on, wondering where the strange noise came from (I was tapping the stock of my rifle with my hand). How I should like to have plugged him, but the track of the elephants was so fresh that I was obliged to refrain; at last they quietly walked away without seeing us. We came to a long check, having got on to a last night's track, but again hitting off the right track away we went for some miles, and at last heard the loud crashing of bamboos ahead. The wind being unfavourable we circled round, and approaching very carefully soon saw a big head; and we heard other elephants beyond. Atley pointed to the head we had first seen. I whispered that I could see no tusks, but he said 'That's a big one'. I crept up to a tree within ten or twelve paces of him as he stood on the other side of a very thin bamboo clump facing me. The front of his head was quite clear, so kneeling down on one knee to obtain a better angle I fired my rifle loaded with a spherical ball, and four and a half ounces of powder; to my astonishment it did not even stop him, and before I could get the other rifle he had turned and bolted. I took a crack at the side of his head as he rushed through the bamboos, and another at his ear; both shots appeared to stagger him. I kept running and watching for a favourable turn of his head, but he never stopped and made for some open forest. In passing through the bamboos he or we had disturbed a bull bison, which ran across the elephant's path, who immediately charged him furiously, and Atley declared struck him with his tusks, which so alarmed the bison that he put on his best pace and soon outran the elephant, who continued to chase him for some minutes. I tried to run on but got so blown I was obliged to give it up.

On the 11th October, 1856, Michael and I started after an early breakfast to Pullikul on the chance of falling in with elephants. Pullikul means 'child's stone'. The Karder women who love their lords come to it, and standing on a flat stone a few yards from the Pullikul, which is a round projecting piece of rock, place a stone on their toes and attempt to pitch it on the rock; if it happens to alight on the rock, the child will be a boy, if it hits and falls back, a girl, and if they fail to strike the rock at all the child will die at its birth. We wandered through the forest till nearly one o'clock without seeing anything but some tracks of bison and the quite fresh 'pug' of a tiger.

It should be mentioned that at this time (1856) the elephants were very numerous in Southern India, and had committed so many depredations in the cultivated districts that the Government had issued an order for all elephants to be killed, and offered a reward for each elephant, male or female; had this not been the case no females would have been shot. We had just sat down to tiffin when Atley pointed to the fresh track of an elephant; as soon as we had tiffed we took up the track. It was not long before we got up to the herd feeding in some open forest; I pointed out the tusker to Michael, whose turn it was, and who went down to him, I keeping more to the left where there were two or three females; on seeing him raise his rifle I cocked mine, when bang it went off. I had got into the bad habit of cocking my rifle without noise by drawing the trigger back as I pulled up the hammer—a most dangerous plan. I was most awfully disgusted at the contretemps and fully expected that Michael would lose the tusker by it. I ran back to get another rifle and returned just in time to see an old female blundering over a prostrate companion. They had given me the Laing rifle and I bowled her over with a shot behind the ear, she falling on the top of the dead one. The row was now

'Heels Over Head.'

something awful, and to my astonishment I found in this short time Michael had dropped the tusker and a brace of females. The row was caused by two little elephant calves; one had got its tail jammed between the two dead females, which made him sing out most lustily, and the other joined in the chorus; added to this were the groans and grunts of one of the fallen elephants and the roaring of another tusker a short distance off, which Michael ran up to and shot. We then ran some distance after another tusker till we were both quite out of breath, and when we stopped, found ourselves near one of the calves. The little beast was roaring like half a dozen tigers—such a queer little brute about the size of a wild boar, and looking like an elephant dwarf at least two hundred years old. We laid ourselves out to catch him, and now commenced as laughable a scene as ever occurred. The little brute was the most perfect caricature of an enraged tusker, charging right and left at everything that came in his way, banging his head up against enormous forest trees, and pushing with all his force against them, apparently under the impression that they must fall beneath his enormous power. On my trying to turn him he furiously charged me, turning as I turned, roaring at me with rage, and when I got behind a tree he came full tilt up against it. At last we boned him by the tail, and held on over a fallen tree like grim death; however, the strong little brute gradually worked his tail through our hands and ran off again. We tore after him and I caught him by his tail again, shouting out loudly for assistance; he dragged us to the edge of a rock and Michael neatly pushed him over it, we holding by the tail so that he could not use his hind legs; after many hard struggles and stretching his tail and trunk to the utmost we secured him, but the poor little beast died the next day.

On the 14th we were undecided where we should go, when the question was settled by Atley reporting that a tusker had been seen on the other side of the Annagundy Pass, with fresh tracks of a herd. We started about nine a.m., riding as far as the top of the pass; we had gone but a very short distance down the other side when we struck on the 'spoor' of the herd; some monkeys in the reeds close by made a sound so exactly like elephants moving off that for a time we thought that they had taken alarm, but it was not so, for after a comparatively short track we came up with them. We could only see a couple of females low down in a nullah. I selected one showing the temple shot, though it was the furthest off, as I funked the shot behind the ear which the nearest gave. This deceived Michael, who thought I was sure to take the nearest; seeing me raise my rifle, he did the same and at my report was considerably astonished to see the elephant he was aiming at fall; he consequently only got a running shot at the other, and failed to drop her. I had fired the big rifle with the conical ball, which only knocked the elephant's head into a bamboo clump on the opposite bank; after staggering about she got on her legs again and commenced climbing up the bank. I now had a capital lesson on the ear shot, for Michael was at my elbow showing me the exact spot where to plant the bullet. On receiving the shot the elephant reared up on end and fell clean heels over head to the bottom of the nullah, such an awful smash—squelch would be a better term. Michael said he had never seen anything like it. She was a very large female; I made her with the measuring tape eight feet seven inches.

In 1863, when at Hassanoor with the late Sar Victor Brooke, he shot the largest elephant ever killed in Southern India. We had started early on the morning of the 30th of July, the native shikaries being very positive about elephants being in the neighbourhood.

We had not gone far before fresh marks and droppings dispelled all doubts, and shortly afterwards we came plump on a tusker standing amongst some low trees. We crept up to within twelve yards of him, but just as B. fired, the elephant had raised his head and was apparently picking his teeth with his trunk; this threw the angle out and the ball went in front of the brain, or rather past it. He wheeled round at the shot, and I caught him an awful smite on the other ear with the Lancaster, which nearly brought him down, but he recovered himself and went off at a great rate. B. took up the running and was very close to him at one time, but he got away, he was not a very large animal, but his ivories were worth bagging. We returned to the bungalow to breakfast, B. a good deal cut up at the loss of the tusker. Soon after breakfast a number of elephants were reported about three miles off in the other valley through which the road passes, so away we went after them; heard them in the valley below us, and presently saw some of them on the opposite side; just then some men minding cattle hearing one of the elephants trumpeting began shouting 'Anee, Anee!' (Elephants, Elephants) which put the whole herd in motion. They all passed along a rather open space of the hill about a quarter of a mile distant. I never saw such a sight—there were at least sixty elephants, the leader being a splendid old bull; on they went, sometimes in twos and threes, sometimes in single file; with two or three small tuskers, and last of all, whipping them in, came a monster; his tusks appeared to be so long that they almost touched the ground; there was an exclamation of surprise from all present. When they had passed we followed and soon came up to them standing in rather an open glade on the hill side, and there was the grand old tusker outside of all. It was my shot by *right*, but my sole desire was that Brooke should bag him. There were so many elephants about, and especially one old female facing us, that it was very difficult to get nearer than thirty paces to the big bull. He was standing looking away from us close to a tree, and we then saw, alas, that he had only one tusk. It was a long shot but we could not get nearer, and as he turned his head I whispered to Brooke to take him behind the ear. The shot only spun him round, and as he exposed his other ear we both let drive, which staggered him tremendously, and with ears cocked forward reeled about like a drunken man; I then ran forward to about twelve yards and planted a ball exactly between the eyes. Brooke followed it up with a couple from his Westley Richard rifle. I thought he must fall, but I believe he was saved by resting on his tusk for a moment; he then recovered himself and bolted. He dashed down into a deep ravine and gave a loud roar; on running up he was nowhere to be seen, so we took up the track; at first there was no difficulty, but this, from the blood ceasing, increased, still, on we went, Brooke manfully sticking to the track, I despairing of ever seeing the grand beast again.

For a good nine miles we followed the track, the greater part of the way at a foot trot; at last we came to the foot of a hill down which the elephant had zigzagged *at a walk.* On rounding some thick bushes the man in front of me pointed, and there was the huge monster standing in some water. Pushing Brooke to the front he steadily raised his rifle, and aiming at the orifice of the ear let drive, and down came the grand old tusker with a crash, sending up the water far above our heads. It was a long shot—twenty-seven yards. I ran down to the elephant, and seeing he was not dead Brooke killed him by a shot in the back of his head, and thus died the largest and toughest old tusker I ever came across; a grand trophy. His tusk measured five feet eleven inches outside the lip, and carefully measuring him we made him exactly eleven feet high with an enormously thick neck; although he showed no signs of great age except in his feet, he must have been, I think, a very old animal. We had seven miles to get home, but right cheerfully we accomplished the journey, Brooke doing the greater part of it with only one shoe. We did not arrive at the bungalow till long after dark.

We devoted the greater part of the next day to cutting out the tusks, and a long business it was. The broken tusk was in a very decayed state, and the foetid odour from it almost unbearable. How the poor brute must have suffered!

In respect to the tusks of this elephant the following letter in the *Field* newspaper, from the late Sir Victor Brooke, settles the question as to their size and weight:

> Sir—Will you kindly allow me to correct a mistake in your correspondent 'Smoothbore's' letter published under the above heading in your issue of the 1st inst. In his letter 'Smoothbore' states that the weight of the large tusk of the elephant shot by me in the Hassanoor hills, Southern India, was eighty-five pounds, and that so long ago as 1870 I confirmed this statement in *The Field*. If I did so, I was myself in

error. When my friend, Mr Sanderson, published his most interesting work entitled 'Thirteen Years Amongst the Wild Beasts in India', he requested me to have the tusks of the elephant weighed and measured carefully, and at page 63 all the dimensions will be found accurately recorded. It will be seen that the perfect tusk weighs ninety pounds, and the broken one forty-nine pounds. The perfect tusk is exactly eight feet in length. Unluckily I cannot remember what the tusks weighed shortly after the animal was killed, but I remember being disappointed at finding they had lost considerably when I weighed them for Mr Sanderson, i.e., fourteen years afterwards.

Victor Brooke.

On this same trip I killed my last elephant. On August 1st, we started up the valley to look for elephants. When three parts up we saw some on the opposite side; it took us some time to get round, and when we did get to the spot they had vanished. After hunting about amidst numerous tracks we at last heard them; creeping up to a tree about thirty yards from them, I saw they were all females. I would not fire for fear of disturbing a tusker, so we watched them for some time, and the way in which they flogged the flies off with twigs was a caution to small boys; at last one of them winded us and they all moved off. Soon afterwards we came on them again, hidden away in some bamboos; we got up close to three females. I moved a little forwards to get the shot; the instant I did so an old lady with a calf at her heels caught sight of me and wheeled round. I had my rifle loaded with a quicksilver hardened ball and four drachms of powder. She was not above fourteen yards off. The ball struck her between the eyes, but the only effect was to turn her round and send her off at the double. I was considerably riled after such a failure, and was sitting on a rock chewing the cud of disgust when our people said there was an elephant close by. Asking B. to stop her if I did not, we stole up to her. I saw that she was the same old female with the young one; I got up to within sixteen yards, and the next moment would have had a good ear shot, but she saw me and instantly gave a trumpet and charged full tilt at us down the slope of the hill. I had to advance a pace or so to get clear of some bushes; taking a steady aim with the Lancaster I sent both balls between her eyes, and through tin hardened bullets they had apparently no more effect than if they had been putty. The Lascar with my other gun had bolted, so there was no help for it but to bolt after him; he fell flat on his face, and I got the rifle from him. In the meantime Brooke had stood like a trump, and had stopped and turned the elephant at seven or eight yards; he wisely did not wait on such ground to fire the other barrel. He said the calf, on its mother turning, threw up its trunk and gave a loud hooray, when away they both went, and we never saw them again. This was very unsatisfactory. We had not, however, gone far when we came upon a fresh herd returning up the hill from their bath; they were all covered with black mud, but there was no tusker with them; we stalked to within twenty yards of them; my two failures had nearly destroyed my confidence. After watching them for some time I took a shot at an old female behind the ear as she turned; it appeared to be another failure, but the next moment she toppled over, falling dead against a tree. She was an extraordinary old elephant; her stumps were worn down to the roots, she had not a particle of hair on her tail, and her general appearance showed signs of great age. The Lascar stood very steady this time, I had pointed out to him the danger to both of us if he ran before handing me the rifle.

A.J.O. POLLOCK

Elephants

I was first introduced to wild elephants when quartered at Bangalore in 1870 by Gordon Cumming, who then held an important position in the Mysore Commission. ...

After muster parade on the 30th June, 1870, I started on ten days' leave of absence with Gordon Cumming, to look for some elephants which were reported to have arrived near Hooliya, a small jungle hamlet some fifty miles south of Bangalore. A drive of thirty-six miles took us to the travellers' bungalow at Kankanhulli, where we found that all our provisions and liquor had been sent on to Hooliya by the amildar (district native official), but it was too late in the day to continue the journey, most of which led through a rocky country covered with scrub jungle; so we slept there, and, starting early next morning, arrived in our camp in Hooliya about noon, after a fatiguing march of fourteen miles, most of which was performed on foot, the ground being too rough and jungly to use our horses. The head shikari met us on our arrival, reporting that the elephants—two tuskers and a cow—were about two koss distant, in some thick jungles towards the River Cauvery, and that he had left two jungle wallahs to watch them. We thereupon held a council of war, deciding to tiffin and start after them without loss of time, as they could not be depended on to stay another night in their

From *Sporting Days in Southern India*. London: Horace Cox, 1894.

present quarters, and might be forty miles away if we waited until next morning.

A walk of over an hour through park-like undulating country, took us to a lonely valley surrounded by steep hills, and about one mile in breadth, through the middle of which a prettily-wooded stream wound down to the Cauvery. The scouts, immediately descending from their trees, came forward to report that the elephants, after drinking, bathing, and skylarking in a small pond, had betaken themselves to feed in a dense thicket of the smaller kind of bamboo, which fringed the stream about half a mile below us. Descending into the valley, we first visited the pond, which was not more than twenty yards square. The margin had once been covered with barroo reeds, but these the elephants had demolished; the place was poached up in every direction by their tracks, the steep banks had also been scaled, and high jinks had evidently been going on all round; indeed, the jungle wallahs reported that this was a honeymooning trip, and that the pond had been the scene of both love and war. Also that the tuskers were rival suitors, and had had frequent indecisive battles, as, although differing in size, the smaller bull had larger tusks than his opponent, which subsequently proved to be true. We then took the tracks up to the thicket, and soon heard the cracking of the bamboos as they were munched by the elephants. Creeping forward we got to within twenty yards of them, but the covert was too dense to see anything, so, having ascertained that there was little or no wind, we lay down at the edge of a small glade, towards which the trio were feeding, with our second rifles on the ground beside us. The crunching of the bamboos got louder and louder by degrees, and at last a huge brown mass, with a pair of gleaming tusks emerged from the jungle on the opposite side of the glade—some thirty yards across, and smelling danger, sounded the alarm by striking the end of his trunk against the ground, thus emitting a metallic noise resembling a log of timber falling on hard ground.[1] His companions then drew up beside him, the female in the centre. After a minute's deliberation they slowly advanced, but in a hesitating manner, trying the wind with their trunks and evidently suspicious of danger. Each man was to take the tusker next him, the cow was not to be fired at, we had

[1] This noise can be heard at a distance of two hundred yards.

a final look at our cartridges, full cocked the rifles, and opened the cartridge pouches so as to be ready for reloading. The elephants now in full view had halted within twenty yards. A rifle in each hand we both jumped to our feet, and ran forward to engage them. At a close range I fired three shots at my tusker's head and one for the other tusker's heart as he swerved off to my right front, his head being obscured by the cow's stern. They all crashed off through the bamboos, closely pursued by us. Seventy yards further on, Cumming's tusker collapsed stone dead in a kneeling position. In addition to his shots in the head, the steel tip of my bullet had, as already mentioned, passed through the body in the line of the heart. After a minute we continued the chase—a stern chase and destined to be a long one—and soon afterwards saw the shadowy outlines of the two elephants who had halted to wait for their companion. As we advanced they moved into an adjacent glade where we again opened fire but without effect, for charging off they crossed the stream into another thicket of 'Seega kye'[2] and bamboos, through which we valorously followed till our clothes were torn to rags. This burst lasted for ten minutes, when we emerged into more open forest for some hundreds of yards, until we again found ourselves in a hopeless brake of male bamboo, so thick that it was impossible to see five yards in front. The tracks separated here, so we did the same, each of us following his own line, it was a regular maze, but by following in the elephant's wake, a view was obtainable for about ten yards in front.

When fifty yards inside the thicket, a loud crashing close to my right was followed by the apparition of the tusker, charging along the back track. He was twelve yards from me, but the right barrel missed him clean, the bullet cutting a bamboo stem just over his head (a record shot). The left barrel, fired when he was almost on top of me, luckily turned him a little, and he passed within a few feet on my left, and thundered away through the bamboos like an express train. Done to a turn I crawled out of the thicket and threw myself upon the ground, where Cumming, having heard my shots, soon arrived, dead beat also. The stream was close at hand where a drink and wet handkerchiefs round our heads soon revived us. We had a good laugh over my curious shot, and a

[2]Thorny acacia.

useful rest of ten minutes before continuing the fray. To avoid the bamboos we then made a detour and soon struck the trail of both the elephants, which led us along the right bank of the stream for two hundred yards where it crossed and entered another dense patch of jungle. On the opposite side of this, we viewed both animals heading towards our left, and, running forward, poured in a volley, a shot from Cumming's 8-bore muzzle-loader bringing the tusker to his knees, but he got up again and bolted away as fresh as paint. Cumming had to halt to reload, but I pushed on and was slowly gaining on the tusker, whose ponderous hindquarters were about thirty yards ahead. The jungle now was easy going, a few scattered clumps of bamboo and no undergrowth, but the position of the tusker disclosed no vulnerable point.

At length, losing patience, the right barrel was fired at the leviathan target in front, in order to provoke a charge; the effect was magical; round he came screaming with rage, ears cocked, and trunk uplifted. He was on slightly higher ground, and came down the slope like a runaway locomotive, but his trunk was still in the way. When about twenty yards distant an overhanging bamboo caused him to lower it, and to expose the bump. As the trigger was pressed, I heard Cumming's bullet—fired from thirty yards behind me—whistle past and 'thud' on the tusker, who, swerving slightly to my left, crashed into a bamboo, and fell dead within twenty yards, getting another shot from the 8-bore as he collapsed. The scouts had spoken the truth, for this tusker was rather smaller than the first, but had longer and more massive tusks; they were cut out very badly by the coolies, who, although specially warned, left some nine inches of each in the skull. ...

Provided the trail of a herd is struck about midday, and is not more than six hours old, it ought to be followed up, even if leading straight away from camp, for elephants generally rest for several hours when the sun is high, and do not recommence feeding until three o'clock in the afternoon. For instance, if at noon a six hours' old trail is hit off, the elephant would have had four hours' feeding (on the march) before the daily halt, about 10 a.m., and in that time would have covered about six miles, therefore three hours are available to catch the herd up before they move again from the halting place, some six miles distant. Another way of looking at the problem is that, in addition to the morning's stroll of, say, twelve miles, another six miles, plus the distance from the finish to camp, must be added for this enterprise, exclusive of that covered after touch has been obtained of the tusker; but this is a feature of the sport, and some keen shikaries will often camp on the trail, continuing the pursuit next day. Solitary males in cool weather frequently dispense with the midday 'snooze' and continue to travel throughout the day, feeding as they go along. My last encounter in the Annamullays was with a wanderer of this sort, not far from Poolakül. At that time (August 1871), the law forbidding the shooting of elephants was actually in force, but I had been in the heart of the jungles for the best part of the preceding six months, and knew nothing about it.

The elephants were just beginning to emerge from the unexplored recesses of the mountains, their refuge during the hot weather, to make their annual foray in search of the young herbage, bamboo else sprouts, &c., in the forest south of Toonacudavoo, the general line of march being by Poolakul, towards the cardamom jungles in the Travancore country, which was forbidden ground. It was therefore necessary to intercept them before they crossed the boundary of British territory, a river some ten miles west of Poolakul. Starting early one morning in a southerly direction, we walked for several hours without finding any fresh tracks of bison, but about noon struck the trail of a large solitary elephant, apparently over six hours old. The tracks of the fore feet measured four feet eight inches clear round the circumference, and as twice this is equal to the height, he was nine feet four inches at least. The shikaries, as usual, were not keen for the undertaking, pointing out that the tracks were stale, and that they were taking us away from camp towards the Travancore march, which was then some eight miles distant; but I insisted on following him for a few hours, believing he would rest for some time in the middle of the day. At the end of an hour we reached the brink of a stream running through a tract of bamboos, the foot prints led down to a salt lick in the steep bank overhanging the water; this had delayed him for a considerable time; he had wandered about and returned to it again, and the red earth bore tracks which proved he was no muckna, but a fine tusker, as my hand could fit easily into the grooves made by his tusks in the soft clay. Thence for another hour we pushed along quickly through the bamboos, finding at intervals remains of sprouts which had been devoured by him, some portions being over six feet long, and as thick as a man's leg. This was a good omen, as it signified delay, although on the other hand the fragments were covered with small insects, and the beetles had raised great mounds of earth close by the droppings. Into the latter Atlay would thrust his foot, and after remaining pensive for some seconds would murmur 'ratri' (last night) in a despairing way, which made me long for Pochello, or Kistiah, or Baloo, or any of the plucky and sanguine Deccan shikaries instead of this listless aborigine. On leaving the bamboos we entered an open part of the forest, with thick patches of cannæ dotted about, and encountered a sow with a litter, which not only barred the way, but twice charged up to within twenty yards without any provocation, for we had halted directly we saw her. However, she retired after the second demonstration, stopping at intervals and trotting back to see that we had not moved.

These beasts are a horrid nuisance when stalking, but it is better to be bullied by them than to alarm the jungle by firing. An hour later, we were stepping over the trunk of a large tree, which had been partly burnt, and I was pointing out to Atlay that some ashes which had been brushed off the elephant's feet, as he passed over, were quite fresh, and had not been washed away by a recent shower, when the second Carder—who was a few yards in advance—came rushing back the picture of terror, and exclaimed 'Ani'—then pushed the rifle he had been carrying into Atlay's hand, and bolted to the rear. We advanced twenty yards, to the edge of a glade, at the opposite side of which, calmly, munching a bamboo, stood the tusker eighty yards off. The glade was full of elephant creeper[3] and longish grass. I then inquired how the wind was. Atlay, caught up some heavy leaves, and let them fall; this convinced me that he was suffering from his companion's complaint, and he ought to have been forthwith deprived of his rifle and sent to the rear. There was hardly a breath of air, and I proposed stalking him for the front shot, but Atlay recommended the ear—so I crept cautiously forward, and got behind a large tree within a dozen yards of the tusker, who showed over two feet of ivory, indicating that his tusks were about five feet long. He fed slowly past towards the

[3]Bauhinia.

left, but did not give an opening for the temple shot, his stern being towards me, and I had no confidence in the rear-to-front shot, at the back of the ear although—as he halted to eat another young bamboo shoot—this was offered most temptingly. At this stage I glanced round to see that my second rifle was at hand, but to my intense disgust found that the perfidious Atlay had withdrawn from the competition, and had taken it off with him! Five minutes elapsed without a satisfactory chance for a shot—except one, when he suddenly turned round and examined me intently, for about twenty seconds, during which trying interval, averting my eyes, I remained perfectly steady; this was from force of habit, for, as a rule, it is the best course to adopt, but in this case it was folly, seeing that the front shot was overlooked, and that in all probability aim could have been taken and the shot fired before he moved. Being satisfied with his inspection he recommenced feeding, and shortly after turned broadside on, exposing the ear shot; in the gloom of the forest the ear-hole was indistinct, but I could wait no longer, so aimed steadily, and fired. He first went a header into the bamboos, and remained motionless for some seconds, leaning against their thick stems; then, recovering himself, he rushed over an adjacent small tree, subsiding against a larger one, which cracked with his enormous weight, as he leaned his body against it, his legs inclined outwards, at an angle to the ground. Although not more than twenty yards distant, he was facing away, so to fire would have been useless. This was a good opportunity to reload; the paper cartridges, however, had become so swollen from damp that they would not enter the breech,[4] which was rather awkward; he soon revived and, cocking his ears, began to try the wind with his trunk, and evidently sniffed the 'tainted gale', for he advanced, encountering a tree on the way, through the side of which he pushed one of his tusks. I now stepped into the open, to get a clearer shot; on he came, in a shuffling sort of way, without elevating his trunk, but clearly intent on business; and when within ten yards I fired for the bump, and down he went on his knees—weak though the second rifle was, it would have been welcome then. The tusker soon recovered his legs, and, turning about, retired very groggily, cannoning against the trees that came in his way; he

[4] Brass cases were not made in those days.

was not blinded by the shot, but simply dazed, though he had sense enough left to cross the Travancore river close by—up the opposite bank of which his track led into the territory of the Rajah, where we could not encroach. Atlay reappeared simultaneously with the elephant's retreat, declaring that if a herd had been there—instead of a solitary rogue—he would have stuck to me all the time. The scene of the skirmish was revisited on the way back; the blood that had fallen from the first wound was in gouts resembling liver, the range being nine yards; the second shot was fired at less than twelve yards range, but to this day I cannot tell where either bullet struck, although it is certain they were both very close to the brain. Four days later two Carders came in to report that a Mulser they had met the day before had brought information of a dead tusker, which had been found towards Nilliambaddy by some jungle-wallahs, who had cut out and kept the tusks. Atlay was sent for, and declared that it was within two miles of where our scrimmage occurred, adding that his clan were not on good terms with the natives of those parts. I was incredulous, but promised that if the tusks were brought in a good reward would be given. Two Carders and the Mulser started off that day to negotiate for them, but after an absence of two days returned empty-handed, and apparently rather the worse for wear, stating that a bargain could not be struck, and that the possessors of the tusks had given them a sound thrashing; this led to a feud, which culminated in a free fight some months later, in which two men lost their lives.

If an elephant is badly wounded, and goes away, as this tusker did, he very seldom succumbs to his wounds; but occasional cases have occurred of their doing so, probably from loss of blood. How this could result from a head shot, it is difficult to say; perhaps an artery may have been cut, the hæmorrhage from which might not prove immediately fatal in the case of so huge an animal. Some years ago an account of an elephant's death from the bite of a cobra appeared in an Indian newspaper, and, to the best of my recollection, nearly twenty-four hours elapsed before the animal died; whereas, in the case of a human being, death supervenes in about the same number of minutes. Atlay, the Carder shikari, informed me that in the year 1867, in the Annamullays, when great numbers of bison died from murrain, many elephants also suffered from the same disease, and that he got three hundred rupees for a pair of tusks he then took from a dead bull elephant. In those days they were in the habit of catching elephants in pitfalls, the remains of which still existed in many parts of these forests, as well as in the Tippicado district of the Wynaad.

The Kheddah operations by Sanderson supplied great numbers of elephants to the Government, and put a stop to the system of pitfalls; but when in Bangalore in 1881, I was informed that the last animal of his first catch of elephants (numbering over fifty), had died that year; and, as they had not survived ten years' captivity, there would appear to be something wrong in this method of capture. I am unable to vouch personally for these facts, but statements to this effect were made to me by more than one person who ought to have known the truth of the case, and whose veracity was above suspicion. When in pursuit of elephants or bison, very dark shikar clothes should be worn, the ordinary khaki colour being much too light for the jungles frequented by them. A friend of mine, who was wearing a light-coloured coat, once had a very narrow escape from a rogue elephant in the Billiga Rungam hills, which he had fired at and knocked down; the brute got up again, and, seeing his light clothing, gave chase, and very nearly caught him.

When bolting from an elephant, endeavour to blink him by turning sharply off, down wind if possible. If in bamboo jungle, it is not difficult to dodge him, but he will catch you within twenty yards if you get into ground where there is undergrowth, which he will brush through like cobweb, while you are struggling in it with difficulty. The late Major Gordon Cumming had a theory that, by laming an elephant with a shot in the foot, he could be killed with greater certainty than by risking the usual head shots, which in heavy jungle result in many animals escaping badly wounded, owing to the difficulty usually experienced in hitting the brain. He told me that one day, in the Sacrabyle jungles, he had followed up a herd, and found the tusker under a tree, standing on three legs, in the way they are in the habit of doing while thus resting in shady spots. He could not get a favourable position for a head shot, so crept up and fired into the sole of one of the hind feet, which was raised from the ground. The poor brute turned round and attempted to charge, but was dead lame, and the hunter had no difficulty in giving him a quietus.

At first sight this appears a cruel method to adopt, but,

considering the large percentage of wounded elephants that escape to suffer prolonged torture, it is more humane than the ordinary plan. In addition to selecting the usual tree of refuge near the firing point, it is very desirable to scan the surroundings, to decide on lines of retreat, free from impediments such as bushes, long grass, and creepers, in case of having to make a bolt of it with an empty rifle, a contingency that sooner or later is bound to occur when elephant shooting. To harden leaden bullets for elephants two ladles are required, one of which must be considerably smaller than the other; into the smaller one pour enough molten lead to make three bullets, add one-tenth of quicksilver, and stir with a bit of iron, so as to mix it well, then cast the bullets without loss of time. If the quicksilver was added to the molten lead in the larger ladle, it would evaporate too quickly. Tin is also used to harden bullets, but, being lighter than mercury, it lessens their penetration, and is therefore less efficacious. There is no sport that can be compared to tackling a solitary tusker, except, perhaps, following up a wounded tiger on foot. In shooting tigers from trees, or from a howdah, there is but little if any danger. The charge of a wounded bison can be stopped or turned by even a badly placed bullet; dangerous though he be, the size of a panther engenders a certain amount of contempt for him; a bear is not a very formidable opponent, although a plucky one as a rule; but in the case of a tusker the fight is a fairer one. Your heavy rifle feels uncommonly light in your hands as you approach him, and study his vast proportions, and you know that on it alone you must depend, and that if he is not killed in the first shot, the odds are pretty evenly balanced between you.

After a victorious fight, you will, however, regret to see your huge antagonist lying dead, his feet and tusks the only portions of his immense frame that can be utilized. One always feels these pangs of remorse after the closing scene with all animals except tigers or panthers.

C.E.M. RUSSELL

The Indian Elephant

I have not gone in for shooting elephants behind the shoulder, and the late Mr Sanderson, after giving this method a fair trial, denounced it as needlessly cruel. I shall therefore confine myself to the usual Indian method of firing only at the brain. Personally, I do not believe that a shot damaging the top of the latter is necessarily fatal—in fact, judging by analogy I am almost certain that such is by no means sure to cause death, but if shot through the middle or lower portions of that organ, the animal dies instantaneously.

Very frequently a bullet passing through the head very close to the brain or possibly through the top of it, floors the creature who may lie stunned for a short while or may at once get up again.

The sportsman must be on the look-out for this and never trust to an elephant being defunct until the fact is beyond all question. Generally speaking, an animal which has been only stunned and floored (not brained) falls quickly and with a loud crash, while one which has been shot dead sinks down slowly and quietly, making very little noise, unless the carcass should crush dry branches or bamboos in its fall.

As soon as an elephant has fallen to the shot, the sportsman should run in close; and if he has any doubts regarding the animal's

From *Bullet and Shot in Indian Forest, Plain and Hill*. London: W. Thacker, 1900.

extinction, should continue firing into his head at an angle calculated to reach the desired spot. The surest sign within my knowledge that a male elephant has been brained is that, a very short time after the fatal bullet has been fired, an organ which is usually hidden is extruded, and a general evacuation ensues. Previous to this, I counsel no faith in the creature's demise.

If the elephant be not brained, he will soon begin to struggle, and attempt to rise. Happy, then, is the sportsman who is accompanied by a gun-bearer upon whom he can rely to stand by him with his second rifle or gun; for it is often exceedingly difficult to finish off an elephant which is floundering about and trying to get up! In the last trip which I made after these animals in a zemindary in the Madura district (Southern India) it took a learned (and sporting) judge and myself all we could do to bag an elephant which had been floored, though I was armed with a double 4-bore and a double 8-bore, and my friend with a double eight, and though moreover the men stood firm. The animal very nearly escaped us, and once, when I was unloaded, he got well on to his legs, and I thought that he was off, but fortunately a useful shot from the judge dropped him again, though he instantly began trying once more to rise. Eventually a bullet from the 4-bore reached his brain and he was ours. ...

In my last trip after elephants, in the Vursinaad valley of the Madura district before referred to, a female (unwounded) charged my friend and myself, her head coming through the cover only ten paces off, as she rushed at us with ears cocked, after making the short, sharp trumpet 'prut! prut!' which elephants generally utter before charging. I had had no big game shooting for a long time, and quite forgot in my hurry to pull the left trigger of my 4-bore. The result was that I pulled the right, both barrels went off, and I was thrown on my back several paces off, but luckily quite unhurt except by thorns. The elephant fortunately was also floored, and was very glad to take herself off after recovering her legs.

A European would have but a small chance of escape by flight if attacked by an elephant on the ground usually frequented by the latter. He would indubitably be caught by thorns or bamboos, or tripped up by branches or fallen canes hidden in the grass; and it is therefore advisable to have a second big gun in reserve, and, if practicable, to engage a man who will stand by his master with it (but who will never dream of firing himself), relying, if attacked, solely upon powder and heavy lead. If unloaded when charged, the sportsman should, if possible, get out of sight behind cover, or into a nullah (if one should be handy), and rapidly reload, and he may then obtain a good chance while the elephant is searching for him, though it is wiser never to be quite defenceless, but to always keep one barrel in reserve in case of accidents, which, with two big guns, can generally be managed.

Elephants often charge upon very slight provocation—sometimes no more than that caused by the smell of man—and females with young calves are particularly liable to do so. I have been charged by quite a small male upon no graver cause than my accidentally trespassing 'between the wind and his nobility'. I was on the track of bison at the time, and, seeing the elephant at some distance off went up near enough to him to estimate his quality, and then finding that he was a little beast with very small tusks, I left him alone, and again took up the tracks of the bison. After we had gone on a short distance, we got to windward of the elephant, when, suddenly, one of the men said in his own language, 'The elephant is coming'; and, sure enough, there was the brute coming down on us in full charge; but an 8-bore bullet in the head staggered though it did not floor him, and the precocious and combative youngster executed a rapid strategic movement to the rear, looking very foolish.

All wild animals, but more particularly elephants, should they be suddenly startled, and so led to lose their heads and make a blind rush, are liable to run into, instead of away from, the very danger which they are seeking to evade. I have had a tusker, who had not the slightest intention of charging, rush so straight in my direction, after I had given him both barrels of my 8-bore and was defenceless (the men with my spare guns having bolted), that I had to get out of his way to avoid being accidentally run over.

This happened in the open, and the tusker was a solitary animal, but I have twice in one trip seen herd elephants, alarmed at getting our wind, bolt straight in our direction. I was then accompanied by a good sportsman and pleasant companion (now, alas! no more), the late Brigadier-General A., who had received permission from the Mysore Government to shoot two tuskers. Upon one of these occasions we had gone out after bison, and were on our way through the forest when we came across a herd of elephants feeding in a valley. We did not interfere with them, not wishing to shoot animals in herds. The General, moreover, had shot his two tuskers (one with a single bullet and other with my aid), so we continued our course down the valley. When we had put, perhaps, two-thirds of a mile between ourselves and the herd, we got into the wind of the latter, and saw them stampeding in the opposite direction. We walked on, until, all of a sudden, a crashing down the hillside above revealed the fact that the animals were rushing straight upon us. On our right, in the direction from which the elephants were coming, stood a thick bamboo clump, and to this I took the General and the men, and we stood behind it to let the elephantine avalanche sweep by.

The herd was steering to pass the clump on our left, but one cow came round on the right and pulled up and faced me. She was so close that her head was within three or four feet of the muzzle of my rifle when I levelled it. There was no time to ask her further intentions, and, moreover, we were between her and her companions, so I shot her dead.

I was very sorry to have been obliged to shoot a cow, but under the circumstances it was inevitable.

Upon the other, and previous occasion in the same trip, a friendly tree was our shelter, and the herd, which had got our wind, filed past on our right within a few paces, and without seeing us. Had there been a shootable tusker in it, this would have been a grand chance for the General, who had not, when this incident occurred, bagged the two elephants, to shoot which he had permission; but the herd was a small one, and the only male in it was not fit to shoot and was therefore allowed to pass unscathed.

It is a curious and unaccountable fact, that, while mucknahs are the exception in India, a tusker is an exceedingly rare animal amongst male elephants in Ceylon. ...

Elephants, in common with bison and deer, appreciate salt in wet weather, and they therefore frequently visit salt-licks in the monsoon; and sometimes, when one of the latter is situated in a nullah, a good idea of the size of the tusks of an elephant which has visited it may be obtained from their impressions in the soft earth of the bank.

A similar approximation may also be sometimes made if a place in which the elephant has lain down to sleep should be found, provided only that the soil be sodden—as is usually the case during the monsoon, which is by far the best time for elephant shooting in Mysore.

It is, owing to the restriction before mentioned, by no means easy to advise a sportsman who may wish to shoot an elephant how to obtain the required permission.

Before the Mysore Government reintroduced the capture of elephants in kheddahs, leave to shoot a tusker was often granted upon application; but now that the same are working, it would, in the absence of powerful interest in high places, probably be refused, unless a really troublesome 'rogue' should prove dangerous to human life, or habitually destructive to property. ...

The hill ranges of the native state of Travancore abound in elephants which are very destructive, and formerly, if leave to shoot one or two tuskers was applied for, it was granted. Recently, however, the Travancore Government has not been so liberal in this respect, though it seems probable that as the planting industry upon those hills is advancing by enormous strides, the complaints of the planters regarding the damage done by elephants may induce the Government to grant occasional permission to shoot a few tuskers.

In jungles owned by private individuals, leave from the proprietor is all that is required, but there are not many such in which elephants exist, the zemindary of Guntamanaikanur, in the Madura district of the Madras Presidency, being a notable exception.

Episodes in Elephant Hunting

A Man-killing Mucknah

I certainly began big game shooting at the wrong end, i.e., before becoming a steady shot by practice at black buck and spotted deer, etc.; I had virtually to commence with elephants and bison. The result was that I failed to bag many animals which would certainly have been mine had I sown my wild oats of over-anxiety to bag, and keenness, upon more commonplace and less exciting game.

The first occasion upon which I ever saw wild elephants was in Assam, and by moonlight. One night, after dinner, I was told that they had invaded the tea estate on which I was then working as assistant-manager, and that they were near the tea-house. Taking an 8-bore rifle, I went out to look for them. Just behind the tea-house, when I got near to the latter, I saw some shadowy sterns disappearing in the gloom, and hastily pitching and pulling, I fired at one of them, and accelerated the retreat of the trespassers.

I then went to bed, and had fallen asleep, when I was awakened by a man who told me that the elephants had returned. Fringing the tea, was a narrow belt of jungle and bamboo, and beyond it lay low ground covered by a great sea of high reed and grass—at that season standing in water. I went out again, and could hear the elephants in the narrow belt, and, approaching the sound, sat down behind a tea bush to await the appearance of one of the animals. Before long the head of a tusker emerged from the bamboo, and I fired at his temple. A great crushing in the jungle ensued, followed by a tremendous splashing, squelching, and popping, as the elephants floundered through the wet, muddy swamp full of high reeds and grass, accompanied by the tusker, who was little, if any, the worse for the scare which he had experienced.

The next occasion upon which I fired at an elephant was shortly after I had joined the Mysore Forest Department. I had at the time never bagged a single head of running game bigger than a jackal.

In January, 1882, I left Mysore with H., of the Forest Department; and upon the fifth day of our trip I met with an adventure which nearly brought my big game shooting days to an abrupt conclusion ere they had well begun.

H. and I had been encamped in tents in the Metikuppa forest. The water supplies in the interior of that forest had nearly all dried up, and our camp was pitched beside a filthy pool, from the mud beneath which, if a stick were thrust down into it, bubbles of gas arose to the surface. Fortunately H. had brought a cask of good water mounted on a cart, and we had plenty of soda-water with us. Frequenting this, and the adjoining forest of Karkenkotta which is bounded on the south by the Cubbany river, was a large and dangerous rogue elephant, a mucknah, who had killed several people, and whom, in the interests of forestry, it was advisable, if possible, to destroy.

He was not then in the Metikuppa forest, as we soon ascertained, so on the 27th January we moved camp to Karkenkotta, marching through the jungle in the hope of finding tracks of the rogue *en route*.

In this we were successful, for we came upon the fresh tracks of a large single elephant. H. and I dismounted from our ponies, and sending the men who were loaded with camp requirements on to Karkenkotta, and accompanied by Kurrabas to track and to carry our spare guns, ammunition, etc., we set off to try to find the rogue. The forest consisted of high timber, now bare and leafless, alternating with bamboo of different ages, the youngest forming dense thickets, and the mature an open jungle of large clumps, with clear spaces between. So hard and dry was the ground, that tracking was very difficult, and after a good deal of very arduous and hot work, we lost the tracks. The men were quite at fault, but making a detour, they struck a nullah, in the now almost dry bed of which a little water still lingered in the deepest pools. Their judgement proved correct, for here again we found the tracks, and ere long we came upon hot dung, so that we knew that the object of our pursuit was now very near to us, and a little further on we heard a crashing of bamboos. Thinking that the elephant had discovered us and was running away, I took the 8-bore and ran up, in order to, if possible, intercept him, when, to my surprise, I saw the rogue standing beside a bamboo clump, in high open jungle, on a gentle slope above me. The dry, crackling leaves which strewed the ground made noiseless progression impossible, even to a Kurraba, and there was no cover beyond sparsely scattered bamboo clumps. Half running and half walking, I closed in quickly and alone, the elephant meanwhile standing facing me, and apparently staring at me. About twenty-five or thirty yards from him, a thin, dead trunk leant at an angle of about forty-five degrees. It occurred to me that this might be useful as a breastwork in case of a charge, so I pulled up behind it, and aiming at the elephant's forehead, I fired. Both barrels went off simultaneously, owing to my having pulled the right trigger, and the elephant, after tottering for a few seconds, fell over with a crash like that of a falling tree. He lay prone, only slightly and convulsively moving his legs. H. then joined me with the men, and I reloaded and went in nearer to the elephant, who began to struggle and try to rise. H. thereupon fired both barrels of his .577 express, and ran away, the men with my spare guns and cartridges following suit. I got back to the leaning trunk and waited until the elephant had finished floundering about and had regained his legs, when I again fired at his head; and once more both barrels went off, whilst the animal stood, swinging slightly from side to side, and looking very shaky. I had but two more cartridges left in my pocket, and I now put these into the rifle and fired again. For the third time both barrels went off, and immediately after the report the elephant came down upon me. I was now quite defenceless, and had to run for it, which I did obliquely, turning a bamboo clump, round which, to my horror, the rogue followed me. I then set off at my best pace down the most open glade which I could see, the elephant gaining on me at every stride, when I suddenly saw H. standing behind a bamboo clump, whose shelter he had gained after he ran away upon the elephant's attempting to rise. I thought, of course, that he must have reloaded, and making a final effort, I reached the clump, with the elephant almost on my heels, and turning it sharp, pulled up beside him. The elephant stopped for a moment, H. said, and twisted his trunk about to smell, but fortunately he had received sufficient punishment; for, having lost sight of me, he went on at a great pace, and crossed the frontier into Coorg. H., I found, was still unloaded, and he told me that his cases had stuck, so it was lucky that the rogue did not prosecute a search for me. I was somewhat amused at H. asking me (rather indignantly) what I had come to *his* clump for!

Now here was a case in which, in my ignorance and inexperience, I had made a great mess of it; but then it should be remembered that had I killed that rogue, he would have been *my first head* of big game, as I had not then bagged even a deer or an antelope.

In the first place, I was in error in supposing that the animal was staring at me before I fired at him, and in firing hastily in consequence of that supposition. Then, directly the elephant fell, the crash with which he came down should have led me to suspect, had I had experience, that he was not brained, while the moving of his legs as he lay would also have afforded conclusive proof of this fact. I ought, of course, to have gone up within twelve or fifteen paces before firing, and, having floored the elephant, to have run in close to his head, and endeavoured to brain him before he could regain his legs.

After this I wounded and lost several elephants, and it was not until the 24th August in the same year (1882) that I succeeded in bagging my first.

My First Elephant

In the Berrambadie forest in Mysore, I was following up a herd of bison, out of which I had already bagged one, when I saw an elephant walking rapidly along in front. The wind was right, and I followed him, waiting for a chance. Presently I heard the Noogoo river in front, and felt sure that the elephant would halt there, nor was I disappointed, for, on topping the bank, I saw him standing in the stream, and throwing water over himself. I took the shot behind the ear, and the elephant fell, but was not dead, for he tried to recover his footing, and as his head bobbed past me (the rest of his body being under water) I fired both barrels of my 8-bore down into it. A jet of blood spouted forth at each shot, and I hastily reloaded, whereupon, as the elephant tried to get up the bank, just in front of me, I brained him. He sank back, some bubbles rose from the tip of his trunk, and I had bagged my first elephant. I had shot a bison and an elephant before 12 o'clock!

I was terribly afraid that the river might rise during the night and the carcass be carried away, so I sent for stout ropes, and had it securely fastened to trees. Cutting out the tusks was, under the circumstances, a work of great difficulty, and it took a large number of men procured the next morning, and working hard from then until late afternoon, to extract them. I was obliged to abandon all idea of preserving the feet. The tusks of this elephant showed about 2½ feet outside of the gum, and when extracted proved to be respectively 4 feet 10 inches, and 4 feet 11½ inches in length, and 15 inches in greatest girth. They weighed 63 lbs. the pair.

In 1883 I bagged three elephants. The shooting of the first two was unaccompanied by any incident worthy of relation, but that of the third was somewhat extraordinary.

The Vanished Elephant

A friend, W——e, who is short-sighted and uses an eyeglass, was in camp with me in the Mysore district, intent on shooting.

We had just marched from Rampore to Kalkerra in the Ainurmarigudi forest, when the news was brought that a tusker had been found for us only three miles off. We proceeded to the place, and saw the elephant in the distance.

W——e now asked me to halt for a few minutes while he mopped his face, and wiped his eyeglass, which had become misty from perspiration. Then we advanced, but the elephant was no longer visible, and we went cautiously, closer and closer, until I wondered what *could* have become of him—still not a sign of him did we see. When we had viewed him, he was moving about in a nullah in which there was much high reed, but now he was quite invisible, and appeared to have vanished into thin air. At last, just in front of us, we saw the elephant lying on his side in a swampy place, his head pillowed on dry ground on our side. We got up to within *less than five paces*, and then W——e fired. At the shot the elephant got up, and as he was crossing our left front in a great hurry, I dropped him dead by the temple shot.

The Insane Tusker

An extraordinary adventure occurred in the case of Colonel and Mrs G., who were in camp with me in the Berrambadie forest in 1884. In that year I had made all arrangements for catching elephants in a kheddah in a pass under the Billiga Rungun hills. Most unluckily the rains failed, there was no fodder, and I had great difficulty in providing food for the few tame elephants which had been placed at my disposal for the work. It was most annoying. I had taken a great deal of trouble, and had constructed a large enclosure, with a small one for roping opening off it, and all was ready, even to the gate of the latter (well studded with sharp nails on the inside), which was lashed up ready for use. It was so arranged that, after the entrance of the elephants, one strike from an axe or chopper, severing a rope, would cause the gate to fall into position, and effectually cut off all retreat. I had imported jute, from which large numbers of elephant ropes had been made, and nothing was required but the advent of elephants into the vicinity of the kheddah. As I have said, however, when the time for the latter to appear had arrived, the rain had *not*, consequently there was nothing to induce them to come into the low-country jungles.

Sick and tired of continued disappointments and enforced inaction, I decided to move the tame elephants into the Berrambadie forest, where there was, I heard, more grass, rig up an impromptu kheddah there, and try to capture at least a few animals.

I was in camp at Moluhollay, where, as I have mentioned, Colonel and Mrs G. came for a few days, in order that the former might try for bison.

Even here, the grass which had sprung up had withered, and the ground was hard on account of the drought.

I set to work in real earnest, selected a suitable spot, and got a stockade ready. One day, when I was going out on this work, I suggested to Colonel G. to take his wife on one of the tame elephants and show her the forest, and he did so, the lady riding a very large tame tusker. On my return to camp from work in the evening, some Kurrabas, who had been out with Colonel G., came from him to tell me that a wild tusker had been for a long time, and was still, following the tusker on which Mrs G. was mounted. The situation appeared to me to be a very perilous one for the lady. The Kurrabas said that the wild elephant wanted to fight with the tame one, and indeed, apart from that hypothesis, it was not easy to understand the wild animal's object in following a *tusker*. The men told me that the Colonel wanted me to bring tame elephants and ropes, and to try to secure the intruder. Taking my 8-bore rifle, and passing through the space in which the tame elephants were picketed, I gave the necessary orders, and then went on to join the Colonel, whom I met quite close to the camp. The sight was a very strange one. First came the tame tusker carrying the lady; next the Colonel, rifle in hand, on foot with the men; and last of all, walking sedately and quietly behind, followed the wild tusker at a distance of only some thirty yards from the tame elephant.

Directly afterwards, the tame females met us, and the wild tusker became uneasy, and went off a little way. I then sent two females to attempt to lead him away, while Mrs G. on her tusker went to her tent. The wild animal, after some hesitation, followed the females, and I kept close behind him, determined, if he should attempt to escape, to shoot him, since there was very great danger lest he should return at night and attack the tame elephants at their pickets. There was also no certainty as to what so strangely behaved an animal might, in a nocturnal visit, do to the tents, so I had fully made up my mind to catch him if possible, and, failing that, to shoot him.

There had been no time for any preconcerted plan. The only thing to be done was for the tame females, avoiding the camp, to lead the tusker into the kheddah, where he could be at once secured.

The idiots of mahouts who were riding the tame females led, however, straight towards the camp, with tents, horses, servants, etc., around, and the tusker began to make off. I ran up to try to turn him, but he held on, increasing his pace, and just as I had reached the high road which the elephant crossed, and as the latter, going at speed, was about to enter the jungle on the other side, I dropped him by a lucky shot behind the ear, and with two more bullets killed him. This elephant appeared to be mildly insane. He had followed the same tusker for hours, taking no notice of the Colonel and the men on foot, though he must often have got their wind. The men on cutting out his tusks found seven or eight huge maggots in his brain, and it is possible that the presence of these irritating pests might account for this animal's extraordinary behaviour.

A Fighting Tusker

In 1882 Captain (now Colonel) W. (late of the 43rd Regiment) was in camp with me at Bandipur, and one day a brother officer of his, who had done very little shooting, and who had never seen a wild elephant, joined us. Next morning W. and his friend went out together and came upon the tracks of a large, solitary male elephant. They followed them up to the Mysore boundary, and then, finding that the elephant had crossed into Her Majesty's territory, where W. had no permission to shoot him, the latter sent one or two jungle men round to give their wind to the animal in the hope of driving him back into Mysore. This stratagem was successful, and the elephant returned. W.'s battery consisted of a double .577 express rifle taking a charge of 6.5 drachms of powder, a double .450 express, and an old, though accurate, single 6-bore muzzle-loading rifle carrying a belted ball, while his friend was armed with a double 12-bore rifle.

The elephant became very uneasy before W. had got in as close as he wished to do, and he had to fire hurriedly with the .577; the single 6-bore being behind and not within reach at the time. Away went the elephant, with W., who had given him both barrels, in hot pursuit, reloading as he ran. As soon as he got fresh cartridges in, he fired one barrel behind the ear, but without effect; and then, as a last chance, he directed the other bullet at the elephant's leg: He was just putting in fresh cartridges after this shot, when he heard the short, sharp war-trumpet of the tusker, and saw the latter with trunk coiled up and ears cocked, charging straight back at the cloud of smoke. There was no big tree behind which to step, so W. took a couple of strides to one side behind a sapling, and gave the elephant the contents of one barrel in the face, and a bullet from the other in the ear, as the tusker brushed past him so close that W. said he could have struck him. Most fortunately, the enraged brute, failing to see W., went on, 'going for', and severely punishing, a bamboo clump, behind which his friend and the men, who had, however, escaped from it long before the tusker got there, had been hiding.

W. then followed the elephant up, and he found that the leg shot had deprived him of all travelling power, for after punishing the bamboo clump, he struck off at an angle, and came to a halt in a thicket. W. then discovered that the caps for his big gun had, by an oversight, been left at home, and that there was only the one cap on the nipple of the loaded piece. He obtained some small caps, however, from his friend's 12-bore cartridges, and by cutting these open, he got them to fit the nipple of the 6-bore.

A great fight then ensued. W. used his own weapons and also his friend's rifle, and he gave the elephant, who charged twice more—but not *home*—many shots, until at last a ball from the big gun, the third which he had fired from it, laid the tusker low. The elephant was of the largest size and very old, and his tusks weighed no less than 123 lbs. the pair.

Grand Trophies

In July, 1886, I was in camp at Karkenkotta, on the road from Mysore to the western coast, with Captain (now Colonel) B. of the Gunners. B. had never fired at an elephant, nor had he a weapon fit for the purpose, though he had obtained permission to shoot one. I had leave to shoot 'rogues' only, and one of these was reported as frequenting the Karkenkotta forest at the time. It was therefore arranged that we should go out together, and that I should endeavour to bag the rogue, while B. should try for any other tusker.

On the morning of July 7th I sent out men in pairs in different directions to try to find the rogue, and news that he had been discovered having reached camp, B. and I went out. The elephant was, however, very badly placed, and he discovered us before I had got well up to him, and a hastily fired shot failed to stop him.

We then went on the tracks of another single elephant, which we followed for a long distance. At last we knew from the signs that the quarry could not now be very far ahead, and we soon saw him moving slowly across our left front. I saw no tusks, and whispered to B.—to whom I had allotted my 8-bore rifle, while I retained my gun of similar bore in case of emergencies—to take care that he was not a mucknah, and B. replied, 'No, I can see his tusk.' The next moment, I saw a foot or so of thick tusk, the rest being hidden in the grass. B. put up the rifle, took a steady aim, and fired, and down went the tusker. We ran in to his head at once, and, by my advice, B. gave him two or three more shots to make sure, but I believe that he was a dead elephant when he fell.

His tusks were a truly magnificent pair, weighing 127 lbs. So long and incurved were they, that one overlapped the other at the tips.

A Stunned Tusker

As an instance of the advisability of making quite sure that an elephant is really dead, I may quote an experience of Colonel—now Brigadier General—P.C. (of the Coldstream Guards) who was shooting in Mysore. He had floored a fine tusker which he believed had fallen dead, and was admiring his prize, and patting his shikarrie on the back in his delight at his triumph, when the latter suggested that his master had possibly better reload. Before he could do so, however, the elephant recovered his legs, and, despite the Colonel's efforts to detain him, made good his escape.

A Lucky Chance

Although elephant shooting frequently entails much hard work before the game is encountered, it sometimes happens that the sportsman chances upon a tusker very unexpectedly. I well remember, many years ago, bagging a tusker when out for an evening stroll in search of spotted deer behind the travellers' bungalow of Karkenkotta in Mysore, but, as is so often the case in elephant shooting, there was nothing remarkable attending the circumstances of his death beyond the luck of the *rencontre*.

I have personally shot, and have assisted friends in shooting other elephants at various times, and have had considerable experience of the sport, though I have (alas!) drilled holes through the heads of a good many of these animals which have escaped, and I regard elephant shooting as a very difficult branch of sport, and also as a highly exciting amusement.

E.E. BULL

Charged by a Rogue Elephant: A Nilgiris Man-killer

(The risks run by anyone who attempts to rid a district of a rogue elephant are enormous. The Rev. E.E. Bull, Chaplain at Coimbatore, describes how he and a party were chased by a rogue which many people believed was a myth. The rogue specialized in murdering human beings, having 'some especially fine top notes' when attacking.)

Somewhere away back in the early twenties a small tusker elephant began to make a sinister reputation for himself at the foot of the Sigur Ghat which terminates practically at the twelfth milestone on the road between Tippacadu and Ootacamund.

It was not an ordinary rogue, that Sigur one; though for that matter rogues are never cast in the ordinary mould.

This one being very small, as elephants go, had to make good in cunning and pertinacity. His range or beat was a comparatively local one. From Tippacadu across to Sigur and then through Annikutti and Serur to the Bhivani and back comprised the scope of his wanderings. Sigur was his headquarters during the dry months of the year, and it was at Sigur that his blackest crimes were committed.

Reprinted from Stanley Jepson, *Big Game Encounters*. London: Witherby, 1938. The period of the story appears to be the early 1920s.—DKLC.

Those who have dared the Sigur Ghat as a quick motor-route to Mysore from Ooty will have noted with admiration the beauty of that quiet corner at the foot of the Ghat through which purl the cool waters of the Sigur River. A dense jungle has grown at the spot; for during the hot weather the region around there is the only bit of country for miles round which sports verdure and affords an adequate shelter from the sun.

There gather herds of elephant to wander down the course of the Sigur River to cool retreats in the Mysore Ditch.

The Rogue, like all rogues, being outlawed by his own kind, frequented the higher ground adjacent to the river or some shady ravine in the valley at the foot of the Ghat. He was very small and could, when on murder bent, conceal himself in a clump of bushes close to a path and await his prey.

His tactics were to await the close approach of his victims and from a distance of some fifteen yards rush out upon them with a deafening scream of hate and rage. He had some especially fine high top-notes, and his pace was consistent with the noise made.

On one occasion he attacked a cart with two men in it, and having brutally killed both men and done away with their identification marks he turned his attention to the cart which he reduced to the proverbial matchwood. The bullocks, on this occasion, he graciously spared.

Singly, men and women were seized and brutally mutilated until their remains retained no semblance of a human body. One instance of his brutality was to seize an aged man and flog him to death against the trunk of a tree until he held only the legs of the battered body by his trunk.

He was fond, too, of persecuting the villagers of Annikutti by camping at the river-crossing near their village and chasing away all who attempted the ford, drew water, bathed themselves or washed clothes there.

He loved to exercise himself with 'two hundred yards on the flat' in pursuit of a human being. One forest guard whom he managed to catch, he playfully hurled aloft on to the spiky fronds of a bamboo clump from where he was rescued in a dying condition the next day.

When he was in residence at Annikutti all 'shikar' operations came to an abrupt end, as none of the bravest would dare to invest his retreat—which was in a valley at the foot of the hills. On many shikar-trips to Annikutti, I was faced with this nuisance as we were restricted to hunt game then at a respectable distance from his lair.

As regards myself, I thought his existence was mythical. I had heard of his reputation and had interviewed the son of the unfortunate victim flogged to death on the tree-trunk, only two days after the tragedy!

I had never seen him and since he was proscribed for short periods only on the report of the tragedies imputed to him, it appeared to me that the authorities treated his individuality as a kind of 'Mrs Harris!' But the notoriety of the flogging incident, with the poetical setting of the tragedy—so primitive in its conception as to rival the 'stoning to death' of the nomadic Israelites—aroused the interest of the authorities at Ooty to put the culprit definitely 'to the horn' in the shape of a Rs 500 reward for his destruction.

But nothing happened, the terror gradually vanished away from the ken of the authorities and the reward again was withdrawn. I discussed this 'nightmare' with Mullah, the old head-shikari of Annikutti who had been Government House shikari in the days when Governors were not vexed with the problems of non-cooperation and could indulge in health-giving recreations such as the chase of beasts of the field.

Mullah had grown old, but I had known him in the halcyon days of yore when a Commander-in-Chief went down before a tiger and Her Excellency could mark four notches on her roll of trophies of royal tiger-land! Mullah is now reputed to be one hundred years old. He looks it!

In the days of which I am speaking he had then all but retired from the chase. He still condescended to accompany me on tiger beats only. I held conclave with him on the subject of this rogue which Mullah averred was 'flesh and blood'—a very real danger. He himself had been chased and narrowly escaped death.

Nor would he ever allow me to go out when the elephant was said to be about unless I was prepared to hunt him with full sanction of the authorities! Mullah knew that I knew about as much about elephants as I did about mastodons, and Mullah put a high price upon his own professional dignity. I happened to be in camp at Annikutti in January 1924–5, with Major M-B. and ergeant M.—

a very old and valued attendant of mine in the field. He is, alas, no more. We had had two weeks' sport and were about to bait for a tiger when the report came in that the rogue had again materialized and taken up his old quarters under the famous 'Honey Rock'. All shikar operations ceased. The bait was already tied up, and although Mullah promised it should be fed, no one except the tenders was allowed to go in that direction.

A few days afterwards, in the morning, the report was made that the cow had been killed by wild dogs. Now I am particularly fascinated by the habits and doings of the 'jungly kutta'. I had heard of him as occasionally demeaning himself to the pilfering of domestic cattle but I had never experienced a robbery of my baits at his hands. And so 'I had me doots.'

Mullah did not think the tenders would dare to lie to him, and gave it as his opinion that a panther might have killed the cow, but that it were madness to go over there. We were daringly restless all that day. We had suffered severely at the hands of this 'bogey', as we deemed the Rogue. So I persuaded Sergeant M.—who wanted no persuasion—to accompany me without shikaris to view the kill, when we should be able either to establish some interesting facts or expose the fallacies of our followers. When it was known that we had started on our venture, Mullah sent his son Chetty with one Karrian—a good tracker—to attend us. We arrived safely—at about 4 p.m.—to view the kill. It appeared to have been killed by a panther.

Around the kill, however, were numerous pug-marks of 'wild dog', which suggested that the pack, on their return from a morning hunt, had come upon the 'kill' and investigated it. Having dared so much, the ruling spirit of the chase became too strong for our attendants, and Chetty suggested a 'sit up' for the panther on some rocks close by.

The place was intersected with deep ravines, heavily wooded, wherein the Rogue was said to be lying up. At 7 p.m., when the light was too bad to shoot, we started for the bungalow two miles away as the crow flies. Having climbed out of the ravine-country on to the flat we followed a path which skirted the decline into the ravines on the edge of which were clumps of bushes. We had handed our rifles to the shikaris. We were walking and conversing in ordinary tones, quite unaware that danger threatened us, when suddenly, half-left ahead of us, with a deafening scream the Rogue hurled himself upon us at the distance of about twenty yards.

Karrian streaked off with the Sergeant following. It was good that I had *them* in front and not Chetty, for I followed their lead. Chetty, whether on purpose or not, bolted to the right with my rifle. We seemed to hear the enemy thundering on our tracks and we ran, blindly, desperately. Now this Rogue generally chased the single one who invariably, in such circumstances, goes off on his own. He had caught all his victims by concentrating on the straggler, and after Chetty he went. This we were not aware of until we had raced half a mile, to stop breathless and alert. The rogue made a bad choice in Chetty, who knew all about him and every jungle-path in that forest. Chetty literally threw him off. For, in about half an hour, he silently rejoined us. We were afraid to move in any direction.

'It is the bad elephant,' he whispered, 'you must follow me without a sound. Don't be afraid, but don't make the slightest sound. He waits for us and will never leave us until we reach the bungalow.'

The lights in the bungalow were visible at two miles! Should we ever enjoy that shelter again! We followed Chetty with creeping tread and managed to cover over a mile without further molestation. We were within half a mile of the bungalow and where there were some ruined stables.

We had entered a sunken road leading to the stables—bounded by a formidable fibre-growth. So high and thick was this hedge that it formed a very adequate defence of our right-flank on which the end of the jungle stood.

We were well in this defile when our enemy, who had waited there, threw himself upon us from a height of eight or nine feet, and undoubtedly would have overwhelmed us had the fibre-growth not withstood him. He raged and plunged, but could not advance. In our panic both the Sergeant and I had nasty falls with our rifles in our hands. Mine bears the marks to this day!

The Sergeant sustained a bad injury to his eye. But it was 'up-and-away' in spite of all this, and we reached the sanctuary of that stable-shed, hardly daring to hope we were safe. But so it was. The elephant was shy of those buildings, and must have retreated chagrined but resolved that he would 'take it out' of the next for this defeat. So ended the adventure. We no longer doubted the existence of the 'bad elephant'.

When we arrived at the bungalow we found Major M-B. and various of our retainers lining the verandah and listening to the sounds of the attack. They had known at once that the 'bad elephant' had got us, and were speculating on the extent of the casualties!

Three months after, we had our revenge when one midday I shot the Rogue, inflicting a serious wound at a spot in the head supposed to be mortal. From that date—though the elephant escaped immediate death—it has never been heard of again in those parts. A report of a dead elephant—small, with small tusks—being found twelve miles from where I wounded the rogue and down the Moyar Valley seems to suggest that I had rid the world in those parts of a very nasty encumbrance to sport, and the jungle-folk of a real danger.

A. MERVYN SMITH

'Peer Bux', the Terror of Hunsur

(Many of Mervyn Smith's chapters from his book, *Sport and Adventure in the Indian Jungle*, were originally published in the *Statesman* around the turn of the century. He contributed regularly to the Calcutta newspapers which carried a number of *shikar* stories. Unlike many *shikar* writers, Mervyn Smith did not only describe his own adventures but also recounted those of others. 'The Terror of Hunsur' is one of his most dramatic stories. It is about 'Peer Bux', a government elephant owned by the Madras Commissariat Department. At certain periods of the year, male elephants go into *must*. They become violent and sometimes attack their own mahouts. A *must* elephant, however, is very different from a rogue. This was always a point of contention amongst British *shikaris* for they were reluctant to kill a very valuable and generally docile animal which occasionally went into fits of uncontrollable anger. Whether 'Peer Bux' was just in *must* or whether he had become a rogue it was hard to tell but he caused havoc in Hunsur, destroying entire villages. The hero of this story is Gordon Cumming who is finally called in to kill the rampaging elephant.)

Peer Bux was the largest elephant in the Madras Government Commissariat Department. He stood nine feet six inches at the shoulder and more than ten feet at the highest point of the convexity of the backbone. His tusks protruded three-and-a-half feet and were massive and solid, with a slight curve upwards and outwards. His trunk was large and massive, while the skin was

Reprinted from *Great Indian Hunting Stories*. Harmondsworth and Delhi: Penguin, 1988. The story is set in the 1870s, perhaps more precisely in 1874–6.—D.K.L.C.

soft as velvet and mottled red and white, as high-class elephants should be. His pillar-like fore-legs were as straight as a bee line from shoulder to foot, and showed muscle enough for half-a-dozen elephants. Physically Peer Bux was the beau ideal of elephantine beauty, a brute that should have fetched fifteen thousand rupees in the market and be cheap at that price, for was he not a grander elephant to look at than many a beast that had cost its princely owner double that sum? He was quiet too and docile, and could generally be driven by a child. Yet with all his good qualities, with all his majestic proportions, Peer Bux was tabooed by the natives. No Hindoo would have him for a gift. He was a marked beast; *his tail was bifurcated at the extremity*. This signified, said those natives learned in elephant lore, that he would one day take human life.

When captured in the *kheddahs* in Michael's Valley, Coimbatore district, the European official in charge of the *kheddah* operations imagined the animal would bring a fancy price; but at the public sale of the captured herd no one would give a bid for him, although his tusks alone would have fetched over a thousand rupees for their ivory. The fatal blemish—the divided tail—was soon known to intending purchasers, and there being no bidders he had to be retained for Government use.

The Commissariat Department was justly proud of Peer Bux. He had done good service for six years. Did the heavy guns stick in the mud when the artillery was on its way to Bellary, Peer Bux was sent to assist, and with a push of his massive head he would lift the great cannon, however deep its wheels might be imbedded in the unctuous black cotton soil. Were heavy stones required at Mercara, Peer Bux would mount the steep ghaut road, and think nothing of a ton-and-a-half load on his back. The Forest Department too found him invaluable in drawing heavy logs from the heart of the reserves. His register of conduct was blameless, and beyond occasional fits of temper during the *must* season once a year he was one of the most even-tempered as well as one of the most useful beasts in the Transport establishment.

The Commissariat sergeant at Hunsur, who had known Peer Bux for two years, would smile when allusion was made to his bifurcated tail and the native superstition regarding that malformation. 'Look up his register,' he would say, 'no man-killing there. Why, I would rather trust him than any other elephant, male or female, in the lines. Just you see that little beggar, no higher than this (showing his walking cane), the *mahout's* son, take him out to the jungles and bring him back loaded with fodder, and lambaste him too, if he won't obey the little imp. He kill a man! Why he wouldn't kill a fly. The (natives) know nothing; they are a superstitious lot.'

But a little while, and quite another story had to be told of Peer Bux. This pattern animal had gone *must.* Fazul, his usual *mahout* (keeper), was not there to manage him (he had gone with Sanderson to Assam), and the new keeper had struck Peer Bux when he showed temper, and had been torn limb from limb by the irritated brute. Peer Bux had broken his chains; had stampeded the Amrut-mahal cattle at Hunsur; had broken into the Government harness and boot factory and done incredible damage; had gone off on the rampage, on the Manantoddy road; had overturned coffee carts and scattered their contents on the road; had killed several cart-men; had looted several villages and torn down the huts. In fact a homicidal mania seemed to have come over him, as he would steal into the *cholum* (sorghum millet) fields and pull down the *machans* (bamboo platforms) on which the cultivator sat watching his corn by night, and tear the poor wretch to pieces or trample him out of all shape, and it was even said that in his blind rage he would eat portions of his human victims. I may here mention that natives firmly believe that elephants will occasionally take to man-eating. It is a common practice when a tiger is killed for the *mahouts* to dip balls of jaggery (coarse sugar) in the tiger's blood and feed the elephants that took part in the drive with this mess. They say the taste of the tiger's blood gives the elephant courage to face these fierce brutes. The taste for blood thus acquired sticks to the elephant, and when he goes mad or *must* and takes to killing human beings, some of their blood gets into his mouth and reminds him of the sugar and blood given him at the tiger-hunts, and he occasionally indulges in a mouthful of raw flesh.

Was Peer Bux *must*, or was he really mad? The *mahouts* at Hunsur, who knew him well, said he was only *must*. Europeans frequently speak of *must* elephants as 'mad' elephants, as though the two terms were synonymous. *Must*, I may state, is a periodical functional derangement common to all bull elephants, and corresponds to the rutting season with deer and other animals. It generally occurs in the male once a year (usually in March or April), and lasts about two or three months. During this period a dark-coloured mucous discharge oozes from the temples. If this discharge is carefully washed off twice a day, and the elephant given a certain amount of opium with his food and made to stand up to his middle in water for an hour every day, beyond a little uneasiness and irritability in temper no evil consequences ensue; but should these precautions be neglected, the animal becomes savage and even furious for a time, so that it is never safe to approach him during these periods. When an elephant shows signs of *must*—the dark discharge at the temples is an infallible sign that he should always be securely hobbled and chained. A *must* elephant, even when he breaks loose and does a lot of damage, can if recaptured be broken to discipline and will become as docile as ever, after the *must* period is passed.

It is wholly different with a mad elephant. These brutes should be destroyed at once, as they never recover their senses, the derangement in their case being cerebral and permanent, and not merely functional. This madness is frequently due to sunstroke, as elephants are by nature fitted to live under the deep shade of primeval forests. In the wild state they feed only at night, when they come out into the open. They retire at dawn into the depths of the forests, so that they are never exposed to the full heat of the noon-day sun.

Peer Bux being the property of the Madras Government, permission was asked to destroy him, as he had done much damage to life and property in that portion of the Mysore territory lying between Hunsur and the frontier of Coorg and North Wynaad. The Commissariat Department however regarded him as too valuable an animal to be shot, and advised that some attempt should be made to recapture him with the aid of tame elephants. Several trained elephants were sent up from Coimbatore, some more were obtained from the Mysore State, and several hunts were organized; but all attempts at his recapture entirely failed. The great length of his fore-legs gave Peer Bux an enormous stretch, so that he could easily outpace the fleetest *shikar* elephants; and when he showed fight, none of the tuskers, not even the famous Jung Bahadoor, the fighting elephant of the Maharaja of M could withstand his charge. Meanwhile the terror he inspired stopped nearly all the traffic between Hunsur and Coorg, and Mysore and Manantoddy. He had been at large now for nearly two months, and in that time was known to have killed fourteen persons, wrecked two villages, and done an incredible amount of damage to traffic and crops. In an evil moment for himself he took it into his head to stampede the Collector's camp on the Wynaad frontier. The Collector was away at Manantoddy, but his tents and belongings were destroyed, and one camp follower killed. Permission was now obtained to destroy him by any means, and a Government reward was offered to anyone who would kill the brute.

Several parties went off from Bangalore in the hope of bagging him, but never got sight of him. He was here today, and twenty miles off next day. He was never known to attack Europeans. He would lie in wait in some unfrequented part of the road and allow any suspicious-looking object to pass; but when he saw a line of native carts, or a small company of native travellers, he would rush out with a scream and a trumpet and overturn carts and kick them to pieces, and woe betide the unfortunate human being that fell into his clutches! He would smash them to a pulp beneath his huge feet, or tear them limb from limb.

Much of the above information regarding Peer Bux was gleaned at the Dak Bungalow (travellers' rest-house) at Hunsur, where a party of four, including myself, were staying while engaged in a shooting trip along that belt of forest which forms the boundary between Mysore and British territory to the south-west. Our shoot thus far had been very unsuccessful. Beyond a few spotted deer and some game birds we had bagged nothing. The Government notification of a reward for the destruction of the rogue-elephant stared us in the face at every turn we took in the long, cool verandah of the bungalow. We had not come out prepared for elephant-shooting, yet there was a sufficiency of heavy metal in our armoury, we thought, to try conclusions with even so formidable an antagonist as Peer Bux, should we meet with him. Disgust at the want of success hitherto of our *shikar* expedition, and the tantalizing effects of the Government notice showing that there was game very much in evidence if we cared to go after it, soon determined our movements. The native *shikaris* were summoned, and after much consultation we shifted camp to Karkankote, a smaller village in the State forest of that name, and on the high road to Manantoddy. The travellers' bungalow there, a second-class one, was deserted by its usual native attendants, as the rogue-elephant had paid two visits to that place and had pulled down a portion of the out-offices in his attempts to get at the servants. In the village we found only a family of Kurambas left in charge by the *Potail* (village magistrate) when the inhabitants deserted it. These people, we found, had erected for themselves a *machan* (platform) on the trees, to which they retired at night to be out of the reach of the elephant, should he come that way. From them we learned that the rogue had not been seen for a week, but that it was about his time to come that way, as he had a practice of making a complete circuit of the country lying between the frontier and the Manantoddy–Mysore and Hunsur–Mercara roads. This was good news, so we set to work at once, getting ammunition ready for this the largest of all game. Nothing less than eight drams of powder and a hardened solid ball would content most of us. K—, poor fellow, had been reading up 'Smooth bore' or some other authority on Indian game, and pinned his faith to a twelve-bore duck gun 'for,' he argued, 'at twenty paces,' and that was the maximum distance from which to shoot at an elephant—'the smooth-bore will shoot as straight as the rifle and hit quite as hard'.

Our horses and pack-bullocks were picketed within one of the out-offices, and all the native servants took shelter inside the other. Great fires we kindled before the out-offices as a precautionary measure—not that we expected the elephant that night. We were in bed betimes, as we meant to be up at daybreak and have a good hunt all round, under the guidance of the Kurambas, who promised to take us to the rogue's favourite haunts when in that neighbourhood. The Dak Bungalow had but two rooms. That in which O— and myself slept had a window overlooking the out-offices. In the adjacent room slept F— and K—. Towards the small hours of the morning I was awakened by a loud discharge of fire-arms from F—'s room, followed by the unmistakable fierce trumpeting of an enraged elephant. There is no mistaking that sound when once heard. Catching up our rifles we rushed into the next room and found F—, gun in hand, peering out through the broken window frame, and K— trying to strike a light. When F— had recovered sufficiently from his excitement, he explained that he had been awakened by something trying to encircle his feet through the thick folds of the rug he had wrapped round them. On looking up he thought he could make out the trunk of an elephant thrust through the opening where a pane of glass had been broken in the window. His loaded gun was in the corner by his side, and, aiming at what he thought would be the direction of the head, he fired both barrels at once. With a loud scream the elephant withdrew its trunk, smashing the whole window at the same time. He had reloaded and was looking out for the elephant, in case it should return to the attack, but could see nothing, as it was too dark. F——'s was a narrow escape, for had the elephant succeeded in getting his trunk around one of his legs nothing could have saved him. With one jerk he would have been pulled through the window and quickly done to death beneath the huge feet of the brute. The thick folds of the blanket alone saved him, and even that would have been pulled aside in a little time if he had not awakened and had the presence of mind to fire at the beast.

No amount of shouting would bring any of the servants from their retreat in the out-office, although we could distinctly hear them talking to each other in low tones; and it was scarcely fair of us to ask them to come out, with the probability of an infuriated rogue elephant being about. However, we soon remembered this fact, and helping ourselves to whisky pegs, as the excitement had made us thirsty, we determined to sit out the darkness, as nothing could be done till morning.

At the first break of day, we sallied out to learn the effects of F——'s shots. We could distinctly trace the huge impressions of the elephant's feet to the forest skirting the bungalow, but could find no trace of blood. The Kuramba trackers were soon on the spot, and on matters being explained to them they said the elephant must be badly wounded about the face, otherwise he would have renewed the attack. The shots being fired at such close quarters must have scorched the opening of the wound and prevented the immediate flow of blood. They added that if wounded the elephant would not go far, but would make for the nearest water in search of mud with which to plaster the wound, as mud was a sovereign remedy for all elephant wounds, and all elephants used it. The brute would then lie up in some dense thicket for a day or two, as any exertion would tend to reopen the wound. The Kurambas appeared to be so thoroughly acquainted with the habits of these beasts, that we readily placed ourselves under their guidance, and swallowing a hasty breakfast we set off on the trail, taking with us one *shikari* to interpret and a gun-bearer, named Suliman, to carry a tiffin-basket.

The tracks ran parallel with the road for about a mile, and then crossed it and made south in the direction of the Kabbany river, an affluent of the Cauvery. Distinct traces of blood could now be seen, and presently we came to a spot covered with blood, where the elephant had evidently stood for some time. The country became more and more difficult as we approached the river. Dense clumps of bamboo and wait-a-bit thorns, with here and there a large teak or honne tree, made it difficult to see more than a few yards ahead. The Kuramba guides said that we must now advance more cautiously, as the river was within half-a-mile, and that we might come on the 'rogue' at any moment. Up to this moment, I don't know if any of us appreciated the full extent of the danger we were running. Following up a wounded *must* elephant on foot, in dense cover such as we were in meant that if we did not drop the brute with the first shot, one or more of us would in all probability pay for our temerity with our lives. We had been on the tramp two hours and we were all of us more or less excited, so taking a sip of cold tea to steady our nerves, we settled on a plan of operations. F—— and I, having the heaviest guns, were to lead, the Kuramba trackers being a pace or two in advance of us. O—— and K—— were to follow about five paces behind, and the *shikari* and Suliman were to bring up the rear at an interval of ten paces. If we came on the elephant, the advance party were to fire first and then move aside. If the brute survived our fire, the second battery would surely account for it. It never entered our minds that anything living could withstand a discharge at close quarters of eight such barrels as we carried. Having settled matters to our satisfaction, off we set on the trail, moving now very cautiously, the guides enjoining the strictest silence. Every bush was carefully examined, every thicket scanned before an advance was made; frequent stops were made, and the drops of blood carefully examined to see if they were clotted or not, as by this the Kurambas could tell how far off the wounded brute was. The excitement was intense. The rustle of a falling leaf would set our hearts pit-a-pat. The nervous strain was too great, and I began to feel quite sick. The trail now entered a cart-track through the forest, so that we could see twenty paces or so ahead. Now we were approaching the river, for we could hear the murmuring of the water some two or three hundred yards ahead. The bamboo clumps grew thicker on either side. The leading Kuramba was just indicating that the trail led off to the right, when a terrific trumpet directly behind us made us start round, and a ghastly sight met our view. The elephant had evidently scented us long before we appeared in view, and had left the cart-track and, making a slight detour to the right, had gone back a little way and concealed itself behind some bamboo clumps near the track. It had quietly allowed us to pass, and then, uttering a shrill scream, charged on the rear. Seizing Suliman in its trunk, it had lifted him aloft prior to dashing him to the ground, when we turned. K— was standing in the path, about ten paces from the elephant, with his gun levelled at the brute. Fire, K— fire! we shouted, but it was too late. Down came the trunk, and the body of poor Suliman, hurled with terrific force, was dashed on the ground with a sickening thud, which told us he was beyond help. As the trunk was coming down K— fired. In a moment the enraged brute was on him. We heard a second shot, and then saw poor K— and his gun flying through the air from a kick from the animal's fore-foot. There was no time to aim. Indeed, there was nothing to aim at, as all we could see was a great black object coming down on us with incredible speed. Four shots in rapid succession, and the brute swerved to the left and went off screaming and crashing through the bamboos in its wild flight. Rapidly reloading we waited to see if the rogue would come back, but we heard the crashing of the underwood further off and knew it had gone for good. We had now time to look round. The body of K— we found on the top of a bamboo clump a good many yards away. We thought he was dead, as he did not reply to our calls, but on cutting down the bamboos and removing the body we found he had only swooned. A glass of whisky soon brought him round, but he was unable to move, as his spine was injured and several ribs broken. Rigging a hammock, we had him carried into Manantoddy, where he was on the doctor's hands for months before he was able to move, and finally he had to go back to England and, I believe, never thoroughly recovered his health. Suliman's corpse had to be taken into Antarasante, and after an inquest by the native Magistrate it was made over to the poor fellow's co-religionists for burial.

Our tragic adventure with Peer Bux, the rogue elephant, was soon noised abroad and served only to attract a greater number of British sportsmen, bent on trying conclusions with the 'Terror of Hunsur', as this notorious brute came to be called by the inhabitants of the adjacent districts. A month had elapsed since our ill-fated expedition, and nothing had been heard of the rogue, although its known haunts had been scoured by some of the most noted *shikaris* of South India. We began to think that the wounds it had received in its encounter with us had proved fatal, and even contemplated claiming its tusks should its carcass be found, and presenting them to K— as a memento of his terrible experience with the monster, but it was a case of 'counting your chickens', for evidence was soon forthcoming that its tusks were not to be had for the asking. The beast had evidently been lying low while its wounds healed, and had retreated for this purpose into some of the dense fastnesses of the Begur jungles. Among others who arrived on the scene at this time to do battle with the Terror were two young officers from Cannanore—one a subaltern in a native regiment, the other a naval officer on a visit to the station. They had come with letters of introduction to Colonel M—, in charge of the Amrat Mahal at Hunsur, and that officer had done all in his power to dissuade the youngsters from going after the 'rogue', as he saw plainly that they were green at *shikar* and did not fully comprehend the risks they would be running, nor had they experience enough to enable them to provide against possible contingencies. Finding however that dissuasion only strengthened their determination to brave all danger, he thought he would do the next best thing by giving them the best mount possible for such a task. Among the recent arrivals at the Commissariat lines was 'Dod Kempa' (the Great Red One), a famous tusker sent down all the way from Secunderabad to do battle with Peer Bux. Dod Kempa was known to be staunch, as he had been frequently used for tiger-shooting in the notorious Nirmul jungles and had unflinchingly stood the charge of a wounded tiger. His *mahout* declared that the Terror of Hunsur would run at the mere sight of Dod Kempa, for had not his reputation gone forth throughout the length and breadth of India, even among the elephant folk? Kempa was not as tall as Peer Bux, but was more sturdily built, with short, massive tusks. He was mottled all over his body with red spots: hence his name Kempa (red). He was a veritable bull-dog among elephants and was by no means a handsome brute, but he had repeatedly done good service in bringing to order recalcitrant pachyderms, and for this reason had been singled out to try conclusions with the Hunsur rogue. With such a mount Colonel M—— thought the young fellows would be safe even should they meet the 'Terror', so seeing them safely mounted on the pad he bid them not to fail to call on D——, the Forest Officer on the Coorg frontier, who would put them up to the best means of finding the game they were after.

They had been gone about four days when one morning the Commissariat sergeant turned up at Colonel M——'s bungalow and with a salute informed him that Dod Kempa was in the lines, and that his *mahout* was drunk and incapable and he could get no information from him. The elephant and *mahout* had turned up some time during the night; the pad had been left behind, and the man could give no information about the two *sahibs* who had gone out with him. Fearing the worst, the Colonel sent for the *mahout*, (elephant driver) but before the order could be carried out, a crowd of *mahouts,* and other natives were seen approaching, shouting '*Pawgalee hogiya! Pawgalee hogiya*!' (he has gone mad! he has gone mad!). Yes, sure enough, there was Dod Kempa's *mahout* inanely grinning and shaking his hands. Now and again he would stop and look behind, and a look of terror would come into his eyes. He would crouch down and put his hands to his ears as if to shut out some dreadful sound. He would remain like this for a minute or two, glance furtively around, and then as if reassured would get up and smile and shake his hands. It was plainly not liquor that made him behave in this manner; the poor fellow had actually become an imbecile through fear. It was hopeless attempting to get any information from such an object, so handing him over to the care of the medical officer, a search party mounted on elephants was at once organized and sent off in the direction of Frazerpett, twenty-four miles distant, where D——'s camp was. When they got about half-way they were met by a native forest ranger, who asked them to stop and come back with him to a country cart that followed, in which were the dead bodies of the two unfortunate officers of whom they were in search. On coming up with the cart and examining its contents a most gruesome sight met their eyes. There, rolled up in a native *kumbly* (blanket), was an indistinguishable mass of human flesh, mud, and clothing. Crushed out of all shape, the bodies were inextricably mixed together, puddled into one mass by the great feet of the *must* elephant. None dared touch the shapeless heap, where nought but the boot-covered feet were distinguishable to show that two human beings lay there. A deep gloom fell on all, natives and Europeans alike; none dared speak above a whisper, and in silence the search party turned back, taking with them what was once two gallant young officers, but now an object that made anyone shudder to look at. The forest ranger's story was soon told: he had been an eyewitness of the tragic occurrence. Here it is:

> The officers arrived two days ago at Periyapatna, a large village half-way to Frazerpett, and while camped there, a native brought in information of a bullock having been killed at his village some four miles off. The *sahibs* determined to sit up in a *machan* over the kill, and go for the tiger when he returned to his meal. They left their camp-followers and baggage at Periyapatna, and accompanied only by himself (the ranger) and the native who brought the information, they rode out on Dod Kempa, took their places on the *machan*, and sent the *mahout* back with the elephant with orders for him to come back at dawn next day to take them back to camp. The tiger did not turn up that night, and the whole party were on their way back to Periyapatna in the early dawn when suddenly Dod Kempa stopped, and striking the ground with the end of his trunk, made that peculiar drumming noise which is the usual signal of alarm with these animals when they scent tiger or other danger. It was still early morning, so that they could barely see any object in the shadow of the forest trees. The elephant now began to back, curl away his trunk and sway his head from side to side. The *mahout* said he was about to charge, and that there must be another elephant in the path. We could barely keep our seats on the pad, so violent was the motion caused by the elephant backing and swaying from side to side. The officers had to hold on tight by the ropes, so that they could not use their guns, when, there in the distance, only fifty yards off, we saw an enormous elephant coming towards us! There was no doubt that it was the rogue, from its great size. It had not seen us yet, as elephants see very badly; but Dod Kempa had scented him out as the wind was in our favour. The *sahibs* urged the *mahout* to keep his elephant quiet so that they might use their guns, but it was no use, for although he cruelly beat the beast about the head with his iron goad yet it continued to back and sway. The rogue had now got within thirty yards, when it perceived us and stopped. It backed a few paces and with ears thrown forward uttered trumpet after trumpet and then

> came full charge down on us. No sooner did Dod Kempa hear the trumpeting than he turned round and bolted off into the forest, crashing through the brushwood and under the branches of the large trees, the *must* elephant in hot pursuit. Suddenly an overhanging branch caught in the side of the pad, ripped it clean off the elephant's back, and threw the two officers on the ground. I managed to seize the branch and clambered up out of harm's way. When I recovered a little from my fright, I saw the rogue elephant crushing something up under its fore-feet. Now and again it would stoop and drive its tusks into the mass and begin stamping on it again. This it did for about a quarter of an hour. It then went off in the direction that Dod Kempa had taken. I saw nothing of Dod Kempa after the pad fell off. I waited for two hours, and seeing the mad elephant did not come back, I got down and ran to Periyapatna and told the *sahib's* servants, and we went back with a lot of people, and found that the mass the elephant had been crushing under its feet was the bodies of the two officers! The brute must have caught them when they were thrown to the ground and killed them with a blow of its trunk or a crush of the foot, and it had then mangled the two bodies together. We got a cart and brought the bodies away.

Simple in all its ghastly details, the tale was enough to make one's blood run cold, but heard as it was, said one present, 'within a few yards of what that bundle of native blankets contained, it steeled one's heart for revenge'. But let us leave this painful narrative and hasten on to the time when the monster met with his deserts at the hand of one of the finest sportsmen that ever lived, and that too in a manner which makes every Britisher feel a pride in his race that can produce such men.

Gordon Cumming was a noted *shikari*, almost as famous in his way as his brother, the celebrated lion-slayer of South Africa, and his equally famous sister, the talented artist and explorer of Maori fastnesses in New Zealand. Standing over six feet in his stockings and of proportionate breadth of shoulder, he was an athlete in every sense of the word. With his heavy double rifle over his shoulder, and with Yalloo, his native tracker and *shikari* at his heels, he would think nothing of a twenty-mile swelter after a wounded bison even in the hottest weather. An unerring shot, he was known to calmly await the furious onset of a tiger till the brute was within a few yards, and then lay it low with a ball crashing through its skull. It is said that, having tracked a noted man-eater to its lair, he disdained to shoot at the sleeping brute, but roused it with a stone and then shot it as it was making at him open-mouthed. He was known to decline to take part in beats for game or to use an elephant to shoot from, but would always go alone save for his factotum Yalloo, and would follow up the most dangerous game on foot. He was a man of few words and it was with the greatest difficulty he could be got to talk of his adventures. When pressed to relate an incident in which it was known that he had done a deed of the utmost daring, he would dismiss the subject with half-a-dozen words, generally: 'Yes, the beast came at me, and I shot him'. Yalloo was as loquacious as his master was reticent, and it was through his glibness of tongue round the camp fire, that much of Gordon Cumming's *shikar* doings became known. Yalloo believed absolutely in his master and would follow him anywhere. 'He carries two deaths in his hand and can place them where he likes (alluding to his master's accuracy with the rifle); therefore, why should I fear? Has a beast two lives that I should dread him? A single shot is enough, and even a *Rakshasa* (giant demon) would lie low.'

A Deputy Commissioner in the Mysore service, Cumming was posted at Shimoga, in the north-west of the province, when he heard of the doings of Peer Bux at Hunsur, and obtained permission to try and bag him. He soon heard all the *khubber* (news) as to the habits of the brute, and he determined to systematically stalk him down. For this purpose he established three or four small camps at various points in the districts ravaged by the brute, so that he might not be hampered with a camp following him about but could pitch in at any of the temporary shelters he had put up and get such refreshments he required. He knew it would be a work of days, perhaps weeks, following up the tracks of the rogue, who was here today and twenty miles off tomorrow; but he had confidence in his own staying powers, and he trusted to the chapter of lucky accidents to cut short a toilsome stalk.

Selecting the banks of the Kabbany as the most likely place to fall in with the tracks of Peer Bux, he made Karkankote his resting-place for the time, while a careful examination was made of the ground on the left bank of the river. Tracks were soon found, but these always led to the river, where they were lost, and no further trace of them was found on either bank. He learned from the Kurambas that the elephant was in the habit of entering the river and floating down for a mile or so before it made for the banks. As it travelled during the night and generally laid up in dense thicket during the day, there was some chance of coming up with it, if only the more recent tracks could be followed up uninterruptedly; but with the constant breaks in the scent whenever the animal took to the water he soon saw that tracking would be useless in such country, and that he must shift to where there were no large streams. A couple of weeks had been spent in the arduous work of following up the brute from Karkankote to Frazerpett and back again to the river near Hunsur and then on to Heggadavencotta. Even the tireless Yalloo now became wearied and began to doubt the good fortune of his master. Yet Gordon Cumming was as keen as ever, and would not give up his plan of following like a sleuth-hound on the tracks of the brute. On several occasions they had fallen in with other parties out on the same errand as themselves, but these contented themselves with lying in wait at certain points the brute was known to frequent. These parties had invariably asked Gordon Cumming to join them, as they pronounced his stern chase a wildgoose one and said he was as likely to come up with the Flying Dutchman as he was with the Terror of Hunsur.

It was getting well into the third week of this long chase, when the track led through some scrub jungle which would not give cover to anything larger than a spotted deer. They had come on to the ruins of an ancient village, the signs of which were a small temple fast falling into decay, and an enormous banyan tree *(Ficus religiosa)*. It was midday; the heat was intense, and they sat under the shade of the tree for a little rest. Cumming was munching a biscuit, while Yalloo was chewing a little *paan* (betel leaf), when a savage scream was heard and there, not twenty paces off, was the Terror of Hunsur coming down on them in a terrific charge. From the position in which Cumming was sitting a fatal shot at the elephant was almost impossible, as it carried its head high and only its chest was exposed. A shot there might rake the body without touching lungs or heart, and then the brute would be on him. Without the least sign of haste and with the utmost unconcern Gordon Cumming still seated, flung his *sola topee* (sun hat) at the beast when it was about ten yards from him. The rogue stopped momentarily to examine this strange object, and lowered its head for the purpose. This was exactly what Cumming wanted, and quick as thought a bullet, planted in the centre of the prominence just above the trunk, crashed through its skull, and the Terror of

Hunsur dropped like a stone, shot dead. 'Ah, comrade,' said Yalloo, when relating the story, 'I could have kissed the Bahadoor's (my lord's) feet when I saw him put the gun down, and go on eating his biscuit just as if he had only shot a bird of some kind, instead of that devil of an elephant. I was ready to die of fright; yet here was the *sahib* sitting down as if his life had not been in frightful jeopardy just a moment before. Truly, the *sahibs* are great!'

A.E. WARDROP

Elephant*

Poor Mada [my head sholaga tracker] was killed by a bear in 1922.

I then went after an elephant, having heard from my friend Mr Van Ingen, the Mysore taxidermist, of one that had been proclaimed a rogue in that district. The Dewan and the officials of Mysore were exceedingly kind to me in connection with this animal as well as with the bison.

The elephant lived in the Begur Range, some fifty miles from Mysore. He had recently killed one man by kicking him, after a long chase down a path; he had also broken up the greater part of a man, cart, and bullocks complete, and was now outlawed. A price of Rs 500 was on his head; so I might, and namely did, keep the tusks when I shot him.

I had studied live elephants in the Mysore elephant stables for hours, from every aspect, as well as a skull in the zoo there, and I had considerable recent practice with the 470 rifle.

My camp was at a pleasant bungalow, close to which lived Mr Channiga-Raya, the forest ranger, well-educated Mysore gentleman, to whose help and society I owe much.

The rogue lived three miles from the bungalow in a patch of jungle a few miles square, bounded by hills on two sides, the

From *Days and Nights with Indian Big Game*. London: Mcmillan, 1923.
*This is a modified version of the original chapter heading.

Cubbany, a tributary of the Cauvery, made a third and a fire-line the fourth side. This last was his favourite haunt.

The road to the jungle ran through young rāgi fields like green wheat, with meadows of black clover-like grass in which fat cattle grazed. Everywhere were the olive and grey tints which, with the sky, make the typical blue Mysore day.

The jungle itself consisted of big trees and bamboos, with, for the most part, a dense undergrowth of grass or young bamboo, which sometimes grew fifteen or twenty feet high. Here and there were lower clearings, with a hundred yards of view but vision was generally much more restricted. Beautiful aisles of bamboo clumps were occasionally to be met with, growing apart like the pillars of a cathedral; the delicate tracery of their boughs overhead was like the arched groin of a roof, and the light below, subdued in the brightest sun, completed the resemblance to a great sacred building.

The elephant was marked down from early dawn before we started. We met parties of Kurubers, wild men of the woods, and these dwindled in numbers until we reached the last two men, who were actually watching the elephant and marking their progress by leaves. It was the military system of advance guard, vanguard, and patrols, admirably carried out by Mr C.

On the first day we came early on the elephant. I could see the back of his head and one ear above the undergrowth. He gave me a shot that I had studied. I crawled to a tree and, resting my rifle, had a perfect shot at twenty yards; but I had to fire through some leaves, and one bamboo twig of the thickness of a pencil was just in front of my foresight. This I chanced, and fired; I heard no noise, and hoped he had fallen dead. Steps, at first towards us and then receding, soon undeceived me. I had missed, and the pencil twig was gone. But my attendants would have none of missing twigs. My name was MUD.

The elephant had not seen us. In the hope that he might take the shot for thunder it were better not to follow and frighten him.

'This is a *shaitan*, and there is witchcraft in it', said old Juman, my bearer. 'It can only be defeated by prayer—and money.'

We tracked the elephant for long next day, and came on him at 6.50 p.m., when I found d the light too bad to fire.

The Kurubers were good fellows. They had a great respect for this elephant, yet they tracked him in all his ways.

On the third day we got news of the rogue before we left the bungalow at 9 a.m., and we saw him by 10 o'clock. He was in thick bamboo; we were thirty yards from him and a little above him. Finding no chance of a good view, I crept forward, parallel to the elephant's path. Presently I got a clear broadside view of an ear, and fired. Missfire. I reloaded and getting once more a clear view of the ear, again pressed the trigger. Missfire. I thought of Juman; the rifle must be bewitched.

On hearing the second click the elephant swung towards us at a walk. I could only see the outline of his head in foliage. I reloaded and fired as best I might into this. If I had waited until he was in the open he would have been on top of us. The elephant seemed to stagger as I fired and then became invisible. Immediately after my shot came a volley, my second barrel and one barrel each from Mr C. and a rabbit of a Forest-guard. None of these hit, but they made a comfortable sound.

The elephant crashed off trumpeting. We followed up the blood tracks. Within half a mile the Kurubers' marvellous instinct spotted him standing still in dense cover. We made a little detour and got within eighteen yards of him. Mr C. was on my left, the 'rabbit' and a Kuruber on my right. I could see a dim silent mass, but devil a mark could I see to fire at. I waited. There was a pull on my left shoulder, as Mr C. urged me to fire. The 'rabbit' also distracted me with his pulling and pointing; then his nerve gave and he fired. I turned to curse him when the elephant, at the same second, strode forward and stood quarter-right towards me, leaning somewhat backwards, trunk raised on high, scenting for his adversaries. I fired. There was a delightful vision of upturned trunk and feet, a heavy thud and all was still.

So died the Rogue of Begur.

An inglorious victory indeed. The poor beast had no chance: stunned by a heavy rifle, he never knew where his foes were. Rogue he was, yet probably as much sinned against as sinning. He had no hairs on his tail, his ears were in ribbons, and he had three recent bullet wounds on him.

His tusks were just over 4 feet. I had reckoned he stood 9 feet 9 inches on a modest measure; but his foot circumference was 54 inches. So I had overestimated his height, on the usual basis of calculation of the foot circumference being half the height.

I went home and then returned to cut out the tusks. The news of the rogue's death had spread. The countryside went out to see him, and I met little groups. of tens and twenties moving and talking freely where none had walked of late.

I found an official telegram on my return, ordering me to Simla at once, so I had to abandon expeditions which I had planned, after two other rogues elsewhere.

In January 1923, after the buffalo shoot, I was able to take advantage of the generosity of H.H. the Maharajah of Travancore, who had given me leave to shoot bison and an elephant, and to keep the tusks.

I got every help from the Dewan and was most fortunate in enjoying the hospitality and help of Col. and Mrs D.-D. I borrowed everything from them, and my shoot ran on very pleasant lines.

For three weeks I worked the country round my host's estate, on the Cardamum Hills and round the Peryar Lake, and shot two sambhur, one bison, and a really good tusker.

The sambhur were both long and lucky shots. The bison was extinguished by the .470 at sixty yards. An easy shot, for we got above him and waited for him to come out into the open.

I was after elephant for ten days' actual hunting. In all the near treks, as well as on our successful day, D.D. accompanied me and helped me more than I can say.

There was a considerable amount of *eter* everywhere. This is a densely matted jungle of close-growing young bamboo, twenty to thirty feet high. A man can only get through it by the elephant tracks. An elephant crashes through it like butter; and when one hears them on the hillside a few yards above one, while groping along the track oneself, one easily realizes that this *eter* is the most serious proposition that Indian big-game sport presents. One also often finds *lantana*, a high matted shrub of the marigold type, which, like the *eter*, is equally suited to an elephant and unsuited to a man. Only, in the *lantana* there is blue sky overhead. In both *eter* and *lantana*, except when shooting along a track, the maximum range of a rifle bullet may be taken as five yards.

Our first day's work was all in *eter* and *lantana*, in a big patch of which D.D.'s shikaris had located a large and well-known tusker that frequented that neighbourhood. We followed this brute for hours, and heard him rumbling but never saw him. Then, unknowingly, we chanced on to a rogue elephant which kept company with the big tusker. The next time we got close this brute trumpeted and went off. We ran along the trail in the *lantana*, for darkness threatened. Suddenly the whole track was darkened by the mass of the charging rogue, trunk upraised, mouth open, absolutely silent, and looking like the side of a house made of gutta-percha. Luckily one shot in the head from D.-D. turned the beast, and I, for one, was glad. I was too slow to fire. D.-D.'s shot was purely in self-defence and did no real damage, for we went to the spot next day, found the rogue had gone right away, and later heard of him in good health.

Where there was no *eter lantana* the grass was generally high, except in the Cardamum forests. There had been unusually late and heavy rains.

The work was severe. Our longest day started with a two-mile walk; then we picked up tracks of a good tusker, followed him fifteen miles, and had a five-mile trek home again.

I spent five days on the Peryar, and was immensely struck, not only with the engineering work on it, but by its beauty, its winding channels, and lonely grandeur. It has all and more than the charm of the lakes in the Trossachs, with the additional attraction that the banks and surrounding heights, instead of being monopolized by the Glasgow Corporation, are in the saner keeping of sambhur, bison, and wild elephant.

Here as well as on the Cardamums I was up with elephant, and examining them daily, but found no tusker good enough to shoot. I might only fire at one. On the Peryar all travelling was by water in a dug-out canoe. We frequently saw sambhur and elephant in this way, and on one occasion ran into a herd of twelve elephants swimming, but there was no good tusker among them.

The elephants swam very freely across the numerous arms of the lake, which were generally several hundred yards wide, and our normal method of picking up fresh tracks was to paddle round the edges of the lake and disembark when tracks were found.

We used to start at about 4 a.m., and those not rowing were glad of a couple of blankets. On our right, low over the lake, the Southern Cross showed brilliantly. Broken by the ripple of our bows, a bright streak of water pointed to the morning star, shining as I have never seen it shine elsewhere.

Finally I had given up all hope of an elephant, and my car was at the door to take me to the nearest rail *en route* to England, when my host suddenly heard news that the big tusker was once again in the neighbourhood. So we had a thirteenth-hour hunt, starting off at peep of dawn in D.-D.'s car.

We got to our ground, and while the shikaris were reconnoitring, D.-D. heard the elephant below us. For elephant and bison shooting acute hearing is a really important asset to the hunter.

After some reconnaissance we closed for action, D.-D. having replaced the shikaris and conducting the stalk. The elephant was in a deep ravine, bordered on the one hand by an open hillside and on the other by a big patch of *eter*. The *col* was covered with man-high grass and was the intercepting feature between the elephant's present cover and the heavy jungle and *eter* of a big valley on the far side.

We got close to the elephant and could see him, but I could get no clear view of his head. He moved up the ravine, so we climbed a little and worked forward to intercept him; but the elephant had got a touch of our wind and was moving on fast. D.-D. turned out of the ravine and climbed along the grassy crest towards the *col*. We were 'all-out', with our wind tested to the utmost.

D.-D. heard the elephant, and signalled to me to hurry up. A last effort landed us in an open patch of grassy hill with some rocks. As the elephant's head appeared out of the cover we threw ourselves down. He was moving at a steady walk up to the col to cross to the next valley. He was seventy yards away and the whole of his head showed above the grass. An earlier reconnaissance by one of the shikaris, from a tree, had satisfied all doubts as to his tusks. I got a quick shot and hit him through the brain, for he reared up on the steep slope and fell over backwards, being hit again in the head by both of us. He fell head down on the track he had just come up and never moved again. His tusks were 5 feet long, 17 inches in girth, and weighed 86 lbs. Double the circumference of his forefoot made him 9 feet 8 inches high.

So ended this happy trip. I caught the boat with a rush, and in all the journey down I thought of much kindness, of unselfish sportsmanship, and of the glorious time I had spent in these wild, beautiful, and little-known mountains.

RANDOLPH C. MORRIS

An Elephant Shoot on the Baragur Hills (Coimbatore District) [1926]

Three solitary tuskers having been proscribed on the Baragurs, the morning of February 28, 1926, found three of us, Major R.E. Wright, IMS, Mr P. Saunders (both of Madras), and myself at Hassanur (North Coimbatore) full of enthusiasm to go after the proscribed rogues. A delay occurred at Hassanur as the top two leaves of my Ford front springs had, we found, snapped, and new leaves had to be substituted which I luckily had with me (the roads round this part of the District being so vile I find it pays to carry nearly all the spare parts of a Ford with me!). We left Hassanur at 2 p.m. and travelled along sixty miles of a perfectly terrible 'road' the last fifteen miles being across fields and along a cart track through the jungle, arriving eventually at the forest bungalow we had decided should be our first stop at 7 p.m. Here we were delighted to find our good servants (who had been sent on in advance) had prepared everything for our arrival, and we were not sorry to tumble into our cots after drinks and an early dinner. We were up before dawn, and having arranged for our kit

Reprinted from *A Century of Natural History*. Ed. J.C. Daniel. Bombay: Bombay Natural History Society, 1983.

to be brought along on pack bulls, we left after a meal at daylight for the second stage of our journey. Nine miles of track (even worse than the day before) took us to the foot of the northern end of the Baragurs; leaving the car here in the bamboo jungle we ascended six miles of steep paved road-way that led from the foot of the hills to Madeswaran Mallai on which stands a famous and very sacred temple, pilgrimages to which, from the surrounding countryside, take place monthly. We had our trackers with us and we were more than pleased to arrive at a shady nalla about a mile from the temple itself, where we threw ourselves down for a well-earned rest. The climb had been a most exhausting one, the path being steep, the sun blazing hot, and the paving stones hard. The shikaris went off to mark down the first elephant. We had arranged that Wright should take the first elephant we came across, Saunders the second and I the third. The bamboos were all in seed, and hundreds of jungle-fowl were feeding on the bamboo rice, and after a rest we amused ourselves stalking them. At about 5 p.m. the trackers returned with the news that they had marked down one of the three rogues, not half a mile from where we then were. We were not long in getting to the place where the men had seen the tusker and we found him with his back turned to us standing among some clumps of bamboos bordering a patch of open ground. We crept up to within about twenty yards of him; and he then got our wind (the wind was all over the place) and his trunk slowly came round, followed by his ponderous body until he faced us. That he spotted us was quite certain as he curled his trunk up and looked as if he meant business. Wright fired, supported by our rifles, which however were not necessary as Wright's shot aimed at the bump above the trunk, found its mark and the tusker collapsed stone dead. The tusks were very curved and massive, the left tusk being more than a foot shorter than the right. The elephant was a very old one and had not one single hair on the end of its tail. The right tusk measured 6 ft 3 in. (weight 64 lbs.) and the left tusk 5 ft (weight 54 lbs). In quite a short time crowds of the inhabitants of Madeswaran Mallai (a village adjoining the temple) came to view the fallen elephant and rejoiced at its downfall, as for five or six years they had had a thin time of it with three rogues roaming through the jungle surrounding their village. Another elephant was reported to be in the vicinity but the light was too bad to make any move other than to the bungalow at Madeswaran Mallai. Needless to state we were very elated at our success that evening. Everything had gone well so far and 'according to plan'. We left early next morning for the spot where we were told the second elephant was last seen, but there was no sign of him, he had evidently been scared off by the shooting. At about 10 a.m. however news came in that the elephant was at a place known as Kokkubarai, some six or seven miles away; and that the third tusker (a fellow with crossed tusks) was also there. This was great news and we travelled as fast as we could up hill and down dale over a rough and stony path and reached the shola which one of the elephants was said to be in, at noon. Sure enough, as we walked quietly along the path bordering the shola, Saunders taking the lead, the tusker came out on the path in front of us, and started to trek along the path, tail on. He soon left the path, and went off at a fair pace along the hillside, and we were hard put to it to keep him in sight. Eventually he slowed down somewhat, and we managed to get above him hoping for a side shot. This we found difficult for some time; and then came our chance. The elephant turned about and started to retrace his steps and then paused; Saunders got in an excellent ear-shot, supported by Wright, and the tusker rolled over dead with a tremendous crash. His tusks were a perfect pair, and each measured (and weighed) the same (length, 5 ft 4 in.; weight, 35 lbs.) By this time we were fairly tired, and wished we could bag the third tusker without another long trek. Little did we realize then that our wishes were to be fulfilled. We were now about twelve miles from our camp and it was a broiling hot day. The third cross-tusked rogue was said to be a fiend, by far the worst of the three, and this was proved to be true. A man who had been sent to keep in touch with the tusker from a safe distance came back with the news that the tusker was standing in a small shola about two miles off. This was not so bad; we felt we could do another two miles anyhow! The elephant had gone along a path that skirted the hillside, and along this path we followed, my tracker Bomma in front carrying my rifle, I next, a local Lingayat third carrying Saunders' rifle, Saunders fourth, another tracker carrying Wright's rifle came fifth, and Wright brought up the rear. We hadn't advanced more than a mile, and were just passing through a patch of infernally thick undergrowth, when Bomma, who had climbed a log that had fallen across the path, suddenly turned round, thrust the rifle into my hands with the word 'the elephant is coming', and retired to the rear. I had visions of the rogue charging along the path and bursting in upon us while we were in the thick stuff, and realized our only chance was to get out of the patch by getting up above the path. To do this it was necessary to retreat a few yards, in my haste I forgot Saunders was close behind me, and turning round I knocked him off his feet! I told him to get up and above the path as fast as he could, and hastening a few steps further, found myself clear of the thick patch and face to face with Wright who being last hadn't been able to take in the situation and couldn't understand why everybody was scattering. He had however seized hold of his rifle. 'Up above the path, quick,' I whispered, and we both scrambled up through longish grass, keeping our eyes on the path expecting every second, to see the tusker appear. I saw Saunders had managed to get slightly higher than we were, and that he was endeavouring to climb up the side of a rock the top of which was flat and level with the hillside. It didn't occur to me then that Saunders had no rifle, and that only our two trackers were with us. The next moment a shrill trumpet rang in my ears, and looking up I saw the cross-tusked rogue bearing down upon us. As I looked he paused for a second, and I realized that I had to shoot quickly and shoot to kill. The elephant was within five yards of me and still closer to Saunders who however flung himself backwards into a crevice of the rock. I flung up my rifle, took quick aim at the bump above the trunk and fired and I heard Wright fire immediately after. The tusker pitched forward, the tips of its tusks about six feet from me, we both fired once more to make sure that he wouldn't rise again; but we need not have done so as the elephant was quite dead; both our bullets had entered its brain. It is hardly necessary for me to say that from first to last the whole affair took a mere fraction of the time it has taken me to write this. When we had sufficiently composed ourselves to take things in, we realized that Saunders was rifleless and that his rifle-bearer was not on the spot. He was discovered some way off with Saunders' rifle still on his shoulder. He had bolted back with it directly he heard Bomma tell me the elephant was coming. I yelled to him to bring the rifle and never did I see a man more visibly ashamed of himself than he was when he rejoined us. The rifle was taken roughly from him by one of our trusty trackers and he was told to clear out in no uncertain terms. Saunders' feelings can be well imagined when he found himself without a rifle and the elephant literally almost on top of him; the elephant for a second had actually placed one of its feet on the rock Saunders was busily climbing! We mounted the rock and Bomma pointed out the spot ahead of us where he had first seen the elephant. It was stationary and facing us when he caught sight of it he said, and had started moving rapidly towards us, presumably on seeing Bomma. The spot indicated by Bomma, and verified by the other tracker was on an examination of the tracks, quite fifty yards from where it was shot, so that the elephant had covered this stretch in very quick time. The local fellow who had brought us news of the whereabouts of this tusker was very emphatic in his statements that he had last seen the tusker a mile further on. The Sholagas declared that our shooting had 'drawn' this rogue, and that it had retraced its steps. It was quite evident that the rogue, had been getting our wind as we approached him (this was impossible to avoid as it was blowing in all directions), had paused, and then moved forward rapidly on seeing Bomma; but why not along the path we were then on? It is my firm belief that the elephant, seeing Bomma disappear, had divined our intentions (or rather his intentions) and raced along the hillside above the path to cut him off, and suddenly coming on a group of us made the pause fatal to him. That his pause was only momentary and he would have been among us the next moment is absolutely certain for we were altogether too close to him. The aftermath was all the more pleasurable in that the affair had been so full of incident and thrilling. The tusks were a splendid pair, the right one 7 ft 7½ in. (weighing 68 lbs.) and the left 7 ft 4½in. (weighing 63 lbs.). There had certainly been a humorous side to the affair, our intense desire to escape from what we considered a death-trap having led us right under the feet of the elephant as it were. We were by now very weary and hot, and felt we could not face the trek back to our camp. We therefore walked back about four miles to a cool evergreen shola and decided to sleep the night there. We sent a man for our servants and kit; we still had our pack bulls in camp and rested till they turned up at about 10 p.m. It was very pleasant dining and sleeping on our cots that night on the open hillside just above the shola. We decided to end up our shoot by motoring southwards through the Baragurs to a place named Tattakerai where another rogue elephant had been proscribed, our intention being to have a go at this one also. We accordingly, next morning, sent off our kit and servants by a short-cut down to a forest bungalow, at Geriki-Kandi, on the Kollegal–Bhavani road, and tramped down with our shikaris to our car. After mending a leak in the hosepipe we started off and were once again motoring along dreadful tracks and by-ways where no car had ever before been seen or heard of. A five-mile short-cut which we took across fields from one village to another in order to avoid an alternative route of fifteen miles was a positive nightmare; how the Ford car stood it beats me and my respect for a Ford was increased a thousandfold on the completion of this journey. The track was good and bad in parts, and where it was bad it was generally horrid, the car having either to climb a series of outcrops of rock or dive into wash-outs and miniature gullies. The tyres were a mass of prickly-pear thorns and we were very soon mending puncture after puncture. On arriving at Geriki-Kandi where we intended to sleep the night we spent a hot and beastly hour or more mending inner tubes. We decided to push on to Tattakerai to make enquiries about the rogue and to return to Geriki-Kandi after doing this. We climbed seven miles of a steep and poisonous ghat and were glad to reach Tattakerai, which is situated on the summit of the Baragurs (4000 ft) and was comparatively cool, the heat at Geriki-Kandi being unbearable. The forest ranger had informed us that the rogue had not been heard of for three months, but on making further enquiries at a village named Oosimallai, a mile along the road from Tattakerai, we learned that the rogue visited the fields there nightly. This was cheering, and we left our trackers there, and motored back down the ghat to Geriki-Kandi. On our arrival we found our servants and kit had arrived, and we were very soon in our cots outside the bungalow. We left at 5 a.m. next morning, giving instructions for our kit to follow us, and arrived at Tattakerai at 6 a.m., and at Oosimallai a little later. Here we left the car and struck off into the jungle with our trackers and two local Sholagas. We did not have to go far before we came on fresh tracks of the elephant and a little later we heard him breaking bamboos. Two of our shikaris were sent to locate him; they unfortunately 'jumped' a herd of bison which crashed into the jungle disturbing the elephant, and causing him to move off into some very thick stuff. On inspection we found that we would gain nothing by following him up into this cover, as it was far too dense. We then climbed a rock on the hillside overlooking the cover in the hopes of being able to locate the elephant. One of our trackers penetrated the cover below us for a short distance in order to climb a tree to get a better view, but with no better success. Soon after his return the elephant moved up to where this man had been, and evidently smelt him as he trumpeted shrilly and kicked the ground repeatedly. This showed that the elephant was inclined to be vicious, and we decided to throw in stones in the hopes of drawing him out. Our plan very nearly succeeded, as on hearing the first stone fall the rogue trumpeted again and charged to the spot where the stone fell. This went on for some time, our stones being hurled nearer and nearer to the edge of the cover. We got the elephant to within about ten yards of the edge of the cover, but nearer than this he would not come; he finally retired some way in, and would not move to stones and taps on trees, etc., so we decided to leave him in peace till the afternoon, in the hopes of his coming out to feed in more open jungle. In the meantime we discovered a way into the outskirts of the cover from below, and took up our position in a favourable place and waited for him to come out; but this he would not do, and as the light was getting very bad, we decided to try to move him by the use of stones again. Stones were therefore hurled into the cover from above and only resulted in the elephant leaving the cover and that jungle in the opposite direction, with a scream. He evidently decided that the jungle was bewitched! We returned to the bungalow at Tattakerai and decided to have one more try for the rogue before closing our shoot. We left next morning for the same spot, hoping to find that the elephant had returned, and we sent two of our trackers in another direction. They soon marked down the rogue and if one of them had brought us word of this we would in all probability have added a fourth elephant to our bag, as they found him in very open jungle. They however stupidly sent a local Lingayat to fetch us, and the man for reasons known only to himself (probably after some heavy thinking) took us down into a deep and hot valley saying the elephant was making down the valley, instead of guiding us back to where our men were keeping in touch with the rogue. We walked up the valley for five or six miles, and when we reached the head of the valley and saw no signs of the elephant having been there at all we were considerably peeved. Even from here it took us quite another half hour to reach our trackers. This delay of nearly three hours lost us the tusker, as by the time we were on its tracks it had gone into thick cover. We cautiously followed it up, this being our last chance as we had to leave the next day. We finally caught a glimpse of the elephant's head half-turned towards us, giving only an eye-shot. This was taken, but either the elephant moved or the aim was not quite correct, the shot failed to bring him down and the elephant crashed off. We never saw him again although we followed him up for a considerable distance. We had to leave next morning, but we left one of our trackers, a good man, who, with a local, was to try and mark the elephant down as I hoped to return later to finish him off. We left at 7 a.m. motoring through the Baragur hills, through Baragur and Tamarakerai, and down the narrow ghat to the plains on the east, and back up to Hassanur, and so ended a most enjoyable and successful shoot, lasting a week and crammed with all the pleasures and thrills of the chase one could desire. We left the extraction of the tusks and the amputation and cleaning-out of the forefeet of the elephants to my two skinners who had experience of this before, and they did their job very well. The tracker left at Tattakerai to follow up the tusker returned several days later with the information that he could find no trace of the tusker, its tracks having got mixed up with those of a herd; and that he believed the elephant was going strong and none the worse for the knock it had received.

H.S. WOOD

Elephants from Above and Below

Only those sportsmen who are fortunate in being posted to Assam or Burma have the best opportunities for this form of shikar, and it is the ambition of every big-game hunter to bag an elephant. In elephant-hunting also one has to depend upon oneself. The hunter must track up the animal by himself as Indian natives have a wholesome dread of the beast and will more often than not bolt at the critical moment.

One would think that such a large animal will leave a distinct spoor, and so it does in soft or swampy ground. But on hard ground the spoor is scarcely visible; at most, a small impression made by the nails of the feet. One must trust therefore to other signs of fresh tracks, such as recent droppings, a freshly-broken branch of tree or bamboo, a crushed leaf or blade of grass.

It is very difficult to see an elephant in thick forest, for if he scents or sees danger he will remain absolutely quiet and motionless. If a tusker, probably the first thing that will attract your attention will be the gleam of his tusks, or, if he is scenting you, his trunk raised and curved forward at the end and be moving a little. A slight movement of the ears may direct your attention to the spot where he is standing. ...

My first elephant was shot not very far from Tammu in the

From *Shikar Memories*. London: Witherby, 1934.

Kubbo-Kale Valley N. and I rode the seventy-two-odd miles that lay between Manipur and Tammu in one day, taking nine hours and changing ponies four times. The going was very rough, and we were very sore next morning. But in spite of this we sallied forth, N. in one direction and I in another. I picked up the tracks of a solitary bull bison, near the site of a deserted village, where it had been feeding on plantain shoots when, all of a sudden, a herd of about thirty elephants passed in line about fifty yards away, from left to right.

A tusker headed the herd, and as I had obtained permission to shoot one, I fired. The animal sunk to his knees, but before I could give him the left barrel a female, with a calf, left the herd and came straight for me. She had her head raised and trunk coiled. I gave her the left barrel in the neck. She came on with blood spouting from her throat and dropped in a sitting position not five yards from me, where she started vomiting large clots of blood. I then turned round for my trackers to get more cartridges, but they had bolted and climbed a tree. I was naturally angry and ordered them to come down. I eventually got a further supply and so was able to put an end to both wounded elephants. It was a narrow escape, for I should surely have been killed had my first shot not felled the female. I therefore learnt a lesson, and that to always carry spare ammunition myself when after dangerous game. Hosts of villagers came for the meat, and by evening not a vestige of flesh remained. She had small tusks, and these I kept, also the feet.

The Darrang district in Assam was a great place for rogue elephants, and, on arrival, I laid myself out to bag one or two. I learnt that there were at the time two of these, one known as the 'Bindikuki rogue', and the other the 'Sesa'. These two had been the terror of the district for a number of years, and no one had seemed to have had the pluck to go after them, despite the tea-gardens in the vicinity, where they did their work of destruction. The Bindikuki rogue had also claimed a few human victims and I asked H., a planter, to send me word to headquarters directly one or both were about.

One afternoon I got a wire saying 'The Bindikuki rogue on the job', and as there was no train, I got a trolley from the station-master and went straight to H.'s bungalow. The village suffering the damage was about four miles from the garden, se we proceeded there at once, and on reaching it saw that practically the whole of the plantain crop had been destroyed, paddy trampled and eaten, and the villagers in a state of panic. The villagers said that the elephant would return towards nightfall. So we waited.

Unfortunately a thunderstorm came on and it rained in torrents; the night was as black as pitch; the elephant did turn up, but I told H. that it was useless going after him in such weather, and that it would be better to return to his home and pick up the tracks next morning. He agreed, and the villagers promised to turn up in force. When we did return to the village there were about twenty men armed with spears, bows and arrows, and a musket or two, ready to go with us.

The tracks led into a very dense forest, and we had not got more than a few yards into it when the elephant trumpeted, and our whole escort bolted, leaving us to contemplate one another. H. said, 'What are you going to do?' I replied. 'Follow him up,' and this we did. The track after a while diverged into two, so H. took the right and I took the left.

I had not gone more than forty yards, however, when I heard a swishing noise, and pressing through the creepers, cane bushes and other jungle I saw the gleam of his tusks. The brute standing about thirty yards from me, head on, but I could not get the frontal shot because his upraised trunk covered the vital spot. He was scenting me but could not see as his sight was obscured by a double cataract of both eyes, as I discovered afterwards. I found, however, that by kneeling I could get a better view, and having done so, I said to myself, 'As soon as you drop your trunk I will let you have it.' After a little while, which seemed a wait of hours, he did so, and I fired. The next moment he came straight at me, his head raised in the air and trunk coiled. I fired again at his neck; there was a spout of blood and he dropped about five yards from me.

I do not think H. had gone very far along his track, for shortly after grassing the rogue down, I received a violent clap on the back from him, and a 'Well done, old chap'. The rogue had a beautiful pair of almost symmetrical sabre-shaped tusks, each weighing 54 lbs., measuring 19 inches in circumference, and 5 feet 4 inches in length. I was naturally pleased, and on examining the body later I noticed four or five bumps under the skin like little, hard tumours. On cutting into these out dropped spherical bullets that some of the villagers must have fired on former occasions from a muzzle-loader and which had penetrated only about two inches below the surface. He had also a scar high up on his forehead, and on examining the bone under this, I found another spherical bullet that had penetrated to about three inches. This old warrior had certainly carried a lot of lead about with him.

I found my first shot had gone rather high, and so had failed to stop him. This rogue was very old; I should think fifty or sixty years of age. The tips of the ears were very much turned down and the skin was wrinkled. The circumference of the forefoot was 57 inches, giving the height approximately at 9 feet 6 inches.

My next encounter was with the Sesa rogue, and the place at which I bagged him was not very far from the spot on which the Bindikuki rogue was shot. It was arranged once more that H. should send me a wire when he appeared, and when the news came I went by the earliest train so Sesa, a railway station on the Tezpur–Balipara Railway, where H. met me. The first thing I came across close to the station was a villager crying bitterly, wringing his hands and saying that the elephant had, during the night, destroyed his whole crop of paddy. It had then apparently gone off to a small tea-garden about three miles from the station and had wrought havoc there by pulling down the roofs of four or five huts, putting the occupants to flight and then consuming all the paddy stored in the interior of the huts.

We picked up his tracks at the demolished huts, and accompanied by H.'s trackers and ten or twelve other men, we proceeded along them.

He had apparently made for some dense forest, and we had been going for some time in this when I heard a loud snoring which the men said was the elephant asleep. But when this got louder and louder our following, as on a former occasion, bolted. Just at this stage H. seems to have contracted a bad attack of cramp, the consequence being that I had to leave him and go on alone. This rogue was usually accompanied by two females, but on this day, fortunately for me, the ladies were not present. But the jungle was awful, for I purposely left the track, judging that the elephant would suspect danger from the direction in which he entered, and also that he would probably scent me. So I made a detour and crawled through some dense ringall jungle on hands and knees.

The snoring now seemed to get feebler, and it was very difficult to locate the direction from which it came, the sound having a sort of echo about it. But whilst creeping along slowly I suddenly caught sight of a large yellow mass in front and not ten yards away, looking for all the world like a huge ant-hill. Even at that small distance it was still difficult to decide that the snoring issued from the great bulk until I noticed that it heaved up and down with each sound.

The first glimpse of the elephant I got was his back, for he had this towards me. It was of no use shooting yet, so I crept nearer and more to my right. From this fresh position I could see his neck and later his huge head. He was lying full length, head on ground, and at a distance of some five yards or so. I crawled no further but fired a rapid right and left into the most prominent part of the occipital bone. The huge brute just lifted his head, dropped it, and never moved again, having been practically killed in his sleep.

It seemed rather a mean thing to do, but how could I have acted otherwise? He was a rogue, had to be killed, and the encounter too close to allow of a more sporting risk to be taken. He was a huge beast and in splendid condition. The circumference of the forefoot was 67 inches, giving his height at 11 feet 2 inches. This is about the maximum height of the Indian species.

The tusks were about 3 feet long, but very thin. I unfortunately did not cut them out on the spot and they were stolen during the night; probably by some of the garden coolies. This dead elephant gave me a lot of trouble. I was constantly getting telegrams asking for its removal, for it was fouling the air for a mile around. So at last I mustered the municipal sweepers, headed by the Jemadar, and when they came back they said, 'It was awful job.' They had to cut it up in pieces and bury each separately. The skull adorns the entrance to the Chotta bungalow at Bindikuki tea estate, and there are the two holes close to each other in the skull made by those bullets.

Another encounter with a rogue occurred near a garden at Orangajuli, situated in the N.W. corner of the Darrang district, and at the foot of the Bhutan Hills.

On my arrival for inspection the garden manager, H., met me with, 'Doc., you are in luck. Yesterday a rogue chased my elephant out of the forest and the D.C. has proclaimed him'; so we started on the following day, after lunch. My wife was with me and we mounted together on H.'s shikar elephant 'Pyari', and H. himself on a borrowed one. We picked up the tracks of the rogue at the place where he had chased H.'s elephant. Siriman, the mahout, asked me to be on the look-out whilst he looked down and did the tracking.

We had tracked the rogue for about two hours when I saw a large, black object about forty yards away, in some high grass. Siriman called to me to fire but what I saw was the back and posterior of the beast, so refrained. But he must have heard us, for he turned his head, without shifting his body and looked round at us. I then took the opportunity of a temple shot and fired. He promptly whizzed round and with a scream and trunk coiled, charged down on us. My second barrel failed to stop him, and the next moment he had almost touched our elephant, but there was just time to push home one other cartridge before he swept us off with his trunk, to place the muzzle of the rifle at his head, and fire without even bringing it to the shoulder.

To our mutual relief the great brute rolled over and then from side to side, with all four legs in the air. He was then finished with a soft-nose bullet.

He proved a huge specimen in the prime of life and condition. The circumference of the foot was 62 inches, giving his approximate height at 10 feet 4 inches. The tusks weighed 58 lbs. each, were 5 feet 6 inches long along the curve, and 19½ inches in diameter. A perfect pair with blunt, conical ends. I gave H. one and took the other.

When returning home we shot a solitary bull bison which charged and gave us a devil of a time. This was indeed a bag to be proud of, and accomplished in seven hours. There was also a Ganesh in the forest, but he was not dangerous so we did not go after him. H.'s garden and surroundings were a sportsman's paradise, for one could get bison any time, also sambhur, peafowl, swamp deer, and bear. He is dead now, but I shall always feel indebted to him for many days of fine shikar and hospitality.

Some little time later my wife and I were trekking across the Cossyah Hills to Shillong, from where we were proceeding to Bombay and then to England. At one of the rest-houses I heard that a proclaimed rogue was about, playing the devil with the crops and chasing natives at a village called Umtopo. The dak bungalow chowkidar said this village was only three miles away, but it proved to be more like six. Natives are always very unreliable as to distances. However, next morning I started with a sporting kit, Selim and a Cossyah, having decided to spend the night in the vicinity of the rogue's depredations.

I got to the village eventually and found everyone very drunk. They informed me that they did not know where the elephant was, so I told the headman that if I did not receive *khubber* by the evening that there would be trouble. I therefore constructed a small hut on a nearby hill and waited events. At about 4.30 two men came rushing up to say that they had seen the elephant in the valley below. There was therefore no time to waste as the shades of night were falling fast. Selim and I tore down the hill, with the two informers. The tracks, leading into 15-foot null (reed), were pointed out to us, and then the men bolted. We followed them and had not gone more than 100 yards when I heard a branch crash and, on looking in the direction, saw a black patch which seemed like the head of the beast. I fired, and away he went, with Selim and I following closely on his heels. There were plenty of blood-tracks, but we had to give up owing to the gathering darkness and find our way out by the help of torches.

I started out next morning very early and found that the elephant had sat down, or rather lain down, not very far from where we had given up the evening before. A fine cast of his tusk was in the soil, and there was plenty of blood. We eventually came up with him in heavy jungle, and the Cossyah with us shinned up trees for a view, but he got away into grass about 15 feet high before I could get a shot at him. He appeared to be a huge brute with a magnificent pair of tusks, but in this sea of grass it was impossible to sight him properly till I climbed a solitary tree and saw that he was going very groggily and rolling from side to side. I tracked him till nearly sundown and then, much to my disappointment, had to give up.

What a weary journey it was to get back to camp. It had been a tramp of nearly nineteen hours and I was thoroughly done up, nor could I spare another day without missing the boat at Bombay.

And now for the sequel. About three months after I reached England, I received a photograph from a certain magistrate, with a letter saying that he had got the Umtopo rogue two months after I had left, and that the tusks were 6 feet 8 inches long. On return from leave my tracker, Singbia, told me that the elephant had been found dead four days after I had left, and so I lost a magnificent trophy.

In the course of hunting other game my wife and I often came on wild elephants. One day we went up the Rowai River to fish, and apart from fishing gear only took my shotgun. On our way upstream I thought I would go and inspect a salt-lick to see if bison had recently visited it. I asked my wife to sit on the river-bank whilst I was away, and when close to the salt-lick a tremendous trumpeting and a rushing occurred. The men shouted, 'Run, run', and we tore down hill. I pushed my wife into the boat and we made for a small island in midstream. From here we could hear elephants on the opposite bank making loud rumblings, so had rather an anxious time. Why that herd charged us I do not know, for a herd of elephants usually moves off when it sees man.

On another occasion, whilst carrying our folding Ford boat through jungle to negotiate some rapids, we heard strange sounds from the opposite bank, and, looking up, saw three elephants gazing at us from the top of a cliff. These moved off after a while, and in like manner did elephants we came on in the Langting forests.

My final experience with elephant occurred when at a last camp in India, on the Dehingi River. A few days before we set out I saw a fakir standing outside my gate, and as I passed through he said, 'Sahib, you are going for shikar. You will run a risk of being killed by an elephant, but take these and they will protect you.' He then handed me some pieces of wood dyed red. I gave him baksheesh, thought his prophecy nonsense, and put the pieces of wood in my pocket.

One day, a little later, I made for the Longari River, near which there were some fine sambhur. I had four men with me at the time. My head tracker was in front and we were following the tracks along the river-bank when, suddenly, as we neared a bend, the trackers jumped back and whispered, 'Hathi'. I immediately seized my .450 from one of the men and looked ahead to find a huge Makna, motionless, and with his ears cocked, about twenty yards away. I had no permission to shoot him, but determined to let him have it if he charged. So we stood gazing at each other for fully five minutes. He then began to kick the sand up with his forefoot, and rapped his trunk on the ground, which meant mischief.

I now thought of the old dodge of making an elephant bolt, so picking up a pebble hit it against my rifle. The huge beast screamed and went at a slow pace up the bank, but stopped at the edge of the forest to look down at us. I then pelted him with stones to make him move, and we never saw him again.

Had he charged, and a bullet had failed to stop him, we might have had a nasty time. What the 'fakir' foretold therefore came true. But how did he know what was going to happen? I rather liked fakirs, and used to have long talks with them about their travels. They often gave me valuable information of shikar as most of them live in the jungle-caves or tramp throughout the length and breadth of India.

Later on, in my account of panther, I tell of how I was unable to secure a single animal without the help of a fakir's pujah.

There are two interesting points in relation to these great beasts—those of 'Elephants Pearls', and the question as to where elephants die. There are, I believe, only two cases recorded of the former being found, perhaps because hunters have not looked for them, but they are considered very lucky, and are worth a fortune.

These 'pearls' are found in the pulp of the tusk. They are about as long as a man's little finger, white and showing some striation. They are not enamel but composed of dentine. My theory is this. At the top of the tusk containing the pulp the dentine is ridged. In the process of development, this ridge, or part of it, becomes detached and falls into the pulp, where it is subject to movement and so gets smoothed down. An authenticated instance is that of one found in a tusker shot by a forest officer in the Chittagong Hill tracts.

JOHN SYMINGTON

Sona Dant, Rogue Elephant

One moonlight night in the forest I fired a shot at a tiger, which disappeared in the heavy undergrowth. Next day with some eight or ten servants and coolies we started out on foot in search of the wounded, or maybe dead, tiger. This, I was told by experienced forest officers and shikaris, is a most dangerous thing to do—in fact it should never be done, for it is almost equivalent, as one forest officer put it, to asking for one's life insurance money. An elephant should always be used for tracking a wounded tiger. We had not been able to get the district elephant, however, as it was at work in some other part of the district and I was keen on getting the tiger.

We had reached a rather open place in the forest where the jungle grass was short and the walking comparatively easy. To our left was a stretch of tall jungle composed chiefly of elephant grass, the average height being eight or ten feet. There was almost a clear-cut, though natural, line running to the north between the short grass area on one side, which looked like a rough park, and the elephant grass area on the other, which had the usual forest appearance of that part of India. Wild cardamoms were growing amongst the tall grass.

From *In a Bengal Jungle*. Chapel Hill: University of North Carolina Press, 1935.

The chowkidar, or watchman, who had accompanied us and who was a born shikāri, thought it quite possible that the tiger whose tracks we were searching for might be hiding in the tall grass. Accordingly we decided that some of the party should keep along the edge while others entered the tall grass area, and that all should move in a northerly direction.

We had moved only a short distance when the trumpeting of an elephant was heard, and then the great rushing sound of a huge body moving through the jungle; at the same time the beaters, who had entered the jungle, appeared at almost flying speed making for the open. I was a short distance within the tall grass area and with rifle in hand took up my position behind a small tree and waited the oncoming of the wild elephant. On it came, but it suddenly seemed to realize that there was danger ahead, for it came to an abrupt stop only a few yards from where I stood. I could not see it—nor could I get even a glimpse of any part of its body, but I knew that it was just there, seemingly almost within touching distance only a few yards from where I stood, where a sapling tree was being violently pushed backwards and forwards. It was pushing this tree with its forehead and trying its strength as an Indian bull digs its horns into the ground and tosses earth into the air before engaging in a fight or attacking an enemy. I stood my ground with my rifle at the ready, expecting every moment that the elephant would charge me. I thought then, and have thought many times since, that it would have been safer to have run at full speed, as all the servants and beaters had done, for in such dense jungle an elephant can be practically on top of one before it can be seen; and there is no use shooting at an elephant with the intention to kill unless it can be struck in one of the few vital spots where it is possible for a bullet to pierce its skin.

I was now alone and I realized the awful solitariness and the danger of my position. My shotgun had been carried off by the fleeing beaters, one or two of whom were never seen again that day. Should my first shot fail, there would be no time for a second at such close range, for my rifle was not an automatic or a double-barrelled one, and there was no companion at my elbow to put in a saving shot. The strain was great while waiting for the elephant to charge or to retreat. The backward and forward movement of the tall sapling ceased, and everything seemed as still as the grave for the next few moments. Was the elephant scenting me and the beaters, and what would be its next move? Suddenly it moved a little distance to the right and then made a rush in an almost opposite direction from the place where I was standing, and at about fifty yards distance I could see the head of another tree swaying to and fro in the air as the elephant butted and played with it. Now was my opportunity to make a getaway, and I accordingly moved out into the more open space in the forest before mentioned.

I collected the servants and beaters and we decided to climb a tree standing on the demarkation line between the tall and short jungle some two hundred yards to the north of us. This we did, all of us who were left climbing into the same tree. It was a large tree and was dead, but of too great a diameter and strength for the elephant to knock over. Here we felt safe, at least temporarily, from another attack and we had a breathing spell.

We had scarcely found positions in the tree when we could see the jungle beginning to move, and the movements were in our direction. We realized that the elephant was coming towards us for we could hear it coming, though it was hidden in the tall grass. On it came to within a few yards of our tree, when it stopped, not directly facing us, but standing facing in an eastern direction with its left side towards the tree. This we knew by the waves in the grass made along its path, but as yet we could not see it. The chowkidar climbed into the higher branches of the tree and, in a low voice, informed me that it was an elephant and a tusker, also that it was a rogue elephant, and asked me to shoot. I climbed up into the tree towards him and from there could see the top of the elephant's head and part of its shoulder, but I could not see the tusks. I think, however, that I could have brought the animal down with one shot. In the circumstances I probably would have been justified in doing so, but there is a fine of some Rs 2000 for killing a female elephant, or any elephant that is not a declared rogue, and for these reasons I hesitated. I wanted to see the tusks with my own eyes and, though we were all in danger, even if the elephant were a female, I did not want, under almost any circumstances however dangerous, to shoot a female elephant. While I hesitated and tried to get a glimpse of the tusks, the elephant moved away a few steps and was again completely lost to view, soon after making off in the direction from which it had come. We clambered down from the tree and moved quickly in the opposite direction, as we could not make up our minds as to the elephant's being a declared rogue. One is allowed to shoot only rogue elephants in India, and to shoot a rogue one must know its size and description so as to make no mistake.

We continued our search for the tiger in another direction and found it dead at the edge of another large patch of tall jungle grass.

The elephant which we had encountered that day was undoubtedly a rogue known to the inhabitants of those parts as Sona Dant, from the yellow colour of its tusks —'sona' also being the word for gold. This rogue elephant had been holding up people travelling the road which followed the Rydak River leading through the forest from the Himalayas to market places further south. It would frighten single pedestrians and hold up groups of people and scatter them in all directions as they fled for their lives. It was a declared rogue, but unfortunately, its measurements and size had been greatly exaggerated in the description given by the Commissioner, part of whose duty it was to declare a dangerous elephant a rogue. This made it very difficult for anyone coming in touch with the elephant with the intention of destroying it to decide whether he was really at close quarters with the rogue elephant or not.

Many months later a pahari, or mountaineer, came to my bungalow with a very sad story of how a tiger had killed two of his cows which had wandered into the forest and how, when he had gone in search of them he had found them both lying dead. He asked if I would go into the forest and try to shoot the tiger. What is sad news to one is good news to another, for, while sympathizing with the pahari in this, to him, very great loss, I was glad to have the opportunity for another tiger hunt, especially as I had the feeling that I would be doing a service to the community. I promised him that if I bagged the tiger he would be recompensed, in a measure, for the loss of his cattle.

It was only a little after daylight when he came to the bungalow, and I immediately mounted one of my ponies and rode up into the forest. On reaching the place I found that two valuable cows had been killed the night before, as related by the pahari, and there they lay about two hundred yards apart. This was in a part of the forest where grew large patches of a certain kind of grass which was used extensively for thatching purposes, almost all the native houses in that part of India being thatched with it. Some of the jungle had been cleared here and there and the cows had wandered about a mile into the forest to graze in these clearings. A narrow footpath led through the forest to the clearing and it was along this path that I had ridden.

We looked around for a hiding place on the ground, for we were convinced that Stripes would return for a meal that night. There was no good place on the ground and good trees for the purpose were scarce in that part of the forest. They were either far too large and too difficult to climb, or too small for a machan. Finally we decided on a half-dead tree within about fifty yards of one of the kills. It was not a good tree, but selecting it was the best we could do in the circumstances, and my men soon had a small machan made up in the clefts of the branches. I got back to the bungalow in time for an early breakfast.

When I returned home in the evening I found everything ready as had been arranged for a visit to the machan to watch for the return of the tiger, and starting out, after a quick supper, I got into the machan as soon as possible. The servants, who were to return for me later, removed the bamboo by which I had climbed up and went back with my horse to the bungalow, leaving me alone.

The cold weather had slipped away, and a feeling of spring was in the air. The peach blossoms were in full bloom, and other trees were beginning to put on their new foliage. The sheesham trees are among the first to burst into leaf, and the soft green colour of their leaves shows up in stretches along the banks of the streams and the lower-lying places that will be streams in the rains. The fragrance of their tiny white blossoms filled the air with sweetness and made me feel that spring had surely come. The months of November and February are, in my opinion, the two best months in India—November before it gets too cold, and February before it gets too hot.

Loading my rifle and shotgun, I placed each in a corner of the machan within easy each and settled down quietly to wait for the return of the tiger. The sun was setting and a stillness was creeping over the forest. The squawking of a wild peacock could be heard in the distance towards the Sankos River, and from below the southern edge of the forest came the familiar sounds of a village as it finished its day's work—its returning herds of cattle and tame buffaloes and men and animals settling down for the night to cook and sup and sleep. The screeching yelps of jackals announced that their nightly hunt for prey had commenced, and their weird calls were answered by an angry chorus of village dogs.

To sit in a machan is fatiguing and very tiresome. The tiger seemed to be in no haste to return to the kill. Perhaps it was extraordinarily cautious, or had sensed some danger, or maybe it had spied the machan in the half-dead tree, which afforded none too much cover.

Several hours passed, and a dim moon now shone through a misty and somewhat cloudy sky. Being tired from my day's work and from watching for the appearance of the tiger, I fell asleep. How long I slept I do not know, but I was awakened by the sound of the tread of an animal and the shaking of the tree. Had the tiger come, and was it trying to climb the tree, or had it already jumped into it? Gently but quickly I raised myself and grasped my rifle. The shaking of the tree continued but nothing appeared at the machan; so peering over its edge I tried to discern what was taking place beneath. Directly below I could make out the hind half of an elephant and concluded that its head must be near the trunk of the tree. I also, almost in the same moment, felt convinced that this was my old enemy Sona Dant, which had disturbed as and put the beaters to flight on a former occasion. On top of this came the impression that if the tree were vigorously shaken some of the dead branches would break and come hurtling down on top of me, and that they were heavy enough to injure me more or less permanently I knew. I was also aware that the trunk end of one branch which supported a corner of the machan was within reach of an elephant's trunk, that it was none too strong, and that if an elephant got hold of it, the machan might be pulled to the ground. Having come to the decision that there beneath me stood a rogue elephant, that I was in immediate danger, and that shooting this elephant would be allowed and probably rewarded by Government, I promptly determined to carry it out if possible.

It was a tiger I had expected and now that I was in the presence of an elephant I remembered that unfortunately my rifle was loaded with soft-nosed cartridges—the right thing for a soft-skinned animal but of no use with an elephant except to frighten it away or, on the other hand, enrage it and make it more dangerous. I silently and as quickly as possible threw one soft-nosed cartridge from the magazine and slipped in a cartridge with a hard-nosed bullet, deciding to take the chance of the first shot's having a fatal effect. I then moved silently to the side of the machan from which I thought that the head of the elephant would be visible and, as I leaned over the edge, the elephant emerged from beneath the machan in a slanting direction. Whether it was making up its mind to have a butt or shove at the tree I do not know. The moonlight was favourable, both for the sights of my rifle and for the head of the elephant, and I could see its tusks gleaming in the moonlight. The huge animal was all alert and sensing danger. It had, no doubt, visited the kill and knew from previous experiences that its enemy Stripes was prowling in the vicinity. I also felt that it knew that man was near, but that it had not yet become aware of his exact position. Just as I aimed for the base of its skull its movements seemed to quicken and a swift motion in some direction seemed imminent, but at that instant the trigger was pressed and, the bullet finding its mark, this great jungle marauder lurched a few steps forward and fell with a crash that shook the earth. It fell on its right side and remained motionless. I have seen only a few killed elephants and each of them fell on its right side, and I have wondered if this was true of all slain elephants. A forest officer of my acquaintance is of the opinion that it is probably true, though neither of us can explain why it should be so.

My next step was to inform the Commissioner of what had happened and this I did by mail next morning. The usual investigation took place and it was decided that the elephant was a rogue. As a reward I was allowed the tusks. In due time the following notification was sent me.

Office of the Divisional Forest Officer
Buxa Division.
Dated Baksa-duar, the 6th April 1924.
Office Order No. 46

Dr. J. Symington of Dumpara Tea Estate is granted free of royalty two tusks (weighing 9 seers, worth Rs 114) of the rogue elephant destroyed by him on the 14th February 1924.

(Signed) Divisional Forest Officer, Buxa Division.

FRANK NICHOLLS

Experiences with Elephants

In 1942, I received a request from the local forest office, to disperse a large herd of elephants which was doing exceptional damage to the villagers' paddy (rice). They had refused to leave the area, in spite of the villagers' efforts to move them with flaming torches of grass fixed on long bamboo poles. Two men, while safely up in some trees, had watched the herd crossing the river and had counted one hundred and fifty-eight elephants.

I sent two elephants to the place early next morning and gave instructions to the mahouts to reconnoitre the forest where the wild elephants were and to ascertain what type of male or males were in charge of this large herd. I also gave them instructions to be at a certain point where I would meet them that evening. I took my .470 rifle, a shotgun and a five-cell torch with me. On reaching the pre-arranged site, the senior mahout said it was indeed a very large herd, that he had been through it twice but he could only find three half-grown tuskers and he was certain that the male or males in control were away for the time being.

As we arrived at the paddy area contiguous to the forest, it was just getting dark and elephants were there in plenty. There were groups of villagers sitting round fires and I gathered from them that the elephants had destroyed approximately ten acres of paddy in three days. Believe it or not, some men were crying: the rice

From *Assam Shikari*. New Zealand: Tanson, 1970.

they had expected to feed their families with for the whole year had been destroyed, and they had toiled for nothing!

We very quietly went into the herd. It was the largest I had seen. I switched on my torch every thirty yards or so and if I kept the light too long on one animal it simply turned its beam end to me. They just continued to pull up the paddy, beating the dirt off its roots by threshing it against their forefeet and eating it. Paddy grows in soft wet soil and more was destroyed by their huge feet than was actually eaten. They ignored us completely—safety in numbers, they most probably thought! I knew that unless I shot the leader of the herd, they would not leave the area. I knew too that he was not far off, probably gone to chase away one of the attentive bachelor elephants which is always keen to decoy one or two of the females from the herd.

After making certain the leader was absent, I went back to my car and told the mahouts I would be back at daybreak the next morning. On my return I found that the whole herd had entered the forest. I followed on my elephant and we soon came upon them. We went quietly through them looking for the fellow in control but there were only the three, half-grown tuskers which had been seen the evening before. We then came out of the forest and proceeded to a river about a quarter of a mile away. Looking from the river-bank towards the hills we saw a huge makhna coming towards us on the opposite side of the river. It appeared to be tracking another elephant, for it was continually raising its trunk and scenting the air on the opposite side of the Boroi River. After coming to within one hundred and fifty yards of us, it decided to go up the river-bank and across a patch of grassland towards some forest. We quietly went down the bank and crossed the river with the idea of intercepting it. On entering the forest, we suddenly came upon a full-grown tusker. It had been badly knocked about and one eye had been gouged out and was hanging on its cheek, and it had some other nasty wounds also.

The large makhna then arrived and made to attack the tusker. Unfortunately the makhna got our wind and turned and went off like a tank before I could get near enough for a fatal shot. Seeing that the tusker had lost an eye, and had many other wounds and it had belonged to the herd, I put it out of its misery. We recrossed the river near the herd and fired two shots in the air from my 12-bore shotgun. This dispersed the herd, which went thundering off into the forest. A week later I enquired as to whether the herd had returned and was informed that it had not been seen again.

Some three months after shooting the one-eyed tusker, I received a message from the local forest officer to say that at the foot of the Dafla Hills, some twenty miles from me, a makhna was chasing everyone it set eyes on, including his subordinates, and would I go and shoot it please. I knew there was a fairly reliable female elephant to be hired near that area, so I made arrangements and got it, but took along my own head mahout and a grasscutter. The latter also knew how to work an elephant, should it be necessary for the mahout to dismount for tracking. It was during the month of March, when everything was terribly dry in this area and the ground as hard as cement.

I arrived at about eight o'clock and we went to a villager's house, not far from the main forest, to enquire of the whereabouts of the makhna. He said he had not seen or heard of it since it had paid a visit to his house one night a week earlier, when it had trampled on his cooking pot and brass plates which his wife had left outside the hut. There was a small stream about a quarter of a mile from his house and I thought it would be a likely place to find footprints, as the main river was some four miles away. On following the bank of the stream for a while we came upon some fresh footprints of an elephant but owing to the very dry conditions we found it difficult to follow these through the scrub jungles.

The mahout dismounted to track the makhna, as it was very difficult to see any marks from the top of my elephant and the grasscutter took his place at the controls. We then made better progress but it was midday before we came to where the elephant had entered a ravine at the foot of the first range of the hills. The ravine was about twenty feet wide, with fairly precipitous sides: an ideal retreat in which an elephant could remain undisturbed during the excessive daytime heat. It really was delightfully cool inside the ravine and where the sides were not too steep overhanging bamboo and creepers were growing, giving some welcome shade and food.

As we proceeded, it appeared that no human beings had ever entered the area but there were signs that elephants, deer and pigs came and went at will. After we had been travelling for an hour, the ravine became more narrow and winding, and I began to realize that there was not much space to turn round in an emergency. We noticed that some very thick bamboos were drooping down and had been obviously pushed aside by the wild elephant as it went up the nala. After going for about another two miles up this ravine, I thought it was time to turn back. My mahout, who had remounted, then suggested that he should go ahead on foot to see if he could spot the elephant round the next few corners. Off he went, while my elephant reached for creepers to eat. I told the grasscutter to keep his mount facing the way the mahout had gone.

After a few minutes, there were loud shouts from the mahout ahead! I could make out that the elephant was charging down the ravine at him and his yells were followed by terrific trumpetings, which sounded louder than usual as we were in a confined space. The wild elephant came round the corner, some twenty yards away like an express bulldozer and hit a clump of thick bamboos which were dropping down from the sides of the ravine. These went off like fire crackers as the segments between the knots cracked open! This terrific noise, in addition to the elephant screaming at us with rage, was too much for the elephant I was on and she turned and bolted back down the ravine with me clinging on top!

The elephant's saddle, just in front of where the rider sits, is fitted with a strong iron bar to hold on to and there is also a six inch wide running-board along either side of the elephant's pad, fixed at each end by ropes to the saddle and on which the feet are rested. I gripped the round iron bar with my left hand and bringing up my rifle with the other, I fired at the vital spot in the wild elephant's forehead just as my mount started to swing round. A .470 double-barrelled rifle weighs eleven and a quarter pounds, so naturally I could not hold it up to my shoulder very steadily or for more than a second or two. The shot did not, however, take effect and merely added to the noise while our speed was soon up to fifteen miles an hour! The grasscutter was powerless to hold the elephant and after she had gone some fifty yards at full blast, some hanging creepers caught the man under his jaw and pulled him off the neck of the elephant and back on top of me. I then found myself gripping the iron bar with my left hand and helping the struggling grasscutter to regain his seat with the other, while still holding on to my rifle.

As the grasscutter regained his seat, I felt something touch me high up on my back. On turning round, I saw it was the wild elephant's trunk endeavouring to get a grip on my coat near my shoulders! For a moment I was frozen with fear and then I immediately drew myself up and forward by the iron bar in front of me, swung round and brought the heavy rifle up to my shoulder, holding it more or less like a revolver and fired. The elephant came down like a ton of bricks, stone dead. As I fired that shot, my topee was swept off and the reader must believe me when I say that it was later found squashed flat under the elephant's trunk!

After going round the next corner the elephant I was on pulled up on her own. A few minutes later we turned back up the ravine and I heard a wailing from my mahout, who had apparently dodged the elephant in some bamboos and was now coming on as fast as he could. I could make out his crying to be *'Hamara sahib morigello!'* which means 'my sahib is dead!' That was his reaction to seeing my topee crushed under the dead beast's trunk! On hearing his wailing, I shouted out that I was not dead and he came running round the corner and looked at me. After we got our breath back we laughed heartily for five minutes while we went over the incident and felt much better for it.

On getting down to inspect the dead elephant, I saw that my two bullet marks were exactly parallel to each other and only four inches apart. That was my thirty-eighth elephant. On getting out of the ravine again I made for my car and drove to the nearest European's bungalow, where Mr Brett lived at Bori, instead of going many miles to my own, as I had a thirst that I would not sell if I could avoid it! On reaching the bungalow my friend said to me, 'Good heavens! What have you done to vour face? Thank goodness my wife is not here to see you!' He led me by the arm to a looking glass and I saw that I really did look a dreadful mess. What had happened was that in our flight from the wild elephant, hanging creepers, some with barbs like fret saws, had been drawn across my face at fifteen miles an hour and had drawn blood which, with the perspiration running out of my hair, I had been wiping all over my face with my hands. However, a wash and a drink soon put me right.

The next morning my right arm failed to function. It was set stiff and I could not move it without pain. The European doctor said it was due to the recoil of the rifle when I fired it like a revolver, without holding it against my shoulder. He advised me to go to Shillong for an X-ray and I went a few days later—a drive of some three hundred miles. That dear friend of mine, Dr Roberts of the Welsh Mission, was there at the time and he put the whole arm in plaster, with strict instructions to leave it for three weeks but to keep moving my fingers, and a few days after the local doctor had removed the plaster the arm had healed.

III
Brushes in Burma

F.T. POLLOK

An Elephant Hunt

In 1856 I had to go to Mendoon on the Matoon, a lovely stream, some forty miles west or south-west of Thayet Myo, which was, until lately, our frontier station on the Irrawady on the right bank. I had been here before, and had various sport under the guidance of an old Burman *shikarie* who had accompanied Ashe of the Artillery (afterwards killed at Cawnpore) into the Arrakan range, where he shot three elephants.

On my arrival I sent for the man and inquired if there was any game about near, for my time was limited, and I could not remain away long from my headquarters, which were at Namyan. He professed to be able to show me a solitary bull elephant with large tusks. I asked him how long it would take to overhaul him.

'If we leave today,' he replied, 'there is a *teh* we can sleep in tonight and get to the jungle he frequents about twelve tomorrow.'

I had been sold before, so only credited about half what he said; but I could spare four days, during which my workpeople would be collecting certain timber I wanted, so telling my headman to dismantle some deserted phoongie houses and to make rafts of the timber for transportation down the Matoon to Prome, and that

From Colonel F.T. Pollok and W.S. Thom, *Wild Sports of Burma and Assam*. London: Hurst and Blackett, 1900.

I'd be back in that time, I put together a few things, which a couple of men carried, and with my two servants started about 10 a.m. Mendoon had been a place of importance, an appanage of the eldest son of the king of Burma, but it had been burnt down and all but deserted during the late war with us. When clear of it we followed bypaths for an hour, then crossed a stream, an affluent of the Matoon, and entered first an Eeinghein and then a teak forest. There was not much undergrowth, and we followed a track for a couple of hours or more made by elephants during the last rains. We then began to climb the spurs of the lower range of hills. Calling a halt I made an *al fresco* meal, giving some food to the Burman, who, having no caste, will eat anything; in fact, they are the most omnivorous people I ever met—nothing comes amiss to them in the way of food.

The meal over, I reclined under a convenient shade and allowed the Burmese to have a smoke, and doled them out a tot of grog. We then started afresh. The ascent became very stiff, and although I was in very good and hard condition, it was very soon a case of 'bellows to mend', but I soon recovered my second wind and was then able to trudge along fairly well. Animals construct these paths as if they had been instructed in engineering, for they wind round and round the hills, gradually ascending, and if we had stuck to them all would have been easy, but the guide would take short cuts, which proved very laborious and fatiguing, as the hillsides were covered with fallen branches of trees and debris of all sorts. About 5 p.m. we were probably at an elevation of 1000 feet, looking back the lovely Matoon looked almost at our feet, though miles away; to the east, in the distance, the mighty Irrawady appeared a mere thread; to the north and west rose the Arrakan mountains, which reach an elevation of some 6000 feet, and are densely wooded for about 3000 to 4000 feet. We could see mist rising here and there from the valleys which lay between us and the main range.

About 5.30 we resumed our journey, and after a climb of another 200 to 300 feet began to descend, and soon came to some *townyahs*, or clearances, made by Karens for growing their hill paddy. These people are very destructive to forests, as they change their location every two years, trusting to the ashes of what they have felled and burnt to manure their crops for that period, then they seek fresh pasture.

Just before dark we came to a *teh*, a raised platform fully 20 feet off the ground, but as there was space on it only large enough to accommodate a couple of men sitting, I did not think it worth while to ascend it, and although I was told there were man-eating tigers about, I decided to take my chance at the bottom, taking precautions to light fires all round. My dinner was soon ready, and whilst I partook of it, all hands but one servant set to work to collect wood.

My meal finished and washed down with a bottle of that divine nectar as it then existed, Bass's pale ale; alas! that firm seems to have forgotten the knack of making the ale which made them so famous in days gone by—or I cannot get it,—for the beer of the present day cannot hold a candle to that which used to be exported in hogsheads to India in the middle of this century, and which, when mature and cooled, was a drink for the gods! Never sleep on the ground if it can be avoided, it is so simple to erect a platform of bamboos or other wood a foot or two off the ground; this done, I wrapped a *cumbly* round me, and with an air-pillow under the head I was soon asleep, and slept like a top till within an hour of dawn, when we were all astir. Drinking a cup of *café noir*, for no milk was procurable, we resumed our march by daylight, and it was a case of ascending and descending all day. The lower spurs of all considerable mountains consist of a mass of teelahs; no sooner have you come to the crest of one than down you go into a valley, cross a rivulet, and ascend a hillock higher than the last, and so on, till the intermediary stage is passed and the base of the mountains itself is reached, which may be at any altitude from 600 to 1000 feet or more. About 6 p.m. we halted at the top of a slope, a stream running down close by. We must have been fully thirty miles from Mendoon. The water of this rivulet was deliciously cool and clear, and I utilized it for cooling a bottle of beer. I delight in water for lavatory purposes, but at my meals I prefer something stronger. Here we soon rigged up sleeping berths and shelter overhead, and were glad to avail ourselves of *razais* as covering, for the air was decidedly chilly. At the elevation we were there were few or no mosquitoes and no sand-flies.

The *shikarie* warned us to be very quiet, as elephants and gaur and occasionally tsine wandered about here, and we could see from their droppings that this was rather a favourite beat of theirs. So only such fires as were requisite for cooking our food were lit in a secluded glen, and then by 8 p.m. extinguished. The night passed without disturbance.

By 5 a.m. we were up and away. We neither ascended nor descended, but went along the edge of the plateau towards where the *shikarie* said were some salt-licks, always favourite resorts of almost all animals. Leaving the cleared spot where we had rested, we entered into a gloomy forest consisting of sal and buttress trees; from the latter an oil or varnish is extracted. These monarchs are of immense girth and height, often 100 to 150 feet above the ground without a single branch; the roots grow out of the main stem fully 5 or 6 feet, and form buttresses which extend to some distance before disappearing into the ground. On the lower lateral branches there are often huge bee-hives pendant, many of them 7 or 8 feet long by 3 or 4 in depth. These attract the bears, that climb up the trees by sticking their claws into the soft bark, and thus rob the bees of their store of food.

The Burmese and Karens copy these beasts; fill a haversack with bamboo pegs, drive one in, rest on that, drive another higher up, and so on, till they reach the site of the coveted prize; they then smoke the bees until they are stupid and partially unconscious, and then walk off with the honey. The process of thus climbing seems hazardous in the extreme, but an accident seldom happens.

Besides these trees there were stupendous clumps of both the male and female bamboos; the former are much prized for shafts for hog-spears, and the latter are converted into a thousand and one articles, in fact an entire house, including the roofing, is often made from bamboos alone—many of them are 3 feet in circumference and make capital buckets.

From an inspection of the country I came to the conclusion, before I could bag my elephant my work lay before me. I had at that time a two-groove, No. 10-bore double rifle, made by old Joseph Lang. I was so pleased with it that I had another made like it afterwards, but at that time I only had one of his and one of Sam Smith's, both noted makers in India. The *shikarie* carried one weapon, I the other. They were muzzle-loaders, of course, as breech-loaders had not come into use then. He led the way, I next, and the coolie about 100 yards in the rear, keeping us just in sight.

About 7 a.m. we came upon the fresh spoors of two elephants;

they had been feeding quietly and moving along leisurely, so we had no difficulty in tracking them. Those who wish to slay these leviathans in their forest homes need be sound of wind and limb, for it is no child's play following them up, for quietly as they feed along they are ever on the move, and get over the ground far faster than one would believe. Occasionally, when the weather is very oppressive, a beast may take a siesta and be caught napping, but where we were the heat was not outrageous, and these two had not made any considerable halt, so it was close on four before we came in sight of them, standing a few yards apart, pulling down and browsing on the tender shoots of the bamboo. The noise they made in rending the bamboos and then converting them into pulp by beating them on a foot, deadened the sound of our footsteps, and I had no difficulty, the wind being in our favour, in reaching a buttress which afforded good shelter and was within easy shot. The two animals differed greatly, they might have been father and son. The one nearest me was an old emaciated male with long tusks, the other was in his prime, very handsome to look at. What a beauty he would have made for a howdah elephant! We had no means of entrapping him, but it seemed a shame almost to devote him to death for the sake of his tusks alone; but what will not a hunter do with the furor of the chase upon him!

Motioning to the *shikarie* to stand close, ready with the spare rifle, I waited until a movement of the old one exposed the temple shot; then, stepping aside, I took a quick but steady aim and let fly.

Down he fell! His companion turned at the sound and gave me a front shot; dropping on one knee, I fired, and he fell stone dead. I thought the first also was as dead as Julius Caesar, and, as I was going towards them, he picked himself up and charged full at me. I fortunately had the spare rifle, and gave him a right and left, and threw myself under the lee of a buttress; as the monster passed, he all but trod on me. He only ran a few yards, and then right-about faced and bore down towards me again, but I had shifted my position further back behind another buttress or he would have had me. I now noticed that he was hunting for me by scent, for one of my last shots had knocked out one eye, and the other had, to a certain extent, paralysed the trunk, and the blood was pouring from the wound into the sound optic. So I retreated behind another tree some 20 yards further, where I found the *shikarie*, who had loaded his rifle. I soon loaded mine—the bullets fitted beautifully—and in pushing them down they made no noise. Being ready for battle again, I stepped clear and gave him the contents of both barrels into the temple, but as I fired he threw up his head, and neither missile reached the brain. On receiving these wounds he blindly rushed forward, a buttress caught his fore-feet, and down he went, such a cropper! I seized the other rifle and gave him two shots as he was attempting to rise, but he bore a charmed life, and I again failed to kill. He then retreated. As soon as I had both weapons ready I took up his trail. Considering the terrible nature of his wounds, inflicted at a distance of only a few yards, and the cropper he had come, it was marvellous at what a rate he went away. We had to follow at a trot, and when he heard us coming he either hid and then rushed at us, or spun round and charged blindly. I fired no less than eleven more shots, but failed egregiously to put him out of his misery. It was getting too dark in the gloomy forest for accurate shooting, and the monster kept his head tossing about as if possessed of a perpetual motion. To hit the brain, except by a fluke, was hopeless, so we left him, determined to follow him to the death on the morrow.

We could not find the coolie with our food; he had disappeared during the scrimmage. To return to camp was not to be thought of; sleeping out for a night is no great hardship to a real hunter, so we went back to the elephant I had slain. We collected sufficient debris to keep our fires going all night, and then, declining to partake of any portion of the flesh of the elephant, which the *shikarie* had cut off and partially cooked, I lay down alongside the elephant, and using one of his ankles as a pillow, and bidding the man light a couple of fires and keep them going, I was soon fast asleep.

When I awoke just before dawn I felt a little hungry, and missed my cup of coffee, but tightening my belt and washing my face in the first little stream we came to, we resumed our chase. He must have got ahead fully ten miles, which we had to make up, so we walked along at a pretty brisk pace. When I was all but exhausted I espied a peacock and bowled him over. We carried him till we came to water, and then kabobed some of its flesh over some embers and made a hearty meal.

We did not overtake the tusker that day, so slept in the jungle again, but felt the cold considerably, for we had been steadily ascending. To make matters worse our fires died out, and we were pretty well benumbed by the morning, and glad to resume our pursuit. Every now and then we came upon where the poor stricken brute had struck the boles of trees, the result of his more than half blindness, and also where he had lain down in a mass of gore. We noticed also that his stride became shorter and shorter, and that he had leant against a tree or two for support—all signs of increasing weakness—so we pressed on with renewed hopes.

The country we were in was pretty open forest, with here and there patches of long grass. We had just passed one, with our eyes riveted on the ground, when there was a fiendish screech, and a bloody form all but tottered on to the top of us! I jumped aside, and fired both barrels into his carcase, close to the shoulder. This reduced him to a slow walk, and he struggled along with his trunk pendant and limp, and altogether his aspect was a woebegone one. I seized the other rifle, ran forward, and as he flopped an ear forward I fired into the space behind it, and staggering along two or three yards, he fell forward—dead!

Poor old beast! Thank God he was at last dead, for he must have suffered fearful agonies. One eye was shot out, the other all but closed by coagulated blood, and he had received numerous wounds, yet the gallant brute never uttered a groan, and died fighting to the last. His tusks were 4 feet 8 inches and 4 feet 6 inches respectively, but thick and straight. By the foot measurement he was just 10 feet 2 inches high.

But now where were we? The *shikarie* climbed a tall tree, took a good look all round, and when he descended, said if we walked quickly we should get to the camp by night. Before we had gone far a sambur crossed our path, which I killed, and as I felt very tired and hungry, I preferred camping out another night in the jungle and to have a square meal at once, to tramping on an empty stomach, with the chance of reaching camp that night.

The Burman soon broiled the liver, cut in slices, which we ate, but Adam's ale was our only drink! We rigged up a shelter overhead, lit a fire, and slept the sleep of the weary till close on daylight. We partook of another meal before starting, and finally reached camp after midday.

The coolie had returned and reported that he had seen me trampled to death by the elephant, so my boy had gone to where the encounter had taken place to pick up master's bones, but finding one elephant dead and evidences that we were in chase of another, he wisely returned to camp and stuck to it until we should return.

After a day's rest I took all hands, and as decomposition had commenced we had no difficulty in extracting the tusks, and soon made our way back to Mendoon, and thence by boat to Namyan, where I got only a day after I was due, but as I was my own master that did not signify.

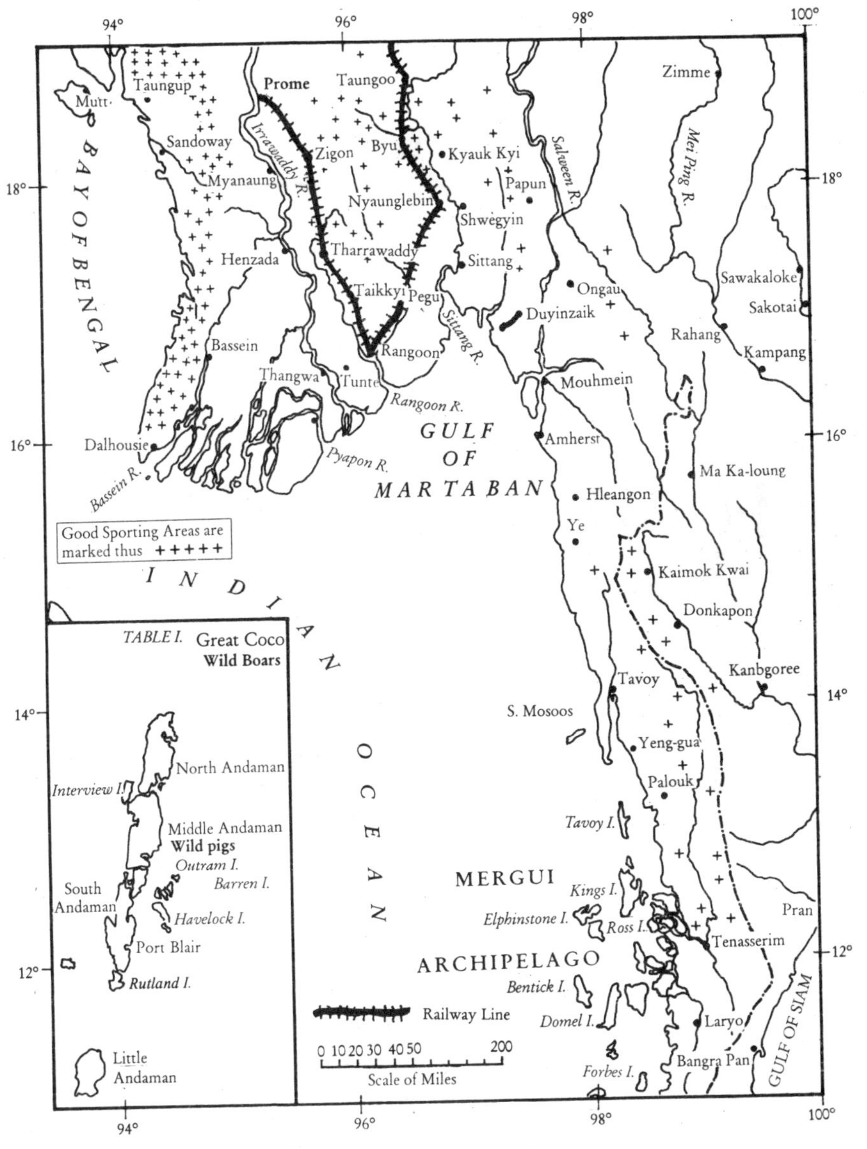

Good Sporting Areas in Lower Burma.

W.S. THOM

Elephants

Elephants are perhaps the most docile, timid, intelligent of animals, and yet when thoroughly roused and in full charge with curled-up trunk they present a most furious and fear-inspiring spectacle. There are two distinct varieties of the Asiatic elephant, although of the same species, to be found in Burma. I quite agree with all Colonel Pollok says on the subject with regard to the marked differences between tuskers and 'hines', or tuskless elephants. The first are known in Hindustanee as 'goondas', the tuskers; the second as 'mucknas', or in Burmese 'hine'. I have no intention of going fully into particulars as to their habits, etc., as Colonel Pollok, whose experience of them is much more varied and greater than mine, has already, in the beginning of this book, dealt with the subject at some considerable length. I should like, however, before relating my experience with them, which covers the death of some twenty-two animals, to give the sportsman some idea as to the method of approaching and shooting them, their haunts, peculiarities, and any other observations which, to one who has never seen an elephant in his wild state, may be of some service. The elephant is, as a rule, very easily stalked, provided one has the wind in his favour. I have often been standing within a

From Colonel F.T. Pollok and W.S. Thom, *Wild Sports of Burma and Assam*. London: Hurst and Blackett, 1900.

yard or two of the hind-quarters of one of these animals waiting patiently for the huge beast to turn round and expose a vital part. Their powers of scent, as is well-known, are very keen, and they can easily detect the presence of a human being at a distance of a quarter of a mile. Their senses of sight and hearing, on the other hand, are far from good; I have often approached an elephant, which was directly facing me, while it rested under the shade of a tree during the heat of the day, and have not been observed. He does not seem to be able to comprehend matters till his head is turned a little to one side, when apparently you come into view more easily; he then immediately backs or wheels sharply round as if on a pivot, and makes off. Under these circumstances a male elephant will not charge once in a hundred times.

At other times I have been within 80 to 100 yards of a herd right out in the open, with hardly a tree or a bush between, and have not apparently been detected although stared at suspiciously, and it was not till a slant of my wind had been obtained by an uplifted trunk that the usual dull rumblings of alarm were sounded, preparatory to a sudden and swift departure. There are various sounds uttered by elephants denoting different meanings, which are well known to all who are familiar with the habits of these animals. Colonel Pollok has remarked on them. It is marvellous how after an alarm a herd will collect together and then swiftly and noiselessly take its departure.

An inexperienced sportsman will often be exceedingly surprised on approaching a cover, which he has every reason to believe contained a number of elephants, to find that not only have they all disappeared, but that there are also no sounds to indicate that they are even anywhere in the immediate vicinity, so quietly, quickly, and orderly have the whole herd in single file melted away. I have never had any difficulty in approaching a solitary elephant or even a herd to within a few yards; gaur, tsine, deer, etc. are very much harder to stalk, their sense of hearing, compared with that of the elephant, being more acute. Elephants will often stampede when suddenly alarmed, and the whole herd will rush off pell-mell in the greatest confusion in different directions with a noise so terrific, especially should it be in bamboo cover, from the smashing and falling of the cane that it somewhat resembles an independent musketry fire. Should the sportsman be in the line of flight in a stampede of this sort he should always stand firm behind the trunk of some tree or solid clump of bamboos. He will then be in perfect safety, as the terrified animals are intent only on getting away as far and as quickly as possible. A herd alarmed in this manner will often travel ten or fifteen miles without stopping. The only danger to be apprehended is from a female elephant when accompanied by a young one, of whose safety she is very solicitous. An old female, when the herd has been alarmed, invariably takes the lead, and the rear is usually brought up by a huge 'muckna' or tusker. The large tuskers more often, however, are the first to get out of danger's way, and are, so far as my own experience goes, never found near a herd, but always on the outskirts, at distances varying from a few hundred yards to a quarter of a mile. A large tusker will often during the night wander away miles from a herd, in order to visit rice fields or a certain favourite banana plantation. These visits are often repeated at intervals, till the animal has either been fired at or in some other manner effectually scared. Elephants in Upper Burma do a great deal of damage annually to the rice crops, and in a single night a herd of twenty animals will utterly demolish a field of rice, in fact they destroy more by trampling on it than they eat.

I remember very well once on a pitch-dark night vainly endeavouring to get a shot at a huge solitary elephant, that night after night visited a certain patch of 'paddy' land in the Twinge jurisdiction of the Tagaung subdivision, Ruby Mines district. The Burmans in this locality, being unarmed, had done their utmost to drive away this animal by making huge bonfires along the paths by which he was known to enter the fields, and by throwing lighted brands at him; all to no purpose, however, as with a slight, suppressed scream of rage and feinting charge he used to put them all to flight. He would then stalk calmly in amongst the standing rice and begin uprooting it; the swish, swish of the earth being knocked off the roots of the rice-stalks as he banged them across his forelegs prior to stuffing them into his capacious mouth was distinctly audible. I succeeded eventually in shooting this animal, which turned out to be a huge 'muckna' or 'hine'. The circumstances connected with his death will be related elsewhere.

No forest can contain a herd of elephants for more than three or four days, as, destroying more than they eat, they consume all fodder in a very short time. They are therefore continually moving about from one locality to another. The denser and more luxuriant the vegetation the better is the chance of falling in with them. Elephants are found at almost any elevation. I have shot them at a height of quite 3200 feet; they do not as a rule, however, remain at such a high elevation for any length of time. During the end of April, May, and June elephants, gaur, and tsine resort to hilly, open places where there is a breeze, and where they can escape from the tormenting gad and other predatory flies which infest the low-lying country. An elephant's skin, although very thick, is just as sensitive as that of many other animals to the proboscis of the various insects which prey upon mammalia. Solitary elephants are always worth following and shooting, as they are usually large and have the best tusks. Should the tracks of an elephant with a diameter of 18 to 20 inches be found, and it prove to be a tusker, it will invariably be noticed that he has one if not two good tusks. Burman hunters say that they can always tell by examining the toe impressions whether the animal possesses good tusks or not, or whether the right tusk is heavier than the left, simply by the deep and distinct impression or otherwise of the two front toes of the fore-feet in the soil. This depends a good deal upon whether the earth is hard or soft at the time. My hunter has often remarked to me of a track, 'Sir, look at the deep toe impressions of this elephant's right fore-foot compared with his left, which is very indistinct; he has only one tusk.' Again, of another fresh track, which shows only the huge circle-like impression of the foot without the toe impression, he would say, 'We need not take on these tracks, sir, it is only a "hine", ah-swe-ma-she-bu', or in other words a tuskless male. I am convinced, from my own experience of tracking up elephants, that large tuskers invariably leave a very distinct and deep impression of the two front toes of the fore-feet in the soil, though a similar impression may sometimes be made, and has, within my own experience, been made, by a huge 'muckna' or 'hine'. I have personally tracked up and shot several large solitary 'mucknas', which had done a great deal of damage to crops, and found that in most cases there was always the huge circular imprint with a perceptible impression of the toes, but the latter not so well marked as in the case of a tusker. A solitary bull should always be approached with the greatest caution, as he is generally an old stager, who is on the alert for the slightest sound, and has often been stalked and fired at by Burman hunters. A solitary bull which has often been fired at or disturbed by hunters generally rests during the heat of the day in dense 'kaing', tall elephant grass, quite impenetrable to the sportsman, or in some thicket where he is practically unapproachable. Sometimes, however, he is found stretched out at full length on his side on some breezy bamboo-wooded slope sound asleep, snoring away quite unconcernedly. ...

My first elephant, a small tusker, was bagged in the Nampan forest in the Shan States of Momeik, Ruby Mines district, whilst on a two months' shooting expedition. My hunters and I were on the move one morning early through the jungle on the look-out for fresh gaur tracks, when the snapping of a twig in a bush skirting a water-course about 20 yards ahead of us attracted our attention. On hearing the sound I thought we had either got on to a herd of gaur or a solitary bull, and immediately pushed forward as quietly and as quickly as the conditions would permit; but what was my surprise on gaining a piece of rising ground to see, not what I had expected, gaur, but a solitary tusker elephant, standing perfectly still, with its ears cocked forward, and trunk up in a listening attitude. It was quite a rude shock to my nerves, as this was my first elephant, and the distance between us only about twenty paces, with no trees or bamboo clump behind which to retreat, so I felt very much inclined to go back quietly by the way I had come. Not wishing to show any signs of funk in the presence of my hunters, I managed to screw up courage to creep up a little nearer, my heart and pulse all the time going like sledge-hammers. When within about fifteen paces I decided to fire for the point of the shoulder from a little behind, in order to rake the vitals and penetrate the heart. Bang! went the report from the heavy 8-bore, followed by an angry, shrill, half-suppressed scream from the elephant, which, wheeling suddenly round as if on a pivot, came straight for us. I hardly waited to see the result of my shot, and, as you can imagine, did record time over and through the bushes and fallen timber, hampered as I was with the heavy 8-bore, which, however, at the time felt like a feather. I very nearly came to grief all the same, as, while jumping a fallen tree, a hidden stump tripped me up and sent me sprawling frog-fashion, rifle and all, on the other side. Moung Hpe, one of my hunters, was fortunately equal to the occasion, as, running up, he at close quarters effectually stopped the charge, by letting the animal have the contents of both barrels of my double-twelve Lang smooth-bore, burning 4½ drams of powder. My rifle and I were fortunately none the worse for the fall, so hastily jamming in another cartridge I ran round to where the elephant was standing in rather an undecided manner, and at a distance of about twenty-five paces succeeded in getting in a right and left behind the shoulder. This seemed to have the desired effect of disabling him, as after first staggering from side to side in the vain endeavour to ascend a slight incline, he lurched heavily to one side against a bamboo clump and then collapsed stone dead in a kneeling position. My last two shots I afterwards found had, after raking his lungs and grazing the heart, lodged in his chest. We extracted the tusks and also took away with us to camp the tail, liver, and heart; the latter is, if my memory does not deceive me, about the size of a Rugby football, or a little smaller perhaps, and is capital eating. The tail stewed or as soup is simply excellent in my opinion. The elephant was afterwards cut up, and the meat divided among my followers, who dried it in the sun and over a slow fire, eventually disposing of it, together with the meat of other animals shot by me at the expiration of my shoot, to the neighbouring villagers, thereby netting a round sum of some Rs 300 to Rs 400. I have always made it a point when out shooting to allow as little meat to be wasted as possible. The proceeds of sale of all meat of animals shot was always given to my hunters, who were afterwards all the more keen in furnishing information as to the whereabouts of game.

My second elephant was bagged under rather peculiar circumstances, and for some days after its death disagreeable arguments by outsiders, who had nothing whatever to do with the matter, and who had never before shot an elephant amongst them, but who were keen on having their say, were continually being raised as to who was entitled to the tusks. The reader will, however, judge for himself.

I was out on a ten days' shoot with two officers from a regiment at a neighbouring hill station, Bernardmyo, whom I had invited to shoot with me. I shall call them A and D; the latter was a hardy old veteran of over fifty, who had lived a long time in the East, and was, besides being excellent company, a keen and enthusiastic sportsman. A was a young subaltern who had not, I presume, been long in the East. Both knew how to use the rifle well. After getting out into the jungle under canvas, some ten or fifteen miles away from any village, we managed to work up separately, each with his own gun-bearers and trackers, towards the Shwe-u-taung range of hills. Our beats were arranged so that we should not interfere with one another's sport. I had not been out half-an-hour before my hunters struck the trail of a herd of gaur; these tracks were, however, according to Moung Hpe, about twelve hours old. Nevertheless, I was determined to stick to them. So we took them on, and worked steadily up a steep ridge. At about midday, after being out since daybreak, my attention was attracted to a herd of elephants trumpeting in the valley to my left, somewhere in D's neighbourhood; not wishing to relinquish the bison, however, or to interfere with D's sport, we held on. We were then at an elevation of some 2500 feet. Whilst moving along in this manner I heard a faint noise on ahead, and suddenly to my surprise a magnificent tusker elephant stalked majestically into view down the same ridge we were on. It was amusing to see how the animal kept the flies from his body by whisking from side to side a small branch covered with leaves which he had broken from a tree, and which he used as dexterously as a lady does her fan. This elephant was a much larger animal than my first, and his tusks protruded from his mouth quite three feet. The wind was fortunately in our favour, or else the animal would soon have scented us and made off. I waited till he had approached broadside on to within about twenty paces, and fired for the temple shot between the eye and ear. The 8-bore was the only weapon with the exception of the double smooth-bore I had in my possession at that time, a single .303 and double 12-bore rifle not having been purchased till a year later, and I had unfortunately left the smooth-bore in camp. As I was on lower ground than the elephant when I fired, I immediately retreated out of the way to one side, taking up my stand behind the trunk of a large buttress tree, which had huge parapet-like projections on either side at the base. The smoke after the shot obscured everything for a few seconds, and the next thing I saw was the elephant rolling down the side of the hill exactly to the spot I had just vacated, where it was brought up by a slight depression in the ground. It was a sight never to be forgotten to see that elephant struggling on its back, with all its four legs in the air, vainly trying to recover its equilibrium, having only been temporarily stunned by my shot, which had passed into the right side of the head, missing the brain by a very little.

An elephant invariably recovers from a head shot wound, when the brain is not touched, as there are no large arteries, the severing of which would cause it to die from loss of blood. Sanderson says, 'A shot that goes through the skull into his neck without touching the brain may kill him, but it will take time.' While the elephant was in this position I was only about six paces off behind the tree already spoken of, vainly endeavouring to extract the empty cartridge case which had somehow expanded in the chamber, so that I should have two shots instead of one to meet him with should he get up. I did not succeed, however, in getting it out. In the meantime my plucky hunter had been doing his best to hamstring the unfortunate beast with his sharp 'dah', or fighting sword; this, however, owing to the frantic endeavours made by the beast to regain his legs, he failed to do, and as I saw that the elephant was about to regain his feet, having got on to his fore-legs, I aimed for the forehead bump shot between and below the eyes, and fired; but whether through nervousness, or excitement, I cannot say, my shot did not reach the brain, nor did it seem to have the slightest effect, as, slowly regaining his hind-legs, he swept majestically down the hillside without uttering a sound, evidently making a beeline for the herd already referred to in the valley below. I was awfully disgusted with my bad luck, or bad shooting, call it which you will. We took on the tracks immediately, and followed on as quickly as possible; after about half an hour's tracking we suddenly heard two shots fired down in the valley somewhere in D's neighbourhood, which showed that he had got on to something. An interval of about half an hour then elapsed, when eight or ten shots were fired at intervals. My hunter, then turning round to me in an excited state, said he was convinced that D had come upon my elephant, which might have been partially disabled by my last shot passing through the forehead into the neck or body, and that he was now all unconsciously killing my animal. This was too much for me; it was about midday, and the whole jungle had been thoroughly disturbed by our shots, so I thought it useless looking for game, and returned to camp, intending, if D had not already killed the animal I had wounded, to take on the tracks next day. Towards evening

D returned to camp triumphantly waving an elephant's tail in his hand, jubilant at having slain his first tusker in Burma. I jokingly said to him that I hoped he had not shot the elephant I had fired at and floored.

Next day, A, D, and myself visited the spot, accompanied by our trackers. The elephant was lying in a kneeling posture with both tusks driven deep into the ground. It was impossible to tell from an examination of the bullet-holes in the animal's head whether any of the shots had been fired by my 8-bore or by D's 12-bore rifle, or the 10 smooth-bore which he was using, as the skin had contracted and the holes appeared exactly alike. I made my hunters take on yesterday's tracks, and after an absence of about three-quarters of an hour they returned, having taken up the trail right up to the spot where D had first fired at the elephant. Poor D would at first hardly believe me when I told him that the elephant now lying dead before us was in reality the one I had wounded. I knew, however, that my trackers would never have played me false over such a serious matter simply to curry favour, so I suggested cutting out the bullets, which we did; and after a great deal of labour, one of my 8-bore, solid, hardened, spherical bullets was to D's utter astonishment and disgust then brought to light. A, who was rather incredulous, suggested weighing the bullet; D was, however, quite convinced that it was mine, and although it had been very much knocked out of shape, the lead was all there, and it certainly presented the appearance of having at one time been an 8-bore spherical ball.

The rule amongst sportsmen is, that the animal belongs to the one who first draws its blood, so long as he sticks to it and follows it up till he kills it; should he relinquish the chase, however, and give up the animal as lost, then any other sportsman would be entitled to shoot. I then proposed to D, who had naturally by this time become very crestfallen, that we should split the difference by taking a tusk each, although I suppose both tusks rightfully belonged to me. D made no demur, but assented to this proposal. The rightful ownership of these tusks was, as I have already said, afterwards made the subject of many a heated argument, and I was often told I had no right to them. This may or may not be the case as it happened; however, I think I was quite entitled to one tusk, if not both. D's first two shots, I afterwards ascertained from the

Burman hunter who was with him at the time (a villager of Chaukmaw, near Sagadaung, Momeik State, Ruby Mines district), had been fired at the head of another elephant altogether, which had gone clean away, practically not having been hit in a vulnerable spot, or even floored. It was while following up the tracks of this elephant, according to the account afterwards given me by D's tracker, that they came upon the one I had wounded standing stock-still under some trees looking quite disabled; it was then an easy matter for D, who mistook it, according to the Burman's story, for the one he had first fired at, and whose tracks he believed he was still following, to pump lead into it, which he did with a vengeance, firing no less than ten shots, the animal being apparently too done up to either charge or put on enough speed to escape. The surrounding country in the neighbourhood was very hilly and rocky, and a wounded elephant would therefore find escape, having a lot of climbing to do, well-nigh impossible. My second shot I afterwards found proved, on examination, to have done all the damage, having entered the body after passing through the neck.

There is no sport which entails a greater amount of endurance and hard walking than elephant hunting, and the sportsman has to be in fairly good condition if he wishes to indulge in this particular branch of big-game shooting with any degree of success. I have repeatedly marched on for miles on the seemingly fresh tracks of a solitary bull elephant, sometimes in despair of ever coming up with the owner, so steadily and over such an immense stretch of country do these animals wander; at other times after walking for many a weary mile I have come on the animal, only to find that he has winded me, and made off. In cases of this sort, should it be after midday, it is well-nigh hopeless to take on the tracks of the elephant again that day, as the animal, if it be a large tusker which has often been disturbed in this manner will travel for miles without stopping once.

One day in July, in the rainy season, while cantering along the road between the villages of Chaukmaw and Pinkan, I came across the large tracks of an elephant; having nothing of any importance to do at the time, I dismounted from my pony, hitched it up to a tree, and waited till my transport and servants arrived. The tracks had a circumference when measured of quite 4 feet 8 inches, which would approximately make the elephant's height to be about 9 feet

4 inches. On the arrival of my men and transport I unlimbered my guns from their cases, a double 8-bore rifle by Tolley, burning 10 drams, and a double 12 smooth-bore, burning 4½ drams, and started on the tracks accompanied by two villagers from Chaukmaw, who were not much use as trackers. The tracks which, according to my companions, had passed the road early that morning, about 3 a.m. probably, held steadily on for about three miles, in which distance the animal had not apparently stopped once to feed, except on an occasional bamboo shoot which happened to be growing within reach of its trunk.

An elephant, in fact no wild animal, cares to cross a beaten track or highway during the day; they often do so, but in great trepidation and fear, and the pace is invariably increased. A gaur, tsine, sambur, barking deer, or pig, will either bound across or trot over quickly after a little hesitation; a tiger will walk across, if not disturbed, with a long, quick, stately step. An elephant will shuffle over noiselessly by turning his head slightly to either side as he passes, to see that none of his human foes are in sight. Should any of these animals suddenly cross your newly-made trail in the jungle, they invariably dash off at a great pace; gaur, tsine, and the deer tribe gallop away with a snort, or a bell; the elephant will back suddenly and make off at right angles, bringing his trunk at the same time down to the ground with a rap, emitting often a sharp, clear, metallic sound of alarm. I have watched a whole herd of elephants which had been alarmed and were going at full speed, recoil from human scent in this manner and refuse to cross the trail, as if they had each one received a severe blow on the forehead.

Within three hours of the time of my taking on the tracks we came upon the animal's fresh warm droppings; this raised my hopes of at any rate being able to come up with the elephant that day. The rain about this time came down in torrents, and in spite of a waterproof cape, so heavy was the downfall that it was with the greatest difficulty that I could keep my cartridges dry. On one or two occasions I almost despaired of ever finding the tracks, as they were often nearly obliterated by the rain. The men with me, however, who were, as I have already said, by no means experienced trackers, stuck to it, stimulated by my promises of plenty of 'sungwe' (reward money), and assisted by my little knowledge of tracking, by making now and again wide casts, always succeeded in striking the trail again. We were at last rewarded by hearing the snapping of a bamboo a few yards ahead. I then tried the wind by striking a match, and blowing it out; the direction taken by the smoke indicated that the wind was fortunately in our favour. Another 30 yards brought me in sight of the tusker, who was standing on the edge of a steep, rocky piece of ground, feeding on some young bamboos. I crept up with the 8-bore to within about twenty-five paces, having just instructed one of the trackers to be in readiness with the 12 smooth-bore should I require it. Fixing on a small bamboo clump in my immediate rear, behind which I could retreat after firing, I walked up to the elephant and fired when about fifteen paces off for the shoulder-shot, after which I immediately retreated under cover of the smoke, which hung in the damp air, to the bamboo clump fixed upon. The elephant on receiving the shot stood perfectly still for a few seconds, and then, with a shrill scream of pain and rage, charged up and passed within six feet of the flimsy bamboo clump behind which I had taken up my position. I had in the meantime succeeded in getting in another cartridge, and as the elephant passed me at a quick shuffle I gave it a right and left immediately behind the shoulder which caused it to stumble slightly. The huge beast on receiving the shots turned round and faced me as if about to charge, but after regarding me for a few seconds in an undecided manner it wheeled round and made off again. My two companions at this critical moment had, on seeing the huge beast loom up alongside the bamboo clump, thought discretion the better part of valour and ascended trees.

The rain all this time had simply been coming down in torrents. After shouting myself hoarse for the two trackers, who looked very sheepish when I began to chaff them for making themselves scarce, we took on the tracks of the elephant, whose route was now plainly indicated, not only by its tracks, but by splashes of blood on the ground and surrounding bushes. We had not gone half a mile before I caught sight of the elephant standing in some open 'indaing', bastard teak forest, 'with its trunk up in the air, through which at intervals blood appeared to be issuing; this was a sure indication that he had been shot through the lungs and was practically disabled. On seeing me approach he made feints of charging, but I could see from the bubbles and bloody froth which dropped from his trunk that he was helpless and that the end was near. I then walked up to him accompanied by a Burman with a spare gun, and at the distance of about ten paces administered a *coup de gráce* by planting a bullet in the centre of the bump with my Lang smooth-bore. The elephant on receiving the shot toppled over on one side with a dull thud, falling on its right side, the heavier tusk being the right one. I have noticed that tuskers, when shot through the brain, invariably, when they fall on their sides, collapse on the side which has the heavier tusk. Elephants very often, on the other hand, when killed by body shots, succumb in a natural life-like kneeling posture.

A piece of the right tusk had, at some time of the animal's life when he belonged to a herd, been broken off in an encounter, or perhaps through an accident. The pulp cavity in both tusks had decreased considerably, showing that the elephant was an old one. It will be noticed that the hollow or pulp cavities of large massive tusks are as a rule very small. ...

Some of my readers, I dare say, think that sportsmen are unnecessarily cruel and callous in their methods of killing game, and no doubt wonder how one can find any pleasure and excitement in doing to death such a harmless beast as a gaur, or an animal so intelligent and useful as the elephant. Granted, but we have all still, more or less, implanted in our breasts a taint of the savage instinct of our forefathers to take life, and there is also a natural craving for some form of excitement amongst the majority of people, which has in some way or other to be satisfied, and what better form of excitement or what more manly and healthful sport could one desire, than the tracking up and stalking of these wary denizens of the jungle? We sportsmen have, however, whilst standing over an animal newly shot, a momentary feeling of regret or remorse, call it which you will, but this feeling is only momentary and is more than counterbalanced by the satisfaction of having obtained another noble trophy.

The largest tusker elephant which it was ever my good fortune to shoot fell to my 8-bore one lovely evening in November 1895. It was then about the beginning of the cold weather, and the evenings and early mornings were quite chilly.

Whilst travelling through the subdivision in the neighbourhood of Twinge, one of the police posts under my charge, I got word of a huge tusker elephant which had, according to rumour, been fired at and wounded by Burman hunters, who were still tracking up the animal. As these hunters had all previously been warned by me not to disturb or shoot any of the solitary elephants, gaur, or tsine in the neighbourhood, there being numerous herds upon which they could indent, I was naturally not a little annoyed at their behaviour, more especially as I had promised them 'sungwe', (Bur., reward money), and plenty of powder and ball, should they furnish me with information regarding the whereabouts of 'solitaires'.

Proceeding to the village of Wapyudaung, which lay within the sphere of my duties and where the hunters lived, I ascertained that the rumour was true, and that three of them had come on a huge tusker asleep, in some bamboo jungle about six miles from Wapyudaung, and that while the animal was lying asleep they had fired simultaneously at his head with their old Tower muskets, and then followed up the beast for three successive days without coming up with it, eventually giving up the chase in disgust, as the animal had not shown any signs of being disabled. Whilst *en route* to Wapyudaung I fortunately met these hunters on their way home on the day of their return from the jungle. They gave me full particulars regarding the locality in which they had relinquished the tracks, but absolutely refused to accompany me, on the grounds that they were foot-sore and tired, and that there was not much chance of my coming up with the elephant, the direction of whose tracks plainly indicated that it was making for the Shwe-u-taung range of hills. No amount of bribes would induce them to come with me, not even the promise of the value of one tusk, should I bag the animal.

It would have been quite a different matter if I had my own hunter, Moung Hpe, with me; he, however, lived at Sittone, a village distant from Wapyudaung some twenty-five or thirty miles, and could not therefore be sent for to arrive in time to take up the tracks. Eventually, I heard that the thugyi or head-man of the village of Ontabu, situated about nine miles from the village of Wapyudaung and about three miles from the spot where the hunters had given up following the elephant's tracks, had at one time been a *shikarie* and tracker of some note. The Wapyudaung hunters had on their way back imparted to the Ontabu thugyi the whereabouts of the elephant's tracks. So, early next day I left for Ontabu with a few coolies, determined to follow up and sleep on the trail of the elephant till I came up with and bagged him. I was all the more determined to do so, after the opposition I had received from the Wapyudaung hunters, who were, I have no doubt, somewhat vexed and disappointed at having lost an elephant whose tusks were worth at least Rs 600. As a tracker the old Ontabu thugyi turned out to be all that could be desired. I started out with eight or nine coolies, taking as little kit with me as possible, and armed with my double 8 and 12-bore rifles.

We struck the tracks of the elephant at about 9 a.m., and followed them all day without coming up with the owner. I camped that night in the jungle, sleeping on a waterproof sheet with a few branches rigged up overhead to keep off the dew. At daybreak we were off again, and soon came on fresh signs of the elephant having been in the neighbourhood. Some cultivators, whose clearing we passed, informed us that the animal had, during the preceding night, eaten and trampled down a large quantity of standing paddy or rice. This was good news to us, although rough on the cultivator, and it showed that the elephant was in no way disabled, nor had it apparently any intentions of making for the Shwe-u-taung range of hills, or leaving the neighbourhood.

Hitherto my tracker was under the impression that the elephant had, as predicted by the Wapyudaung hunters, headed for the Shwe-u-taung hills, but now he informed me that it had altered its line of flight, and from various signs *en route*, we noticed that it had quite settled down again and got over its recent alarm, as it had begun to zigzag from one place to another, and had fed on several bamboo clumps, which had been stripped bare of their leaves. My coolies, boy, and Burman 'lugale', or servant-of-all-work, were now instructed to follow my hunter and myself at a respectable distance, while we moved cautiously forward. At the same moment, the loud cracking sound of a breaking bamboo was distinctly audible some way ahead. It was amusing at this juncture to see with what longing eyes my servants and coolies looked about them for suitable trees amongst whose branches, should the elephant charge, they would find a safe retreat. I then lit a match, blew it out, and noticing that the current of smoke was in our favour, I moved quickly and noiselessly forward. The elephant had in the meantime moved into a shady patch of tall young bamboos, whose stems were nowhere thicker than a man's wrist, and about 12 or 15 feet high; there was also a number of small saplings, but not one of a sufficient thickness to furnish a retreat in case of a charge. We could now distinctly hear the animal as he stood in the shade lazily flapping his ears.

I have always found it the best policy, when possible, before firing at large game such as elephants, rhino, gaur, or tsine, to fix on a good solid bamboo clump, tree-trunk, or rock, behind which to retreat after firing in case of a charge. It is not always necessary, of course, and there is not always a retreat available, but it should always be taken advantage of when possible, as it is quite unnecessary to risk your life and become foolhardy.

An elephant or gaur, I have always found, when disturbed or wounded will invariably be found standing or resting in cover, head on towards the point by which danger is expected, namely, the trail by which he has just entered. Animals have sufficient instinct to know this, and, as happened in this case, I found the elephant standing facing me. I crept up to within about twenty paces, backed up by my gun-bearer, and then for the first time got a glimpse of ivory that convinced me that for once the Burmans had not exaggerated, and that the animal now standing before me was the possessor of the best pair of tusks it had ever been my good fortune to see, and which now seemed within easy grasp.

The animal's head was unfortunately hidden amongst the bamboo leaves and branches, sufficiently to prevent my obtaining the head-shot; so creeping quietly round, fearful of treading on dry leaves or twigs, I gradually worked round to his flank. The wind must, however, have shifted, as wheeling suddenly round with a low sharp snort of alarm, like the sound emitted from a steam-pipe when suddenly turned on, off he sailed away at a great pace through the slim bamboos, which bent, cracked, and waved about beneath his strides like reeds. I immediately dashed away in his wake, determined to get in a shot somewhere, with the intention eventually, of course, of following him up to the bitter end, even though I should have to sleep on his trail for another week.

After keeping up with the animal in his immediate rear for some 200 yards, and finding that I could not outflank him so as to obtain a raking shoulder-shot, I fired in desperation at the huge target that presented itself, my shot apparently taking effect under the tail. The effect was magical in the extreme, and, contrary to all my expectations and experiences with elephants, the huge beast wheeled round with a shriek and charged straight down upon me at a great pace. I was too breathless and jumpy from the sharp run I had just undergone with the heavy 8-bore, to shoot straight, and having only one chamber loaded I fired wildly, aiming for the bump or forehead shot, jumping to one side immediately after.

The shot could not have hit the elephant, as he did not stop or swerve from his course in the slightest. My friend with the 12-bore was *non est*, poor man; he thought, I have no doubt, that the weight of three-score years and ten warranted his getting out of danger's way. As can be imagined, I did not wait to see any more, but dashed off at a tangent, jamming in two cartridges as I fled, the heavy 8-bore, although weighing quite 18 lbs., feeling as light as a feather. I was, however, in the pink of condition and as hard as nails. The elephant caught a glimpse of me as I dashed to one side, being then not quite ten paces off, and swerving round slightly towards me, stood for a few seconds, after which, wheeling round, he sailed away again in the direction he had first taken when fired at by me.

After collecting my men, who scrambled like so many monkeys down from the various trees outside the patch in which the elephant had taken up his quarters, and instructing them to follow behind slowly, my tracker and a gun-bearer and I took on the tracks, and kept steadily on. It was then about 9.30 a.m., and my guide informed me that he did not think we would come up with the animal that day, as we would not be able to travel very quickly, owing to the many difficulties which would be thrown in our way, such as the tracks becoming mixed up with those of other animals, a herd of which had been seen in the neighbourhood.

Some people may imagine that to track an elephant is a very simple matter, and so it is in wet weather, when the ground is wet and soft and the elephant leaves a deep impression. It is a very different matter, however, in dry weather, on hard stony ground or on hard laterite soil, when the ground is bare and denuded of all vegetation.

I know from experience that it is really much easier often to track up a solitary gaur or tsine under these circumstances than an elephant, whose flat feet leave hardly any impression. The utmost capabilities of my tracker were on this occasion called into play about an hour after we had taken on the tracks; in fact, on one occasion, for half an hour I almost despaired of ever finding them again, as they had become so mixed up with those of a herd which had been in the vicinity the day before, so that it was almost impossible to distinguish between them. Some of the best Burman *shikaries* and trackers I have known have been at sea when it came to the tracking up of a solitary bull elephant, but were, on the other hand, in their element when on the trail of a gaur or tsine; the reason for this being that some hunters made a living by mostly following and shooting elephants, whilst those who were afraid to tackle these monsters stuck to the other game. After making a number of wide detours or casts we did, however, eventually, strike the trail, and immediately pushed on again.

It was now well on to the evening, and, as tracking was made much easier by the ground being softer and covered with more vegetation, I suggested to my hunters that we should push on as quickly as possible, leaving the coolies and servants to follow. This we did, each of us scanning eagerly the ground, with the determination of not again losing the trail.

After having covered some eighteen miles of country from the time I fired at the elephant, we struck the banks of the Pethaung stream, which was about 30 yards wide, strewn with huge rocks and boulders and high shelving banks. The elephant's tracks now headed downstream, and as there did not seem to be much chance of our coming up with him that evening, it being then about 5.30 p.m. and some time past sunset, I called a halt, and sent back the tracker to ascertain how far off our coolies were. About a minute or two after his departure, my gun-bearer and I were startled by hearing a crash in the jungle on the opposite bank some 150 yards downstream, and at the same time an elephant, with a magnificent pair of tusks, walked down the side of the bank into full view, and came up the middle of the river-bed in our direction, and stood motionless beside a pool, facing us 50 yards off. My gun-bearer and I were fortunately lying down out of sight at the time, resting under an overhanging clump of bamboos by the river-side, and also hidden by a few low stunted bushes which were growing in midstream close to us. At this moment the all-unconscious tracker, who was fortunately some way off, began blowing on a hollow bamboo, with the intention of bringing up the coolies. The elephant, fortunately, did not seem to notice the noise, and after standing in midstream for about half a minute, lazily flapping his ears, he began to move upstream slowly towards us. The wind was, fortunately, in our favour, so wriggling into a kneeling posture, I crouched down to receive him with the 8-bore when he came near enough. My gun-bearer in the interval, who was sitting crouched down behind me with my spare rifle, was in a great state of excitement, as he was continually urging me to shoot, saying: 'Shoot, sir, shoot; he will wind us and be off!' The elephant in the meantime was walking along steadily and slowly towards us, with the intention of apparently returning along the route by which he had come. I waited till he approached to within about 15 yards, and then taking a steady aim with the 8-bore, fired for the bump or forehead-shot. On receiving the bullet he swerved quickly to one side, with a loud, sharp, shrill scream of pain and anger, and made for the opposite bank. Before reaching it, however, he received my left barrel; the ball, a hardened spherical one, entering behind the right shoulder, penetrating the heart, and bringing him to the ground after a preliminary lurch or two, where he lay uttering a low, deep, rumbling sound, resembling distant thunder, while life ebbed away. I rushed up, having in the meantime reloaded, thinking he might get up again, but saw from the way the blood gushed out that the heart had been pierced. He was a magnificent beast, with massive tusks.

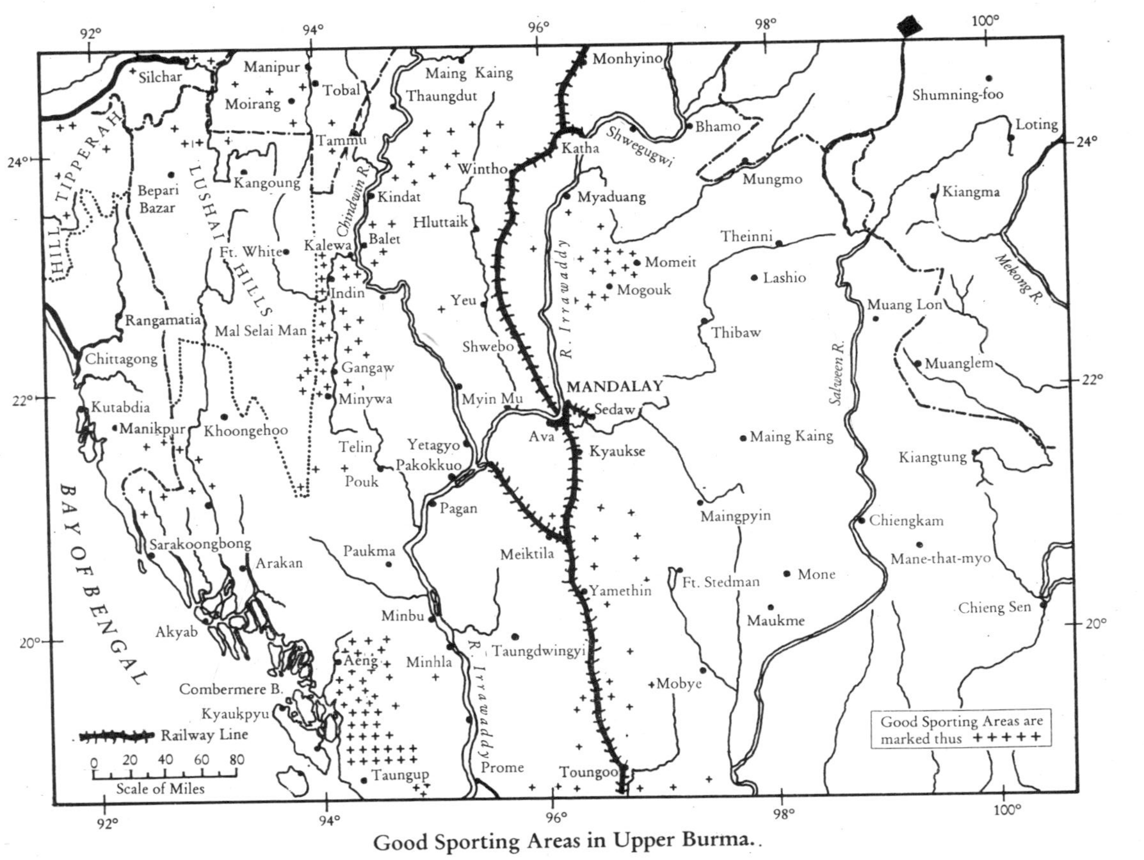

Good Sporting Areas in Upper Burma..

G.P. EVANS

The Indian Elephant

Some apology is, perhaps, needed for this book. An excellent book on big-game shooting in Burma, entitled *Wild Sports in Burma and Assam*, by joint authors Colonel Pollok and Mr Thom of the Burma Police, has already been written, and, therefore, an additional book may seem superfluous. But Colonel Pollok wrote of shooting in Lower Burma many years ago, and, from the nature of the country, was obliged to do practically all his shooting from the back of an elephant. The present book, like Mr Thom's portion of the work referred to, treats of shooting in Upper Burma only, and on foot. Although Mr Thom's experiences and mine coincide in the main, there is a difference, due in part to the localities in which we have hunted. Mr Thom did most of his shooting in one district, the Ruby Mines. I have never been to the Ruby Mines, but have shot in the districts of Upper and Lower Chindwin, Shwebo, Sagaing, Meiktila, Magwe, and Yamethin; that is to say, in the wet and dry zones alike. This would appear at first sight to make but little difference. In reality it affects the subject considerably, not on account of a wider experience, which I do not claim for a moment, but because the habits of animals differ in some degree according to the locality in which they are found. Mr Thom's experiences with elephants, for instance, were gained

From *Big-Game Shooting in Upper Burma*. London: Longmans Green, 1911.

chiefly while following single beasts, as one would naturally expect in the hilly country of the Ruby Mines. Mine, on the contrary, with few exceptions, were obtained with herds in the dry zone. Then, again, 'tsaing' found in the indaing forests of the dry and intermediate zones differ considerably in habits from those roaming in the bamboo jungles of the hills. 'Thamin' appear to call for a somewhat lengthier notice than that accorded to them in 'Wild Sports'. Finally, Mr Thom had exceptional facilities for obtaining the best trackers in his district, and in writing of them he seems to have lost sight of the difficulties under which less fortunate individuals have laboured. In making these remarks I trust I shall not be misunderstood. I merely wish to point out that circumstances alter cases. I gratefully acknowledge that when I first began to shoot big game in Burma, Mr Thom's portion of the book above mentioned was of the greatest assistance to me. But I found myself so often hampered by incompetent trackers, as well as by my own ignorance, that I determined, when I had gained sufficient experience, to commit that experience, to print, in the hope that newcomers might avoid the pitfalls into which I had myself fallen. ...

It is hoped that the list of shooting localities at the end of the book, and the glossary of Burmese words likely to occur daily in the jungle will be of use to those who are new to the country.

G.P. Evans

Strand Hotel, Rangoon
August 25, 1910

An account of the hunt which ended in the death of this elephant may be worth giving. During October 1907 I was out in the Lower Chindwin district trying to locate the whereabouts of a big herd of elephants, which for some days had been doing damage to cultivation. Three days were spent in fruitless journeys from village to village in the area in which the herd had committed depredations, until I began to think that the elephants had left the district altogether; but on the fourth day perseverance was to be rewarded. I had with me at the time a Mohammedan orderly, by name Allah Din, a bit of a scamp, but a most useful ally, as he spoke Burmese like a native of the country, and was, moreover, a very plucky fellow. The only thing against him was that at a critical moment he was apt to lose his head, and I had eventually to dispense with his services after he had twice bolted during a stampede of elephants, in one of which he was caught, narrowly escaping with his life. He got off without a bone being broken, the elephant fortunately contenting himself with kicking him once between fore and hind legs, and then leaving him. But it was over a month before he could walk without the use of a stick. This does not sound as if he had displayed any courage, but, as a matter of fact, nothing could be more plucky than the way in which on this, and on many former occasions, he had crept along unbidden at my heels, right into the middle of a big herd of elephants in thick jungle, armed only with an ordinary Martini-Henry rifle, and sometimes not even this. It was only after the shot had been taken, and the stampede in our direction had followed, that he was seized with an unreasoning panic which he was unable to overcome. It is only fair to add that in his youth Allah Din had been caught by a tiger which he had wounded, and which he insisted on following up alone in long grass. The tiger inflicted severe injuries, mauling him badly, and biting his arm through to the bone, breaking it in two places. Allah Din recovered after a long spell in hospital, but this adventure had doubtless shaken his nerve. I have entered on this digression because Allah Din was, as you will see, mainly responsible for my bagging this elephant, the tusks of which were the finest trophy I ever obtained.

But to hark back to my subject. Early on the morning of the fourth day I moved camp some ten miles in the direction of a village, Thapan, not far from the township of Budalin. As we got near the village we were met by an excited party of villagers, who reported that the herd had visited their cultivation overnight, and was now pretty certain to be found in the Thapan jungles, some three miles from the village. Here was news indeed! Leaving word for my kit to be taken on to the village, Allah Din and I started off at once, accompanied by three villagers as trackers. It was now past eight o'clock, and though I felt pretty sure of getting up to the herd, the chances were that we should find the elephants resting in thick cover instead of feeding, thus making the search for a big tusker difficult. On approaching the jungle, which was bordered by a large sandy nullah, or 'choung' as it is called in Burma, I was disappointed at not finding any traces of the herd, and began to think my men were mistaken. But they were positive that the elephants were somewhere in that jungle, so we retraced our steps and tried in another direction, and at last hit off the fresh tracks of the herd. There had been no recent rain, and it proved a difficult business to follow the trail over an open grass plain. In due course we reached the choung, and to my delight heard the elephants feeding in the jungle on the opposite bank. The cover, however, was very thick, and when I did get a glimpse of the herd it consisted, apparently, of a few animals only—all cows and small tuskers. We watched these for some time, during which the trackers got more and more excited, gesticulating and whispering whenever an elephant showed itself. There was one tusker somewhat larger than the others, with tusks weighing perhaps 40 lbs. the pair. The trackers, who would not keep still, kept urging me to shoot it, with the result that there was a trumpet of alarm, and the herd made off across our front, entering the choung and heading for the open plain we had lately passed over. Telling the trackers to stop where they were, I ran after the elephants, in two minds as to whether to shoot the tusker. Now that they were vanishing, the tusks I had despised a minute or two ago seemed a desirable trophy, although I had secured several larger pairs. The elephants presently slowed down into a fast walk, showing that they were not seriously alarmed. They had probably heard the Burmans, but had neither seen nor winded us. Again I was troubled with compunctions, and as the herd lessened its pace, I decreased mine also. Not so Allah Din. Always impetuous, he was running hard after the elephants, although unarmed, and was now some twenty yards or more ahead of me. Suddenly I saw him stop dead, point to the left, and then come running back to me, wildly waving his arms. Thinking he was urging me to follow the herd (for I had stopped running), I said to him as soon as he reached me, 'I am not going after them. He is only a small tusker.' Allah Din was too winded to speak at first, but presently he gasped out, 'It isn't that, but I have just seen an enormous tusker close by on our left.' I was at a loss what to make of this, as we were on an open plain with a few trees growing at intervals and with no cover even for a deer to hide in, much less an elephant. A patch of thick jungle, however, stretched away to the left, and hid the plain in that direction from view. Allah Din now went on to explain that, just as he had got level with this strip of jungle, he had seen a lot of elephants, as he expressed it, standing out in the open, and that there were several tuskers among them, and, in especial, one huge elephant with magnificent tusks. I followed the orderly somewhat doubtfully, but as soon as we had got level with the strip of jungle above mentioned, such a sight met my eyes as I had never before witnessed. There were about to a dozen elephants quietly standing right out in the open, nearly all of them bulls, with several good tuskers among them. One of them towered above his fellows, but I could not see his tusks, as a cow stood alongside hiding the lower portion of his head. Allah Din, however, assured me that this was the beast whose tusks he had seen, so I proceeded to stalk him without more ado. Luckily I had the wind. At first everything went well, but when within a hundred yards of them I suddenly came almost on top of a wretched little tusker, who was standing, fortunately, with his back to me, under the shade of a tree. I was in terror that he would discover me; but no, there he stood peacefully dozing in happy unconsciousness of my presence, and allowed me to pass him within ten yards. The remainder of the detachment was on the far side and a little in advance of the big fellow, with the exception of the cow, who was standing close up against him on the near side, both animals being broadside on to me. Bent double, I crept up to them, with Allah Din, as I afterwards found, close on my heels. He must have followed very noiselessly, for I had forgotten all about him in the excitement of the stalk, and only discovered his presence when I had fired. I was now within ten yards of the bull, but his tusks were still hidden behind the cow. Only those who have hunted big game can realize my feelings as I stood within a few paces of one of the finest elephants in Asia, unable to take advantage of a chance which comes to a man once in a lifetime. To fire without getting a glimpse of his ivories was not to be thought of. Allah Din in his hurried glance might very easily have mistaken him for another elephant, and I might find after all that I had shot a worthless 'hine' or tuskless male. At the imminent risk of discovery, I edged away to try and get a view of his head behind the cow. At this moment the cow threw up her trunk. I had a fleeting glimpse of a magnificent tusk, which seemed to my excited imagination even bigger than I afterwards found it to be. The next moment her trunk was down again, but I had seen all I wanted to, and crept back again to my former position. I did not dare to try for the earhole, as this would have necessitated getting level with the eye of the cow, who must then have seen me. Slowly I raised the rifle. The silence was intense. I could hear my heart thumping loudly beneath my shirt. The great ears of the bull came forward, exposing the fatal spot behind the ear, but the next second, with a resounding flap, they were back again. Again they flapped to and fro, without giving me a moment in which to take aim. This would never do. It could only be a matter of seconds before I was discovered, and then good-bye to the chance of a lifetime. I determined to fire the instant the ears again went forward, and breathlessly waited for a movement. There they go again. Now or never! Bang! At the shot the bull and cow wheeled round as on a pivot, and rushed off trumpeting loudly. Quick as they were, the rest of the elephants had a start of them. The herd, or rather the detachment, made straight across the plain for dense jungle, with my bull bringing up the rear. Never shall I forget the disappointment of that moment. I had eyes only for the bull, and dashed off wildly in his wake, with but the faintest hope of overtaking him before he reached the sanctuary of the jungle. But luck was on my side. About 200 yards from where the elephants had been resting was a deep nullah, and into this they disappeared one after the other, reappearing in a few seconds as they climbed the opposite bank. I pulled up dead, and the moment the huge back of the bull came into view as he ascended the steep bank I pressed the trigger. For a few paces he went on as if untouched, and then suddenly collapsed in a sitting position. My bullet had caught him fair in the spine, and had paralysed his hind quarters. I do not think I ever ran faster in my life. In much less time than it takes to tell it, I had scrambled into the nullah and up the opposite bank, and had fired at a distance of a couple of yards into the earhole. But the poor beast in his agony kept tossing his head, and rooting up small bushes with his trunk, making it difficult to take a steady aim. My shot had no effect, but a second attempt was successful, and the elephant rolled over dead by the side of a big tree, which held the body up, and prevented it collapsing altogether on its side. My delight can be imagined. Allah Din and I, with the perspiration streaming down our faces, pump-handled each other till we were tired. The point of the smaller tusk was firmly imbedded in the ground, and the massive forelegs were doubled up underneath the animal. By dint of twisted creepers, and much hauling on the part of the three Burmans who had now joined us, and ourselves, we at length got one of the forelegs sufficiently out from under the body to measure foot, and I remember wishing that Sanderson had been there to see the size of it. I imagine it would have altered his views regarding the height to which the Indian elephant occasionally attains.

On our arrival at the village a bullock cart was dispatched to bring in the head, attended by the villagers *en masse,* each man armed with a dah to assist in decapitating the fallen monster, and, incidentally, to cut off as much meat for himself as possible. I sent Allah Din to superintend the operation, with strict injunctions that no meat was to be taken until the head and feet were safely in the cart. The head was sent in in triumph to Budalin next day, as much meat as possible having been removed from the skull, and a deep grave was duly dug for its temporary resting-place, and kept well watered. At the end of a fortnight the skull was dug up, and the tusks removed by hand. The feet, after being thoroughly cleaned out—a difficult and lengthy business—were cured in the jail at Monywa, and, as waste-paper boxes, now make a very imposing addition to my collection of trophies.

I cannot pretend to have felt many qualms of compunction when I have been lucky enough to knock over a big beast. One generally has to work pretty hard for the shot, and at any moment the tables may be turned on the hunter. Moreover, elephants are mischievous brutes: the amount of damage a herd will do to cultivation has to be seen to be realized. I confess I did feel mean when I bowled over my first elephant, a youngster with tusks about 3 ft long and weighing something like 12 lbs. the pair. But I have never since been guilty of such a crime, and I may, perhaps, be allowed to plead in extenuation that not only was it my first elephant, but that I had only a few hours previously let off this very elephant, or one just like him, because I was unwilling to fire a shot while a chance remained of bagging a finer animal. When, during a stampede, he gave me a second chance, it was too much for poor human nature as exemplified in the person of a beginner. I tried to console myself with the reflection that I had erred in common with Sanderson and other noted Nimrods of bygone days, when they first essayed the finest of all sports. But it was a very poor sort of consolation, and I felt heartily ashamed of myself.

A certain amount of harm is done by native shikaris, and occasionally by subordinates in Government employ; but these people cannot afford, as a rule, the rifles necessary for the killing of heavy game, so their attentions are generally confined to patting an unwary deer over a water-hole. I remember, however, in Burma once meeting a subordinate in the Public Works Department who informed me that he knew of the whereabouts of a herd of bison, and suggested that I should accompany him and wipe out the lot! He had already killed a cow and wounded a bull from this very herd, and was extremely pleased with his performance.

In Burma, as in India, elephants are now protected by a special Act, and it is illegal to shoot them except in self-defence, or when actually doing damage to cultivation. But it is not difficult, I believe, to obtain permission to kill one elephant, and in many parts of Upper Burma during the latter part of the rains elephants do so much damage to rice cultivation that permission to go after a particular herd is readily granted by the local authorities. Occasionally, in certain districts where elephants have been doing constant damage, the Elephant Act is treated as a dead letter for the time being, permission being given to all and sundry to drive the elephants from that part of the district which has received too much attention from their frequent visitations. Then, again, elephants may be shot in independent territory, with the sanction of the reigning sawbwa, or prince; but such places are very inaccessible, and require much time to reach, and very complete arrangements, since no villages will be met with, and all provisions, including fowls, eggs and rice, have to be carried. The beginning of the cold weather would be the best time of year in which to make a trip to one of these out-of-the-way places. It would be quite impossible to shoot there in the rains and at the same time avoid malarial fever. Worse still, the sportsman's servants would be knocked over by fever to a certainty, when the shooting trip would perforce come to a speedy termination. The hot weather—March, April, May and the beginning of June—would be the most favourable time for wandering through the jungles, as the undergrowth would then be low. Tracking, however, owing to the dry state of the ground, would be difficult. Personally, if I intended to make a lengthy trip after elephants in independent territory, I would choose the cold weather, taking my chance of finding the beasts in thick cover. During November the ground would still be damp from the recent rains, while occasional showers might be expected in December and January. However, since in most years elephants are pretty certain to be doing damage to cultivation in Burma proper during the latter part of the rains, it would hardly be worthwhile making a long journey—possibly of several weeks—into independent territory, when permission to shoot one or more close at hand could probably be obtained without difficulty. In the rains elephants wander into the dry zone, finding sufficient cover in the thick scrub which grows in certain tracts, and are often to be found within a few miles of villages, too close to be pleasant to the unfortunate cultivators, whose crops they ravage during the night.

As regards the pursuit of elephants, the writer's experience differs from that of many sportsmen. So far from having to cover huge distances after elephants, he has almost invariably found them easier to locate,[1] and easier to come up with, than any other species of heavy game. Of course, if one particular beast is the object of pursuit, and if tracks are followed which are perhaps two days old, a long, stern chase may be expected. But where elephants are plentiful it is rarely long before fresh traces are found, or the animals themselves are met with. Indeed, the difficulty very often is to avoid them when after bison or tsaing, and elephants are in the neighbourhood. Sooner or later you are bound to run up against them, probably spread right across the tracks of the animal you are following. This is always a nuisance. The trackers, who are all right after bison, don't in the least fancy close quarters with a herd of elephants, and the trouble is to get past. Apart from everything else, a Burman is a very child for curiosity, and even if not actually afraid to pass the elephants, he will think nothing of wasting half an hour or more watching the herd feeding at a safe distance, while all the time your bison is getting farther and farther away. By the time you have got past, the tracks of the bison will possibly have been lost, or, what amounts to the same thing, have been trampled over by the elephants, so that they cannot be distinguished.

But *revenons à nos moutons*. Many of my readers will want to know how to set about shooting elephants in Burma. They will

[1]Locate here refers to the approximate marking down of animals in a particular jungle or area after tracks have been found, and does not include the journey from village to village in quest of information.

want to know the best time of year in which to shoot, and the best districts to go to. Those who are new to the sport may wish to know also how to find the big tusker in a herd, and the best weapon to slay him with. I will endeavour to put myself in the place of a man new both to Burma and to elephants, and to give him such information as my own experience suggests as likely to help him. With regard, then, to weapons, I recommend a D.B. high-velocity 450–400 rifle. As to districts, it depends on whether a man has obtained permission to shoot an elephant under any circumstances, or whether he is restricted to a certain animal or herd doing damage to cultivation. The same may be said with regard to the time of year. To the man who has obtained the sanction of the local government to kill an elephant, I would say try the districts of the Upper Chindwin, the Ruby Mines, the Arracan Hill Tracts, Shwebo, Mandalay, or Magwe. Anywhere, in fact, where elephants are to be found throughout the year (see the list of districts, with their respective possibilities as regards sport, at the end of the book.) To obtain sport in the districts above mentioned, the latter end of May and the whole of June would be the best months. The undergrowth is still low, while the ground is soft enough for tracking. A month earlier it is like iron; a month later the undergrowth has sprung up to a height which may vary from four to eight feet or more, while the leaf-shedding trees and bushes have donned a new garb in grateful recognition of the early monsoon showers—all very pretty and artistic, but exceedingly trying to the hunter. Therefore, if shooting outside the dry zone, do not be beguiled into trying for elephants in the cold weather, except in independent territory, when, in view of the long journey entailed, and the constant marching when you get there, it might be advisable to postpone the trip till the cooler months.

Although in Burma proper the sportsman will probably be limited to one elephant—should he succeed in obtaining sanction to kill one at all, by no means a certainty—he will have plenty of opportunities of shooting bison, tsaing, and other game in the districts mentioned: a further reason for choosing the months of May and June for his shoot. The selection of a particular district will depend on the time at the sportsman's disposal. If his time is practically unlimited, the Arracan Hill Tracts offer a greater variety of game than most other districts, and may give him a rhino. If stationed in a good game district my advice is to shoot in it, and to resist the temptation to go farther afield. The sportsman will naturally obtain more help from the local authorities in his own district than in others where he is a stranger. In Burma, at all events, sportsmen and officials are usually very generous in putting acquaintances, and even strangers, on to the best shooting grounds in their district, and in helping them to get good trackers, transport, &c.; but they consider, very naturally, that they have the first claim to the shooting in their own districts, and they do not view with delight the prospect of being invaded by sportsmen from other parts of Burma. So that, before deciding to shoot in a district other than the one in which you may happen to be stationed, it is as well to ascertain the nature of the reception awaiting you. This applies, of course, equally to men coming out from England, and over from India, to shoot in Burma.

But bearing in mind the Kheddah operations in Burma, and the prohibitions of the Elephant Act, I would not advise anyone who is especially keen to hunt elephants to apply to the Local Government for permission to shoot one. This of course would only be advisable in the case of those who want to shoot a variety of game—bison, tsaing, thamin, &c.—and who wish to add an elephant to the bag. If elephants are the *raison d'être* of a hunting trip, I would say, time your arrival for September, and confine your attentions to the dry belt. During the latter part of the rains elephants wander into the dry zone to escape the insect pests of the damp regions. As the feeding is very limited in extent, the animals soon find their way to the paddy-fields, and before long reports of damage come in from all quarters. Permission is then given to drive off the elephants, and who so competent to effect this meritorious action as the sportsman, with his modern high-velocity rifle? Off he goes, therefore, armed with a chit from the Deputy Commissioner containing the necessary sanction. But even this precaution, though desirable, is not actually necessary. So long as elephants have really been doing damage in the district, it will suffice to obtain verbal permission to shoot such animals as are known to be the offenders, always provided that they are still engaged nightly in their felonious practices. The prospective sportsman may ask, 'How am I to know that the herd I am after is the one which is doing the damage?' Well, there is small chance of a mistake in this direction. The sportsman travels from village to village, making inquiries as he goes, until finally he arrives at one close to which the elephants have fed on the paddy-fields the night before. The herd will have made for thick scrub jungle just before daylight, and will be found within a few miles of the village. These are the culprits, and if not driven off they will be certain to pay another visit to the paddy-fields during the night. They take very little notice of the shouts and tom-tomming of the villagers, being well aware that for all their noise they can do no harm. Even shots fired at night only have the effect of driving them off for a few hours, when back they come again.

Perhaps it would be as well to describe in detail the process to be followed by the sportsman from the time he first gets information of elephants doing damage to the happy moment when a big tusker lies dead before him. In the first place, then, 'khubbar' is essential, and the best way to obtain it is to have a friend at court in the person either of the Deputy Commissioner, the Assistant Commissioner, the Sub-divisional Officer, or the Deputy Superintendent of Police. If elephants are on the rampage reports will assuredly be brought in, together with applications from the villagers for guns and ammunition. Before the men get back to their villages the elephants will probably have departed to fresh woods and pastures new, and the guns will be utilized for shooting deer. But they will be issued none the less, in view of the likelihood of the elephants returning sooner or later. This is the time for the sportsman to get 'khubbar'. Burmans, like all Orientals, are very dilatory in their movements and if the sportsman seizes his opportunity he will be able to forestall them, arriving at the scene of action long before they are back in their respective villages. It should be borne in mind that when they do get back, they will not confine themselves to firing from their 'tehs' in the paddy-fields at night, but will march in a body to the jungle where the elephants are resting, and will scare the herd by firing volleys on the outskirts of the cover. The elephants will, of course, retreat, for perhaps twenty miles or more, and though they will return later on, since no real damage has been done, the sportsman's chance for the time being will have vanished with the elephants. It is therefore a great advantage to be first in the field. Guns may be issued, perhaps, to half a dozen villages, so that one lot, at all events, is pretty certain to have a bang at them, with the result that the elephants will clear out of that part of the district for the time being. Although, as I have said, elephants take little notice of shouts, or even shots, at night, when actually on the paddy-fields, they take quite another view of the matter when followed and fired at during the day.

We will suppose, then, that the sportsman has lost no time in dogging the elephants from village to village, and has at last located them in thick scrub some few miles from the paddy-fields. Now comes the tug-of-war. Long before you see the herd you are informed of its vicinity by the loud trumpeting of the older beasts, and the squeaking of the youngsters, while the deep rumblings of the herd and the crash of branches torn off the trees tells you that the elephants are unsuspicious and still feeding. Your Burmans now begin to point excitedly, and suddenly develop a suspicious politeness, assigning to you a prominent position which you could well dispense with. The noise the huge brutes are making is almost drowned in the beating of your own heart, which is thumping under your shirt in an absurdly noisy and officious manner. Keeping the wind, you now get up to the herd, and presently make out the legs or head of a cow or young tusker, which, all unconscious of your presence, is lazily pulling down a branch here and there, and ramming it into its capacious maw. It is now a case of thus far and no farther with your Burmans, who if not already up trees will take to them on the very first note of alarm. In any case, they have no intention of getting closer. After all, they have brought you up to the herd, and that is as much as you can expect from the ordinary villager. You now begin to creep in among the elephants, and will have ample opportunity of recognizing the difficulty, not to say danger, of trying to find a big tusker in thick cover with elephants all round you, and invisible until you stumble on a beast only a few yards distant. After getting as far as you can, and failing to discover a big tusker, you sneak out again, and try from another point. It is exciting work, especially if the herd is slowly feeding towards you. The big tuskers are generally in rear of the herd, in a little group all by themselves, with one or two cows. I have, however, on several occasions found them right in the middle of a herd surrounded by females. A herd, if of any size, is seldom united, but is split up into several detachments, each of which must be separately searched for a big tusker. Sooner or later, in trying to avoid a young tusker or a cow, you will, on rounding a bush or bamboo clump, come suddenly almost on top of a cow with calf. These are nasty customers, and if a man is very close are apt to charge on suspicion. If all goes well, and you have pushed on boldly but quietly, always of course paying the greatest attention to the wind, you are pretty certain to come on a big fellow at last, if there is one in the herd. The trouble now is to get up to him. There are probably half a dozen elephants all round him, and it may take a lot of manoeuvring to get within a dozen yards or so. You cannot get too close. The closer you are the safer you are, as the herd is less likely to stampede in your direction. Wait till he gives you a fair chance, aim carefully at his head, and look out for a stampede. At the shot there will be a rush, the whole herd will close up and then stampede—in which direction it is impossible to say. If they come straight down on you, your only chance is to stand absolutely motionless behind a bamboo clump or tree, if there is one available; otherwise, in the open. To run is fatal. A stampede by a big herd of elephants in one's direction is a trying ordeal, but it is not as dangerous as it appears if one keeps cool and does not attempt to move. The huge beasts are merely intent on escaping, and will pass by on either hand, mistaking one for a tree. Any movement attracts attention and induces pursuit. If, during a stampede, an elephant is seen coming straight towards you, a shot or a shout will turn him aside. This is the only time it is permissible to shout at elephants, unless one wishes to provoke a charge. When a herd is suspicious, and stands motionless just before moving off, a shout will probably result in one or more of the animals charging at once.

As a result of your shot one of three things will happen. Your elephant may be knocked over and lie dead as mutton, with a bullet through his brain; or he may merely be stunned, and lie bellowing on the ground; or he may wheel round and make off. To take the last case first. If the ground admits of it, rush after him at once and try to get alongside for the ear-shot. If you cannot manage this, fire under his tail and look out for squalls! He will probably wheel round and charge on the spot, thus giving you the chance of a forehead shot. This should turn him, if it doesn't drop him. As he turns to continue the retreat, you may have time to give him a shot in the ear. He will not go far now. He has three shots in the head and one in the tail, and is sure to be in an uncommonly bad temper; he will wait for you in the thickest patch of cover he can find and will charge out at you as soon as he sees or hears you. And so the game goes on until, in one of his charges, your bullet finds the brain, and over rolls the huge beast like a shot rabbit. If your first shot has knocked him over and merely stunned him, his bellowings will acquaint you with the fact. Lose no time in getting up to him, and giving him his quietus before he finds his legs. An elephant's head is a mass of cellular tissue, and a shot anywhere except in the brain won't bother him much. I need hardly say that if you let him get away you may make up your mind to having seen the last of him. If you have luckily found the brain, further proceedings will cease to interest him, and all that remains to be done is to cut off his tail and walk home in triumph. ...

A charging elephant carries his head high, and a shot aimed at the bump above the trunk would merely glance off, and would certainly not stop a charge. In this case aim at the base of the trunk low down, almost on a level with the mouth. The shot will travel up towards the brain, and if it misses the exact spot, will do so by a few inches. An elephant's trunk is extremely sensitive, and the combined effect of the blow on the trunk and the passage of the bullet close to the brain will in itself suffice to turn a charge, and possibly to knock the animal over. Should he still come on, a second bullet in the same place, or even a little lower, will almost invariably turn him, and give you time, possibly, for a shot in the ear as he makes off. A charging elephant coils his trunk in his mouth and so gives a fair chance. *I have* read of elephants charging with trunk thrown up, but am glad to say have never met with such an inconsiderate brute, and do not believe that one elephant in a hundred would be likely to carry his trunk in this position while actually charging. It is dead against the animal's normal habit and instinct. In such a case I should be inclined to shoot straight at the elephant's eye and hope for the best. If unsuccessful, the shot would, at all events, have the effect of bringing down the unruly member to its natural position, and a second bullet aimed at the base of the trunk would probably induce a more reasonable frame of mind. It is indeed fortunate for some of us that a charging elephant is not so tenaciously vindictive as a wounded buffalo, who, when charging, refuses to be stopped except by death alone. If this were so one would have little chance against an elephant charging from a few paces' distance. Escapes, indeed, from a wounded buffalo are only made possible by the fact that under ordinary circumstances the beast charges from some way off, fifty paces or more, giving the hunter time to get in a couple of cool shots, and so rake the animal from stem to stern. When a buffalo lies 'dogo', and comes out unexpectedly at a few paces' distance, the chance of a hurried shot striking the nostril, and so reaching the brain, must be slight indeed, and it is under these circumstances that men get caught through no fault of their own.

One hears occasionally of animals charging at the shot. What happens, I think, generally in these cases is that the beast is momentarily stupefied, fails to locate the sound of the shot, and in its first rush comes in the direction in which it has been facing. This has happened to the writer when shooting both bison and tsaing, but on catching sight of him the animal has immediately swerved and gone on. The result, of course, may be different in the case of a beast suspicious of danger who has seen its enemy, as, for instance, a tiger crouched and watching the man in front of him. Here the animal not only scents danger, but sees before him the person from whom it is to be apprehended. The shot confirms his suspicions, and a charge is just as likely to be the result as not.

It is commonly supposed that the most dangerous form of elephant shooting is the pursuit of a rogue. I do not think that this is the case, and the majority of men who have hunted elephants will probably agree with me. It is true that a rogue will charge on sight, but this very fact is in one's favour, as when doing so he presents a favourable opportunity for the head shot. I can state from experience that a rogue is just as easily turned as any other elephant; when wounded he behaves as any other elephant will under the circumstances, that is, he goes on and waits in the thickest patch of jungle he can find, and comes out like a gigantic Jack-in-the-box as soon as he sights or hears you. Sooner or later he exposes himself badly, until finally a bullet in the brain rolls him over.

It is a great advantage to have only one beast to deal with. When interviewing a herd the sportsman runs a double danger, possibly before a shot has been fired. The first is that a stampede may occur at any moment in his direction, and the second that, also at any moment, he may unexpectedly stumble on to a cow with a calf. A herd of elephants, unlike a herd of bison or other big game, spreads out and covers a large area, and as the herd is almost invariably in thick jungle, individual elephants are met with very suddenly. It is extremely unpleasant, on making a detour to avoid a young tusker or a cow, to come almost face to face with another cow with a butcha beside her. If at such close quarters she finds you out, a charge will probably be the consequence. She is taken by surprise, and her maternal fears induce her to assume the offensive, when if she were alone she would probably sheer off. If merely suspicious, she may take a couple of strides up to the bush or clump behind which you are crouching, and at the slightest sound she will be on top of you. More than once the writer has been held up in this uncomfortable predicament, hardly daring to breathe, with a huge brute standing stiff with suspicion almost over him. Fortunately, on these occasions the wind has held, and the elephant, after what has seemed hours but was really only a few seconds, has come to the conclusion that there was something uncanny about that bush, though what it was she didn't quite know, and has sheered off, with her calf at her heels. This constitutes the chief danger of elephant shooting, and it is one which must be expected, if a point is made of thoroughly searching a herd for a big tusker. It is curious, by the way, to note how readily elephants interpret the various sounds and movements made by individual members of a herd. There is no mistaking their attitude when one of their number signals 'man'. There is absolute stillness for a few moments, then a rush as the herd closes up, and off they go with many a shrill scream and trumpet, as they crash through the dense undergrowth as if it were tissue paper. A short, sharp trumpet proclaims that one is discovered. But if the sportsman happens to be very close to an elephant in a herd, and the beast is alarmed, it will quietly move off with hardly a sound, and, in spite of this, the whole herd will know as if by magic what is taking place and will silently follow suit. Similarly, in stalking single elephants, when the animal sights or hears a man at close quarters, there is a quick rush, followed by absolute silence. The novice creeps cautiously in the elephant's wake, supposing it to be standing close at hand listening. Not a bit of it! That elephant is quietly making tracks for all it is worth, and has no intention of pulling up until it has placed many a mile between itself and its pursuer.

I shall not easily forget my first interview with a herd of wild elephants, and how disappointed I was at what I thought was the mysterious behaviour of the herd. I was after bison at the time, at the foot of the Chin Hills, and had never seen or heard wild elephants. I had an old tracker with me who proved to be quite useless. It was a regular case of the blind leading the blind. We were making our way one evening across an open plain bordered by thick jungle, when suddenly an unearthly scream rent the air. I looked at the Burman, who returned the compliment, evidently as fogged as I was myself. 'What is it?' I whispered. 'Pyoung' (bison), he said. The sound was presently repeated, and seemed to come from a corner of the thick jungle ahead of us. Somehow I didn't think it could be bison. I had an idea that bison lowed or bellowed like domestic cattle; but I supposed he knew. The idea of elephants never occurred to me. Well, we skirted the jungle, and presently approached the spot from which the weird sounds had proceeded. As we were moving along I heard the squelching of muddy water just inside the cover, as if some large animal were having a bath. Cautiously I peered into the thick bush, and caught sight of the hind quarters of an elephant rolling from side to side. The brute was enjoying a mud bath. The Burman got a glimpse of it at the same moment, and calling out 'Sin la dé! sin la dé!' ('Elephant, elephant, it is coming!') took to his heels, and was half way across the plain before one could say Jack Robinson. At the same time there was a noise as of huge corks being drawn from invisible bottles, and I got a momentary glimpse of the retreating hind quarters of the elephant. I heard a slight brushing of the jungle about fifty yards away to my left, and a similar sound on my right. This was succeeded by absolute silence. I now realized that we had surprised a herd of elephants. After waiting for a few moments in the expectation of hearing further sounds, I cautiously crept along in the wake of the beast we had surprised, expecting to find it standing waiting for me a few yards farther on. The jungle was abominably thick, being of the wild-rose persuasion, and as I crept along the narrow elephant track, stumbling over creepers every now and then, and being held up by 'wait-a-bit' thorns every few yards, I found myself thinking what a horrible place it was to be caught in if the beast charged. Needless to say, the great, muddy footprints were all I saw of that elephant, and after following them for about half a mile, I gave it up in disgust, and regained the plain, there to find my tracker looking rather ashamed of himself. He told me he had once been caught by elephants, and that was the reason he was so afraid of them—a palpable fairy tale, since anyone who had once got close enough to elephants to be chased by them, would certainly have recognized their trumpet. It is, perhaps, hardly necessary to add that I got no bison with this man either; in fact, I doubt whether he had ever before either seen or heard wild elephants or bison. The quiet disappearance of the herd was a revelation to me, and one by which I have since profited.

Elephants getting the scent of a human being invariably announce the fact by a sharp scream, which is instantly followed by a rush, as the animal or the herd makes off. All animals appear to fear the scent of man much more than the sight of him. One may sometimes get up to a beast after it has heard the approach, or even caught a glimpse, of its pursuer, and has bolted. But let the breeze bring but a whiff of the dreaded taint to the sensitive nostrils, and the animal is off for good.

Tracking elephants is often difficult work. One would suppose that the great feet would leave an unmistakable imprint, and so they do in sand and on damp soil. But when the tracks lead over dried leaves and stony soil, the spongy feet form practically no impress, unless there has been recent rain. A displaced leaf, an inch or so of upturned soil, a broken branch, are often the only signs to guide your trackers, who, unless they are really good men, will be certain to lose the tracks before very long. I shall have more to say about trackers elsewhere, but I may remark *en passant* that few things are more annoying than to follow tracks for several hours, and eventually have to give them up. A Burman objects more than most Orientals to saying that he cannot do what is required of him. He therefore very often sets out gaily to track, knowing in his heart of hearts that as soon as the tracking becomes difficult he will be unable to follow. At first everything goes well. The tracks lead, we will say, across a sandy nullah and enter bamboo jungle, where they keep round a hill. The soil is loose and heavy, and the elephants' feet have sunk in at every step. After a while a ridge is reached, and here difficulties begin. The tracks cease to become patent to the eye, and check follows check in rapid succession. Other tracks cross and recross those which you are following, and your Burmans keep up a flow of discussion as they peer about, trying to hit off the original tracks. 'That's old.' 'No, I think it's new.' 'It's yesterday's tracks.' It's last night's', and so forth. This goes on for some hours during which you have, perhaps, covered three miles of country. Presently, seeing that matters look pretty hopeless, you say, 'Can't you find the tracks?' And you are then told, 'No, we can't follow them—they have got mixed up with others—many elephants have gone this way,' and back you trudge to camp, anathematizing under your breath the Burman and his annoying little ways. This sort of thing will happen over and over again with indifferent trackers under circumstances in which a good tracker would have little difficulty in picking out the tracks. Of course, in really hard, dry weather the best trackers can do little; but such men will follow tracks over all kinds of soil as long as the ground is sufficiently damp to leave the faintest possible impression of the animal's footprints. Such trackers are rare, in Burma at all events, and in most cases the sportsman will have to rely on the local moksoh or shikari, who is often merely a coolie, and has probably never seen big game at close quarters. It is, however, consoling to know that nearly every Burman in the remoter villages can track after a fashion, that is to say, infinitely better than most Europeans. Given heavy rain overnight, your village tracker will certainly bring you up to elephants or bison; but let two or three days of dry weather succeed the rain, and unless he is an experienced tracker, he is sure to lose the trail before very long. It follows, therefore, that in Burma a man must possess both patience and time to wait for the opportunity, and to seize it when it offers. Even in the rains a break of ten days is not unknown, and if, after the first three or four days of that break, the sportsman attempts to track without first-class trackers, he will have his trouble for nothing.

When following single elephants I have always found that as soon as overnight tracks were found, one came up with the animal within four or five hours at most. In this respect I may, perhaps, have been fortunate, but it has happened so frequently that there must be some other explanation, and I think it is this. Elephants are very deliberate sort of creatures—very unsuspicious, though quick to take alarm when danger threatens. Both bison and tsaing are shy beasts, avoiding man's proximity as much as may be. But the elephant doesn't concern himself particularly. I suppose his great bulk gives him a feeling of security; at all events, he takes his ease when and where he will like a gentleman. After his midday siesta he begins to feed at about 3 p.m., and wanders along as he goes, taking his time about it till 11 p.m., or thereabouts, when he rests for four or five hours during which time he may lie down. At 3 a.m. or so he again begins to feed, moving slowly along, stopping for hours, maybe, in some place where the bamboo fodder particularly tempts him. As soon as the sun gets up he moves into thicker jungle, and from about 9 a.m. to 3 p.m. stops feeding, and quietly dozes the hours away. Let us suppose that one strikes tracks at 6 a.m. which the animal has made at 8 p.m. the previous night. The tracks themselves show us how leisurely have been his movements. They zigzag here and there as the beast has turned aside to pull down a branch or to rub himself against a tree. A little farther on he has, perhaps, stopped for half an hour to make a hearty meal. In the three hours during which he has been walking and feeding he has, perhaps, covered three miles. So that if you have been moving at two miles an hour you will arrive by 7.30 a.m. at the place where he has stopped to rest for the night. He is now some four hours ahead of you, but during those four hours he has moved very leisurely, making long halts here and there, perhaps covering another four or five miles in all, so that, tracking slowly but steadily, you come up with him at 9 a.m. or thereabouts, to find him still feeding if you are lucky.

I can only call to mind two occasions on which I have had a really long trudge after elephants. Once when I followed a herd which had got our wind. This herd went for about fifteen miles before again halting in thickish cover. I had started some hours before dawn, and had found the elephants at about 7 a.m., or a little after. The day was cloudy, with a changing breeze, and the herd went off in double-quick time just as I was worming my way up to a tusker. It was evening before I came up with them again, to find them busily feeding. I got my tusker after some trouble, arriving in camp during the small hours of the morning, dead-beat but triumphant. The other time was when following a rogue which I had wounded in the head a month before. Here again the animal was alarmed. We had struck the fresh tracks of a herd which, however, had been doing no damage. I explained to my trackers, one of whom was the headman of the village, that I was not at liberty to follow the herd, and that if I couldn't find the rogue's tracks I would return to the village. I was accompanied at the moment by a nondescript collection of villagers who had come out to meet me armed with 'dahs' to cut up the meat, as somehow they were under the impression that I had already killed an elephant. They were disappointed that I would not follow the herd whose tracks we had just found, but seeing that I was in earnest, they spread themselves out to look for traces of the rogue. Presently they came racing back in a great state of excitement to say that they had almost tumbled on top of an elephant sleeping in some thick scrub a few yards off. I could hardly credit this at first, but on going to the spot there were the footprints of a huge elephant, which had been lying down fast asleep within twenty yards of us. The tracks were at once recognized as those of the rogue, and having, with great difficulty, got rid of my following, I started with my two trackers and my orderly to follow the trail. It was now about 10 a.m., and at 1 p.m. I halted for a couple of hours, so as to come up with the beast in the evening, when I hoped it would be feeding. We got up to him at 4 p.m., and the first indication I had of his whereabouts was a short rush in a patch of thick scrub in front of me. I was afraid I had again alarmed the beast, and that he would go for miles, but he quickly dispelled my doubts. Both trackers had taken to trees, and I saw neither of them again until the elephant was killed half an hour later. I had entered the patch closely followed by the orderly, and had covered, perhaps, two hundred yards when, with a fiendish scream, the rogue charged out at us from some dense cover on my right. For some seconds I could distinguish nothing but the bending foliage as the huge brute tore his way through the thick cover, but presently he burst out, trunk tightly coiled, ears cocked and head held high. I waited till his head was clear, and gave him the right barrel at about fifteen yards. I was using a 10-bore Paradox by Holland with a steel-cored bullet, and aimed low down at the base of the trunk about two feet below the bump. The smoke hung round me like a pall, but stooping below, I saw to my dismay that he was not even checked. I had just time to step aside, so as to clear the smoke, and to give him the left barrel in the same place. This was enough for him, and brought him up when he was all but on me. He slid for some little distance with the impetus of his charge, as he rammed his great forefeet out in front of him to check himself. The next second he had wheeled round and crashed back into the jungle, but I had just time to jerk open the breech, slip in another cartridge, and give him one in the ear before he vanished. It was a very close thing. I suppose he was not five yards from me when he received the second bullet. After waiting a few moments to compose our nerves, I explained matters to the orderly, Allah Din, who was then new to the game but full of pluck. I knew the elephant would not go far, but would wait for us in the nastiest bit of jungle he could find. If I led, tracking, there was every chance of the elephant taking us unawares, and getting a bit of his own back and something over. I told Allah Din that if he would do the tracking I would follow at his heels, keeping a sharp look-out. He was quite game, in fact, too much so, as he wanted to run after the elephant. He was an impetuous chap, and later was caught by an elephant when out with me, as already narrated, and nearly killed, owing to suddenly losing his head during a stampede and trying to run. On the present occasion he would go too fast, and I had to be constantly whispering to him to take his time. After going some three hundred yards or so he stopped suddenly and held up his hand. We had just got out of an abominably thick bit of stuff and were about to enter another. Listening intently, I could now hear the elephant ahead of us kicking up clods of earth, a sure sign that he was badly wounded and bent on mischief. At this moment, inadvertently, I trod on a dry twig, which snapped with a slight crackle. There was a shrill scream from the elephant, and out he came. The orderly dodged aside, caught his foot in a creeper, and lay sprawling directly in front of the charging elephant. Lucky for us it was that we were almost in the open. As the beast emerged from the dense cover I gave him a bullet in about the same spot as before, viz. the base of the trunk, low down. He rolled over to the shot like a rabbit, and as the smoke cleared I saw his huge carcass lying motionless on its side in front of me. The bullet had found its billet this time, and the elephant had died instantaneously. He measured 9 ft 7 in. at the shoulder and had only tusk; that, however, was a beauty, and weighed close on 40 lbs. The other tusk had been broken off at the root, probably in a fight with another tusker. I took a huge bunch of maggots the size of a football out of the broken tusk; the poor beast must have endured agonies from toothache. No wonder he had turned rogue! This particular elephant had done a lot of damage for years. And was said to have killed several villagers. He used to hold up a certain position of a cart-road, and give chase to all and sundry passing thereon. Shortly before he was shot he had chased a Burman who was quietly riding along this road. The pony wanted no urging, and while galloping along with the elephant in close pursuit, the Burman had the presence of mind to snatch off his 'gaung baung'—the silk fillet Burmans wear round their heads in lieu of a turban. He threw this down, and the elephant stopped to tear it into shreds, while the man made good his escape. From first to last I do not think this elephant covered more than eight miles from the time we had startled him when asleep; but had he been other than a rogue he would doubtless have gone considerably farther before pulling up.

While on the subject of rogues, I believe that in nearly every instance the animal will be found to be suffering from some physical hurt which occasions constant pain, and so turns an inoffensive beast into a savage man-hunter. It may be a broken tusk, as in this case, or old bullet-wounds which have left festering sores. Sanderson's rogue was found to have had his tail bitten off at the root. Maggots swarmed at the stump, and must have caused the poor beast intense suffering. And then, think of the indignity of it! Who wouldn't be soured by such an outrage! It reminds one of the story of the German student who, having his nose cut off in a duel, stooped to recover the precious organ in order to clap it on again before it got cold. But before he could execute his design, his unfeeling adversary had put his foot on it and squashed it into a pulp! If the injured man thereafter went about with murder in his heart who could blame him?

Female elephants are often addicted to the practice of biting off each other's tails—a piece of spite that apparently isn't always confined to the feminine sex. Tuskers as a rule, however, are above this sort of thing, and possibly Sanderson's poor rogue suffered from the jealousy of a discarded flame. I once heard a tusker fight taking place in very thick jungle on the outskirts of a herd. But in trying to get up to them I alarmed the herd, which decamped, together with the combatants. The scene of the fight, however, left no doubt as to the fierceness of the struggle. The ground was ploughed up in all directions, saplings and branches were strewn everywhere, while here and there clots of blood showed that more than one thrust had penetrated the thick hides of the antagonists. I was sorry to have missed what would have been a unique sight; but, considering the denseness of the jungle and the excited state of the combatants it was, perhaps, just as well for me that I failed to obtain an interview. As it was, I only got to the place by crawling on my hands and knees, the intertwining creepers and low-hanging branches preventing a more comfortable attitude.

The exact time of year during which elephants breed is uncertain; but as the young are generally dropped in the late autumn, and the period of gestation lasts about twenty months, it is probable that the breeding season is during the hot weather and commencement of the rains. I once caught a young elephant early in November. I had come unexpectedly on elephants in long kaing grass, and the herd had stampeded without giving me a chance. While debating whether to follow them up, I was surprised to hear an elephant roaring a little way off. I made my way to the spot with cocked rifle, expecting to find a tusker on the rampage; but there stood a baby elephant about 8 ft high, bellowing out his grievance like a wounded bull. His unfeeling mamma had decamped leaving her offspring behind. We sneaked up behind him and while my orderly clutched his tail, I threw myself on him and closed him round the neck. But the little brute managed to drag us for a hundred yards or so before we could pull him up. Finally, we got the orderly's 'puggri' round his throat, and frog-marched him into camp. For half the way he fought like an obstreperous pig, making side rushes every now and then into the jungle, and squealing without cessation. But presently he seemed to realize that he had to go, and so might just as well go quietly, and thereafter we had no further trouble. He jogged quietly along in front of the orderly, who drove him as one would a pony. In two days he became absolutely tame, and would rush for his milk whenever he caught sight of me. He was a grand little bull, and I had great hopes of rearing him; but alas! there was nothing better than condensed milk to feed him on, and in spite of every care he died on about the tenth day. I don't suppose he could have been more than a month old. He nearly ruined me in condensed milk, for he used to polish off about four or five tins a day. Young elephants are always very delicate, and it is believed to be impossible to rear them by hand.

Female elephants are very solicitous for their young when with them; but, judging from this instance and others I have heard of, if anything happens to separate the mother from the young one, the former, unlike most animals, will not return to look after it.

At the first note of alarm all the babies in a herd disappear as if by magic. They have all got under their mothers' tummies. A young calf can cover ten or fifteen miles without undue fatigue, helped over bad places by its mother. The trunk of a baby elephant is an inert, wobbly piece of flesh about a foot in length, and quite useless for drinking purposes. The young suck the cows with the mouth, in common with the young of all animals. The cows have their teats, two in number, in front, between their forelegs. They give birth to one calf at a time, twins being rarely heard of. An old cow is invariably the leader of the herd, and when alarmed the tuskers take a line of their own. When travelling, elephants move in single file, the tuskers generally bringing up the rear. Elephants have very poor sight; but when resting during the day and not feeding, their hearing is often acute. When feeding they make so much noise that they can be approached without difficulty. The sense of smell is highly developed, more so than in most animals.

It is often difficult to know what to do when a herd is found just after they have stopped feeding. When it can be managed, it is best to wait till the evening, when they will wander into thinner jungle and commence to feed. But in the rains the weather cannot always be relied on; the wind may veer round, and the herd depart as silently as shadows. When the herd is at rest, the risk of alarming it before finding a big tusker is greatly increased, so that whenever possible it is wise to wait till they have begun to feed again.

As a last word, let me caution beginners against attempting to follow elephants into really dense jungle or high kaing grass. No good can possibly result. It is like pursuing them in the dark. The elephants themselves in such places can only follow elephant paths, and if anything should occur to turn the herd, they will stampede back on their tracks, a practice they are rather given to. There is then no hope for the hunter, shoot he never so straightly. He may turn the foremost elephant, but he will be overrun by those pressing on in rear. I have tried it myself; but it is a foolish game, and one which will sooner or later bring certain disaster in its train. Nearly all accidents that occur when after elephants are caused by the sportsman foolishly following a herd or a wounded elephant into cover so thick that he can move neither to right nor left in the event of a charge, and cannot see more than a yard or two in front of him. It will be found that in hunting elephants quite sufficient risks are run in the ordinary course of the business, without going out of the way to look for trouble.

Appendix

Shooting Localities

The following list of districts in which shooting is to be obtained in Upper Burma does not pretend to be a complete one. Those districts only are mentioned in which the writer has himself hunted, or which are known to him to hold game. The barking deer is omitted, as it is found everywhere.

Yamethin	Northern portion: thamin; and in the hills to the east, bison, tsaing, elephants and bear.
Meiktila	Eastern portion: thamin, sambur (scarce). Farther east in the hills, bison, tsaing, bear and (in the rains) elephants.
Magwe	Thamin; and in the eastern portion, bison, tsaing, sambur, elephants.
Mandalay	Elephants, bison, tsaing and deer.
Sagaing	Thamin; and in the northern portion, elephants occasionally in the rains.
Pakokku	Thamin; and in the hills to the west, bison, serow, gooral and bear.
Northern Shan States	Everything except thamin; but a long journey would have to be made into independent territory to get shooting.
Lower Chindwin	Eastern portion: thamin, and elephants in the rains. Western portion: bison, tsaing and sambur.
Shwebo	Everything except, perhaps, rhinoceros. Elephants in the northern portion all the year round. In the southern portion: thamin, and elephants in the rains.
Chin Hills	Practically nothing. Mahsir fishing.
Upper Chindwin	Everything except thamin. Rhino scarce.
Arracan Hill Tracts	Everything except thamin, and tsaing. A good district for rhino and serow.
Katha	Everything except thamin, and possibly rhino.
Myitkyina	Everything except thamin; excellent mahsir fishing.
Ruby Mines	Everything except thamin.

V.M. STOCKLEY

Asiatic Elephant

The method of elephant shooting is to find tracks fresh enough to be worth taking on and to follow them till you come up with the game. This applies to all other heavy game.

In the case of elephants you may be further guided by the noise they often make in feeding, or their occasional trumpetings and rumblings, even when at rest. Shooting in April in the Katha District, I found elephants almost solely by hearing them, my men not being able generally to track on the then hard ground, though occasional signs might help us as to which direction to take. But elephants were numerous there. As a rule it is no use hunting if your men are not able to track.

Most authorities agree that elephant shooting, if fairly and regularly carried on, is more dangerous than any other kind of big game hunting. It is certainly very hard and exciting work to follow and slay the mighty beast in his own forest domains. The impressive size and bearing of the game, the idea of power it conveys, both in its appearance and in the loud noises made when moving and feeding, or in a stampede when a herd rushes along like an avalanche through the jungle, conduce to this excitement.

From *Big Game Shooting in India, Burma and Somali Land*. London: Horace Cox, 1913.

I have never been charged by an elephant. Sanderson's description of the charge is worth quoting. He says:

> The wild elephant's attack is one of the noblest sights of the chase. A grander animated object than a wild elephant in full charge can hardly be imagined. The cocked ears and broad forehead present an immense frontage; the head is held high, with the trunk curled between the tusks to be uncoiled in the moment of attack; the massive forelegs come down with the force and regularity of ponderous machinery; and the whole figure is rapidly foreshortened and appears to double in size with each advancing stride. The trunk being curled and unable to emit any sound, the attack is made in silence, after the usual premonitory shriek, which adds to its impressiveness.

The best season in Burma and India for heavy game shooting is from the latter part of May till the middle of July: during the first part of the rainy season, in fact, before the rain has become too continuous and the jungle too dense. At this time of the year there may be many days in succession, cool and cloudy with light rain, or only occasional showers, softening the ground and the strewn leaves, making quiet movement possible and tracking generally easy, and therefore forming perfect shooting weather.

In hunting elephants or the other kinds of heavy game, it is as well to make up your mind before starting as to whether or not you wish to be prepared to sleep out in the jungle if necessary. For if you do, more impedimenta (requiring more men) must of course be taken—such as sufficient blankets, a waterproof sheet or valise, a sleeping suit, a towel, change of underclothing, spare pair of socks and boots (for everything you wear during the day will have become soaked from one cause or another), and extra rations, in addition to the things ordinarily taken only for the day, which in my case consisted of a water-bottle, a tiffin tin, and a large waterproof shooting bag (with shoulder strap) containing a light waterproof 'slip on', a flask of brandy, a field dressing, measuring tape, skinning knives, compass, extra cartridges, etc. My tiffin tin was an old biscuit box divided by sheets of tin into three compartments, carried in a leather cover, fastening with buckle and strap, and furnished with a shoulder strap. The tin lid made a good plate, and besides the food, I put in it a small folding knife, fork, and spoon, a little metal salt holder, and a couple of the smallest sized Liebig's extract jars with their corks for holding butter, jam or other condiment.

The gunbearers' extra things also have to be carried as they should be unencumbered beyond a rifle.

To be prepared for sleeping out is no doubt the right way to follow the heavy game. The feeling that you can remain out if necessary is very satisfactory when you are tracking either wounded or unwounded animals. You know it will not be easy for them to shake you off, as you need not give up following in order to get home by night. Your jungle men with their axes or dahs will soon run you up a shelter against rain and dew when necessary. The forest supplies all the required materials.

An objection to sleeping out in the jungles during the rains is undoubtedly the liability to malarial fever (the great game-preserver) from so doing. To guard against this, quinine should be taken regularly. I have found fifteen grains taken twice a week fairly effective. I am no advocate of alcohol, but I will give Kinloch's recipe against fever in his own words, though he does not state the amount of quinine. He writes:

> Early in September of the same year, I disregarded all warnings about jungle fever and set out to have another try for elephants in the Sewalikhs. I took the precaution of swallowing a glass of sherry with a good dose of quinine every morning when I got out of bed, and I never had a touch of fever.

An early morning start should be made, for if lucky enough to find fresh tracks, the earlier in the day they are found the better, since it is an advantage to come up to elephants (or other game) before they have settled down for their midday rest. Animals are more likely to see or hear you when they are resting than when on the move or feeding. It is especially important to approach elephants when they are feeding, on account of the noise they usually make covering any sound of your own approach.

When you come upon big enough tracks that are palpably not too old to investigate, the first question to decide is their age. If a fall of rain has occurred the previous evening or during the night, not followed by further rain, it will be a great assistance in deciding the point, as it will usually be evident whether the track was made before or after the fall. I have always deferred to the opinion of the jungle men with regard to the age of the tracks. The civilized man can rarely compete with aboriginal man in this respect, nor in the art of tracking. Even tracks pronounced of the previous forenoon are worth taking up for a mile to see what they look like then, and the state of any dung that may be come upon, which will always be a great aid in judging the age or freshness of tracks. If they are still considered of the previous forenoon they may be dropped and later ones worked for, but it is often wonderful how quickly tracks become fresh. The reason of this is that elephants (more so than other heavy game) move very slowly while feeding—not more than half a mile an hour, and often considerably less, according to my own experience, and that they halt and rest occasionally for a few hours. Your rate of tracking will probably be about two miles an hour if the state of the ground is favourable. If difficult, it might be only a mile an hour, but it would in most cases average at least one mile and a half, taking the good with the bad, unless, as sometimes happens, much time is lost in unravelling the wanderings and loiterings of feeding elephants, or the track of a single one you wish to hold on to, from others it has become mixed up with. So tracks though pronounced, say, of the previous afternoon, if found by ten o'clock in the morning, may be followed with a fair chance of coming up to the elephants during the day.

The order of march I generally adopted when tracking in Mong Long, before the tracks became very fresh was as follows, there being about twenty-five yards distance between the men or parties named: the tracker (or trackers)—the interpreter (a pensioned Goorkha soldier settled in Burma)—a gunbearer—a gunbearer—shooting-carrier—the syce (ponykeeper)—myself (riding when possible) with a shooting-carrier.

By this means the pony was kept well to the rear, and in hot weather I saved myself as much walking as I could though it was often impossible to ride, and even very difficult at times to get an unridden pony along in the jungle-covered hills. If the weather is cool or you are fit enough to walk all day when it is hot, it is of course better to walk with the trackers and leave the pony at home. You then move less encumbered, avoid the chance of any sound made by the pony, giving warning to game, and are always ready for anything.

With the idea of being more independent of men, who are sometimes difficult to engage, I once tried a pack pony for carrying things required by the party when prepared to sleep out, and found that in whatever manner I arranged the small load, it was too wide to admit of the pony getting through the denser parts of the jungle. If only out for the day I found two carriers sufficient, one to carry my own things, and one those of the gunbearers. If going prepared to sleep out, four carriers were necessary; and in that case the little column could be further lengthened, so as to place the pony a greater distance to the rear. I could halt everyone at any time by a low whistle and signal, which was passed forward till it reached the tracker. On tracks becoming very fresh, the information was passed back to me by signal, and I went forward—carrying a rifle—to join the tracker (or trackers) with one of the gunbearers, the syce taking charge of the pony accompanied by the rear shooting-carrier. This was necessary, as the syce not knowing the jungles, in case he got into difficulties with the pony and temporarily lost sight of the next party in front, required a jungle man to help him. The column or chain would then be shortened by two links, or closed up by fifty yards, but the pony would still be about a hundred yards in rear of the leading party, composed of the tracker, myself, and a gun-carrier. The short distance of twenty to thirty yards between the connecting links of the chain was necessary in the thick jungle occasionally passed through, in order that the men might keep in sight of each other, though even if from any reason they did lose view, it was usually easy for them by following the trail of those in front (and sometimes by listening) to soon catch them up again.

If the wind is on your back it is useless following very fresh tracks. The only thing to do is to judge the probable line of the game (elephants usually head in one general direction), and endeavour by a wide movement forward to come in on their head or flank.

On elephants being heard not far off, or seen, or quite fresh signs (such as hot dung) come upon, the signal would be passed back to halt, while I (after taking the wind) pushed on with the tracker, the interpreter, and a gunbearer. The best way to take the wind is to strike a match and blow it out, when the smoke will show the direction of the slightest stir in the air.

After appreciating the situation by a closer approach, I went forward either alone or accompanied by a gunbearer. If I was unsuccessful in obtaining a shot, owing to the elephants moving on too fast or to their taking alarm, the men in rear were called up, the order of march re-formed, and the tracking resumed.

This order of march and method I have generally adopted in principle when following all kinds of heavy game.

Approaching a herd of elephants to find a good tusker is very difficult work. You have to be constantly considering the wind. You may come on females with young unexpectedly, or find them, and other elephants not worth shooting, bearing down on you, and being perhaps unable to get out of their way in time, may be charged. In any case, if you are discovered the alarm will be given. It is said an elephant suddenly finding itself in the presence of a man, is more likely to attack him than any other animal would be. The best herd tuskers are often by themselves, a quarter to half a mile from the main body. If you can so find them, it will be an advantage in having only a single animal to deal with. When with the herd the good tuskers are generally with the rear detachments. 'You will be guided in your movements as much by what you hear as by what you see. The chances are if you are not fairly quick in finding and shooting a good tusker, you will soon be winded or stumbled on by some of the animals, and the whole herd alarmed. Elephants are not so easy to see in thick forest as might be supposed from their size. The dark shadows cast in such jungle accord with their colour (as with that of all heavy game), and may hide them, though within thirty yards, unless you catch the movement of their ears or tails, which are hardly ever at rest, and which indeed generally give you your first information. The part of the head or body where you wish to plant your bullet will frequently be hidden by grass or branches in the most aggravating manner.

Before firing it is as well to have a substantial tree or bamboo clump handy, behind which to retreat if necessary after your shot. In case of a stampede the herd may otherwise run over you. I have never experienced this danger though stampeding herds have passed me thirty or forty yards away. It is one, however, to take into account.

The most awkward cover in Burma in which to approach elephants is the thick stemmed 'kaing' grass—a dense growth, soft, 10 ft to 15 ft high. You cannot move in it quietly, you cannot run a yard without being tripped up in the tangle round your feet, and you cannot see an elephant in it sometimes when within but half a dozen paces, though you can hear it to any extent—the noise made by the huge animals in feeding and forcing their way through this kind of cover being alarmingly loud, and covering any noise made by yourself in struggling through it. It is a risky matter hunting in grass like this, for there is usually nothing to break an elephant's charge or rush, such as a tree, and while you are bound fast, so to speak, amongst the thick stems and undergrowth, an elephant can go through it easily.

It is, of course, a much simpler affair to approach a solitary elephant than to find a good tusker in a herd. Further, the old solitary tusker offers the best trophies.

The head and shoulder shots are those usually taken in elephant shooting. With regard to the former, a great many elephants have been lost by trying it. The brain is very small proportionately to the size of the head, and if it is missed, the animal is little the worse. The skull contains a mass of bony cells that seem to be unaffected by bullets lodged in them. An elephant that gets away after head shots only is rarely recovered. One evening at dusk in the Katha District, when returning home, I heard elephants a little way off, and diverged with my Burmese hunter (who rejoiced in the easily pronounced name of Mo-Mo) to approach them. Stopping by a tree to listen, we heard an elephant crashing through the dense jungle towards us. A big looking tusker's head showed not a dozen paces from me. He continued slowly moving on, passing me within a few yards. I tried the temple shot (with an eight-bore rifle) as I could see his head better than any other part. He nearly fell but recovered himself and made off. I had reserved my left in case he attacked, and by the time I could see he was not going to do so, the opportunity for using the second barrel in the thick cover had passed. Mo-Mo I noticed had climbed up a tree. There was a blood trail which we followed the next morning. The blood, however, soon ceased and we never saw the elephant again—which indeed I had not expected to do, as it was a head shot, though Mo-Mo had expressed his opinion we should find the elephant dead. ...

Though it is not the fashion to say so, I consider the shoulder shot the best and certainly the more generally useful. It allows for slight errors of aim, and in all the varied circumstances of firing at heavy game in jungle after perhaps a good deal of hard work on both body and mind, errors small or great may easily occur.

If fairly well placed, the lungs will be penetrated, and you must get your elephant in a short time. Many a man who has lost his elephant by trying the head shot would have secured it if he had taken the shoulder.

The heaviest rifles, however, will not always stop a charging elephant, especially if made down a slight incline with full way on—as once happened so Sanderson, who, though armed with a four-bore, and sure that he planted his right on the bump between the eyes (but perhaps a trifle high), was run over before he could use the left, and narrowly escaped being trampled on as the elephant rushed almost over him, bespattering him with blood from a wound in the side. The animal—a big tusker—had charged him simply from catching his wind, without any provocation from himself, but was in a bad temper at the time owing to having just been worsted and wounded in a fight with another tusker.

A hit I have found immediately fatal—though I have never intentionally tried it—is one striking about the centre of the side of the neck. I have dropped two elephants dead by this shot. They were flukes on my part, as I was aiming at the head on one occasion, and the shoulder on the other, and, in consequence of the elephant moving through jungle, did not hit where I aimed. One of them sank quietly into the kneeling position, that has been referred to as indicating an instantaneously fatal shot. This and the brain shot are the only two that can be depended on to cause instant death. Even if shot through the heart, elephant (and other big game) have been known to go several hundred yards before falling.

Some sportsmen recommend running after elephants after firing at them, in hopes of obtaining further shots before they get well under way. I have always done this with bison and buffalo, but rarely with elephant. I think running after or at them would very likely provoke a charge. Their appearance is rather overwhelming, and I suppose impresses me and makes me cautious; for the thought of being charged has never prevented me running after the other kinds of heavy game. After firing at elephants I generally prefer to hold my ground, and follow them up later on if necessary with due deliberation and precaution.

In following a wounded animal I always carried my rifle, accompanied by my, second-gun bearer, and walked with the trackers, who worked under my close protection. The order of march for the rest was as already detailed. In passing through thick cover you should make the trackers go slowly, however easy the trail, and devote your attention to keeping a sharp look out. If the signs are so fresh as to give reason to believe that the game may be only a short distance away, it is as well to occasionally send a man up a tree to command view, especially if possible before entering any dense grass cover. These precautions apply with even greater force to other kinds of heavy game, which, on account of their lesser size, are more difficult to see, and better able to conceal themselves and lie in wait for the hunter, than elephants.

Sanderson says that in following wounded elephants he used to send his trackers on ahead, and follow them with his gunbearers at a hundred yards distance. He considered this the safest plan for the trackers, as he was of opinion they could work better and be more on the alert than if he closely accompanied them. On their signalling the presence of the game, he could come up (as he puts it) 'with a knowledge of the position of the enemy'.

I should not like to adopt this method. My view is that the trackers require the close protection of the gun (or guns), and all trackers I have worked with have seemed to entirely agree with me. In dense cover they cannot tell at what moment they may be charged by a wounded animal. Moreover, whether the jungle be open or close, you may lose good chances if you are not with them.

You must push up to wounded animals whatever the nature of the ground or jungle. In Burma the worst kind in which to do this is 'kaing' grass, previously described. But it should be done.

If the animal is known to be in a small bit of particularly dense cover, other means of moving it to more favourable ground may first be tried, such as giving it the wind from the outskirts, firing, shouting, throwing stones, or setting fire to the cover, but the conditions usually make any of these measures impracticable or futile.

If your first approach to a herd (or a single elephant) has been unsuccessful and you have alarmed them without obtaining a shot, you will follow up and hope for better luck next time. I have found that elephants which have winded me generally go straight away for five or six miles before stopping or slackening again to rest or feed. This means three to six hours tracking, according to the nature of the ground, before again coming up with them.

If they have only seen or heard me they have usually moved but two or three miles, and occasionally less than a mile, before resuming their feeding and loitering.

If they are alarmed a second time, however, from whatever cause, they will probably go away for many miles before again slackening, and you may as well give them up unless you are prepared to sleep on their tracks. You may, in fact, hope to get a second chance of approaching the same elephants in one day, but, as a rule, not more. This generally applies to all heavy game.

Sometimes you strike the trail of animals (single or herds) that are making steadily for some distant part, and you may follow it all day without seeing them.

My first elephant was secured (but not killed) by the head shot. We had been trying to move a herd out of kaing grass by setting fire to it (the month was April), but had failed, the grass being too extensive, though it burnt splendidly, with a crackling roar. Late in the afternoon, on our way home, we diverged towards some water in the vicinity of which elephants might be found at that time of the day. There a man climbed a high tree and in a few minutes sighted some elephants about a quarter of a mile away. Having taken the wind, we went towards them. The sun was now getting low in the horizon. On arriving near the elephants, we found they were in ordinary grass and bush jungle, more open than usual, but without any trees within a hundred yards of them. I approached with my second-gun bearer under cover of tussocks of grass and bushes to about twenty yards from a tusker—the only one I could make out. He was three-quarters facing me, and I had a better view of his head than any other part of him. I aimed between the eye and ear-hole, close to the eye, judging for the brain, and fired.

Getting clear of the smoke, I saw another elephant making off. The one fired at had dropped to the shot. Going up, I found him lying on his side breathing heavily, so gave him a finisher, judging for the heart. It was evident the bullet had not penetrated the central portion of the brain though it possibly grazed its surface. Perhaps the elephant was only stunned by my first shot, and would have soon got on his feet again but for the second. I measured him 8 ft straight between uprights at shoulder and foot up the line of the fore leg. He was not therefore full grown. The tusks proved to be 3 ft long and 9 in. in circumference at gum.

Though I had only obtained a very moderate prize, I felt elated at bagging my first elephant, as we paddled down an arm of the Irrawaddi homewards, the burning grass together with the setting sun making a lurid blaze in the distance.

Later in the month I had moved a couple of marches northwards and established myself in the clean rest house of a very small village, called Ngarde, on the Shwelli river—a tributary of the great Irrawaddi. Most villages in Burma have a travellers' rest house, which though affording primitive accommodation, is more roomy than a tent, and much cooler in hot weather. It consists generally of one room, about 20 ft by 15 ft, raised on a wooden understructure of posts and cross beams 5ft or 6 ft above the ground. To be well raised off the ground is a precaution against fever, and all Burmese houses are so built. Some rest houses are pleasantly situated within the grounds of the village temple, pagodas, and the priests' quarters. It is sure then to be clean—in fact the whole enclosure is so kept, and well swept every day. There are generally some fine shady trees, and palm groves in it. Staying in one of these out-of-the-world old-time places, you feel it was just the same in character perhaps a thousand years ago; the priest in the same kind of yellow robes, the big bell sounding in the same solemn way, and the village children repeating their lessons and chanting their prayers morning and evening in the temple, even as at present.

The priests are the children's instructors, and are served by them in many ways. In the morning a procession may be seen of the children under charge of some of the priests, bearing the latter's daily food from the village through the temple grounds to their kitchens.

On arriving at one of these rest houses the village women and girls bring you water, firewood, etc. The headman will also come, and some other men. The Burmese are a lively, pleasant people, and a good deal of chatter, banter, and laughter, will go on while they are depositing the things they have brought on the verandah. The young women are mostly good looking, fond of bright coloured clothes, and have none of the shyness of their Indian sisters.

The Ngardi rest house was not in the temple grounds, which were small. The boundary fences were separated by a distance of fifty to a hundred yards as well as I remember. The priest owned a flourishing banana garden, outside the actual temple precincts. On the second night of my arrival there, after an unsuccessful day's hunting, I was smoking a cigarette and thinking of turning in, when Mo-Mo entered and announced there was an elephant in the priest's garden, and proposed we should try to shoot it. I put on a shooting coat over my sleeping suit and we sallied forth. The night was too dark to see properly, and my light-coloured pajamas showed up with painful distinctness. The men with me were stripped except a waist-cloth, and practically invisible. So, if the elephant attacked it would be sure to single me out. I therefore felt rather uncomfortable! Arriving near the plantation, we heard the robber breaking about inside it, no doubt thoroughly enjoying the bananas. We entered the enclosure and, creeping on, I tried to make out the elephant, perhaps now about thirty yards from me, but it was pitch dark in the shade of the plantation and I could distinguish nothing, though the position of the animal was indicated by its blowing, tearing and crunching—a giant at supper. By this time I think we were all in a pretty nervous condition, and agreed with remarkable unanimity that it would be better not to shoot, and that there was no place like home. So we beat a noiseless retreat. I formed the rear guard, rifle in hand, hoping all the time the elephant would not catch sight of my pajamas and come on to investigate. I really felt quite pleased when I found myself in the house again, but decided that this sort of thing was not good for the digestion after dinner!

We went to the garden just after daybreak and found the depredator had made a wreck of it. We took up his tracks (by their size a tusker's) which led into high kaing grass. In less than an hour's tracking we heard the elephant. The grass was dense, but I determined to try for a shot, so telling the men to stay where they were, the wind being right, I approached the elephant as quietly as I could in the difficult cover, accompanied by my second-gun bearer—a military policeman named Kadir Baksh. Guided by the sounds of the elephant's movements in the grass and his blowing, which covered the sound of our own movement (though he was much less noisy than an elephant usually is in such cover), I got within twenty yards of him. I could see a tall piece of grass swaying about where he was. Kadir Baksh at this juncture adjured me to go no closer. We neither of us really liked the job. Nevertheless, it was no use stopping where we were, so I waited till the noise made by the elephant as he fed was greater than what would be caused by ourselves, and then seized the opportunity to advance while it lasted. Progressing thus slowly and laboriously, I must at length have arrived within a dozen yards of the animal, without being able to see the smallest bit of him. In trying to get nearer still, there was a sudden rush through the grass and away crashed the elephant. He had either heard or winded us. Calling up the men, we held a consultation. It seemed hopeless work following up in this impossible cover. Mo-Mo proposed to try a drive. The grass was not much more than a mile across in any direction, and the opinion was not only that the elephant would remain in it, but that from the direction of the trail he was in a certain portion of it whence he might be driven across a rather open space the men knew of, and perhaps offer a shot. Mo-Mo arranged the drive for which he collected eleven men. I was posted commanding the open space—a strip a few hundred yards long and five to fifteen wide. The wind was right as regards myself, but would blow generally from the beaters towards the elephant, which would help in moving him and sending him in my direction. The whole affair was, of course, very speculative with so few men in such an extensive cover, since unless the game could be made to cross the limited length of open I should obtain no chance of a shot. Mo-Mo, however, disposed his men skilfully, and the drive was well carried out by all concerned. After a long wait (for it took an hour or two to get everyone into position) a crashing in the high grass showed the elephant was making my way. Listening to his progress, I placed myself where I judged I should see him well if he held on his course, and he shortly emerged on to the open strip about sixty yards from me, and stood broadside on but partly covered by grass—a fine looking tusker. I gave him my right, aiming half way up the shoulder, and then fired the left as he disappeared in the further cover. I felt I had hit him well with my first shot. After a little time we followed him up. His trail through the kaing grass was easy to take on. ...

I killed my finest elephant in the Mong Long jungles, previously described. We started at six o'clock on a June morning. At nine o'clock we came upon what were pronounced to be the previous day's tracks of an elephant. If so, they were perhaps not worth following up, but I gave the order to do so, as I have often found (as already stated) that tracks of heavy game, considered at first to be a day old, become marvellously fresh after being followed for a mile. It so happened in this case. In a quarter of an hour the tracks, and also some dung, were pronounced to be of the night. In another quarter of an hour to be of the morning, and dung was found corroborating this. In half an hour therefore, the tracks had changed from those of the day before to the early morning. At ten o'clock dung was come upon considered only two hours old. In an hour, therefore—or in two miles—the traces had changed from being pronounced say eighteen hours old to two hours old.

About 10.30 we suddenly saw the elephant—a fine solitary tusker—standing facing us some seventy yards away to our right. My pony was being led about 150 yards behind, and at that moment made a crash getting through the jungle. The tusker turned in the direction of the sound and took a few steps towards it. This move exposed his right shoulder; there was no time to be lost; he would have discovered the men and pony coming along behind us in a few moments and been off. I therefore fired at once right and left at his shoulder, on which he went about and sailed away with his head held high. I got in another shot at his stern, aiming for the liver, before he disappeared, and ran on some way in hopes of sighting him and putting in some more, but failed in this, and so took up the tracks again. There was a good blood trail from the shoulder shots. ...

The trackers kept on the trail well, only once being at fault. At two o'clock we again sighted the elephant standing broadside on, fifty or sixty yards ahead. I put in two more body shots as near the shoulder as I could without delay, as these opportunities cannot be lost under such circumstances, and the tusker continued his retreat. He was not a fighter. I hurried after him and got within fifty yards, looking out for a chance of an effective shot. He now walked slowly, evidently hard hit, and I further lessened the distance between us. Suddenly he swung majestically round towards me. I reserved my fire as I thought he was going to charge. But he was too far gone. He made several steps towards me and fell with a crash—dead. Hurrah! a good tusker at last. He had not fallen in a position in which he could easily be measured at the shoulder, so I passed the tape round the fore foot, which measured 4 ft 7 in. in circumference. His height was, therefore, at least, 9 ft 2 in. The foot straight across at its widest part measured 19 in. The tusks were 2 ft 2 in. showing outside the gum, and 15 in. in circumference there. On being extracted, the right tusk proved to be 4 ft 3 in. in length, the left 4 ft 2 in. and they weighed 61 lbs. the pair.

S. EARDLEY-WILMOT

How John Nestall Escaped the Elephant

It is but a few months ago that John Nestall[1] was the picture of health and vigour; his iron nerve and splendid physique were the envy of many who had spent more years than he in the enervating climate of Burma. To-day he seems to be listless and gloomy, his hair is streaked with grey. He is nervous in the extreme, and takes no interest in sport; indeed, whereas formerly all his conversation was of big game, he now changes the subject or leaves the room when the talk threatens to take a sporting turn. His friends speak of him as 'poor Nestall!' and fear that he will never be the same man again; but their verdict is probably the outcome of the well-known pessimism of friendship which entitles one to make the worst of one's comrade's mishaps. In point of fact, it is much more likely that in time his nerves will resume their tone, and that he will be as enthusiastic as before. I, the recorder of this incident, hazard this opinion from personal experience, as I also was once reduced to an almost similar condition, the result of an unfortunate encounter with a tiger. Yet I recovered sufficiently to again enjoy sport which had temporarily become a terror to me.

From *Leaves from Indian Forests*. London: Edward Arnold, 1938.
[1]For obvious reasons, this name is not the real one.

It happened in this way. Nestall, accompanied by two friends—the three mounted on a couple of elephants—was proceeding in the course of his duties through the dense mountain forests of Upper Burma, when the track of wild elephants was observed. In that country time is not of much moment, and during eight or nine months of the year you live a jungle life. Supplied with a few of the necessaries, but none of the comforts, of existence, you wander through pathless forests, your nightly shelter being a 'lean-to' of bamboos covered with a tarpaulin; your food, eggs and fowls, if you happen to come across the scattered villages, and if not, then only the meat the forest provides to season the 'damper' or rice which forms the staple sustenance of yourself and your followers.

Thus, when elephants were discovered in the vicinity it meant, first, sport; secondly, perhaps a valuable trophy; and, lastly, meat for the whole camp. With these incentives it is not surprising that Nestall should have decided on following the trail and endeavouring to secure one of the herd.

So long as absolute silence is maintained and the approach is made up-wind, nothing is easier than to arrive within shooting distance of wild elephants when the sportsman is mounted on a trained animal. You see, the intruder is mistaken for one of the herd, and the noise made in crashing through the jungle is not so alarming as the stealthy approach of man or beast; for any attempt at secrecy is invariably the signal for distrust. In these circumstances it may well be imagined that no long period elapsed before the herd was sighted, and it was found to comprise, besides some ten or twelve females and calves, a male of noble proportions and warrantable tusks. Unfortunately, however, when manoeuvring to secure a shot at close quarters the elephants got the wind of the sportsmen, and, as is usual in the case of an unknown danger, the leader of the herd advanced to reconnoitre and, if necessary, defend his precious charge.

The most carefully-trained elephants can never be said to be quite trustworthy; they are liable to sudden fits of nervousness when there may be no real cause for alarm, whereas actual danger would probably be met without flinching. Such a *contretemps* took place on this occasion, and resulted in a senseless stampede, the wild tusker, attracted by the commotion and determined to make the intruders pay dearly for their temerity, following heavily in the rear. In the frenzied rush through the dense forest Nestall was swept off his mount by an overhanging branch, and found himself, happily unhurt, though much shaken, defenceless on the ground. On the one hand could be heard the clatter of his departing comrades, and on the other the advance of the infuriated wild elephant of great proportions. It says much for Nestall's presence of mind that, dazed as he was, he at once grasped the situation and recognized that safety lay not only in ascending a tree, but also in selecting a stem of suitable thickness from whence he might in confidence await the onslaught of his foe and haply also the return of a rescuing party. Near at hand he espied the dead trunk of a large tree, and separated from it only by a foot or two stood a sapling of convenient size for climbing. In a moment (one's brain works rapidly at such times) Nestall had swarmed up the sapling and sat, at a height of some fifteen feet from the ground, on the edge of the dry stump, which he now for the first time ascertained to be hollow.

His position even now was not an enviable one, for he was exposed to the heat of the afternoon sun while the tusker was questing around in the vicinity searching for his victim. Nestall was also worried by the knowledge that it might be long before the stampede of the trained elephants could be stopped, and further, that even then it might be too dark to take up the return trail to his assistance. Therefore he realized that he might well be forced to pass the night in his present position without food or sufficient clothing, and suffering also from the effects of his fall, which now began to cause him some inconvenience. His mind, however, was speedily diverted from these thoughts by the arrival of the tusker under the tree; and whether it was the moral shock of mutual recognition or that physically produced by a furious charge on the sapling—or perhaps both combined—the result was that Nestall lost his balance and fell, not to certain death on the earth below, but into the hollow tree, where he found himself in temporary security.

For some moments Nestall congratulated himself on his fortunate escape, and struck by the humour of the position amused himself by picturing the astonishment of his friends on their return, and the rage and wonderment of the tusker outside, who was continuing his search for the enemy who had so miraculously disappeared. By degrees, however, as the excitement wore off and he began to feel wearied and sore from his unusual experiences, the prisoner found his forced confinement irksome and wished for some way of escape.

He learnt that the soil on which he stood was composed of masses of rotten wood and fungus which raised him above the earth level, but still not sufficiently to enable him to reach, either by stretching or jumping, any hold for his hands on the edge of the trunk. He then endeavoured to pile the debris of decaying wood to one side so as gradually to raise himself to the requisite height; but in this attempt after many efforts he remained unsuccessful, for the standing room was so limited that there was no space to build a mound large enough for his requirements. Up till now he had not thought seriously of his position, but when it dawned upon him that without help there could be no exit from this living tomb the depression and terror which suddenly overwhelmed him amounted almost to despair. But not for long did he give way.

The sun was now setting, and the forest was deathlike in its stillness; the air became cold and damp, and, to add to the pangs of hunger and thirst which now commenced to assail him, he had to contend against the pain of bruises, which during the first excitement he had hardly noticed. Knowing that it would be useless to waste his strength in futile endeavours to escape from his prison, he decided to lose no chance, but to pass the night wakefully, shouting at intervals, though he had faint hope that he could be relieved before daylight, or that the sound of his voice would penetrate far into the forest.

It is needless for me to enlarge on the terrors of that time; briefly it may be stated that alternate periods of despair and hope—the latter growing shorter as his strength failed in the struggle against cold and pain—were happily followed by the sleep of exhaustion.

When Nestall awoke the day had broken and a new fear gripped his heart. Had his companions returned and passed him by when sleeping? In a frenzy he shouted and beat his prison walls with hands and feet till obliged from weakness to desist. Then he felt indifferent to his fate and passed hours in a state of exhaustion and stupor which he mistook for resignation. That it was not so was proved when at noon the sun poured its vertical rays upon him; the intense heat aggravating all his sufferings, which now became intolerable. Then, once more rebelling against his fate, he wasted his strength and energy in despairing efforts for freedom, leaping against the side of the tree, clinging with bleeding hands to any small projection, but only to fall back time after time, and finally to acknowledge that his fate was stronger than he.

It was late that afternoon when his dulled senses first heard in the distance the tones of wooden bells which in Burma all trained elephants carry suspended from their necks. The sound came as might a sudden reprieve to a wretch about to suffer at the hands of the executioner; but the revival of hope was almost as much of a shock as had been in the first instance the recognition of his hopeless position. Again he had to pass through the agony of uncertainty. Would his friends arrive within saving distance of his prison? Would they hear his feeble cries for assistance? He determined to wait—to husband his strength; to shout only when he judged that his rescuers were near enough to hear him. Meanwhile the sonorous tones of the wooden bells continued, and even appeared to come closer and closer—then ceased altogether! Evidently a halt had been called and matters were being discussed. When the sounds were resumed they appeared to Nestall to be fainter; he listened intently, and in a few seconds was convinced of this fact.

He knew then that his life depended on the results of the next few minutes; he shouted again and again for help until his cries died away in almost inarticulate moans of despair; then he remembered nothing more till he awoke to find himself lying in the shady forest, whilst his friends were applying the simple remedies they possessed in the endeavour to restore him to consciousness. It was far into the night before they reached their little camp, and Nestall sank into a sleep, broken all too frequently by sudden awakenings to the horror of despair till he recalled the circumstances of his escape and present safety.

The delay in his rescue was readily explained. The stampede of the elephants had not been arrested till dusk; the night was spent in endeavouring to find the position of the camp, and it was not till nearly noon that a start had been made laboriously to follow up the trail of the previous day. The cries uttered by Nestall as he listened to the sound of the retreating elephants had been faintly heard; they had ceased ere his friends reached his place of confinement, and it was merely a lucky chance that induced them to examine the hollow trunk. A hat lying at its foot, a shred of clothing above, had suggested a more detailed investigation, with the happy result that Nestall had been extracted from his prison and restored again to liberty.

Such are the facts of Nestall's case. There are those who smile at its recital—who point out that his sufferings were due merely to the want of mental control; that he would equally soon have been saved if he had not given way to his fears. To such arguments no answer is possible, but when listening to them one may be excused for believing that had these critics been placed in similar circumstances—nay, if they had been even left solitary to wander these vast forests—they would not have extricated themselves without even more serious consequences.

W. S. THOM

Some Experiences Amongst Elephant and the Other Big Game of Burma 1887 to 1931 [1933]

Big game shooting nowadays is, I am afraid, very much decried. People look askance upon anyone who may happen to have shot a few more animals than other people and refer to them as butchers. The filming and photography of wild animals in their natural state is now to the fore. In my day, however, one could not go in for that sort of thing unless one had a big banking account, as cameras for that kind of work 25 and 30 years ago cost a mint of money. Cameras have, however, now been perfected to such a pitch, that this kind of hobby can be indulged in more easily, whilst they are not quite so expensive. ...

In the hey-day and first flush of my shikar days sportsmen did not think so much of game preservation as they do now.

There were no game preserves or game licences when I came to Burma in 1886, and many sportsmen did not worry so much regarding the numbers of animals shot by them provided the animals could be considered warrantable trophies, and nearly every

From *A Century of Natural History*. Ed. J. C. Daniel. Bombay: Bombay Natural History Society, 1983.

sportsman tried to beat his neighbour so far as the size of the head or the length and weight of a pair of tusks were concerned, whilst he had also to consider the question of recouping himself for the expenses incurred and the cost of his weapons and ammunition, etc. Nowadays all that sort of thing is gone. A man who slaughters game for the sheer love of shooting and bagging animals is no longer tolerated. There is no doubt of course that we all to some extent inherit in our breasts the savage instincts of our forefathers. A great deal has been written and is still being written and done on the subject of big game preservation everywhere; but so far as I can see little or nothing can be done to stay the final destruction of all big game not only in this Province but in India and in Africa. The spread of civilization, the motor car, the modern high-powered rifle, new roads, the woodman's axe, the Arms Act and Rules, electric contrivances for night shooting, poaching by people of the country and the fact that the Forest Department is under-staffed, are all factors which are now slowly but surely tending to bring about the steady diminution of game. It is of course admitted that the necessities of civilization must come first in the scheme of things and the preservation of fauna must take second place.

The European hunter makes little impression on wild life. He is usually a keen sportsman or else he would not hunt in the feverish localities he visits in search of big game. The native hunter is in quite a different category. The difficulties of bush and climate do not thwart him. But why go on; one could write pages on this subject. The fact that such animals as the Malayan Tapir (*Tapirus indicus*) which, so far as this Province is concerned, is only found in Tavoy and Mergui, and the Rhinoceros, two species (*Rhinoceros sondaicus* and *Rhinoceros sumatrensis*) are now entirely preserved, may retard for some years the process of extermination so far as they are concerned. I think I shall not be wrong in stating that the only Tapir and Rhinoceros of Burma that we shall see finally will be animals that have been preserved in Zoos or in Museums. This in my opinion is the order in which animals in Burma are likely to disappear as the years roll on: (1) Tapir (*Tapirus indicus*), (2) Rhinoceros (*Rhinoceros sondaicus* and *Rhinoceros sumatrensis*), (3) Thamin (*Cervus eldi*), (4) Hog Deer (*Cervus porcinus*), (5) Tsine, i.e. the Banting (*Bibos sondaicus*), (6) Bison or Gaur (*Bibos gaurus*), and (7) Elephant (*Elephas maximus*). The *Felidae*, i.e. tigers and leopards, which one might include as big game, will also disappear when large areas of land become thickly populated, causing a subsequent decrease and thinning out of forests and undergrowth owing to the great demand for fuel, and as cultivation spread with consequent diminution of all the remaining deer tribe such as Sambar (*Cervus unicolor*), Hog Deer (*Cervus porcinus*), Barking Deer (*Cervulus muntiacus*) and Mouse Deer (*Tragulus javanicus*). Serow or the Burmese Goat-Antelope (*Nemorhaedus sumatrensis*) and Goral (*Cemas goral*), which are generally found in precipitous rocky localities, will probably be the last to disappear, as they are not easily got at except with low-trajectory, small-bore rifles, which the majority of the people of this country fortunately do not possess. I would be inclined to protect Serow altogether, as in some places they can be easily beaten out of cover and shot with ordinary 12-bore shot guns with cartridges loaded with buck shot. All the bird life of the country is being rapidly thinned out. Some birds are shot and some snared by the people for food, whether they be egrets, Imperial pigeons, hornbills, Sarus cranes, paddy birds or beef-steak birds.

Crows, parrots, vultures, owls, sparrows, hawks, and perhaps doves and green pigeon will probably outlast the rest, with snipe, teal, duck, woodcock and geese coming next. Peafowl, pheasants, jungle fowl, partridges and quail will last till no cover for them exists. When I first came to Burma in 1886 I have seen the horizon in some districts white with egrets, herons, ibises and other waders and water birds. There are very few places indeed now where this can be seen. Snipe and all water birds are being snared wholesale all over Burma. I have not mentioned pigs. No one bothers much about wild pig. They multiply rapidly and are good eating. Besides, they do much harm to the crops of the people; as do parrots and monkeys. It really does not matter what becomes of them. ...

Much has already been written on the elephant by experienced sportsmen, who have shot in Africa, in India and Burma, as to how and where to shoot elephants and the kind of rifle to use, but in case some of my readers have not studied the books of such famous elephant hunters as F.C. Selous, Newman, Sutherland, Stigand, Bell, Burton, Sanderson, Chapman, Kirby, Rainsford, court-Treatt and a host others, I shall discuss the matter here again as clearly and as briefly as possible. I am entirely in agreement with Major C. Court-Treatt, author of *Out of the Beaten Track*, when he says,

> Assuming that the purpose of all sport is the attainment of adventure and, the exercise of skills, I dare to maintain that elephant hunting can legitimately be regarded as the greatest of all sports; and, since only the elephant hunter is qualified to dispute it, my assertion is not likely to meet with any great volume of dissent. Adventure there is in plenty and hard work too; and the hunter needs to be highly skilled in the habits and anatomy of the animal before he can be enrolled into the spiritual membership of elephant hunters. ...

The best time of the year for tracking elephants is during the rains, when the ground is soft and their tracks are more easily followed, especially when they are feeding in bamboo jungle. As a rule the animals possessing the best tusks are solitary, but a monster with very fine tusks is sometimes found leading a herd or on the outskirts of a herd. I found it much easier to follow up the tracks of a solitary tusker elephant than to stalk into a herd with the object of picking out an animal with the best tusks. As some as not, a slant of one's wind or scent is obtained by some member of the herd, usually a female, or a young tusker, when a warning is given, and the whole herd either slips quickly and quietly away, or stampedes without giving the hunter a chance for a shot. Woe betide the sportsman if the stampede is in his direction, as sometimes happens, if he cannot get behind a decent sized tree or bamboo clump in time. The danger of a stampede is that he is liable to be confronted by some infuriated cow elephant with a calf or some bull possessing small tusks or some cantankerous 'muckna' or tuskless male. On these occasions he may have to shoot in self-defence, when the usual report will have to be made to the Forest Department, which will probably fine him, and if a tusker, annex the tusks. The easiest way out of the difficulty where a herd of elephants in a panic stampedes towards you, is to stand perfectly still behind a tree, or bamboo clump, as their sight is far from good, and take the risk of their passing you without having seen you; or, if they do happen to see you, there is always the chance that they will hurry on all the more quickly to avoid you. On the other hand, I have known of herds of elephants to charge deliberately in a body towards the sportsman on scenting him, without having been disturbed in any other way, but they were generally herds that had been harassed a great deal by being frequently fired on by persons armed with inferior weapons. The danger is then very great, and unless the sportsman's nerves are in good order and he has also had long experience with elephants, he should contrive to get out of their way as quickly as possible either by climbing a tree or by making a clean bolt for it. There is no mistaking the sounds emitted by a herd of elephants that means business as it comes charging, shrieking and trumpeting along. A succession of angry screams and trumpetings will be emitted first, which will convey the warning and the sounds of thumping feet and the breaking of branches will then follow. The sportsman's Burman hunters, if they have not already made themselves scarce by ascending the nearest trees, as they are sometimes inclined to do, should be able to warn him of the danger and advise him what to do and which direction to take. Elephant shooting is easy enough if you have good eye-sight, are fleet of foot, and know how to shoot straight, and above all are using a good rifle. The latter is about as important as all the rest put together. In the good old days I made a point of never following the tracks of a solitary tusker elephant unless these measured 18 or 20 inches from toe to heel. I refer only to impressions of the forefeet. ... A solitary tusker usually sleeps on his side flat on the ground like a horse with all four legs stretched out straight. I remember once coming across a solitary bull elephant asleep on the ground which was making use of an ant heap as a pillow. The dung of an old elephant is also generally of a coarse texture and fibrous looking. Tuskless male elephants, called by the Burmans 'haings' or 'hines' and by Indians 'mucknas' are generally big fellows with powerful trunks. A big 'muckna' is usually feared by the members of any herd to which he may belong and he is a very dangerous animal when he becomes a rogue and turns solitary. As a rule there is no mistaking the tracks of a 'muckna' or 'haing' for they are generally more circular and less elongated than the forefoot impressions of a tusker. No sportsman ever shoots or is permitted to shoot a female elephant in India or Burma unless compelled to do so in self-defence, simply because, unlike the African species, they carry no tusks. ...

To escape from a charging elephant, it is not safe for a hunter to run in a straight line for any distance, for he has a better chance of eluding the animal by going off at right angles, especially if he is running up wind, that is to say, if his scent is being carried towards the approaching elephant. The screams of an infuriated, wounded, charging elephant are terrifying, and awe-inspiring in the extreme, and woe betide the hunter if he trips and falls or is overtaken, for he would be pounded into pulp and every bone in his body would be broken. An elephant usually seizes a human being with his trunk and dashes him against the ground or against his own knees, and then flings him away into the air or strikes him a terrible blow with his trunk. Sometimes he kicks his victim with his forefeet, or after seizing him with his trunk throws him to the ground and kneels upon him, if he does not drive his tusks through his body. In nearly every case a fatal injury is inflicted. ...

The photograph of the large wild tusker which was taken in the Thayetmyo Yoma hills is perhaps one of the finest photographs ever taken of a wild tusker. He was coming out of high elephant grass and, as there was a deep ten-foot wide nullah in between, a few yards only separated us. The lens used was a 17½ inch Ross' Telecentric, a perfect picture being obtained. It may be asked why I did not shoot this fine specimen. My reply is that I had shot quite a number already and would much rather have the photograph I obtained. I had a heavy rifle with me at the time which was being carried by a very faithful staunch old hunter of mine, Maung Tha Yauk by name, who never once let me down on all the numerous occasions on which he accompanied me into the wilds, and who has not long since gone to *Nirvana*. May we meet again in the Elysian fields of that mysterious land about which we talk such a lot but know nothing, to relate there all over again the details of the many hairbreadth escapes and encounters we shared together. Will I ever see his equal again? To Tha Yauk, one of the finest hunters, trackers and characters it has ever been my good fortune to know, I owe much of whatever success I have attained in the pursuit of Big Game.

A large tusker photographed in the Thayetmyo Yomah.

IV
The Most Dangerous Game: Encounters in Ceylon

SAMUEL WHITE BAKER

The Rifle and Hound in Ceylon

The love of sport is a feeling inherent in most Englishmen, and whether in the chase, or with the rod or gun, they far excel all other nations. In fact, the definition of this feeling cannot be understood by many foreigners. We are frequently ridiculed for fox-hunting: 'What for all dis people, dis horses, dis many dog? dis leetle (how you call him?) dis "fox" for to catch? ha! you eat dis creature; he vary fat and fine?'

This is a foreigner's notion of the chase; he hunts for the pot; and by Englishmen alone is the glorious feeling shared of true, fair, and manly sport. The character of the nation is beautifully displayed in all our rules for hunting, shooting, fishing, fighting, etc.; a feeling of fair play pervades every amusement. Who would shoot a hare in form? who would net a trout stream? who would hit a man when down? A Frenchman would do all these things, and might be no bad fellow after all. It would be *his way* of doing it. His notion would be to make use of an advantage when an opportunity offered. He would think it folly to give the hare a chance of running when he could shoot her sitting; he would make an excellent dish of all the trout he could snare; and as to hitting his man when down, he would think it madness to allow him to get up again until he had put him *hors de combat* by jumping on him.

From *The Rifle and Hound in Ceylon*. London: Longmans Green, 1854 (new imp. 1904).

Their notions of sporting and ours, then, widely differ; they take every advantage, while we give every advantage; they delight in the certainty of killing, while our pleasure consists in the chance of the animal escaping.

I would always encourage the love of sport in a lad; guided by its true spirit of fair play, it is a feeling that will make him above doing a mean thing in every station of life, and will give him real feelings of humanity. I have had great experience in the characters of *thorough* sportsmen, who are generally straightforward, honourable men, who would scorn to take a dirty advantage of man or animal. In fact, all real sportsmen that I have met have been tender-hearted men—who shun cruelty to an animal, and are easily moved by a tale of distress.

With these feelings, sport is an amusement worthy of a man, and this noble taste has been extensively developed since opportunities of travelling have of late years been so wonderfully improved. The facility with which the most remote regions are now reached, renders a tour over some portion of the globe a necessary adjunct to a man's education; a sportsman naturally directs his path to some land where civilization has not yet banished the wild beast from the soil.

Ceylon is a delightful country for the sporting tourist. In the high road to India and China, any length of time may be spent *en passant*, and the voyage by the overland route is nothing but a trip of a few weeks of pleasure.

This island has been always celebrated for its elephants, but the other branches of sport are comparatively unknown to strangers. No account has ever been written which embraces *all* Ceylon sports: anecdotes of elephant-shooting fill the pages of nearly every work on Ceylon; but the real character of the wild sports of this island has never been described, because the writers have never been acquainted with each separate branch of the Ceylon chase. ...

We had just arrived at an angle of the mountain, which, in passing, we were now leaving to our left, when we suddenly halted, our attention having been arrested by the loud roaring of elephants in a jungle at the foot of the hills, within a quarter of a mile of us. The roaring continued at intervals, reverberating among the rocks like distant thunder, till it at length died away to stillness.

We soon arrived in the vicinity of the sound, and shortly discovered tracks upon a hard sandy soil, covered with rocks and overgrown with a low, but tolerably open jungle at the base of the mountain. Following the tracks, we began to ascend steep flights of natural steps formed by the successive layers of rock which girded the foot of the mountain; these were covered with jungle, interspersed with large detached masses of granite, which in some places formed alleys through which the herd had passed. The surface of the ground being nothing but hard rock, tracking was very difficult, and it took me a considerable time to follow them up by the pieces of twigs and crunched leaves, which the elephants had dropped while feeding. I at length tracked them to a small pool formed by the rain-water in the hollow of the rock; here they had evidently been drinking only a few minutes previous, as the tracks of their feet upon the margin of the pool were still wet. I now went on in advance of the party with great caution, as I knew that we were not many paces from the herd. Passing through several passages among the rocks, I came suddenly upon a level plateau of ground covered with dense lemon grass about twelve feet high, which was so thick and tangled that a man could with difficulty force his way through it. This level space was about two acres in extent, and was surrounded by jungle upon all sides but one; on this side, to our right as we entered, the mountain rose in rocky steps, from the crevices of which the lemon grass grew in tall tufts.

The instant that I arrived in this spot, I perceived the flap of an elephant's ear in the high grass, about thirty paces from me, and upon careful inspection I distinguished two elephants standing close together. By the rustling of the grass in different places I could see that the herd was scattered, but I could not make out the elephants individually, as the grass was above their heads.

I paused for some minutes to consider the best plan of attack; but the gun-bearers, who were behind me, being in a great state of excitement, began to whisper to each other, and in arranging their positions behind their respective masters, they knocked several of the guns together. In the same moment, the two leading elephants discovered us, and, throwing their trunks up perpendicularly, they blew the shrill trumpet of alarm without attempting to retreat. Several trumpets answered the call immediately from different positions in the high grass, from which, trunks were thrown up, and huge heads just appeared in many places, as they endeavoured to discover the danger which the leaders had announced.

The growl of an elephant is exactly like the rumbling of thunder, and from their deep lungs the two leaders, who had discovered us, kept up an uninterrupted peal, thus calling the herd together. Nevertheless, they did not attempt to retreat, but stood gazing attentively at us with their ears cocked, looking extremely vicious. In the meantime, we stood perfectly motionless, lest we should scare them before the whole herd closed up. In about a minute, a dense mass of elephants had collected round the two leaders, who were all gazing at us; and thinking this a favourable moment, I gave the word, and we pushed towards them through the high grass. A portion of the herd immediately wheeled round and retreated as we advanced, but five elephants, including the two who had first discovered us; formed in a compact line abreast, and thrashing the long grass to the right and left with their trunks, with ears cocked and tails up, they came straight at us. We pushed forward to meet them, but they still came on in a perfect line, till within ten paces of us.

A cloud of smoke hung over the high grass as the rifles cracked in rapid succession, and the *five elephants lay dead* in the same order as they had advanced. The spare guns had been beautifully handed; and running between the carcasses, we got into the lane that the remaining portion of the herd had made by crushing the high grass in their retreat. We were up with them in a few moments; down went one! then another! up he got again, almost immediately recovering from V.'s shot, down he went again! as I floored him with my last barrel.

I was now unloaded, as I had only two of my double-barrelled No. 10 rifles out that day, but the chase was so exciting that I could not help following empty-handed, in the hope that some gun-bearer might put one of V.'s spare guns in my hand. A large elephant and her young one, who was about three feet and a half high, were retreating up the rugged side of the mountain, and the mother, instead of protecting the little one, was soon a hundred paces ahead of him, and safely located in a thick jungle which covered that portion of the mountain. Being empty-handed, I soon scrambled up and caught the little fellow by the tail; but he was so strong that I could not hold him, although I exerted all my strength, and he dragged me slowly towards the jungle to which his mother had retreated. V. now came up, and he being loaded, I told him to keep a look-out for the mother's return, while I secured my captive, by seizing him by the trunk with one hand and by the tail with the other; in this manner I could just master him by throwing my whole weight down the hill, and he began to roar like a full-grown elephant. The mother was for a wonder faithless to her charge, and did not return to the little one's assistance. While I was engaged in securing him, the gun-bearers came up, and at this moment I observed, at the foot of the hill, another elephant, not quite full grown, who was retreating through the high grass towards the jungle. There were no guns charged except one of my No. 10 rifles, which someone had reloaded; taking this, I left the little 'Ponchy' with V. and the gun-bearers, and running down the side of the hill, I came up with the elephant just as he was entering the jungle, and getting the ear-shot, I killed him.

We had bagged nine elephants, and only one had escaped from the herd; this was the female who had forsaken her young one.

Wallace now came up and cut off the tails of those that I had killed. I had one barrel still loaded, and I was pushing my way through the tangled grass towards the spot where the five elephants lay together, when I suddenly heard Wallace shriek out, 'Look out, sir! Look out!—An elephant's coming!'

I turned round in a moment, and close past Wallace, from the very spot where the last dead elephant lay, came the very essence and incarnation of a 'rogue' elephant in full charge. His trunk was thrown high in the air, his ears were cocked, his tail stood erect above his back as stiff as a poker, and screaming exactly like the whistle of a railway engine, he rushed upon me through the high grass with a velocity that was perfectly wonderful. His eyes flashed as he came on, and he had singled me out as his victim.

I have often been in dangerous positions, but I never felt so totally devoid of hope as I did in this instance. The tangled grass rendered retreat impossible. I had only one barrel loaded, and that was useless, as the upraised trunk protected his forehead. I felt myself doomed; the few thoughts that rush through men's minds in such hopeless positions, flew through mine, and I resolved to wait for him till he was close upon me, before I fired, hoping that he might lower his trunk and expose his forehead.

He rushed along at the pace of a horse in full speed, in a few moments, as the grass flew to the right and left before him, he was close upon me, but still his trunk was raised and I would not fire. One second more, and at this headlong pace he was within three

'Caught at Last.'

feet of me; down slashed his trunk with the rapidity of a whip-thong and with a shrill scream of fury he was upon me!

I fired at that instant; but in a twinkling of an eye I was flying through the air like a ball from a bat. At the moment of firing I had jumped to the left, but he struck me with his tusk in full charge upon my right thigh, and hurled me eight or ten paces from him. That very moment he stopped, and, turning round, he beat the grass about with his trunk, and commenced a strict search for me. I heard him advancing close to the spot where I lay as still as death, knowing that my last chance lay in concealment. I heard the grass rustling close to me; closer and closer he approached, and he at length beat the grass with his trunk several times exactly above me. I held my breath, momentarily expecting to feel his ponderous foot upon me. Although I had not felt the sensation of fear while I had stood opposed to him, I felt like what I never wish to feel again while he was deliberately hunting me up. Fortunately I had reserved my fire until the rifle had almost touched him, for the powder and smoke had nearly blinded him, and had spoiled his acute power of scent. To my joy I heard the rustling of the grass grow fainter; again I heard it at a still greater distance; at length it was gone!

At that time I thought that half my bones were broken, as I was numbed from head to foot by the force of the blow. His charge can only be compared to a blow from a railway engine going at twenty miles an hour.

Not expecting to be able to move, I crept to my hands and knees. To my delight there were no bones broken, and with a feeling of thankfulness I stood erect. I with difficulty reached a stream of water near the spot, in which I bathed my leg, but in a few minutes it swelled to the size of a man's waist. In this spot everyone had congregated, and were loading their guns, but the rogue had escaped.

My cap and rifle were now hunted for, and they were at length found near the spot where I had been caught. The elephant had trodden on the stock of the rifle, and it bears the marks of his foot to this day.

In a few minutes I was unable to move. We therefore sent to the tent for the horses, and arrived at 6 p.m., having had a hard day's work from 5 a.m. without food.

SAMUEL WHITE BAKER

Brothers in Arms Against the Game of Ceylon

My friend Palliser and I were out shooting on the day previous, and we had spent some hours in vainly endeavouring to track up a single bull elephant. I forget what we bagged, but I recollect well that we were unlucky in finding our legitimate game. ...

The earliest grey tint of morning saw us dressed and ready; the rifles loaded; a preliminary cup of hot chocolate swallowed, and we were off while the forest was still gloomy; the night seemed to hang about it although the sky was rapidly clearing above. ...

We almost made sure of finding our friend of yesterday's track, and we accordingly kept close to the edge of the river, keeping a sharp eye for footprints upon the sandy bed below.

We had strolled for about a mile along the high bank of the river, without seeing a sign of an elephant, when I presently heard a rustle in the branches before me, and upon looking up, I saw a lot of monkeys gamboling in the trees. I was carrying my long two-ounce rifle, and I was passing beneath the monkey-covered boughs, when I suddenly observed a young tree of the thickness of a man's thigh, shaking violently just before me.

From *Eight Years in Ceylon* (1856). New Impression. London: Longmans Green, 1902. The title is not in the original.

'Curious Shot at a Bull Elephant.'

It happened that the jungle was a little thicker in this spot, and at the same moment that I observed the tree shaking almost over me, I passed the immense stem of one of those smooth barked trees which grow to such an enormous size on the banks of rivers. At the same moment that I passed it, I was almost under the trunk of a single bull elephant, who was barking the stem with his tushes[1] as high as he could reach, with his head thrown back. I saw in an instant that the only road to his brain lay through his upper jaw, in the position in which he was standing; and knowing that he would discover me in another moment, I took the direct line for his brain, and fired upwards through his jaw. He fell stone dead with the silk patch of the rifle smoking in the wound. ...

I was out shooting with a great friend of mine, who is a brother in arms against the game of Ceylon, and than whom a better sportsman does not breathe, and we had arrived at a wild and miserable place while *en route* home after a jungle trip. Neither of us was feeling well; we had been for some weeks in the most unhealthy part of the country, and I was just recovering from a touch of dysentery; altogether we were looking forward with pleasure to our return to comfortable quarters, and for the time we were tired of jungle life. However, we arrived at a little village about sixty miles south of Batticaloa, called 'Gollagangwelléwevé' (pronunciation requires practice), and a very long name it was for so small a place; but the natives insisted that a great number of elephants were in the neighbourhood.

They also declared that the elephants infested the neighbouring tank even during the forenoon, and that they nightly destroyed their embankments, and would not be driven away, as there was not a single gun possessed by the village with which to scare them. This looked all right; so we loaded the guns and started without loss of time, as it was then 1 p.m., and the natives described the tank as a mile distant. Being perfectly conversant with the vague idea of space described by a Cingalese mile, we mounted our horses, and, accompanied by about five and twenty villagers, twenty of whom I wished at Jericho, we started. By the by, I have quite forgotten to describe who '*we*' are, F.H. Palliser, Esq., and myself.

[1]There are very few elephants with regular tushes (tusks) in Ceylon, and their very small ivories are called 'tushes'.

Whether or not it was because I did not feel in brisk health, I do not know, but somehow or other, I had a presentiment that the natives had misled us, and that we should not find the elephants in the tank, but that, as usual, we should be led up to some dense thorny jungle, and told that the elephants were somewhere in that direction. Not being very sanguine, I had accordingly taken no trouble about my gun-bearers, and I saw several of my rifles in the hands of the villagers, and only one of my regular gun-bearers had followed me, the rest, having already had a morning's march, were glad of an excuse to remain behind.

Our route lay for about a quarter of a mile through deserted paddy land and low jungle, after which we entered fine open jungle. Unfortunately, the recent heavy rains had filled the tank, which had overflowed the broken dam and partially flooded the forest. This was in all parts within 200 yards from the dam a couple of feet deep in water, with a proportionate amount of sticky mud beneath, and through this we splashed until the dam appeared about fifty yards on our right. It was a simple earthen mound, which rose about ten feet from the level of the forest, and was studded with immense trees, apparently the growth of ages. We knew that the tank lay on the opposite side; but we continued our course parallel with the dam until we had ridden about a mile from the village, the natives for a wonder having truly described the distance.

Here our guide, having motioned us to stop, ran quickly up the dam to take a look out on the opposite side. He almost immediately beckoned us to come up. This we did without loss of time, and knowing that the game was in view, I ordered the horses to retire for about a quarter of a mile.

On our arrival on the dam there was a fine sight. The lake was about five miles round, and was quite full of water, the surface of which was covered with a scanty, but tall, rushy, grass. In the lake, browsing upon the grass, we counted twenty-three elephants, and there were many little ones, no doubt, that we could not distinguish in such rank vegetation. Five large elephants were not more than 120 paces distant; the remaining eighteen were in a long line, about a quarter of a mile from the shore, feeding in deep water.

We were well concealed by various trees which grew upon the dam, and we passed half an hour in watching the manoeuvres of the great beasts as they bathed and sported in the cool water. However, this was not elephant shooting, and the question was, how to get at them. The natives had no idea of the sport, as they seemed to think it very odd that we did not fire at those within a hundred paces distance. I now regretted my absent gun-bearers, as I plainly saw that these village people would be worse than useless.

We determined to take a stroll along the base of the dam to reconnoitre the ground, as at present it seemed impossible to make an attack, and even were the elephants within the forest there appeared to be no possibility of following them up through such deep water and heavy ground with any chance of success. However, they were not in the forest, being safe, belly and shoulder deep in the tank.

We strolled through mud and water thigh deep for a few hundred paces when we suddenly came upon the spot, where in ages past the old dam had been carried away. Here the natives had formed a mud embankment strengthened by sticks and wattels. Poor fellows! We were not surprised at their wishing the elephants destroyed; the repair of their fragile dam was now a daily occupation, for the elephants, as though out of pure mischief, had chosen this spot as their thoroughfare to and from the lake, and the dam was trodden down in all directions.

We found that the margin of the forest was everywhere flooded to a width of about 200 yards, after which it was tolerably dry. We therefore returned to our former post.

It struck me that the only way to secure a shot at the herd would be to employ a ruse, which I had once practised successfully some years ago. Accordingly we sent the greater part of the villagers for about half a mile along the edge of the lake, with orders to shout and make a grand hullaballoo on arriving at their station. It seemed most probable that upon being disturbed, the elephants would retreat to the forest by their usual thoroughfare; we accordingly stood on the alert, ready for a rush to any given point which the herd should attempt in their retreat.

Some time passed in expectation, when a sudden yell broke from the far point, as though twenty demons had cramp in the stomach. Gallant fellows are the Cingalese at making a noise, and a grand effect this had upon the elephants; up went tails and trunks, the whole herd closed together, and made a simultaneous rush for their old thoroughfare. Away we skipped through the water straight in shore through the forest, until we reached the dry ground, when, turning sharp to our right, we soon halted exactly opposite the point at which we knew the elephants would enter the forest. This was grand excitement; we had a great start of the herd, so that we had plenty of time to arrange gun-bearers, and take our positions for the *rencontre.*

In the mean time the roar of water caused by the rapid passage of so many large animals approached nearer and nearer. Palliser and I had taken splendid positions so as to command either side of the herd on their arrival, with our gun-bearers squatted around us behind our respective trees, while the non-sporting village followers, who now began to think the matter rather serious, and totally devoid of fun, scrambled up various large trees with ape-like activity.

A few minutes of glorious suspense, and the grand crash and roar of broken water approached close at hand; we distinguished the mighty phalanx headed by the largest elephants bearing down exactly upon us, and not a hundred yards distant. Here was luck! There was a grim and very murderous smile of satisfaction on either countenance as we quietly cocked the rifles and awaited the onset: it was our intention to let half the herd pass us before we opened upon them, as we should then be in the very centre of the mass, and be able to get good and rapid shooting.

On came the herd in gallant style, throwing the spray from the muddy water, and keeping a direct line for our concealed position. They were within twenty yards, and we were still undiscovered, when those rascally villagers, who had already taken to the trees, scrambled still higher in their fright at the close approach of the elephants, and by this movement they gave immediate alarm to the leaders of the herd.

Round went the colossal heads; right about, was the word, and away dashed the whole herd back towards the tank. In the same instant we made a rush in among them, and I floored one of the big leaders by a shot behind the ear, and immediately after, as bad luck would have it, Palliser and I both took the same bird, and down went another to the joint shots. Palliser then got another shot and bagged one more, when the herd pushed straight out to the deep lake, with the exception of a few elephants, who turned to the right; after which, Palliser hurried through the mud and water, while I put on all steam in chase of the main body of the herd. It is astonishing to what an amount a man can get up this said steam in such a pitch of excitement. However, it was of no use in this case, as I was soon hip deep in water, and there was an end to all pursuit in that direction.

It immediately struck me that the elephants would again retreat to some other part of the forest after having made a circuit in the tank; I accordingly waded back at my best speed to *terra firma*, and then striking off to my right, I ran along parallel to the water for about half a mile, fully expecting to meet the herd once more on their entrance to the jungle. It was now that I deplored the absence of my gun-bearers; the village people had no taste for this gigantic scale of amusement, and the men who carried my guns would not keep up; fortunately, Carrasi, the best gun-bearer, was there, and he had taken another loaded rifle, after handing me that which he had carried at the onset. I waited a few moments for the lagging men, and succeeded in getting them well together, just as I heard the rush of water, as the elephants were again entering the jungle, not far in advance of the spot upon which I stood.

This time they were sharp on the *qui vive*, and the bulls, being well to the front, were keeping a bright look-out. It was in vain that I endeavoured to conceal myself until the herd had got well into the forest; the gun-bearers behind me did not take the same precaution, and the leading elephants both saw and winded us, when at a hundred paces distant. This time, however, they were determined to push on for a piece of thicker jungle, which they knew lay in this direction, and upon seeing me running towards them, they did not turn back to the lake, but slightly altered their course in an oblique direction, still continuing to push on through the forest, while I was approaching at right angles with the herd.

Hallooing and screaming at them with all my might, to tease some of the old bulls into a charge, I ran at top speed through the fine open forest, and soon got among a whole crowd of half-grown elephants, at which I would not fire; there were a lot of fine beasts pushing along in the front, and towards these I ran as hard as I could go. Unfortunately, the herd seeing me so near, and gaining upon them, took to the ruse of a beaten fleet and scattered in all directions; but I kept a few big fellows in view, who were still pretty well together, and managed to overtake the rearmost and knock him over. Up went the tail and trunk of one of the leading bulls at the report of the shot, and trumpeting shrilly, he ran first to one side then to the other, with his ears cocked, and sharply turning his head. I knew this fellow had his monkey up, and that a little teasing would bring him round for a charge. I therefore redoubled my shouts and yells, and kept on in full chase, as the elephants were straining every nerve to reach a piece of thick jungle, within a couple of hundred paces.

I could not go any faster, and I saw that the herd, which was thirty or forty yards ahead of me, would gain the jungle before I could overtake them, as they were going at a slapping pace, and I was tolerably blown with a long run at full speed, part of which had been through deep mud and water. But I still teased the bull, who was now in such an excited state, that I felt convinced he would turn to charge.

The leading elephants rushed into the thick jungle closely followed by the others, and, to my astonishment, my excited friend, who had lagged to the rear, followed their example. But it was only for a few seconds, for, on entering the thick bushes, he wheeled sharp round and came rushing out in full charge. This was very plucky, but very foolish, as his retreat was secured when in the thick jungle, and yet he courted further battle. This he soon had enough of, as I bagged him in his onset with my remaining barrel by the forehead shot.

I now heard a tremendous roaring of elephants behind me, as though another section was coming in from the tank; this I hoped to meet. I therefore reloaded the empty rifles as quickly as possible, and ran towards the spot. The roaring still continued, and was apparently almost stationary, and what was my disappointment on arrival, to find, in place of the expected herd, a young elephant of about four feet high, who had missed the main body in the retreat, and was now roaring for his departed friends. These young things are excessively foolhardy and wilful, and he charged me the moment I arrived. As I laid the rifle upon the ground, instead of firing at him, the rascally gun-bearers, with the exception of Carrasi threw down the rifles and ran up the trees like so many monkeys, just as I had jumped on one side and caught the young elephant by the tail. He was far too strong for me to hold, and, although I dug my heels into the ground and held on with all my might, he fairly ran away with me through the forest. Carrasi now came to my assistance, and likewise held on by his tail; but away we went like the tender to a steam-engine; wherever the elephant went, there

‘Attack on the Herd.’

we were dragged in company. Another man now came to the rescue; but his assistance was not of the slightest use, as the animal was so powerful and of such weight that he could have run away with half a dozen of us unless his legs were tied. Unfortunately, we had no rope, or I could have secured him immediately, and seeing that we had no power over him whatever, I was obliged to run back for one of the guns to shoot him. On my return, it was laughable to see the pace at which he was running away with the two men who were holding on to his tail like grim death, the elephant not having ceased roaring during the run. I accordingly settled him, and returned to have a little conversation with the rascals who were still perched in the trees. I was extremely annoyed, as these people, if they had possessed a grain of sense, might have tied their long comboys (cotton cloths about eight feet long) together, and we might have thus secured the elephant without difficulty, by tying his hind legs. It was a great loss, as he was so large that he might have been domesticated and driven to Newera Ellia without the slightest trouble. All this was occasioned by the cowardice of these villanous Cingalese, and upon my lecturing one fellow on his conduct, he began to laugh. This was too much for any person's patience, and I began to look for a stick, which the fellow perceiving, he immediately started off through the forest like a deer. He could run faster than I could, being naked, and having the advantage of bare feet; but I knew I could run him down in the course of time, especially as, being in a fright, he would soon get blown. We had a most animated hunt through water, mud, roots of trees, open forest, and all kinds of ground; but I ran into him at last in heavy ground, and I dare say he recollects the day of the month.

In the mean time, Palliser had heard the roaring of the elephant, followed by the screaming of the coolies, and succeeded by a shot. Shortly after, he heard the prolonged yells of the hunted villager, while he was hastening towards my direction. This combination of sounds naturally led him to expect that some accident had occurred, especially as the cries indicated that somebody had come to grief. This caused him a very laborious run, and he arrived thoroughly blown, and with a natural desire to kick the recreant villager who had caused the uproar.

If the ground had been even tolerably dry, we should have

killed a large number of elephants out of this herd; but, as it happened, in such deep mud and water, the elephants had it all their own way, and our joint bag could not produce more than seven tails; however, this was far more than I had expected when I first saw the herd in such a secure position.

J. EMERSON TENNENT

Elephant Shooting

As the shooting of an elephant, whatever endurance and adroitness the sport may display in other respects, requires the smallest possible skill as a marksman, the numbers which are annually slain in this way may be regarded less as a test of the expertness of the sportsman, than as evidence of the multitudes of elephants abounding in those parts of Ceylon to which they resort. One officer, Major Rogers, killed upwards of 1400; another, Captain Gallwey, has the credit of slaying more than half that number. Major Skinner, the Commissioner of Roads, almost as many; and less persevering aspirants follow at humbler distances.[1]

From *The Wild Elephant*. London: Longmans Green, 1867.

[1]To persons like myself, who are not addicted to what is called 'sport', the statement of these wholesale slaughters is calculated to excite surprise and curiosity as to the nature of a passion that impels men to self-exposure and privation, in a pursuit which presents nothing but the monotonous recurrence of scenes of blood and suffering. Sir S. Baker, who has recently published under the title of *The Rifle and Hound in Ceylon*, an account of his exploits in the forest, gives us the assurance that '*all real sportsmen are tender-hearted men, who shun cruelty to an animal and are easily moved by a tale of distress*', and that although man is naturally bloodthirsty, and a beast of prey by instinct, yet that the sportsman is distinguished from the rest of the human race by his '*love of nature and of noble scenery*'. In support of this pretension to a gentler nature than the rest of mankind, the author proceeds to attest his own abhorrence of cruelty by narrating the suffering of an old hound which, although 'toothless', he cheered on to assail a boar at bay, but the poor dog

But notwithstanding this prodigious destruction, a reward of a few shillings per head offered by the Government for taking elephants was claimed for 3500 destroyed in part of the northern province alone, in less than three years prior to 1848; and between 1851 and 1856, a similar reward was paid for 2000 in the southern province, between Galle and Hambangtotte.

Although there is little opportunity in an elephant battue for the display of proficiency as a shot there is one feature in the sport, as conducted in Ceylon, which contrasts favourably with the slaughterhouse details chronicled with revolting minuteness in some recent accounts of elephant shooting in South Africa. The practice in Ceylon is to aim invariably at the head, and the sportsman finds his safety to consist in boldly facing the animal, advancing to within fifteen paces, and lodging a bullet, either in the temple

---

recoiled 'covered with blood, cut nearly in half with a wound fourteen inches in length, from the lower part of the belly, passing up the flank, completely severing the muscles of the hind leg, and extending up the spine; his hind leg having the appearance of being nearly off'. In this state, forgetful of the character he had so lately given of the true sportsman, as a lover of nature and a hater of cruelty, he encouraged 'the poor old dog', as he calls him, to resume the fight with the boar, which lasted for an hour, when he managed to call the dogs off; and, perfectly exhausted, the mangled hound crawled out of the jungle with several additional wounds, including a severe gash in his throat. 'He fell from exhaustion, and we made a litter with two poles and a horsecloth to carry him home' (p. 314). If such were the habitual enjoyments of this class of sportsmen, their motiveless massacres would admit of no manly justification. In comparison with them one is disposed to regard almost with favour the exploits of a hunter like Major Rogers, who is said to have applied the value of the ivory obtained from his encounters towards the purchase of his successive regimental commissions, and had, therefore, an object, however disproportionate, in his slaughter of 1400 elephants.

One gentleman in Ceylon, not less distinguished for his genuine kindness of heart, than for his marvellous success in shooting elephants, avowed to me that the eagerness with which he found himself impelled to pursue them had often excited surprise in his own mind; and although he had never read the theory of Lord Kames, or the speculations of Vicesimus Knox, he had come to the conclusion that the passion thus excited within him was a remnant of the hunter's instinct, with which man was originally endowed to enable him, by the chase, to support existence in a state of nature, and which, though rendered dormant by civilization, had not been utterly eradicated.

This theory is at least more consistent and intelligible than the 'love of nature and scenery', sentimentally propounded by the author quoted above.

or in the hollow over the eye, or in a well-known spot immediately above the trunk, where the weaker structure of the skull affords an easy access to the brain. The region of the ear is also a fatal spot, and often resorted to,—the places I have mentioned in the front of the head being only accessible when the animal is 'charging'. ...

Generally speaking, as regards the elephants of Ceylon, a single ball, planted in the forehead, ends the existence of the noble creature instantaneously: and expert sportsmen have been known to kill right and left, one with each barrel; but occasionally an elephant will not fall before several shots have been lodged in his head. ...

The shooting of elephants in Ceylon has been described with tiresome iteration in the successive journals of sporting gentlemen, but one who turns to their pages for natural traits of the animal and his instincts is disappointed to find little beyond graphic sketches of the daring and exploits of his pursuers, most of whom, having had no further opportunity for observation than is derived from a casual encounter with the outraged animal, have apparently tried to exalt their own prowess by misrepresenting the ordinary character of the elephant, describing it as 'savage, wary, and revengeful'.[2]

These epithets may undoubtedly apply to the outcasts from the herd, the 'rogues' or *hora allia*, but so small is the proportion of these that there is not probably more than one *rogue* to be found for every five hundred of those in herds; and it is a manifest error, arising from imperfect information, to extend this censure to elephants generally, or to suppose it to be an animal 'thirsting for blood, lying in wait in the jungle to rush on the unwary passer-by, and knowing no greater pleasure than the act of crushing his victim to a shapeless mass beneath his feet'.[3] The cruelties practised by hunters have no doubt taught these sagacious creatures to be cautious and alert, but their precautions are simply defensive; and beyond the alarm and apprehension which they evince on the approach of man, they exhibit no indication of hostility or thirst for blood.

[2]*The Rifle and Hound in Ceylon*, by Sir S. Baker, pp. 8, 9. 'Next to a rogue in ferocity, and even more persevering in the pursuit of her victim, is a female elephant.' But he appends the significant qualification, '*when her young one has been killed*' (ibid., p. 13).

[3]'*The Rifle and Hound*, p.13.

An ordinary traveller seldom comes upon elephants unless after sunset or towards daybreak, as they go to or return from their nightly visits to the tanks: but when by accident a herd is disturbed by day, they evince, if unattacked, no disposition to become assailants; and if the attitude of defence which they instinctively assume prove sufficient to check the approach of the intruder, no further demonstration is to be apprehended.

Even the hunters who go in search of them find them in positions and occupations altogether inconsistent with the idea of their being savage, wary, or revengeful. Their demeanour when undisturbed is indicative of gentleness and timidity, and their actions bespeak lassitude and indolence, induced not alone by heat, but probably ascribable in some degree to the fact that the night has been spent in watchfulness and amusement. A few are generally browsing listlessly on the trees and plants within reach, others fanning themselves with leafy branches, and a few are asleep; whilst the young run playfully among the herd, the emblems of innocence, as the older ones are of peacefulness and gravity. ...

They evince the strongest love of retirement and a corresponding dislike to intrusion. The approach of a stranger is perceived less by the eye, the quickness of which is not remarkable (besides which its range is obscured by the foliage), than by sensitive smell and singular acuteness of hearing; and the whole herd is put in instant but noiseless motion towards some deeper and more secure retreat. ...

If surprised in open ground, where stealthy retreat is impracticable, a herd will hesitate in indecision, and, after a few meaningless movements, stand huddled together in a group, whilst one or two, more adventurous than the rest, advance a few steps to reconnoitre. Elephants are generally observed to be bolder in open ground than in cover, but, if bold at all, far more dangerous in cover than in open ground.

In searching for them, sportsmen often avail themselves of the expertness of the native trackers; and notwithstanding the demonstration of Combe that the brain of the timid Singhalese is deficient in the organ of destructiveness,[4] he shows an instinct for hunting, and exhibits in the pursuit of the elephant a courage and adroitness far surpassing in interest the mere handling of the rifle,

[4] *System of Phrenology*, by Geo. Combe, vol. 1, p. 256.

which is the principal share of the proceeding that falls to his European companions.

The beater on these occasions has the double task of finding the game and carrying the guns; and, in an animated communication to me, an experienced sportsman describes

> this light and active creature, with his long glossy hair hanging down his shoulders, every muscle quivering with excitement; and his countenance lighting up with intense animation, leaping from rock to rock, as nimble as a chamois, tracking the gigantic game like a blood-hound, falling behind as he comes up with it, and as the elephants, baffled and irritated, make the first stand, passing one rifle into your eager hand and holding the other ready whilst right and left each barrel performs its mission, and if fortune does not flag, and the second gun is as successful as the first, three or four huge carcases are piled one on another within a space equal to the area of a dining room.[5]

It is curious that in these encounters the herd never rush forward in a body, as buffaloes or bisons do, but only one elephant at a time moves in advance of the rest to confront, or, as it is called, to 'charge', the assailants. I have heard of but one instance in which *two* so advanced as champions of their companions. Sometimes, indeed, the whole herd will follow a leader, and manoeuvre in his rear like a body of cavalry; but so large a party are necessarily liable to panic; and, one of them having turned in alarm, the entire body retreat with terrified precipitation.

As regards boldness and courage, a strange variety of temperament is observable amongst elephants, but it may be affirmed that they are much more generally timid than courageous. One herd may be as difficult to approach as deer, gliding away through the jungle so gently and quickly that scarcely a trace marks their passage; another, in apparent stupor, will huddle themselves together like swine, and allow their assailant to come within a few yards before they break away in terror; and a third will await his approach without motion, and then advance with fury to the 'charge'.

In individuals the same differences are discernible; one flies on the first appearance of danger, whilst another, alone and unsupported, will face a whole host of enemies. When wounded and infuriated with pain, many of them become literally savage;[6] but, so

[5]Private letter from Capt. Philip Payne Gallwey.

[6]Some years ago an elephant which had been wounded by a native, near

unaccustomed are they to act as assailants, and so awkward and inexpert in using their strength, that they rarely or ever succeed in killing a pursuer who falls into their power. Although the pressure of a foot, a blow with the trunk, or a thrust with the tusk, could scarcely fail to prove fatal, three-fourths of those so overtaken have escaped without serious injury. So great is this chance of impunity, that the sportsman prefers to approach within about fifteen paces of the advancing elephant, a space which gives time for a second fire should the first shot prove ineffectual, and should both fail there is still opportunity for flight.

Amongst full-grown timber, a skilful runner can escape from an elephant by 'dodging' round the trees, but in cleared land, and low brushwood, the difficulty is much increased as the small growth of underwood which obstructs the movements of man presents no obstacle to those of an elephant. On the other hand, on level and open ground the chances are rather in favour of the elephant, as his pace in full flight exceeds that of man, although as a general rule, it is unequal to that of a horse, as has been sometimes asserted.

The incessant slaughter of elephants by sportsmen in Ceylon, appears to be merely in subordination to the influence of the organ of destructiveness, since the carcase is never applied to any useful purpose, but left to decompose and to defile the air of the forest. The flesh is occasionally tasted as a matter of curiosity: as a steak it is coarse and tough; but the tongue is as delicate as that of an ox; and the foot is said to make palatable soup. The Caffres attached to the pioneer corps in the Kandyan province are in the habit of securing the heart of any elephant shot in their vicinity, and say it is their custom to eat it in Africa. The hide it has been found impracticable to tan in Ceylon, or to convert to any useful purpose, but the bones of those shot have of late years been collected and used for manuring coffee estates. The hair of the tail, which is extremely strong and horny, is mounted by the native goldsmith, and made into bracelets; and the teeth are sawn by the Moormen, at Galle (as they used to be by the Romans during a scarcity of ivory) into plates, out of which they fashion numerous articles of ornaments, knife-handles, card racks, and 'presse-papiers'.

Hambangtotte, pursued the man into the town, followed him along the street, trampled him to death in the bazaar before a crowd of terrified spectators, and succeeded in making good its retreat to the jungle.

'SNAFFLE'

After Elephants on the Kambukenaar River

It might be supposed after our experience near Chilaw, that Will and I would be content to let 'my lord the elephant' severely alone; but as a matter of fact the encounter had only increased our desire to bring one or more of the mighty pachyderms fairly to hand. Although we had learned that in that case the elephant had died of his wounds, F— was his probable slayer, and we wanted to kill one ourselves. Nearly a year elapsed without our having any opportunity to do so, although I had assisted at the death of my first buffalo in the interval, and very nearly at my own at the same time. The incident may bear relating, especially as it points a moral. During a short trip to one of the immense ruined cities of Central Ceylon, I had met at a rest-house on the road no less a person than V—, the elephant-shot *par excellence* of the day, who, with F—, before mentioned, had formed the Prince of Wales' bodyguard on his elephant shoot in 1876. ...

After this I may be allowed to pay my tribute to the honest Irish heart that is still for ever—the more so, perhaps, as a buffalo

From 'Snaffle', *Gun, Rifle, and Hound in East and West*. London: Chapman & Hall, 1894.

was the immediate, and an elephant the more remote, cause of V—'s death. Long-continued success over his gigantic game (the last time I ever saw him he told me he had just killed his hundred and second elephant) had perhaps made him over-bold. One day he was following up an elephant in full flight, and I believe had actually hold of the brute's tail. The maddened animal kicked out behind, hurling V— far away, and nearly breaking all his ribs. Abscess of the liver supervened on the blow, as it often does. He was, however, successfully operated on, and returned to Ireland to recruit. It was at the end of his leave I saw him last, quite restored to health. Not long after he shot a buffalo, which in falling pinned him down by its weight. Before he could extricate himself, the herd either charging or in mad flight, dashed past, and one of the great hooves struck him again in the fatal spot. Again abscess supervened, and this time death followed, and the Ceylon elephants lost their deadliest foe.

Will had been acting as Government Agent for some months at Hambantota, a most uninteresting spot on the east coast, where he was the only white man. ... Therefore when Will wrote to me and informed me that his relief had sailed from England, and asked if I were game for a month up the coast, I was delighted to reply in the affirmative.

Not much more than a month later I embarked on the Colonial Government steamer in company with Will's relief. The day after we left Colombo we were at Galle, and thence we reached Hambantota by daylight the following day. I was soon ashore, for my tents and share of stores had come by road, and also gone on. ...

Before the sun was up we had said good-bye to Hambantota, for we had a long drive before us. Will's Arab trotted gaily along, and with a halt for lunch we reached the carts before dark, and a very imposing show they made; but rice soon goes when there are a dozen mouths to feed, and there was literally no chance of supplies before us.

Among the other retainers waiting for us were two who would play a very important part in our next month's existence. These were the 'trackers', the best known of whom, Sin'Appu by name, Will, with characteristic good-heartedness, had made over to me. He was a little, old, very dirty-looking native, his natural ugliness not being improved by various scars, of different dates, but all produced by wild animals, mostly by bears. Small and mean as he looked he had the courage of a hero, and would stand perfectly unmoved with a second rifle though a charging elephant was within a few yards.

I know no native hunters who in any respect approach the Ceylon trackers in their power of following up an animal. They will take up the track of an elephant, and follow it for hours over every description of ground, even slab rock where to a European eye no trace of any kind could be seen, through a maze of other tracks, till at last they can point to the track into which the water is still oozing, and you know it is time to get ready your weapons.

The trackers reported that there were plenty of elephants between us and the Kambukenaar River, which here forms the boundary between the southern and eastern provinces of Ceylon, and after some consultation we decided to pitch our standing camp there. This was important, as sending back a note by Will's groom to that effect placed us within the possibility of communication with the outer world if it became necessary.

The dog-cart left next morning to travel 150 miles back to Colombo. As there were no roads at all before us, it was useless to try and take it further. That day we travelled on as there was no chance of game, and the next morning we again started at dawn. ...

The jungle we were entering did not at all respond to the popular idea of tropical forests, for it consisted of dense thorn-covert mostly about five feet high, only to be penetrated by the well-worn game paths. Further on we reached very different scenery—the well-known and lovely 'Park country', where large grass-covered rolling plains alternate with clumps of fine trees and covert. This is the height of perfection in a shooting country, but at this time we were a good many days' march from the 'Park'. ...

Next morning the rising sun found us already *en route.* The beauty of those tropical mornings will always remain with me. All was grey a minute back, but swiftly the red ball rises on the horizon. In ten minutes it is day, the dewdrops shine on every leaf, and our long shadows are surrounded with a luminous outline. I believe this is scientifically called a *perihelion*, and I have only seen it in Ceylon. A peacock screams defiance from yonder stump, and the great black *wandara* monkeys greet the day with loud guttural cries like cheers, 'Houwah! Houwah!' We cannot linger, however.

If you stand a minute the grass all round writhes with land-leeches hastening to the banquet you provide; and see the velvety look of the dead branch by your elbow. It is covered with ticks. Brush against it, and a score of them will soon be burying themselves in your skin, each one burning like a red-hot knitting needle. Besides, Sin'Appu turns round with a grin, pointing to a branch freshly broken. The giant game is before us, and while we hasten after the trackers let me describe the animal we are seeking. ...

The trackers advanced rapidly, we following with some difficulty. At last the tracks became burning fresh, and Sin'Appu signed to us to uncase the rifles, for mackintosh covers are a necessity in these damp jungles. A short further advance was made, and then it was obvious the herd were beyond a low ridge covered with higher jungle, whence low rumblings and breaking of branches were plainly audible. Sin'Appu wormed himself up to the ridge, and returning reported seven elephants, three just in front and the rest rather to the right. We decided in whispers that I should form the right attack, Will waiting till I gave the signal. Sin'Appu led me about sixty yards up, and then we noiselessly ascended the crest. Before I could drop behind a tree there I had seen an elephant, and that so close to me that my heart beat quick. Nothing strikes the beginner at this sport so vividly as the nearness which is necessary for success, for shooting at less than twenty yards' range is obviously unfamiliar to all. In this case I could hardly believe we were unseen, for it seemed to me I could almost touch the great brute. It was a nice bull, and when I saw it was standing carelessly flapping its ears. I signed to Sin'Appu to give the signal. He slipped back to do so, while I raised my 12-bore. At the report of Will's rifle I fired, but the bull only staggered, and my second shot was ineffective. Trumpeting loudly the herd crashed off in all directions. I seized my second rifle and ran as hard as I could after mine. This particular valley was a bit more open, so with a desperate spurt I ranged alongside till I could see the jaw-bone, and fired under the ear. This shot brought him down on his head, but before I could reload he was up again and, whether in confusion or rage I know not, swung round towards me. I had meanwhile got my wind a bit, and as I was not five yards from him had not much difficulty in finding the fatal spot this time, and my first elephant fell. Will, who had had more time, had done even better, for he had dropped his dead on the spot, and might have shot another had anything good come his way, which it did not.

That night we tasted the hunter's delicacy, elephant's trunk, but I can't say I think much of it. The foot is also said to be good eating, but is rather an expensive dish, as Rowland Ward was paying a guinea apiece for them at this time. Not that we sold any of ours, but they were in great demand for presents, making as they do capital footstools, liqueur stands, cigar cabinets, and other nicknacks. ...

Towards evening Will's tracker turned up, and reported that he had found a solitary elephant—'a nasty, dangerous brute', he added. The elephant had charged him, but he had dodged among the trees. Although these solitary elephants wander a great deal, we were anxious to pit ourselves against a 'rogue', and decided to go in quest of him on Sin'Appu's return. ...

The elephant had slightly shifted his quarters, but at last trackers hit on a pool where he had been drinking, and thence they traced out nearly all his night's wanderings. By this time we were getting a bit beat, but the freshening tracks kept us going. Presently Sin'Appu whispered that the *hora* (rogue) had noticed us. Sure enough he had circled round several times to get our wind, and had then withdrawn, no doubt to clear fighting ground.

The trackers now advanced very cautiously, till at last they stopped and stole back to us. They had seen the solitary. We, in our turn, crept forward and made out the head and back. It struck me that the head looked odd. The elephant was among some thick trees, and evidently quite on the alert.

We returned to our followers, and held council of war. We were in a mass of the dense thorn-jungle I have described, and could see two game paths, though which led to the present position of the elephant was doubtful. However, we decided to divide our forces. Will had the shot, and elected to follow the left-hand path while I took the right.

As I had expected, before a shot was fired, I heard a crash, and saw the elephant charge out at my friend. I heard two shots, but to my surprise the second rifle did not follow suit, and I saw the elephant—for I could plainly see his head over the thorns—halt among the smoke. His trunk, which had been curled up out of harm's way, was down now, and I guessed he was up to mischief, so fired. With another scream he dashed on, as I knew, to turn his attentions to me. However, he surprised me after all, for though he could not come direct through the thorns, he did find a short cut, and burst out within a few yards before I had finished reloading. Sin'Appu coolly handed me the other rifle, and took the open one, but the time was so short that I believe I must have fired both barrels at a range of less than four yards. A blow from his shoulder or forefoot sent me spinning, upsetting Sin'Appu in my fall, but the rogue never paused. Charging through the smoke, he made off. We had just about picked ourselves up, and reloaded the rifles, when, to my joy, Will and his man appeared following up the tracks.

'What a brute!' he said. 'He was on me like a shot. Before I could change rifles he had knocked us both flying, and was standing between us, feeling for me in the smoke. I was trying to reload without his hearing me when you fired. You all right?'

'Right as a trivet, bar a bruise or two. Neither bones nor spectacles broken. So let's get on, and keep together in future.' We had rather a weary tramp, though, before we saw the rogue again. Five bullets in the head—afterwards counted—had made him pretty sorry for himself. When we did get to him at last, he summoned up resolution to charge, but it was only a half-hearted attempt, for a barrel from each of us turned him, and we followed, jubilant, at top speed. Will was the faster, and ranged up alongside. This was too much for our adversary, and he turned towards him. This gave me a chance, but blown as I was I only brought him to his knees, when Will ran in and gave the *coup-de-grâce.*

After we had sat for some time on the prostrate body of our game in order to recover our breath, we proceeded to examine him. No wonder I had thought his head presented an abnormal appearance, for his right ear was almost entirely gone, while of his left not half remained. His tail also was gone, leaving only a ridiculous excrescence, little bigger than one's fist. The trackers say that these mutilations are done by other bulls in fighting, and I am inclined to believe it, for the only other solitary elephant shot during the trip had also half his tail missing. These rogues no doubt take up a solitary existence after being driven away from their herd by other bulls, a fact which also tends to prove the mutilation is the work of a conqueror. The elephant was a very fine one; measuring as accurately as we could we made him nine feet six

'Saw an Elephant, its trunk already outstretched towards me.'

inches high, a result checked by the circumference of his forefoot. With the exception of one he was the largest we got that trip.

Next day we reached the Kambukenaar, and after some search found a suitable and pretty spot to encamp on. ...

This camp continued to be our headquarterrs for over a fortnight, though on two occasions we ourselves with one cart slept a few miles away. Elephants were not forthcoming the first few days of our stay there, and our bag varied between buffalo and spotted deer; sambur were not plentiful. Sometimes we went out separately, and sometimes together. ...

It was during our subsequent attack upon the 'Veddah's herd', as we called them, that an incident occurred which, although it might have ended seriously, was sufficiently laughable. I, who had had the shot, had killed a nice bull after three shots, and my chum had gone off in pursuit of another. I was reloading and looking after him when I heard a warning shout from Sin'Appu, and turning round saw an elephant so close on me that its trunk was already outstretched towards me. I just had time to spring behind a tree, and as the brute shot headlong past I saw a calf trying to follow. I did not want to injure the poor brute, but it charged myself and the tracker twice more, and each time so savagely that I thought I should have to fire. Fortunately there were plenty of trees amongst which we could dodge the infuriated mother, and at last she made off, driving her calf before her. Will soon returned, having also killed an elephant. ...

I had some compensation next day. It was a very rainy morning, and I left camp late with my tracker. As we had no knowledge of game, I had one big rifle and one Express with me. We got on a ridge overlooking a large extent of jungle. The first thing I picked up with the glass was a large herd of spotted deer, but it was early in the day to rest content with those. When shortly after I made out five sambur I decided to go after them, as we had not seen many that trip. Accordingly I started off, but half-way I saw some buffaloes, and again changed my mind. Game seemed to be on the ascending scale that day, for in less than a quarter of an hour Sin'Appu, who rather despised all game smaller than elephants, caught me by the elbow and pointed out one of the great brutes moving out into the open. In examining the herd which followed this leader I caught sight of another elephant a great deal further off. He was apparently alone, and of great size, his colour, almost black, tending to add to his bulk. Although to attack an *alion* (solitary) single-handed and with one rifle was a bit risky, I had got confidence at the work, and determined to disregard the herd. Both the herd and the rogue were working down-wind, but the latter was a quarter of a mile behind them and quite that much further from me. I hurried on, passing close behind the herd, which dashed off on getting the wind, but the bull apparently didn't notice the noise, and plodded calmly on. I felt pretty sure he was heading for a biggish jungle not very far on, and ran on thither. When I got on the outer edge I found he was coming down a game track leading straight to the covert. This made it a certainty, and enabled me to wait at exactly the right spot. At four yards there was no excuse for a miss, and he fell stone dead to my first shot. This was undoubtedly the largest elephant shot during the trip. When we came to examine him, we found an old wound on his head. I made Sin'Appu open it with his axe, and we came on an old belted ball of large bore, such as were commonly used for big game shooting thirty years before. It is possible the animal had carried this about all this time, but nevertheless these old weapons turn up at times among the natives (who, however, rarely molest an elephant), and also among the planters. At all events, it had plenty of powder behind it, for it was nearly buried in the skull, and had certainly been there some years.

Shortly afterwards we made our second short trip away from camp. The night had been wet and the jungle was soaking when we left our cart. We had not gone far when I noticed a buffalo turn up a side-track. I told Will, who was leading, and he uncased and loaded his rifle. It was lucky for him that he took this precaution, for as he arrived at the spot the bull charged out of the jungle so suddenly that it seemed to me, looking on from behind, that the rifle touched the brute before I saw the flash. At all events it was so close that the great head actually fell on Will's foot. It never moved again, for, perhaps more by luck than judgment, the bullet had crashed right through the spine, half-way between head and withers.

This was not to be the only bit of luck Will was to have that day, for as we were returning to our cart, whither the trackers had preceded us with a couple of spotted deer, an utterly unexpected event took place. An elephant burst out of some jungle to our right, and crossed the glade, going at a fair pace. Will had his 12-bore ready, and before I could realize his intention, had fired. To my surprise and astonishment the great brute rolled head over heels like a rabbit, and lay dead. Considering it was about forty yards away, and the killing circle on the side of an elephant's head is about as big as the palm of one's hand, it was a wonderful shot.

'Ghastly fluke,' remarked Will, 'but I thought I mightn't have another chance.'

Now it so happened this was the last elephant killed that trip.

Next day we were back at the old camp, and the following night we lay for the last time smoking by the light of the camp-fire by the Kambukenaar. Not that, of course, a fire is required for warmth in that climate, but it serves the triple purpose of warding off at once wild beasts, fever, and mosquitoes. There was a great charm on those nights, after a hard day, in listening to the hundred noises of the jungle. At times they would all be silenced for a minute by the scream of a leopard, or even by the deep trumpet of the lord of the jungle himself.

'Ma certie!' quoth the Scotch skipper of the *Serendib*, as our roughly-secured trophies went on board at Hambantota. This was the result of our month's shoot and I think it deserved his astonished commendation: Seven elephants, five buffaloes, nine spotted bucks, two sambur stags, one leopard (in addition to that killed by Sin 'Appu, the skin of which he presented to me), one alligator—total, twenty-five head of big game, besides peafowl, jungle-fowl, and other birds.

Select Bibliography

A Century of Natural History (1983). Ed. J.C. Daniel. Bombay: Bombay Natural History Society.

Alter, Stephen (1988). Ed. *Great Indian Hunting Stories*. Delhi & Harmondsworth: Penguin.

Baker, E.B. (1887). *Sport in Bengal*. London: Ledger, Smith.

Baker, Sir Samuel White (1854). *The Rifle and Hound in Ceylon*. New imp. London: Longmans Green, 1904.

——— (1855). *Eight Years in Ceylon*. New imp. London: Longmans Green, 1902.

——— (1890; 1898 imp.). *Wild Beasts and Their Ways*. London: Macmillan.

Baldwin, Capt. J.H. (1883). *The Large and Small Game of Bengal*. London: Kegan Paul

Big Bore (1924, new edn). *A Guide to Shikar on the Nilgiris*. Madras: S.P.C.K. Depot, Vepery.

Blanford, W.T. (1888–91). *The Fauna of British India including Ceylon and Burma–Mammalia*. London: Taylor & Francis.

Bloomfield, A. (1871). 'The Mad Elephant of Mandla' (Cond. version of ms. copy pub. in *Hornbill*, 1981 [3]; 1981 [4] and 1982 [1]).

Braddon, Sir Edward (1895). *Thirty Years of Shikar*. Edinburgh: Blackwood.

Bull, Rev. E.E. (undated; early 1920s?). 'Charged by a Rogue Elephant: Nilgiris Man-killer'. In Stanley Jepson (1938).

Burton, Maj. General E.F. (1885). *Reminiscences of Sport in India*. *London*: W.L. Allen.

Casserley, Major Gordon (Earlier than 1913?). *Life in an Indian Outpost*. London: Werner Laurie.

Champion, F.W. (1st edn undated). *Jungle in Sunlight and Shadow*. London: Chatto & Windus.

——— (1927). *With a Camera in Tiger Land*. London: Chatto & Windus.

Daniel, J.C. (1998). *The Asian elephant: A Natural History.* Dehra Dun: Natraj.

Eardley-Wilmot, Sir S. (1930). *Leaves From the Indian Forest.* London: Edward Arnold.

Elliott, Major-General J.G. (1973). *Field Sports in India:* 1800–1947. London: Gentry Books.

Evans, Major G.P. (1911). *Big-Game Shooting in Upper Burma.* London: Longmans Green.

Fletcher, F.W.F. (1911). *Sport on the Nilgeris and in Wynaad.* London: Macmillan.

Forbes, Major. (1840). *Eleven Years in Ceylon.* 2 vols. London: Richard Bentely.

Grove, R.H. et al. (1998). *Nature and the Orient.* Delhi: OUP

Hornady, William T. (1885). *Two Years in the Jungle: Experiences of a Hunter and Naturalist.* London: Kegan Paul.

Hamilton, General Douglas (1892). *Records of Sport in South India.* London: R.H. Porter.

Handley, L.M.H. (1933). *Hunter's Moon.* London: Macmillan.

Hewett, Sir John (1938). *Jungle Trails in Northern India.* London: Methuen.

Hobson Jobson (1886; Bengal Chamber edn 1990). Eds Henry Yule and A.C. Burnell. New edn William Crooke. Calcutta: Rupa.

Hornady, William T. (1885). *Two Years in the Jungle: Experiences of a Hunter and Naturalist.* London: Kegan Paul.

Hunter, W.W. (1897). *The Thackerays in India and Some Calcutta Graves.* London: Henry Froude.

Jepson, Stanley (1938). Ed. *Big Game Encounters.* London: Witherby.

Kinloch, Brigadier-General A.A.A. (1869–76). *Large Game Shooting in Tibet, Himalayas, Northern and Central India.* London: Harrison, 2 vols. 3rd rev. & enlarged edn, Calcutta 1892: Thacker Spink.

Knighton, William T. (1854). *Forest Life in Ceylon.* 2 vols. London: Hurst & Blackett.

Marshall, Edison (1950). *Shikar and Safari.* London: Museum Press.

Morris, R.C. (1926). 'An Elephant Shoot in Baragur Hills'. In *A Century of Natural History.* Ed. J.C. Daniel. Bombay: Bombay Natural History Society, 1983.

Newcombe, A.C. (1905). *Village, Town, and Jungle Life in India.* London: Blackwood.

Nicholls, Frank (1970). *Assam Shikari*, New Zealand: Ton Song Publishing House.

'The Old Shekarry' HAL (1860). 2nd edn. *The Hunting Grounds of the Old World.* London: Saunders, Otely.

Pandian, M.S.S. (1998). 'Hunting and colonialism in the nineteenth-century Nilgri Hills of south India',. In *Nature and the Orient*. Ed. R.H. Grove et al. Delhi: OUP.

Peacock, E.H. (1933). *A Game-Book for Burma and Adjoining Territories*. London: Witherby.

Percy, Lt. Col. Reginald Herver (1894). 'Elephant (*Elephas indicus*)' in 'Indian Shooting' *Big Game Shooting*. vol. 2., Badminton Library. London: Longmans Green.

Pollock, Lt. Col. A.J.O. (1894). *Sporting Days in Southern India*. London: Horace Cox..

Pollok, Col. F.T. and W.S. Thom (1900). *Wild Sports of Burma and Assam*. London: Hurst and Blackett.

'Red Feather' (1923). *Memories of Sporting Days*. London: Longmans Green.

Russell, C.E.M. (1900). *Bullet and Shot in Indian Forest, Plain and Hill*. London: W. Thacker.

Sanderson, G.P. (1878; 7th edn 1912). *Thirteen Years Among the Wild Beasts of India*. Edinburgh: John Grant.

Smith, A. Mervyn (1904). *Sport and Adventure in the Indian Jungle*, London: Hurst and Blackett.

'Snaffle' (1894). *Gun, Rifle and Hound in East and West*. London: Chapman & Hall.

Stebbing, E.P. (1926). *The Diary of a Sportsman Naturalist in India*. London: John Lane.

Steel, J.H. (1885). *A Manual of the Diseases of the Elephant*. Madras: Lawrence Asylum Press.

Stockley, Col. V.M. (1913). *Big Game Shooting in India, Burma and Somali Land*. London: Horace Cox.

Storey, H. (2nd ed. 1907). *Hunting and Shooting in Ceylon*. London: Longmans, Green.

Stracey, P.D. (1963). *Elephant Gold*. London: Weidenfeld & Nicolson.

——— (1967). *Reade: Elephant Hunter*. London: Robert Hale.

Symington, John (1935). *In a Bengal Jungle*. Chapel Hill: University of North Carolina Press.

Tennent, Sir J. Emerson (1867). *The Wild Elephant*. London: Longmans Green.

Thom, W.S. (1933). 'Experience Amongst Elephant and Other Big Game'. In *A Century of Natural History*. Ed. J.C. Daniel. Bombay: Bombay Natural History Society, 1983.

Walker, E.L. (1923). *Elephant Hunting and Shooting in Ceylon*. London.

Wardrop, Maj. General A.E. (1923). *Days and Nights with Indian Big Game*. London: Macmillan.

Williamson, Captain T. (1807; 1808 edn). *Oriental Field Sports*. London.

Wilson, Lt. Col. Alban (1924). *Sport and Service in Assam and Elsewhere*. London: Hutchinson.

Wood, Lt. Col. H.S. (1934). *Shikar Memories*. London: Witherby.

Glossary

alion (Sri Lanka): Solitary animal.

ani/anay (Tamil): Elephants.

ankus/haunkus: Hooked goad for driving elephants. Another common word for it is *gajbag*, a term coined by Emperor Akbar (1542–1605) as his Turkish courtiers and attendants tended to mispronounce *ankus* as *angoj* (Abu'l-Fazl Allami, *Ain-i-Akbari*, 1596–7).

baru grass (Hindi): Also 'kala mucha'. A perennial grass used as fodder. Common English name: 'Johnson grass' (*Sorghum halepense*).

butcha (Hindi): Baby.

charjama: Light riding harness for elephants which can accommodate four or more persons sitting back-to-back facing the flanks, with protective rails at both ends. There are many variations in the design of this type of harness.

chena land (Sri Lanka): Patch of forest land 'which is cleared for the purpose of raising a single crop, after which the ground is abandoned, reverts to jungle again' (Tennent). This seems to refer to the slash-and-burn type of cultivation with a very long cycle.

choung (Myanmar): Large, sandy nullah.

Cossyah: A member of the Khasi tribe which inhabits the Khasi Hills.

Cossyah Hills: Khasi Hills, now in Meghalaya in north-east India.

cutcherie/cutcherry/catchari: An office of administration or court-house up to the district level; in Bengal also the office of an indigo planter or zamindar which has the character of a magistrate's or collector's office *(v. Hobson-Jobson)*.

dah/dao: Sometimes wrongly described as a fighting sword; a long-bladed, all-purpose knife for everyday use.

dwasala (from Persian): The intermediate type between *koomeriah* and *mirga* (q.v.) body-structure of elephants; used by Sanderson.

elephant pearl: There are many confusing accounts of 'elephant pearls' or *gaja moti* or *gaja mukta*. The explanation given in Wood (1934, ch. III) is the one most generally accepted. These 'pearls' growing in the hollow of a tusk can be recovered only from a dead animal. The

Tamil Nadu Forest Department has several such 'pearls' in its stock, some of very irregular shape (baroque) and considerable size. The late Rajkumar Prakritish Chandra Barua of Gauripore, Assam, had a specimen collected from a young tusker which had died in captivity. It was a smooth, oval growth, very pearl-like in shape, embedded in the hollow of the tusk. It is still in the family's possession. Necklaces of 'elephant pearls' are frequently mentioned in ancient Sanskrit literature.

Ganesh/Gunesh: Loosely, an elephant with a single tusk, as in the icon of the deity Ganesha.

gaungbong (Myanmar): The strip of silk Burmans wear round their head.

gomashta: A clerk.

goonda/goondah: There is some confusion over the meaning of this term referring to adult male elephants. Pollok (q.v.) takes the Indian usage of the term as synonymous with tuskers, whereas it is not generally used in southern India at all. Stracey (1963, p.148) explains clearly what the term signifies among elephant men in north-east India: . ... 'this is the term for a large makhna [also spelt as *makna* or *muckna*] among elephant men, but it may be used loosely to include any large and probably dangerous male elephant. The Hindustani meaning of the word is a bad character or rowdy.'

goor: Unrefined cane sugar or jaggery

guddie: A part of the elephant's riding gear or harness which consists of a thick pad made usually of gunny, split in the middle to make room for the spinal column, and stuffed with dried grass, coconut husk or the pith of *sola* (*Aeschynomene aspera*).

hathi (Hindi): Elephant.

'Hathi ata hai': The elephant is coming.

hine/hinge (Myanmar): Tuskless male elephant. See makna/makhna/muckna. Pollok and Thom (1900) see, wrongly, tuskers and *mucknas* as separate subspecies.

hora allia: A term used in Sri Lanka for 'rogue' elephants. It is not always clear if it signifies all unattached male elephants, or applies exclusively to aggressive, killer male elephants. Baker in his two books on hunting in Ceylon sees 'rogues' everywhere, and is not very helpful.

horo (Sri Lanka): Tennent (q.v.) equates the term as used in Sri Lanka with *goondah* (q.v.)

howdah: A box-like structure tied on an elephant's back to carry people. Designs of *howdah* vary according to their intended use—from the gorgeous silver-and-gilt, heavy State howdahs used in pomp and ceremony, to a simple, light frame (they can be more substantially built), the sides covered with plaited cane strips or wire netting, sometimes flippantly called 'chicken coop', where the sportsman stands for a better view when beating tall grassland for game.

howdah elephant: A large, sturdy and staunch elephant suitable for carrying a sportsman in a howdah, as different from a 'pad elephant' used only for beating the cover and loading up with bagged game.

jungle wallah: A man of the forest; used also of forest officers (jocular).

kabobed (v): Made into kabab or kabob; meat cooked on wood or charcoal fire, usually on spit.

kheddah: Literally, 'to drive or chase'; chasing or driving elephants into a stockade for capture. Properly, this is the 'kheddah method' of capture. Loosely to some people, not the elephant men themselves, 'kheddah' has come to mean the stockade itself, and any capture of elephants using a stockade, 'kheddah method of capture'.

khubber: News, information; in the context of shikar information of game, such as a kill by a tiger.

khuni hathi: A murderous elephant.

kohl: A glen.

koomeriah: The most prized body-structure in elephants. The term is used by Sanderson with illustration. Big body-barrel, big head, thick muscular limbs, short legs, particularly hind ones. The term through Sanderson has acquired general currency with a touch of the 'royal' in the name—*koomeriah* (from *koomar*, a prince). The name actually used by elephant men in north-east India is less glamorous: *'koomra'* (pumpkin), i.e. having a round compact body like a pumpkin. Another etymology can be hazarded here: *koomra* by metathesis from *koorma* (tortoise), short legs, thick round body, and thick marked shell (in the case of elephants a thick, wrinkled skin).

koonki/koonkie: In current usage the term means an elephant, male or female, trained in elephant-capture operations. Sanderson (1878) uses the word in this sense. In the second half of the nineteenth century the Dacca Kheddah Establishment under the Commissariat Department of the Army started large-scale capture of elephants in Assam, especially Garo Hills and Chittagong Hill Tracts (now in Bangladesh), and the Dooars in North Bengal. Trained elephants and experienced mahouts were brought from Chittagong, Sylhet, and Mymensingh and plains Tripura (all in Bangladesh now) for this purpose. The majority of these elephants were females. Many believe (pers. comm. Rajkumar Prakitish Chandra Barua [deceased] of Gauripore, Assam) that hearing the word *koonki* being used by mahouts to refer to trained elephants most of which happened to be females, the term became associated with trained elephants irrespective of gender whereas in the literature from East Bengal the word *koonki* means female elephant (*Sri Rajamala* [in Bengali], 2nd vol, ed. Kali Psasanna Sen Vidya Bhusan, 1337 Tripura year; Surya Kanta Acharyya Choudhury, *Shikar Kahini* [in Bengali], 1313 BS [Bengali year]; Brajendra Narayan Acharyya Choudhury, *Shikar O Shikari* [in Bengali], 1332 BS; Bhupendra Chandra

Singha, *Banjangal O Shikarer Katha* [in Bengali], Calcutta: Orient Longman's, 1970). In Captain Thomas Williamson (1808 edn) also *koonki* (misspelt *koomki*) means a female elephant: '*koomkies*, i.e. female decoy elephants' as distinct from domesticated male elephants. In the thirties and early forties of this century in Mymensingh district I heard all female elephants, irrespective of whether trained in capture operations or not, being referred to as *koonkies*. *Hemakosha*, the first authorized lexicon of the Assamese language (*Hemakosha or an Etymological Dictionary of the Assamese Language* (1900) by Hem Chandra Barua; ed. Capt. P.R. Gurdon and Hem Chandra Gosain, Gauhati, Assam) labels the word as Hindi and explains the word as 'female decoy elephant'. *Hobson-Jobson* mentions the word as a term used in Bengal. Thus there seems to be little doubt that it is a loan word in Assamese, the meaning of which later got diluted to signify any elephant, male or female, trained in the capture of elephants.

koss (Hindi; a corruption A the Sanskrit word *krosh*): A measurement of distance of 8000 hands or slightly over two miles.

kraal: A small enclosure.

Langting forests: Now in North Cachar Hills civil district of Assam.

Madrassia: A person from the province of Madras (now Tamil Nadu); in northern or, especially, eastern India a general term for all hailing from southern India.

mahout: Elephant driver.

makna/makhna/muckna: Tuskless male elephant; not a separate subspecies, as claimed by Pollok and Thom (q.v.), but an intra-specific variation. Sanderson is obviously right here.

mirga (by metathesis from Sanskrit *mriga*, deer): A term also used by Sanderson. A type of body structure in elephants: thin, long limbs, small head, light body; usually faster than the *koomeriah*-type elephants, but generally, sadly lacking in courage and endurance, and rarely as staunch and dependable as a *koomeriah*. This particular usage has sanction in ancient elephant lore in India.

moksoh (Myanmar): Shikari.

mudda: The Sri Lankan term for *must* (q.v).

munshi: A clerk or assistant.

murrain: The fatal epidemic disease referred to by this term is probably anthrax.

must/musth: A condition in adult male elephants signalled by the swelling of the temples and a malodorous (to most people) exudation from the temporal orifices. This is commonly, but not always, accompanied by violent and aggressive behaviour when a domesticated animal has to be kept chained up. The other physical symptom is continuous dripping of urine from a half-extended penis. Female Asian elephants also sometimes show discharge from the temporal orifices for a short duration, without however any change in the behaviour pattern.

pheel/pil khana: Elephant stables, stalls, or picketing ground.

phoongie house (Myanmar, formerly Burma): Flimsy structures on stilts made of bamboo and available local timber.

rao: A dry river bed.

razai (Hindi): Quilt.

ryot: In the specific Anglo-Indian context, the term means 'a tenant of the soil; an individual occupying land as a farmer or cultivator' *(Hobson-Jobson).*

sal: A hard-wood tree (*Shorea robusta*). Pollok and Thom (1900) refer to *sal* in Burma, though the distribution of *sal* is not known to extend further east than central Assam or what used to be the undivided Darrang civil district of Assam.

shikar: The sport of shooting and hunting game. In north and north-east India, various methods of capturing elephants are called different kinds of shikar such as *gad shikar* (stockade method of capture); *kheddah shikar* (capture by driving); *mela/peti shikar* (capture by noosing). All these are forms of sport, i.e. shikar, whereas killing an elephant was just *mara* (killing), putting it outside the scope of proper shikar or sport.

shikari/shikarie/shikaree/shekarry (Hindi, Bengali, Assamese): Literally, a sporstman-hunter. *Hobson-Jobson* gives three special meanings of the term: (i) 'a native hunter who either brings in game on his own account, or accompanies European sportsmen as guide and aid'. This is the commonest use of the term in Anglo-Indian shikar literature. (ii) 'The European sportsman himself'; (iii) 'a shooting boat used in the Cashmere lakes', the last usage obviously a corruption of Kashmir's shikara, a particular type of boat.

sot: A flowing stream.

sowari elephant: Riding elephant, used with light harness.

sunwe (Myanmar): Reward money.

teelah (Hindi, Bengali): Hillock.

thugyi (Myanmar): Village headman.

tiffin (Anglo-Indian and Hindustani): In Anglo-Indian households, luncheon.

townyah (Myanmar): Slash-and-burn cultivation.

veranda: An open gallery round or in front of a house.